Treating Schizophrenic Patients

A CLINICO-ANALYTICAL APPROACH

Michael H. Stone, M.D.
Harry D. Albert, M.D.
David V. Forrest, M.D.
Silvano Arieti, M.D.

MCGRAW-HILL BOOK COMPANY
New York · St. Louis · San Francisco
London · Montreal · Paris · Tokyo · Toronto

FOR

David and John

Daniel and Susannah   *Jared and Eric*

Thomas H. Quinn, Michael Hennelly, and Karen Seriguchi were the editors of this
book. Christopher Simon was the designer. Teresa Leaden supervised the production. It was set in Baskerville by Creative Graphics, Inc.

Printed and bound by R. R. Donnelley and Sons, Inc.

Library of Congress Cataloging in Publication Data
Main entry under title:

Treating schizophrenic patients.

  Includes bibliographies and index.
  1. Schizophrenia—Addresses, essays, lectures.
I. Stone, Michael H.   [DNLM:
1. Schizophrenia—Therapy.   WM 203 T783]
RC514.T688 1983   616.89'82   82-12749
ISBN 0-07-001917-7

1 2 3 4 5 6 7 8 9   DODO   8 9 7 6 5 4 3

ISBN 0-07-001917-7

Contents

Contents

Preface

This book was the outgrowth of an all-day seminar on psychotherapy with schizophrenic patients, given by the authors for three successive years (1977–1979) at the annual meeting of the American Psychiatric Association, under the directorship of Dr. Silvano Arieti.

In their original format, these seminars consisted of three rounds of presentations, each followed by an interval set aside for participation from the audience. Among the numerous ways in which our presentations could have been organized, the one we felt most suitable for the seminars was structured according to conventional phases of treatment: "early," "middle" and "late." This system is reflected in several of the present chapters. Most, however, are devoted to topics that, while relevant to the broad theme of psychotherapy with schizophrenic patients, cut across the arbitrary divisions of time. The sections on dangerous patients (Dr. Albert), on humor (Dr. Stone), and on schizophrenic language (Dr. Forrest) are examples. The subject matter of such chapters derives in no small part from the interests of our audiences, whose members addressed many lively questions and comments to us concerning the use of confrontation, the place of humor, the indications for adjunctive pharmacotherapy, etc.

Dr. Arieti's untimely death in the summer of 1981, besides inflicting on the psychiatric profession the loss of one of its most eloquent spokesmen, renowned particularly, of course, for his contributions to the psychotherapy of schizophrenia, prevented him from completing his portion of the book. We are pleased to have his essay on new and revised procedures as our opening chapter. Meanwhile, we hope that the chapters we have subsequently added will convey the spirit, if no longer the letter, of Dr. Arieti's teaching.

Our profession has also been graced in mid-century by another psychoanalyst widely acclaimed for his psychotherapeutic work with schizophrenic patients: Dr. Harold Searles. By a happy coincidence, the three of us were supervised by Dr. Searles during the years of our training at the New York

State Psychiatric Institute. What Arieti and Searles may owe to their mentors, Harry Stack Sullivan and Frieda Fromm-Reichmann, we owe, in our turn, to Arieti and Searles.

We cannot bring forth our book on the psychotherapy of schizophrenia without drawing attention to its timeliness and purpose. Some would contend that neuroleptic drugs, ninety-day limits in many hospital insurance plans, and a growing emphasis on group and milieu therapy have rendered long-term intensive, individual psychotherapy with schizophrenics costly, scientifically unsound, and anachronistic. We hope to satisfy the skeptical reader in such a way that he may join us, in recognizing the problems and therapeutic challenges we have dwelt on in this book, and in agreeing with us that psychotherapy with schizophrenic patients, while in many ways an art, is by no means a lost art.

Indeed, the recent advances, including those in the area of pharmacotherapy, have, if anything, made a greater number of schizophrenic persons amenable to psychotherapy than was hitherto the case. This book does not attempt to provide a handy digest of what has already been said well. Though we have included some material on the historical roots and theoretical underpinnings of this method, we have done so by way of providing a background for the major portions of the book, whose intent is mainly *practical*. We wish to specify and to spell out adaptations in treatment approach we have found helpful with our schizophrenic patients. The book will answer more to the needs of those who, having only recently begun their venture into this therapeutic realm, require something of a foundation. Several chapters, however, have been earmarked for seasoned therapists who may seek to refine and hone further an already well-established technic. Because schizophrenic patients so often require, even transitorily, other varieties of treatment besides verbal therapy in the dyadic encounter, we have incorporated into all sections of the book an *integrated* approach, emphasizing the humanistic understanding of the schizophrenic's dilemma, but drawing attention as well to the use and timing of other interventions (medication, group therapy, behavioral modification, etc.) when and if these are deemed appropriate. Our comments have been illustrated with many clinical vignettes in the hope that they will enliven the text and at the same time imbue the reader with some of the enthusiasm shared by the authors for the so often gratifying work with schizophrenic patients.

It is customary in a book such as this to express gratitude to those who figured most significantly in helping to form and polish it. Arieti and Searles would be the first to understand that our indebtedness, as great as it is to them, is greater still to our patients. We cannot thank them, from whom we have learned so much, by name, and have, indeed, disguised our allusions to them in our various clinical illustrations to the point of unrecognizability. (These necessary, if novelistic, distortions may at times create, inadvertently, the impression of actual persons). We hope we have translated some of the lessons we learned from them into more effective therapeutic skills with which to enhance their comfort in life and their self-fulfillment.

Special thanks are due Dr. Clarice Kestenbaum, whose careful reading and critique of the manuscript were responsible for many improvements in content and in style. Similarly appreciated were the encouragement and forebearance and, following her thoughtful review of the second draft, the insightful suggestions provided by Gail Albert. Lynne Stetson Forrest inspired a fresher and more immediate approach in dealing with creative and emotive matters, which might otherwise have been conceptualized more indirectly by a scholarly temperament.

The book would not have come into being but for the continued support and helpful recommendations of Thomas Quinn, Editor-in-Chief of Social Science. Though long in gestation, the book was quick in delivery, owing to the skillful and unusually efficient editing of Michael Hennelly. His efforts could not begin, however, until the manuscript had been prepared, typed, and proofed, first by Mrs. Roseanne Pennino and again by Mrs. Sharon DellaVecchia, both of whom brought to their work a competence and craftsmanship every author searches for in a secretary, but finds only through good luck.

1

Psychotherapy of Schizophrenia

NEW OR REVISED PROCEDURES

Silvano Arieti, M.D.

Until twenty to fifteen years ago the treatment of schizophrenia was predominantly a hospital procedure, whether it consisted of a course of electric shock treatment or of prolonged psychotherapy. Even after the first great innovators in the field of psychotherapy of schizophrenia—Harry Stack Sullivan, Frieda Fromm-Reichmann, John Rosen, and some of their major pupils, like Lewis Hill, Harold Searles, Otto Will, and others—made their important contributions, psychotherapy of schizophrenia was still considered mainly a form of hospital treatment.

The first edition of my book *Interpretation of Schizophrenia,* which appeared in 1955, was among the first writings to advocate office treatment of the schizophrenic patient. The procedure aroused immediate interest, but in the same year chlorpromazine and other tranquilizers started to be used on a large scale. The majority of psychiatrists became more and more interested in the pharmacological approach, which promised quicker results and yielded more visible effects.

Considerable progress has been made in the pharmacological field. Lately, however, interest in psychotherapy of schizophrenia has been rekindled, for several reasons. What Frieda Fromm-Reichmann, other pioneers, and we, their followers, have tried to do, could not be completely ignored. Some therapeutic ways have, so to say, rubbed off, even on those who were not at first receptive. Psychiatrists have become gradually aware that the therapeutic encounter cannot consist only of writing a prescription and evaluating the manifest symptomatology; the anguish, the conflict, the impact of the suffering, or the impact of the denial of that suffering, have to be investigated. Moreover, psychiatrists have come to the realization that what they can at times learn relatively easily from the psychodynamics and psychotherapy of some schizophrenics can be immensely useful in the treatment of patients belonging to other and less serious categories, provided certain modifications are made. Most important, the schizophrenic patient has become a common office patient, by no means limited to a hospital environment. The practice of many psychiatrists consists to a considerable extent of ambulatory schizophrenics.

Also, some preconceived notions about the psychotherapy of schizophrenia are rapidly losing ground. The psychotherapist is not *a priori* or in an absolute manner against drug therapy. Drug therapy may be given in conjunction with psychotherapy, in many cases an effective therapeutic combination. Drug therapy is particularly valuable in establishing a certain distance between the patient and his symptoms; the relationship between therapist and patient can develop more easily, the socially alienating aspects of the symptomatology abate, and hospitalization is avoided.

Also losing ground is the notion that the psychotherapist considers schizophrenia an exclusively psychogenic disorder. Contemporary psychotherapists have accepted the findings of the major studies on the subject, according to which schizophrenia is the result of a set of etiological factors, organic and psychological. We would now argue that it is probably enough to diminish one of the two components to disrupt the set, thereby either preventing the disorder or minimizing the likelihood of its appearance. If the disorder has already appeared, it seems plausible that, by removing or altering one of the two components, a condition will develop in which schizophrenia will no longer be possible, or if possible, will be ameliorated. Since at the present time we cannot change the genetic code of individuals, it seems much more promising to change the psychological factors.

Basic Principles

To start with, it may be important to formulate as clearly as possible what seem now to be the basic principles underlying the psychotherapy of schizophrenia.

The first principle has to do with combating anxiety. General psychodynamic psychotherapy and especially classic psychoanalysis necessitates the mobilization of anxiety; that is, anxiety is as a rule not necessarily avoided and may even be increased if we want to bring about results. Psychotherapists of the schizophrenic, at least in the first and middle stages of treatment, on the other hand, must aim at causing no or very little anxiety and do their best to diminish the anxiety already present. This is a difficult goal when we deal with psychological processes that are customarily fraught with anxiety. Although a minority of psychotherapists differ on this point, it is generally appreciated that the schizophrenic patient is fragile: a return of anxiety may suddenly demolish months of treatment. Nevertheless, although we do not want to increase anxiety, we do not want to blunt other emotions. This explains also the psychotherapist's cautiousness in administering drug therapy. He is reluctant to use massive doses, which, true, remove many symptoms, but which may also bring about a blunting of affect or even a state of depersonalization. The procedures to be illustrated later in this volume will show how we try to achieve results without eliciting more than a modicum of anxiety.

The second principle states that, whereas as a rule the aim of a physician, including the psychiatrist who uses drug therapy exclusively, is *restitutio quo ante* (a return to the premorbid condition), the psychotherapist does not consider this return a desirable goal. In fact, the so-called premorbid condition of the schizophrenic was already morbid, although in a less obvious way. A return to a prepsychotic condition would mean to settle for the retention not only of a biological vulnerability but also of a psychological one. The potentiality for psychosis would thus persist.

The third principle seems almost a contradiction of the second. In a considerable number of cases we do not achieve a complete cure but a state of "delicate balance." Our main aim becomes that of maintaining this state. Some patients require this type of treatment indefinitely, some require it only for a few months, others for years, before independence from treatment can be achieved. What I mean by "delicate balance" is a particular way of living—satisfactory and productive on the whole, but still precarious in certain respects. The patient has lost his symptoms, has acquired insight into the major psychodynamic mechanisms of his remote and recent history, and his life has been enriched in many ways, even in comparison to the way he was before the onset of clinical manifestations of the illness. Nevertheless, he remains vulnerable to the difficulties of life, to tasks that average people can master, and to misinterpretations in interpersonal exchanges. His tolerance for discomfort and frustration remains low. With intervention, the therapist corrects these trends and helps the patient to navigate in these insecure waters.

The fourth principle, and most important, is that we must see treatment as a way by which the patient proceeds toward self-acceptance. Contrary to what he may show in his manifest symptomatology, the patient at the outset does not accept himself.

First Approaches

Of the many clinical pictures with which schizophrenia may initially present itself, we shall consider the two most common ones—not so much for the purpose of describing their complicated features, as to comprehend their general meaning.

In the first of these pictures, we immediately recognize a state of profound withdrawal, not a withdrawal of a mythical energy or cathexis, but an attitude toward the world, a desire to escape. Often this desire is covered by a feeling that the world is not worth looking at or contacting, not worth participating in. In this picture we recognize also an infinite fear of the world, and an infinite distrust of people. The patient once had a very low self-esteem and did not accept himself; now he has switched positions. Others should not be accepted, and he should keep away from them. They are there to hurt him, to make him feel unacceptable. Any contact with others will bring harm.

In a second common picture, projection prevails over withdrawal. We see a person busily defending himself. Whereas before the onset of the manifest illness he considered himself worth and deserving only contempt, the "accusation" now comes from others. But the accusation has undergone a metamorphosis caused by schizophrenic cognition. He is accused of being a spy, a murderer, a pervert. He feels rejected and persecuted. When we are confronted with a delusional picture of this type, we may go further and even understand the basic significance of the major part of the symptomatology the first time we see the patient. Often the main delusion is the clue that will lead to the denouement of the patient's drama.

A patient may think, for example, that his wife is putting poison in his food. He really believes his wife is poisoning his *life,* but he cannot accept that belief. For if she disturbs his life, *he* may have something to do with their marital difficulties—a realization he dare not acknowledge. Another patient may have an olfactory hallucination. He smells a bad odor that seems to emanate from his body. We can be fairly sure that he attributes to his body what he thinks of himself, namely, that his rotten personality "stinks." It is easier for him to blame his body than his character. Another patient, while he was in a teen-ager camp, believed that people were going into his closet and drawers at night, taking out his clothes, and putting female clothes in their place. He was still concerned with his identity, especially gender identity. Another patient felt that some mysterious, unidentified people from other planets were controlling his thoughts. He had never felt free in life. He felt that his way of thinking was conditioned by distant, extremely remote people who meant nothing to him and yet were capable of chaining him to their ways. Other patients believe they are the Virgin Mary or Jesus Christ. The delusion of being Jesus Christ is common today. How insignificant must these patients feel if they identify with those whom they not only consider their ideal but who are far above human proportion! Thus the focal symptom becomes a symbol of a life drama, of a tragedy that is still being lived.

To understand the basic drama puts us in affective rapport with the patient, increases our desire to guide him to a position in which he can re-accept himself. But we cannot help him by explaining, prematurely, the meaning hidden by his manifest symptomatology. First we must learn to communicate with him. Certainly we cannot deprive him of his delusions when he still needs them. A belief that he is Jesus Christ may be the only protection from greater disintegration.

I have referred to two pictures, each representing one of the two major characteristics of schizophrenia. The withdrawal picture reflects mostly a disorder in relatedness; that is, an interpersonal disorder. The paranoid picture reflects predominantly a cognitive alteration, an intrapsychic disorder. In most cases there is a mixture of the two.

No matter which is the prevailing picture, the first stage of therapy will tend to deal with the interpersonal aspect of the disorder. The first task is the establishment of relatedness. If we do not succeed in this task, treatment cannot go beyond the initial stage. The ability to establish relatedness with a schizophrenic is not a mystical, irreducible quality, or an innate talent that a few privileged therapists possess, but certainly at the present stage of our knowledge it is the least scientific part of the treatment.

First of all, we must clarify what is meant by "relatedness." This concept not only includes rapport or contact with the patient; it also embraces the classic psychoanalytic concepts of transference and countertransference, seen in their simultaneous occurrence and in their reciprocal influence. Although it also includes the psychoanalytic concept of object relations, it does not consider such relations in a one-way direction or as an energy emanating from the individual to the object, but—at the personal level—as an interrelation between two or more individuals, rather in the manner of the I-Thou relationship, in Buber's terms.[1]

Typically, the schizophrenic has always had difficulty in relating to others, perhaps stemming from the difficulty he had with the first Other, his mother. Difficulties with others are reflected upon the self and produce deviation in the development of the self. In the preschizophrenic and schizophrenic, difficulties manifest themselves as anxiety in dealing with others,

[1]Buber (1953).

as actual distrust, fear, and misinterpretation of others. The therapist is also an *other* for the patient. He must do his very best to counteract the patient's anxiety. He must assume an attitude of active intervention, offer warmth, confidence, and reassurance, and make attempts to remove the fear that is almost automatically aroused by interpersonal contact. He may offer short interpretative formulations that he has grasped in his first meetings with the patient. They are passing remarks and not detailed interpretations. The importance of these early explanations lies in conveying to the patient the impression that somebody understands his troubles and empathizes with his feelings. They should not be confused with the deeper interpretations that will be appropriate at a later time. The therapist may find useful on occasion some nonverbal meaningful acts, like touching the patient, holding his hand, walking together.

The therapist should, during this early stage of therapy, ask as few questions as possible pertaining to the symptomatology or to conflict areas. Some psychiatrists still use methods that have been transmitted from a time when questions and answers had a purpose of demonstrating whether a patient was legally insane and could be committed. In the earliest stage of treatment the task of the therapist is not that of obtaining information from the patient, no matter how useful that information would be, but of establishing relatedness. Patient and therapist must learn to know and trust each other.

Attack on Psychotic Symptoms

In the treatment of schizophrenia a considerable number of psychotherapists place exclusive reliance on the establishment of relatedness. To be sure, symptoms do at times disappear or decrease in intensity as soon as relatedness is established. In my experience, although this is true in some cases, in the majority of cases the symptoms persist or return if the patient has not acquired insight into his psychological mechanisms and has not changed his vision of himself, others, life, and the world.

Although psychodynamic interpretations are much better known, interpretations concerning mechanisms and forms of schizophrenia are also important and are generally given at an earlier stage of treatment. With some special technical procedures, the patient is helped to become aware of the ways in which he transforms his psychodynamic conflicts into psychotic symptoms. He then becomes able to intercept or to arrest the phenomenon and to relinquish the symptoms. I have described these techniques elsewhere,[2] but as a paradigm of this procedure I shall repeat here, with some modifications, the treatment of hallucinations. Before illustrating the tech-

[2]See Arieti (1955).

nique, I must stress again that the establishment of relatedness is a prerequisite for the application of subsequent modalities. If relatedness is not established, the patient cannot even listen carefully, and whatever we tell him makes no impression. Moreover, as I have already mentioned, the symptom is in a certain way needed. The patient is not going to give it up, nor is it advisable that he give it up, until the need for it is decreased or we are able to offer compensation. With the establishment of relatedness we convey to the patient the feeling that he is no longer alone in facing his anxiety. The therapist is with him to share the burden. In what follows I shall take into consideration only auditory hallucinations, but the same procedures could be applied to other types of hallucinations after proper modifications have been made.

With the exception of patients who are at a very advanced stage of illness or with whom no relatedness whatsoever can be reached, it is possible to recognize that hallucinatory voices occur only in particular situations, that is, *when the patient expects to hear them.*

For instance, a patient goes home after a day of work and expects the neighbors to talk about him. As soon as he expects to hear them, he hears them. In other words, he puts himself in what I have called "the listening attitude."

If we have been able to establish not only contact but relatedness with the patient, he will be able under our direction to distinguish two stages: that of the listening attitude and that of the hallucinatory experience. At first he may protest vigorously and deny the existence of the two stages, but later he may make a little concession. He will say, "I happened to think that they would talk, and I proved to be right. They were really talking."

A few sessions later another step forward will be made. The patient will be able to recognize and to admit that there was a brief interval between the expectation of the voices and the "hearing" of voices. He will still insist that this sequence is purely coincidental, but eventually he will see a connection between his putting himself into the listening attitude and his actually hearing. Then he will recognize that he puts himself into this attitude when he is in a particular situation or in a particular mood—for instance, a mood in which he "perceives" hostility, as it were, in the air. He has a feeling that everybody has a disparaging attitude toward him; he then finds corroboration for this attitude. He "hears" them making unpleasant remarks. At times he feels inadequate and worthless, but he does not sustain this feeling for more than a fraction of a second. The self-condemnation almost automatically induces him into the listening attitude, whereupon he hears voices of other people condemning him.

When the patient is able to recognize the relation between his mood and the listening attitude, a great step has been accomplished. He will not see himself any longer as a passive agent, as the victim of a strange phenomenon or of persecutors, but as somebody who has a great deal to do with what he experiences. Moreover, if he catches himself in this earlier stage of the listening attitude, he has not yet descended to abnormal ways of thinking (from which it would be difficult to extricate himself). He is, so to speak, *in the process* of falling into the seductive world of psychosis, but may still resist the seduction and remain in the world of reality. He will intercept the mechanism; through our help, he acquires the power to do so.

If an atmosphere of relatedness and understanding has been established, patients learn with not too much difficulty to catch themselves in the act of putting themselves into the listening attitude at the least disturbance, several times during the day. Although they recognize the phenomenon, they sometimes feel that it is almost an automatic mechanism they cannot prevent. Eventually, however, they will be able to control it more and more. Even then, there will be a tendency to resort to the listening attitude and to the hallucinatory experiences in situations of stress. The therapist should never tire of explaining the mechanism to the patient again and again, even when such explanations seem redundant. Such explanations will seldom prove truly redundant, as the symptoms may reacquire an almost irresistible attraction.

Elsewhere I have described related techniques for the treatment of delusions and ideas of reference (Arieti, 1975). If the patient masters these techniques, he will no longer see himself completely at the mercy of others or of obscure forces, but as moving toward mastery of his own condition, even if he remains unhappy. Thus these procedures not only aim at eliminating symptoms, but also at increasing the self-esteem of the patient, who now sees himself reacquiring control over some important psychological events of his life.

In spite of our cautiousness some patients experience either anxiety or depression when they lose the psychotic symptoms. The occurrence of depression during recovery from schizophrenia is generally not a serious threat. The symptoms may have been lost too soon, and the patient misses them. He has not yet been able to replace them with healthy structures in his life. We must help him develop these structures, in a gradual manner. If he feels guilty, we must explain to him that this is partially due to the reintegration of the self-accusatory feelings that he had projected onto the external world when he was paranoid.

More serious is the recurrence of excessive anxiety, which may bring about a relapse. This may be prevented by prompt intervention. An example will clarify this point. A woman used to hear a hallucinatory voice calling her a prostitute. Now, with the method described above, we have deprived her of this hallucination. Nevertheless, she experiences a feeling, almost an abstract feeling coming from the external environment, of being discriminated against, considered inferior, looked upon as a bad woman, etc. She almost has a wish to crystallize or concretize this feeling into an hallucination. If we leave her alone, most likely she will hallucinate again. If we tell her that she is projecting into the environment her own feelings about herself, she may become infuriated. She may say, "The voices I used to hear were telling me I was a bad woman, a prostitute, but I never had such a feeling about myself. I am a good woman." The patient, of course, is right, because when she hears a disparaging voice, or when she is experiencing the vague feeling of being disparaged, she no longer has a disparaging opinion of herself. We must instead point out to the patient that there was one time when she had a bad opinion of herself. Even then she did not think she was a prostitute, but rather had a low self-esteem, such as she thought a prostitute would probably have.

In other words, we must try to reenlarge the patient's psychotemporal field. As long as he attributes everything to the present, the patient cannot escape from the symptoms. Whereas the world of psychosis has only one temporal dimension—the present—the world of reality has three: past, present, and future. Although at this point of the illness the patient tends to live exclusively in the present, he retains a conception of the past, and such a conception must be exploited. We direct the patient to face longitudinally his deep feeling of inadequacy. What concerns the past no longer arouses much anxiety and can be better understood by the patient. The explanation, however, will help him face the present with less anxiety.

At an intermediate stage of treatment we gradually pass, as a general rule, from interpretations that concern the structures of the symptoms to others that refer to content and its dynamic impact. At this stage the patient is able to tolerate a certain degree of anxiety. This procedure is adopted especially in connection with some symptoms that are multifaceted, inasmuch as they can be called at the same time hallucinatory, illusional, delusional, and referential. For instance, a patient may have the idea that people are laughing at him. He actually hears them giggling and laughing, and so he turns his head; he looks at them and sees them smiling sardonically. Actually they may not be smiling at all, or if they do smile, they may do so for reasons that have nothing to do with him. Again we must help the patient recognize that he sees or hears people laughing at him when he *expects* to see or hear them. At this point the patient may be ready to recognize that he feels people *should* laugh at him because he is a laughable individual. He "hears" them laughing because he believes that they *should* laugh at him. What he thinks of himself becomes the cause of his symptoms.

For the patient it is a painful matter to acknowledge that he thinks so ill of himself. In this case, too, the psychotic mechanism will dissolve when it is understood both formally and psychodynamically, and when the patient, with the help of the therapist, is able to tolerate the unpleasant psychodynamic meanings. Again I must repeat that one of the most important skills of the therapist resides in evaluating whether the patient is ready to tolerate the full awareness of certain meanings. In some delusions and ideas of reference there are elements that are valid at a realistic level as well as at a symbolic level. For instance, the boss of a patient used to hit an out-of-order water cooler, ostensibly to make the water flow. The patient interpreted the gesture as equivalent to hitting her. Later discussions seemed to indicate that the patient was not referring to a totally irrelevant occurrence. Her boss was, it seemed, given to acts of displaced hostility, some of which probably were meant for her.

The patient is praised for this insight, but the insight is enlarged to include not only the realistic episode but its symbolic meaning. The coincidence between psychosis and reality is exploited to make contact with the patient and to develop consensual validation in some areas.

This kind of insight I call "punctiform" because it concerns a small segment of reality. Although it is important and should be acknowledged, it should not be confused with the ideas of antipsychiatry psychiatrists who see in the expressions of the schizophrenic patient a revelation of the supreme truth.

This opens up important questions. We must agree with R. D. Laing and related authors that there are grains of truth in what the patient tells us; but let us not see these grains for more than they are, or we may do a disservice to the patient. We may admire the patient at times for removing masks, for saying what other people do not dare to say. But we must also recognize that the fragments of truth he uncovers quite often assume grotesque forms, and that he will apply these grotesque forms to the whole world, so that whatever insight he has achieved will be less pronounced and less profound than his distortion. And his distortion not only has no adaptational value, but is inimical to any form of adaptation even in a liberal community of humankind.

The Quasipoetic Stage

In my studies of schizophrenia I have in practically every case come almost to the point of admiring the pathology as a form of creativity. Such admiration should not lead anyone to the adoption of schizophrenia as a guide for living or as a philosophy of life, but it may help the therapist, especially at an intermediate stage of treatment that I call "quasipoetic."

When the patient tells us that a man from a distant planet controls his thoughts, we may admire the metaphorical content of the delusion. This "man" is the patient's father, toward whom he felt so emotionally distant, as if he were on another planet, and whom the patient experienced as wanting to control his ideas or the direction he wanted to give to his life. When another patient tells us that invisible rays pierce him and cause him harm, he will usually be referring to the hidden or hard-to-detect ways in which society has harmed him.

The patient uses what is for us metaphorical language; from what he tells us, we can indeed learn some hidden truths, as we would learn from a poet. But is the patient a poet? He is not. The difference, described by me elsewhere (Arieti, 1972), lies between the primary process of the schizophrenic and the tertiary process of the creative person. The patient is not at all aware of the metaphorical meaning of his delusions; he accepts them literally. For him it is literally true that a bad odor emanates from his body, that his wife poisons his food, that a man controls his thoughts from a distant planet, that invisible rays go through his body. He is like a dreamer who, while he is dreaming, thinks the dream is true. The dream is true, of course, not just as an act of life, but also in its symbolic content. It is as true as the poetry which, in its metaphorical revelations, discloses to us ways and feelings deeper than those usually attached to a daily reality. It is one of our tasks to guide this pseudo-poet, the patient, to reality, but to a reality that will be less anxiety-provoking than before yet, hopefully, not prosaic. An example will explain what I mean.

Marie was a 19-year-old girl when I first saw her. She was in a catatonic state, completely immobile, like a statue. I shall not repeat the first approaches to treatment of the catatonic patient, which I have described elsewhere (Arieti, 1955) and shall mention here only some aspects of the case pertinent to the point I wish to make. When Marie emerged from her catatonic state, she was still partially withdrawn and retained peculiar postures, movements, and gait; but other symptoms, like paranoid thinking and delusions, dominated the picture.

Marie thought that the man she was in love with had become a vampire and had bitten her on her neck. She felt she had recently been crucified. She still could feel the stigmata in her hands. When relatedness was established, she became capable of talking coherently and of explaining the sequence of events which had led her to the acute episode. She said that the man she had fallen in love with was a young priest who, at first, was her priest, confessor, then spiritual guide, friend, boyfriend, and finally lover. He was the first and only man in her life. Now he was going to return to his native country. She felt abandoned, cheated. In spite of his profession of love during the beginning of their relationship, Donald was not going to leave the Church and marry her, but leave her and remain in the Church. She also felt extremely guilty because she had agreed to have sexual relations with her own priest. She was now afraid of being followed, bitten, persecuted, killed by a vampire. She became more and more convinced that Donald had become this vampire. She remembered that during the period of catatonic immobility she felt that if she moved, the whole universe would collapse and she would be responsible for the cataclysm. When she became less catatonic and predominantly paranoid, she made a number of puns and neologisms. She also had the habit of spelling backward some words whose meanings were important to her. Thus "God" became "dog"; the word "lived" became "devil," and "live" became "evil." Numbers also brought about interesting associations. When I asked her how old Donald was when he became her lover, she said, "28." When I remarked that he was quite a bit older—she was only 19—she replied, "Doctor, we are the same age. Two and eight make ten, and one and nine make ten." Then she added, "Like Sartre's book." When I asked her to explain, she replied, "I mean the book *Being and Nothingness*. Being is one, and zero is nothingness. One and zero together make ten again." Then she went on to explain that civilization is based on the number ten, the decimal system. Three is the perfect number because it represents the Holy Trinity; two represents human imperfection. Three and two together, that is, the holy and the profane, make five, the fingers of one hand; and two hands make ten.

During her rapid recovery, the metaphorical meanings of her symptoms were explained to her. This man who was supposed to be her religious, spiritual guide took advantage of her, reduced her to a puppet that would do anything he wanted. He made only a sexual object of her and was going to abandon her. No wonder she believed he was not a man, a member of the human race, but a vampire who had sucked her blood. With her delusion she wanted to maintain respect and love for the image of man. No member of the human species could do what had been done to her; only a vampire could. She felt guilty for having allowed herself to participate in this love affair. Her moral foundations, her universe of values, were crumbling when she agreed to Donald's requests. No wonder she had attributed a sinful meaning to all her actions, to all her movements. She had become catatonic in order not to act. By becoming so involved with Donald, her priest, who at first she considered close to God, she had turned the values of the Church upside down, and "God" had become "dog." She felt she had "lived" intensely with this man; but "lived" became its reverse, "devil"; and of course to live with this man became "evil." She was very much surprised when I told her that I would temporarily use her language and retain the number 10 to characterize her relation with this man. She was number one and had tried to retain her unity and identity, whereas Donald had revealed himself to be a zero. Marie has made a quick, almost total recovery. Some residues of the illness persist. It was essential, at a certain stage of her treatment, to explain to her the metaphorical truth hidden in her symptoms.

I consider it important to stress that in the process of returning to reality, many patients must go through a poetic stage, in the sense of understanding the metaphorical or symbolic truth of the symptoms. The return to reality is gradual and slow because, unfortunately, the patient's reality is often sad and made even worse by his vulnerability and particular sensitivity. No wonder he wants to escape from it. No wonder we must be extremely careful in promoting his return. We must do whatever we can to improve his reality. That is our double task: on one side, we must help to change the environment realistically. On the other, we must help the patient to modify his misperceptions of his environment, especially in regard to his interpersonal relations.

A last word about Marie. A year later, when she was much better, she asked me what my age was. I told her, "64." Her face beamed, and in a humorous and exuberant mood she added, "What an astounding coincidence, Dr. Arieti! Six and four make ten."

Psychodynamic Analysis

At a more advanced stage, treatment consists more and more of a psychodynamic examination of the patient's life history, of his present and past attitude toward others and himself.

Many psychotherapists (for instance, Laing) believe that schizophrenia occurs solely because of what has been done to the patient. "What has been done" refers especially to events in childhood. According to this school of thought, the family is responsible, and the mother is the major culprit; as a matter of fact, she has been labeled "the schizophrenogenic mother." Many therapists, myself included, used to accept the version of the parents, and especially of the mother, given by the patient at a certain stage of treatment. The psychotherapist used to encourage the patient to stress alleged or real wrong-doings of the parents. Blaming the family was a way to regain self-esteem and self-assertion. According to some research I have made, this vision of the parents is incorrect in 75 percent of the cases. Seeing the patient as a human being who became schizophrenic solely because of what was done to him may be a compassionate appraisal, but in my opinion it is also an oversimplification. I believe it is more accurate to say that the patient becomes schizophrenic because of *what he does with what was done to him.* And what he does depends on many factors.

Let us therefore discuss some psychodynamic concepts that use different formulations. In the childhood of future schizophrenics, we generally find, if we investigate carefully, a deviation from what we can consider a normal family environment. The deviation consists predominantly of an environment characterized by a greater than average level of anxiety, hostility, detachment, or instability, stemming generally from members of the family. This deviation, however, would in itself be remedied by the regenerating and self-correcting mechanisms of the organism and of the psyche; this happens in the case of many individuals. But in the case of future schizophrenics, other circumstances do not permit this correction to take place, so that the effect of the initial deviation not only persists but is amplified by subsequent chain-effects. Circumstances that do not permit a healthy adaptation to initial adverse circumstances may be biological or hereditary. The future schizophrenic would appear to be more sensitive than the average child to adverse environment and psychological pain. The timing of adverse contingencies may not permit the psyche to recuperate between one blow and the next. Finally, compensatory mechanisms, like the presence of useful parental substitutes, may be absent.

Complementary to these environmental circumstances, we must consider the contribution made to its own pathology by the patient's emerging self. For instance, the mother may have definite negative characteristics, including those we have mentioned, but the schizophrenic-to-be responds more profoundly to them in that particular context or because of his own biology. He may ignore or be less affected by the positive qualities of his mother: the mother who is the giver, the helper, the assuager of hunger, thirst, cold, loneliness, immobility, or other discomfort. Thus the child who responds mainly to the negative aspects of mother will tend to create a whole (in terms of a mental representation) of these negative parts. The resulting whole will be a monstrous transformation of the real mother. Similar remarks can be made about the self-image of the future patient. It is not true that the self consists only of reflected appraisals. The sensitive child does not respond equally to all appraisals and roles attributed to him. Elements that hurt him more and in some cases that please him more stand out and are integrated disproportionately. Thus the self, although related to external appraisals, is not a reproduction of them but in some cases a grotesque representation. The representation of the self that the patient retains would stupefy the parents if they were aware of it.

These images of mother and of the self—one image being the major representative of the external world (that eventually will become the neighbor, any others, humankind), and the other being the representative of the individual himself—will affect, at conscious and unconscious levels, all the subsequent life of the individual. They are built not only by external contingencies, but by the patient himself. A large part of the psychodynamic literature has made the error of seeing the child, the adolescent, and the young adult as completely molded by external circumstances, a passive agent at the mercy of others, either parents or society. Although these environmental forces are of great, often crucial importance, we should not forget other factors. The person, even at a young age, is not a *tabula rasa,* a sponge that absorbs whatever is given to him, without his adding individuality and creativity to what he receives and thus contributing to his transformation.

A few concluding words about the mothers of schizophrenic patients. If some have not been good mothers, we have to consider this fact in more definite terms: a mother might not have been ''good'' for a particular child in the particular family situation in which she found herself. Thus we can recognize three different factors acting concurrently: the mother (or her neurosis); the family, with all its difficulties and troubles; and the child, with his own biological predisposition and sensitivity.

During this long psychodynamic part of the treatment we must individualize both the contribution of the patient himself and that of his environment to the crescendo of insecurity, formation of prepsychotic personality, faulty defenses, and, finally, the emergence of the psychosis. Certainly the initial conflicts of members of the family have to be individualized and assessed in their impact on the patient. How the original angle of deviation and the supposed defenses gave origin to false signals of threat, which led to deformations of introjected images and distortions of interpersonal relations, are areas to be investigated as thoroughly as possible.

Family's Role in Rehabilitation of the Schizophrenic Patient

I want to devote the last part of this presentation to the therapeutic role of the family in the psychotherapy of the schizophrenic. Many authors have already suggested that the family should participate in the gigantic therapeutic task; it will not be repeated here what has been described by other authors in detail. I shall focus only on the differences between my approach and others. In the majority of cases my aim is not that of bringing to light how the parents have reduced the patient to a scapegoat, or because of their narcissism have ignored, victimized, or actually expelled from their feelings the patient, or subjected him to incestuous overstimulation, deprived him of his individuality or ego boundaries, or encouraged him to suicide. Very seldom do I aim at showing how parents have perpetrated so-called id-binding, ego-binding, or superego-binding in ways exceeding by far those of the average family. Were these my aims, as they once were, I would continue to find these conditions in significant qualitative or quantitative degrees only 25 percent of the time. In approximately 75 percent of the cases my aim is a different one: not liberation from the family, but reintegration into the family. The emphasis is no longer on the family as a source of pathology, but as a major instrument of restoration to health.[3]

What I want to discuss is the role of a family that, for various reasons—economics, working conditions, reluctance, psychological difficulty, etc.—is not able to be in active family psychotherapy and yet has to participate in the task of rehabilitation.

Let us consider the patient who has been diagnosed a schizophrenic and who now lives with his family. He may be back from the hospital or may have never been in a hospital. Let us further imagine that, whether or not there was an acute episode, at present the patient is considerably better.

What does it mean to have in the family a person who has been diagnosed a schizophrenic? What does it mean to live with the patient day by day? This topic has been relatively neglected in the recent literature. And yet with the welcome trend to discharge the patient from the hospital as soon as possible, the role that the family can play at this point must be reasserted and examined from a different outlook. For the large number of patients who do not recover completely from the initial attack and who remain a serious problem, we may borrow an expression used by President Truman, and say that the buck stops here, in the family. There is no other or better place to turn, no place where enlightenment and guidance from the psychiatrist are more needed and appreciated. Day hospitals and halfway houses are available only for a restricted number of patients.

Of course, there are limitations to what the family can do. Whereas the psychotherapist engages with the patient in a common exploration of the inner life of the patient, the family members are engaged with him in an external exploration, in rediscovering that the external world is not so terrible as it once seemed, but is a place where the patient, too, can find his own niche, and much more than that.

When a patient returns home, I usually introduce the family to the arduous task. First of all, the reality of the patient's return must be faced squarely. A new factor has been added, and the family atmosphere is no longer the same. To make believe that everything is just as it was is masking

[3]See Arieti (1977).

reality; it requires the imposition of mechanisms of denial that are soon likely to produce harm. The aim is not to transform the family members into psychiatric nurses, but to make them understand better the problems that are involved so that they can add this understanding to their affection and personal concern. I wish to make the family aware that a family member has a great advantage over even the best nurse. For the family, the patient will always be a person, not a clinical case. The relative knows what the patient likes and does not like. As clearly as I can, I show the family that the sociological attitudes they have adopted in the past have definite educational values, but they may have disastrous effects when they are imposed on or adopted by the patient. I point out to the relatives that, while they do not intend to punish the patient for his unconventional behavior, in reality, they do punish him in subtle ways unless they train themselves to do otherwise. The family member may avoid him, or stay with him as little as possible; not talk to him or talk in brief, curt sentences; refuse to listen to him or to give him explanations; have a patronizing attitude; be in a hurry in every interchange with the patient; show a perplexed, annoyed, bored, or disapproving facial expression, or at times even an air of consternation.

A considerable amount of time is spent discussing the patient's areas of vulnerability and how to avoid them. Another topic is the language of the patient: how to avoid misinterpretations both on the part of the patient and on the part of the relative. Attention has to be given to why and how even simple remarks like "What did you prepare today for lunch?" can be interpreted by the patient as malicious insinuation.

An important part of the instructions to relatives is how to behave when the patient makes such drastic announcements of decisions like becoming engaged, married, moving to a different state or country, or leaving the husband and going to live with another man. The delaying technique, trying to persuade the patient to wait for a time when he feels more at ease with such projects, is the proper attitude. If the patient insists, however, and cannot be persuaded to postpone his actions, the best thing is to go along and to be of as much help as possible. The same thing could be said for the recovering schizophrenic woman who wants to become pregnant. Pregnancy and motherhood are real challenges for "normal" women. To deliberately invite such a complication while recovering is not recommended.

Contrary to what was advocated until not too long ago, it is not correct to assume that a patient should be told the truth about unpleasant, unexpected news, like the death of a dear one or a demand for divorce. It is not true that he is able to take everything, even if he presents an air of indifference. The patient has to be prepared for the truth. The truth, of course, eventually has to be communicated to him, but only when he has built enough defenses with which he will be able to face it. A complaint that one often hears from relatives is the following: "I want to be genuine, authentic. Since Jean came back, I have to watch every word I say to her. I can't be spontaneous any more. But I don't know if what I'm doing is right. Maybe by being artificial like this, I'm doing some harm. I believe in being authentic." Such doubts, posed to oneself or to the psychiatrist, are legitimate and worthy of full consideration. The relative must analyze further what he means by authenticity. To watch one's words before talking to Jean does not necessarily mean to lose one's authenticity. But to act as if a serious illness had not occurred to a person close to us is not to live authentically. It is authentic and more beneficial to realize that on account of the patient's particular vulnerability and sensitivity, we must modify some of our ways and refrain from using words or phrases that may sound ambiguous or even threatening to him. Moreover, let us remember that in recognizing areas of vulnerability for the patient, we may discover where and how we have been unintentionally insensitive and perhaps even callous. We may recognize that we have wanted to impose our ways because we considered them more appropriate, more efficient, more in agreement with what society expects, or simply because we liked them better.

In summary, living day by day with a recovering schizophrenic is a difficult task, but not an insurmountable one. It can be rewarding not only for the patient but for everyone concerned.

Every member of a family who participates in this reintegrative effort will understand that by helping the schizophrenic we may also help ourselves. We become less impervious to veiled hostility, less blind to what we do not want to see, more apt to understand a voice of dissent, even if it is expressed in an awkward or exaggerated manner. We become better able to listen to words we are generally inclined to ignore because they come from sources that seem irrational, meek, or inappropriately humble.

There, where modern psychiatric science and our hearts meet, is the place in which help for the schizophrenic is to be found, and in which hopes for further recovery are conceived, nourished, and activated.

2

Introductory Comments on Psychoanalytically Oriented Treatment of Schizophrenia:

INTEGRATION OF THEORY AND THERAPY

Michael H. Stone, M.D.

> The schizophrenic patient and the therapist are people living in different worlds and on different levels of personal development with different means of expressing and of orienting themselves. We know little about the language of the unconscious of the schizophrenic, and our access to it is blocked by the very process of our own adjustment to a world the schizophrenic has relinquished. So we should not be surprised that errors and misunderstandings occur when we undertake to communicate and strive for a rapport with him.
>
> Frieda Fromm-Reichmann (1939, p. 416)

Psychotherapy with schizophrenics is a topic much broader than its brief title would suggest. Schizophrenics span the whole range of adaptational levels, from the fairly well functioning ambulatory patients, to the more populous ambulatory but marginally functioning, to the hospitalized cases. Among the latter will be found patients for whom the restoration of at least the premorbid level of function is quite feasible, and still other patients whose chronicity defies our current therapeutic capacities. The topic is broadened further by our having to take into account the fact that amenability to psychotherapy depends in some measure on preexisting personality patterns. The schizophrenic patient who is incapacitated only to a mild degree—socially, say, but not occupationally—but who has the kind of paranoid features that predictably alienate most other people, will tend to improve but little with verbal psychotherapy. The same schizophrenic label, if applied to an acutely delusional person who, in his premorbid state, got along reasonably well with his fellow man, and who is capable of forming a cooperative relationship with his therapist, may make rapid strides once the acute psychosis has subsided, and may eventually outpace the never-psychotic but highly abrasive patient in the previous example.

In our era many more modalities of treatment are available, or have advanced to a higher level of efficacy, than was the case a generation ago. Seldom will a schizophrenic patient with serious impairments improve to his maximum ability with one-to-one verbal therapy alone, but, on our part, we are no longer limited to such a narrow base of operations as prevailed in the era of, say, Ernst Simmel (1929) or Ruth Mack Brunswick (1929). Since our verbal psychotherapeutic efforts will, especially in the case of hospitalized schizophrenic patients, be one of perhaps half a dozen treatment approaches, it behooves us to know how one-to-one psychotherapy is best integrated within the overall treatment. Many difficult clinical judgments enter into the equation, and the equation itself, containing so many variables, cannot be set forth in a mathematically neat fashion. What balance to strike, at any given moment, between a supportive and a psychoanalytically oriented ("expressive") mode is one relevant question. How many sessions per week, and of what length, is another. Under what circumstances is expressive therapy most likely to benefit the patient? Which schizophrenic patients will, sooner or later, have the best chance of realizing some benefit from analytically oriented exploration of their psychic conflicts? Beside these questions rests another set of important considerations, applicable particularly to work with inpatients. Which life-tasks has the schizophrenic patient mastered sufficiently well that we may relegate them to the background as we evolve our initial plans for comprehensive treatment; which tasks has the patient failed to master? Freud compartmentalized life into two broad arenas in his famous response about the essence of life: Love and Work. In thinking about a comprehensive therapy for schizophrenic patients it will, with all deference to the master, be useful to analyze life into a somewhat larger number of compartments.

On the most primitive level, for example, one must be able to conduct life via strategies that, at the very least, safeguard the existence of the individual. One must eat and sleep properly, pay attention to traffic signs, and so forth. Acutely ill schizophrenic patients, even without being overtly suicidal, cannot always be counted on to pay attention to these simple ground rules of *self-preservation*. One step above self-preservation is a level relating to *civility*. Civility relates to the whole complex of patterns for interacting with one's fellow man in harmonious ways, demarcating appropriate boundaries between ourselves and the territories of others, sensing and respecting—deferring to, if you will—the feelings of others, maximizing one's comfort and success by putting the other person at ease, and so on.

Schizophrenic patients, those in the hospital particularly, often display alarmingly little knack (and not much predilection) for getting along in the world of strangers. I think in this connection of a borderline schizophrenic young man who, in the dormitory of the ward, fell into the habit of masturbating in front of his bunk-mates and then drinking his semen. To this day I have only a dim appreciation of the psychodynamic currents and cross-currents that underlay this behavior. What was so striking about this custom was the gross insensitivity it manifested to the sensibilities of those in the patient's immediate vicinity. In some instances of this sort (usually they will be less blatant) the schizophrenic patient is so out of touch with the feelings of ordinary people (in a way that manic-depressives seldom are) that he has to be carefully and repetitively taught to realize the impact his behavior has on others.[1]

Patients whose self-preservative instincts are intact and who are civil enough to keep their neighbors' hostility to a minimum, may nevertheless fail at life-tasks one level higher: *getting along with one's original family.* One's parents and siblings will regularly make allowances for behavior or verbalizations not so easily tolerated by others. Many schizophrenic patients are ''arrested'' at this level of interpersonal development: having conquered self-preservation and civility to some degree, they nevertheless get along so disastrously within the confines of their home as to become ''extruded,'' landing either in our office or the hospital.

Other schizophrenic patients will master these first three steps, only to fail at the next—*to perform adequately at some remunerative job* (or, in the case of an adolescent, at his school assignments). Inability to work, whether because of disorganized thinking or suspiciousness about the intentions of one's coworkers, naturally condemns one to perpetual dependence on the original family, or, where this resource is unavailable, on various benevolent institutions.

We might have inserted a previous step—*the ability to play and to amuse oneself when alone*—ahead of the ability to work, inasmuch as it is generally easier to play than to maintain a job. But the two tasks are often inextricably intertwined: patients who can keep themselves together at their place of employment, but who panic if left alone in their apartment during the evenings or weekends for want of the simplest ''sublimatory'' capacities, tend to ''decompensate'' to the point of no longer being able to work, either.

At all events, beyond the level of harmonious life with the family of origin lies the level of *intimacy with a sexual partner,* with whom one would endeavor to create a new family. This is the highest level of human function with respect to the psychological demands made upon the individual. Neurotic patients who are considered appropriate cases for psychoanalysis will customarily be found to have progressed to the point where their problems center chiefly around such life-tasks as separation from the family of origin, selec-

---

[1]The man from the preceding example, however, knew that his fellow patients would find his habit repugnant: he hoped to get himself ''kicked out'' (as an unwanted or untreatable patient), so he could return home. Lessons in civility were not so much required as a special type of behavior modification, coupled with interpretive psychotherapy.

tion of a marriage partner, or the establishment of good relationships with their children. Neurotic patients usually have at least a few close friends; many schizophrenic patients have never had a close friend. Difficulties in making friends may have arisen for any one of several reasons: some schizophrenic patients are terrified of interpersonal closeness, lest their sense of identity become swamped by the other person; others may not suffer from this type of ego-boundary problem, but may be so unable to resonate empathically with other people as to appear eccentric, "freaky," or otherwise unappealing to potential friends. The schizophrenic who tries to "cheer up" a mourner at a funeral by cracking a joke would exemplify this type of difficulty. Still other schizophrenic persons suffer a life-long *anhedonia,* most likely on a constitutional basis (see Rado, 1956), and intimacy is shunned as harboring too many sources of danger and discomfort, in comparison to its all too meager sources, for them, of pleasure and excitement.

It should not be surprising, in the light of preceding comments, that few schizophrenics, even borderline schizophrenics who have never exhibited signs of psychosis, lead lives that are trouble-free with respect to intimacy. Problems in achieving intimacy will often remain as stumbling-blocks to further progress long after our psychotherapeutic efforts have helped the schizophrenic patient establish some measure of autonomy and self-support through work.

I have dwelt at some length on levels of function and life compartments to demonstrate the correspondences that exist between these tasks and the kinds of specialists, within the broad field of psychiatry, that have been created to help schizophrenic (and other) patients negotiate these tasks—and the interpersonal transactions related to them. It is not for nothing that the hospitalized schizophrenic patient finds himself surrounded by an array of mental health experts from many disciplines: nursing, social service, occupational therapy, and so on.

In Table 2-1 I have attempted to portray these correspondences in schematic fashion. Readers familiar with Von Bertalanffy's systems theory (1968) will recognize in this schema the "systems approach" as I have applied it to the therapy of schizophrenics.

By way of illustration, one can imagine a schizophrenic patient, actively delusional and in poor contact with reality, who is admitted following a heated argument at home with his parents because of his refusal to come out of his room or to bathe during the preceding month. Such a patient may require the services of seven or eight specialists before achieving his maximum gain. Besides effective nursing care he will need the intervention of the social worker to help resolve problems at the patient-family interface.

TABLE 2–1

PSYCHOTHERAPY WITH SCHIZOPHRENICS: RELATIONSHIPS BETWEEN AREAS OF BREAKDOWN AND THERAPEUTIC SUBSPECIALTIES

	Major Life-Task	Manifestations of Failure	Treatment Modalities Relevant to Correction	Relevant Mental Health Expert
1.	Self-Preservation	suicidal behavior	nursing care	nursing staff, physician
2.	Civility (good relationships with strangers)	rudeness, violence	nursing care, behavior modification	nursing staff, behavioral therapist
3.	Good relationships with family of origin	disharmony with family; rudeness, abusiveness, etc., confined to family members	social service, family therapy	social worker
4.	Recreation	anxiety when alone	recreation therapy	recreational therapist
5.	School or work	incapacity to work (or to complete school) and to sustain oneself independently	occupational therapy	occupational therapist
6.	Good relationships with friends	avoidance of others; being shunned by others	group therapy, behavior modification, psychotherapy	group therapist, behavioral therapist, psychotherapist
7.	Intimacy with (potential) marriage partner	shallow existence devoid of close, lasting and meaningful relationships	analytically oriented 1:1 psychotherapy	psychotherapist, psychoanalyst

Note: Gross failure at Tasks 1–5 is usually incompatible with ambulatory function.

Someone trained in behavior modification technics may be called in, perhaps when the acute psychotic symptoms have begun to subside, to help win the cooperation of the patient in the task of forming more acceptable personal habits. Problems in the areas of work and leisure will be addressed by recreational and occupational therapists. The patient's negativism and alienating social facade may then be dealt with in group therapy. If he begins to experiment with forming friendships, or moves on to the beginnings of a more intimate relationship with a sexual partner, he will need the special skills of the analytically oriented psychotherapist, who may, up to this point, have been acting as a coordinator of the other specialists clustered around the patient during the earlier phases of treatment, but who now becomes the central figure in therapy. In "systems" terms, as the patient reaches the level where problems in dyadic relationships are all that remain to work on, the dyadic relationship of therapist-patient moves into paramount importance—the position once occupied by the nursing staff, social worker, or behavior modification expert during earlier phases of the work. In the acute psychotic phase some form of pharmacotherapy will probably have been necessary, administered in some instances by the psychiatrist in charge of the case, in other instances by a consultant psychopharmacologist.[2]

Since the focus in this book is on verbal psychotherapy with schizophrenic patients, we will be paying special attention to conflicts and problems relating to the hierarchically higher levels of interpersonal relatedness, as these were outlined in Table 2-1. Examples will be drawn from behavior therapy and group therapy, but the majority of the clinical vignettes and the theoretical or practical comments related to them will have their origin in experience with a two-person field: the schizophrenic patient and his therapist. The terms "psychoanalytically oriented" or Kernberg's modification of it—"expressive"—will be used interchangeably to qualify this type of psychotherapy.

A book on psychotherapy with schizophrenic patients must also give special emphasis to methods for handling problems peculiar to schizophrenia

---

[2]Further recommendations regarding the pharmacotherapeutic approach during the acute phase may be gleaned from the article by Cazzullo (1976); during the chronic phase, from the contribution of Munkvad et al. (1976). For another systems view of the integrated treatment of schizophrenia, where special attention is paid to the family, Fleck (1976) should be consulted, along with others who focus on family factors, including Stierlin (1976) and Reiss and Wyatt (1978). An integrated approach focusing on milieu is outlined in Paul (1980); the benefits of an "intensive" milieu for inpatients have been put forward recently by Gunderson (1980). Psychosocial treatment integrating individual, group, and family approaches has been described by Mosher and Keith (1980).

itself, rather than to psychosis in general. This means we will be particularly concerned with the consequences of the chronic ego-boundary disturbances so frequently encountered among schizophrenic patients. These are certain eccentricities of thought, speech, and behavior common to schizophrenia but not common to manic-depression or the "organic" psychoses; these, too, will be singled out here for special attention. Paradoxical situations crop up again and again in expressive therapy with schizophrenics; often these are manifestations of the neatly divided ambivalence of the patient, who may have as much, or a little more, emotion invested in the direct *opposite* of what he is stating, as in the stated message itself. Likewise, those who do intensive work with schizophrenics must be equipped with strategies to counter the *anhedonia,* which casts a grayness and, often, an atmosphere of despondency over the life of the patient. In the earlier phases of treatment especially, the schizophrenic patient so seldom says what he means, or means what he says, that we must become adept at making instantaneous translations of symbol-laden, encoded messages to their everyday equivalents, and we must develop a knack for shifting quickly to whatever layer of discourse contains the affects which are most importantly influencing the patient at any given moment. An example may help to clarify this last point; it derives from a personal anecdote, mentioned in the course of a teaching session, by the noted clinician Louis Linn:

> Once, when Dr. Linn was on duty at the emergency ward of Bellevue Psychiatric Hospital, a schizophrenic man, very belligerent and paranoid, drew a gun on Dr. Linn during an interview. Dr. Linn, with a coolness and clinical savvy not all could summon at such a moment, quietly asked, "What are you afraid of?"—whereupon the gunman relaxed and put his weapon on the table.

What may have prompted this extraordinarily intuitive and empathic response on the part of someone whose more ordinary feelings would have been terror? Dr. Linn sensed that, because he *ought* to have felt terror—and indeed experienced some moments of terror, initially—the patient was most likely himself operating out of sheer terror. But because the patient could not cope effectively with whatever was inducing this panicky state, he acted in such a way, as schizophrenic patients so regularly do, as to "laterole" this feeling-state into another person. Furthermore, the terror must have been uppermost—more intense, for instance, than anger at Dr. Linn, since he was a total stranger, capable of inspiring (in a *realistic* way) neither love nor hate. The comment "What are you afraid of" is a therapeutic translation of the instant realization, This guy is certainly trying to make *me* feel afraid! The comment dives below the level of the explicit and gets underneath, to where the dominant but unstated affects resided: the patient was afraid (but too proud, too unaware, or whatever, to start talking about it). The full plaintext of what the patient was communicating might have read like this: "I'm scared out of my mind! I don't dare *tell* you I'm scared because I'd lose face, but I at least can make you feel my fear—because when I point this gun at you—I don't really mean to shoot—you'll *know* the kind of fear that's eating me up!" Dr. Linn's remark demonstrated his recognition of the patient's inner state, and shows how, when therapist is resonating ideally with his patient, one "unconscious" can speak to another.

In any extended psychotherapy, of course, our ultimate goal is to help the schizophrenic patient grow more comfortable with his inner feeling states, so that he can speak about them, however embarrassing they might be, with some candor. This would obviate the need for the kind of indirection and externalization resorted to by the man with the gun. How much better for him to have been able to say, straightaway, that he was in a state of panic because (as an example) some men in the street looked as though they were calling him a faggot and that he himself often feels very uncomfortable about just how much of a man he really is, etc., etc. For want of such candor and self-knowledge, the schizophrenic patient is at the mercy of the few individuals gifted with the ability both to sense the patient's hidden affects and messages and to address them appropriately and with the proper timing.

We have not only to ferret out hidden meanings (often of a sort rarely encountered in analytic work with neurotics), but we must also be alive to the many gradations that usually exist in the continuum of meanings—and in the continuum of possible responses—so that we can teach the schizophrenic patient how he might react more flexibly to situations he habitually perceives in an all-or-none way. The paranoid patient, for example, who regards admission of any psychological problem as a confession of weakness, who must pose as "all strong" lest he appear "all weak" (see Guntrip, 1962), needs to be educated about the much more complex set of values by which the bulk of the world lives. It can, after all, be an act of courage for someone to confess a weakness, the more so if he has hitherto regarded such admissions as sure signs of even greater weakness.

Failure to grasp the secret meanings of our schizophrenic patients' utterances and gestures, is, of course, not the only stumbling block to our therapeutic efforts. It frequently happens, with neophyte therapists more often than with experienced ones, that we understand the meaning, or rather the barrage of meanings, the patient wishes to convey, we may even understand the place within the hierarchy of importance that each of these mean-ings momentarily occupies; but we may not know what to do next. We may feel inhibited from expressing some particular thought or feeling of our own, lest we "harm" the patient. Schizophrenic patients, meanwhile, have a strong penchant for inducing in us their own uncomfortable affects. Fur-thermore, the schizophrenic patient will experience us as not only har-boring the very affects and attitudes he cannot acknowledge in himself, but as harboring them in a way that is directed *against* him. This tendency, called "projective identification" (see Ogden, 1979), is not restricted to schizophrenics and may be seen also in work with borderline patients of all types. But projective identification may be a particularly difficult type of transference distortion to unravel, where schizophrenic patients are con-cerned. Owing to their (generally) weaker hold on reality, they will be slower to grasp the differences between the therapist as he really is and the therapist as they imagine him to be.

· · · · ·

Although Harry Stack Sullivan and others trained in his approach have pointed out that schizophrenics share many qualities with the rest of the population, and are more like other people than they are different, still it is the differences that include the pathological. The differences become the focus of our concern as therapists. Furthermore, a valid case could probably be made for the claim that each schizophrenic—perhaps because of the au-tism and solipsistic thinking peculiar to their condition—is more "differ-ent" from other schizophrenics (in experience, in perceptions of the world around him, and so on) than neurotics are different from other neurotics. Learning to understand neurotic persons (in the course of psychoanalytic training, for example) is rather like learning a new language. Learning to understand schizophrenics is like learning a separate language for each patient.

One may then well ask: if the idiosyncratic qualities of patients under this heading seem to defy generalizations, what can be taught in the psychother-apy of schizophrenia? Even though the variety we encounter in the clinical situation is infinite, however, there are useful generalizations. It is seldom a successful maneuver, for instance, to tackle the delusions of a paranoid patient head on. It is not as often helpful to encourage free association in schizophrenics as it is with neurotics, because schizophrenics are already flooded by primary process material by the very nature of their illness, and tend toward divergent rather than covergent thinking if left to their own de-vices. They would tend all too often to wander onto topics that lead nowhere. Instead of free association (which always has a measure of directedness in neurotics and leads to material of greater emotional meaning), the schizophrenic's associations tend toward randomness.

What is *not* teachable in the psychotherapy of schizophrenia is a precisely specific program of therapeutic interventions. As in chess, there are a few opening moves that can be taught and discussed, a few do's and don'ts; beyond that the staggeringly large numbers of meanings and possible responses make the programming of interventions impossible and push us into the territory of intuition. But clinical intuition can be improved, through teaching, to well exceed what it might be in the natural state. The art of psychotherapy can be taught through example, through analogy. Supervision by seasoned clinicians, along with written material, can provide a less-experienced therapist with a large array of examples—in effect, a dictionary of examples, capable of being systematized and drawn upon at a later date. The more similar the therapist is to a supervisor or to the contributors of a book, the easier it will be to assimilate the kinds of responses encountered in these sources. The closer his patient resembles one or another patient described in a clinical vignette, the more applicable will be the intervention used by supervisor or author. Also, as a means of becoming better acquainted with the hidden (and usually, unconscious) elements in his own personality—in order both to understand more readily the symbolism of the patients' words and acts and to acknowledge more comfortably one's countertransference feelings as they emerge in the course of psychotherapy—a personal analysis is considered essential by those who specialize in the intensive therapy of schizophrenics.

Even without much training, the fledgling therapist enjoys one great advantage over most of his schizophrenic patients. Almost surely, the patient sees life in stark terms, as full of hazards, perhaps even the threat of annihilation, at every turn. And to deal with these hazards, the patient sees himself as having very few options, and probably no *effective* options. This drastically abbreviated set of coping strategies contrasts strongly with the therapist's set. Most therapists, like most people, do not experience ordinary social problems, work conflicts, and the like, in life-or-death terms. We are able to generate a number of possible countermoves to most difficult situations. For this reason, we will usually be able to serve as a "mind-expanding" agent for the schizophrenic patient, teaching him alternatives that would otherwise never have occurred to him.

When we ourselves are at an impasse, it is, of course, our own minds that must be expanded—through supervision, personal analysis, or the written word. Supervision and literature on psychotherapy with schizophrenics should, incidentally, be viewed as complementary, since each has certain advantages and drawbacks. Supervision tends to be more useful with the case at hand. The personality and peculiarities of the therapist can also be dealt with in the intimacy of the supervisor-therapist relationship. And since schizophrenic patients, more so than neurotic patients, tend to get personal with their therapists, put them on the spot more often, and abide less by the ordinary boundaries of the patient-therapist relationship, they will awaken countertransference feelings more often, and of a more disturbing nature, than will be the case in analytic work with psychoneurotics. Here supervision can be very helpful. But no one supervisor or group of supervisors possesses the experience reflected in the corpus of writings on our subject; and because supervision dwells mostly on moment-to-moment interactions with particular patients, it seldom offers the systematic discussion or the concentrated presentation of unusually illustrative examples such as can be found in the literature. Both supervision and the recorded experience of clinicians can help therapists acknowledge, accept, and integrate the many stormy and embarrassing feelings—contempt, hatred, erotic interest, etc.—that schizophrenic patients will predictably awaken in their therapists at unpredictable moments.

Feelings of symbiotic oneness with a patient, for example, can be highly unnerving. During my residency training I had occasion to work with a young schizoaffective woman who had been brutalized by both parents— verbally, by her mother and physically, by her father. Her own personality inclined toward the paranoid, partly for reasons that seemed all too justifiable in light of her mother's hostility and her father's violence. The "reasonableness" of her mistrust, however, did not make her scornfulness or outbursts of rage any easier for me to bear—the more so for their being mobilized by (to my way of thinking) the most trivial signs of inattention. My being away from the hospital over the weekend, for example, or her catching sight of a squash paddle in the office closet (a sign that I sometimes "stopped" being a serious physician to go out and have a good time), would trigger blasts of vilification. After several months of enduring these attacks (the experience was rather like living in the vicinity of Mount St. Helens), the atmosphere in our sessions gave way to one of serenity and tenderness. She spoke very little, and stared at me with affection as unalloyed as the hatred in her glances of a week before. Sometimes she would seem, especially if she were wearing a sweater similar in color to the back of her chair, to blend into the furniture. This impression of her having somehow merged with her inanimate surroundings was perhaps an extension of the even eerier feeling of my having merged, transitorily, with this patient. Similar aberrations in one's sense of ego boundary are, of course, a regular accompaniment of romantic infatuation—which, for most men, may be the only paradigm for such experience. But the largely asexual mother-child symbiosis would seem to be an even more powerful paradigm for these experiences of merging, and may indeed constitute the template upon which the ontogenetically later-occurring boundary-lessness of first love is ultimately fashioned. It is unsettling to be adored, because the importance one suddenly acquires in the life of another person imposes on us an immense responsibility. This is doubly true in the therapeutic encounter, because, no matter how typical and necessary such adoration is in the course of recovering from a schizophrenic illness, the therapist will tend to experience it (along with whatever emotions are stirred up in him) as unprofessional, too personal, a manifestation of things having gone awry in the treatment. Nonetheless, if recovery depends on the patient's passing through a stage of symbiotic oneness, then the emergence of this stage must be endured, even welcomed. To be cast in the role of a mother, especially the mother of a quite young infant, may be particularly disturbing for male therapists, the more so if instabilities in their sense of masculinity exist. With the patient in question, several weeks of thrice weekly sessions were spent in this nearly silent, visual drinking-in of one another, whereupon she become able to put into words the inchoate feelings of having had no sense of closeness with her mother, which had for so long made her feel at once deprived and alienated from her fellow human beings. This patient went on to make a splendid recovery, fostered in no small measure by the excellent supervision I received, which rendered more comprehensible, and more endurable, the uncanny symbiotic state in which the patient and I had been so disconcertingly enmeshed.

With respect to the therapist's mind-expanding function, the following vignette can serve to illustrate how the narrow range of options available to the mind of the schizophrenic patient may be broadened via the "auxiliary ego" of the therapist. The patient in this vignette was experiencing a sense of entrapment because she could think of only two ways of dealing with a difficult situation, neither of which allowed her any relief from anxiety. The therapist, without delving into her past, or into the psychodynamics of an uncomfortable mother-daughter relationship, was able to show her a way out of her predicament simply by coming up with other, less anxiety-engendering alternatives.

> A woman in her mid-thirties was living alone after the break-up of her marriage. She was an amateur musician of considerable skill, though she never had the sangfroid to perform in public. Her mother and brother were particularly intrusive and controlling individuals, and took turns trying either to pry into the patient's per-

sonal affairs or to run her life. She could not as yet stand up to either relative, and felt guilty in advance at the thought of hurting their feelings were she to refuse a request. At the same time, she was exasperated at the outlandish ways in which they would inconvenience her. She dreaded the ring of the telephone, since it was almost sure to be one or the other of them about to buttonhole her for half an hour in the course of asking for some favor she could neither refuse nor comfortably accede to. She prayed only to be allowed a few uninterrupted hours each day in which to practice her piano, but seldom would more than an hour go by without a call. Not to answer the phone, however, seemed unconscionable to her, since (a) it might annoy the relative, who, she supposed, would make even more trouble for her in the immediate future, and (b) she was anyhow merely an amateur, who could not rightfully claim that she needed to practice without picking up the phone—a privilege she assumed inhered only to the status of professional musicians. Besides, what if it were a friend that called? What to do? Since she was not yet psychologically prepared to decline requests or cut short the calls from her relatives (those capacities were not to develop for another two or three years), I felt it more practical to suggest a mechanical solution to her dilemma. If she were to install a second, unlisted phone in her house, she could give the new number just to those people whom she wouldn't at all mind hearing from. She wouldn't have to fear missing a truly important call from her children or her employer. Once she took this step, she became much less anxious, since she didn't mind the occasional and brief interruptions from the "good" phone, and simply turned the "bad" phone off until she had finished practicing or until she mustered the courage to confront her mother and brother. This freedom, I suspect, actually hastened the day when she no longer needed such a device. In her now calmer state, she was able to utilize her psychotherapy more effectively, developing the courage and sense of entitlement to stand her own ground—presumably at a more rapid pace than she could have, so long as she was being unnerved by her relatives.

The preceding clinical example demonstrates one of the ingredients that may be distinguished within the day-to-day flow of psychotherapy with schizophrenic patients. Different authors have stressed one or another component as being critical to the therapeutic process. Gedo (1980), for example, has emphasized the importance of building up the patient's *ego skills* through objective means. My advice about getting a second phone represents an intervention of this kind. Kohut (1971) has stressed the therapist's *empathy;* Gill (1981) would focus on the vicissitudes of the *transference* relationship as "the" curative factor (perhaps more so with better integrated patients, and not so much with schizophrenics); the British objects-relation school (Guntrip, 1967; Fairbairn, 1944) draws attention, as do the Sullivanians, to the *interpersonal* relationship (Sullivan, 1956). Psychodynamic *interpretations* have been underscored by various psychoanalytic authors as key elements, especially when these interpretations effect "transmuting internalizations" in the patient's psyche (i.e., produce some beneficial structural change in the mind).

In my view, all these ingredients are important, just as their advocates maintain. But I don't think one can generalize about how they could be arranged hierarchically. Intensive analytically oriented psychotherapy, by definition, requires attention to transference distortions. But the degree to which transference/countertransference issues occupy the center of the therapeutic stage will vary from one schizophrenic patient to another and will vary from one phase to another in the treatment of any particular case. It might be less humiliating, for example, for a male schizophrenic patient with pronounced paranoid and obsessional features to speak of missing a female therapist before her vacation, whereas to express such yearning for a male therapist might be tinged to an unacceptable degree with homoerotic overtones. In the latter situation, transference issues of this sort may be difficult to broach for a long time.

The most finely honed empathic skills may go for naught during certain periods when the schizophrenic patient is so out of touch with some significant conflict as not to betray it in any detectable way within the therapeutic setting. Intuition will not tell us what is on the dark side of the moon. In hospital work, therapists are less at the mercy of their empathic capacity, of course, because what is concealed during the sessions is often revealed, through behavior, to the nurse or the attendant.

Few schizophrenic patients, even those who start out and remain ambulatory, can reach their maximal level of improvement without devoting some time to the acquisition of "ego skills." The attentional deficits and boundary confusion so characteristic of their condition often render them both out of tune with the needs and feelings of others and handicapped in learning how to grasp what makes other people tick.

One such patient was a borderline schizophrenic engineer I had worked with for many years. Though successful, he was an isolated, lonely man with peculiar habits that annoyed or repelled those with whom he came in contact. He showed no awareness of the margin of error ordinary people accept as a part of life. Once, he demanded a shopkeeper to take back an attaché case because the period after one of the gold monograms was misplaced. The store manager was irate—which left my patient quite baffled. Honest mistakes, a repairman's lack of punctuality, were experienced as malicious acts. But if he dropped cigarette ashes on his dentist's rug, or left peach pits on the magazines of a consultant's waiting room, he could not understand why either should become offended. As he grew somewhat more aware of his eccentricities, and of their impact on others, he was able to speak more candidly, even poignantly, about his insensitivity:

> "I just don't understand people, how they work. I don't even care a whole lot, frankly. People's natures don't fascinate me the way I suppose they fascinate you. I care about people only to the extent of what they can do for me. But I feel like an outcast, outside the pale of ordinary human existence."

The earlier years of psychotherapy with this man were concerned primarily with dynamic factors and transference distortions. The latter years were devoted to teaching him tact and diplomacy. In time, he acquired a better "feedback mechanism" for understanding social situations. This led to some mellowing of his otherwise abrasive facade and to distinct improvements in his relationships with friends and coworkers.

Therapist-Theory Interplay

Sutherland (1980, p. 832) has mentioned, in his article on the British object-relations school, that therapeutic styles are influenced by the personalities of the theoreticians who recommend one or another approach. To this truism, I would add that theoretical formulations are influenced by the personality of the theoretician, and not merely by the particular sample, out of a complex set, with which the theoretician becomes most familiar. *Cognitive style* enters into the picture, for example. There would appear to be biological differences, relating in part to the fine structure of the dominant versus the nondominant hemispheres and to their interrelationship, that influence which of us operates particularly well in an intuitive (nondominant hemisphere mediated) way and which of us excels at sequential, analytic understanding of new material. I believe that many of the differences between Searles' views and those of Kernberg can be resolved if we take into account the basically intuitive mode (however highly refined through experience) by which Searles functions, in contrast to the highly analytical, category-oriented mode we encounter in Kernberg's formulations.

Theoretical differences (and differences in therapeutic recommendations) are shaped, of course, by sample differences. Searles and Fromm-Reichmann spent considerably more time working with severely ill schizophrenic patients than did Arlow and Brenner. The schizophrenic patients on whom Arieti and Szalita have based their theoretical comments represent a less-often or less-continuously hospitalized group than those to whom Fromm-Reichmann or Searles (in his earlier work at Chestnut Lodge) devoted their efforts. Balint, Winnicott, Fairbairn, and Guntrip, of the British school, worked with fairly regressed schizoid patients—patients who were at the very perimeter, if not quite outside, the domain of "analyzability."

Kohut and his followers, whose work may be seen as a natural progression of the British school's (especially of Fairbairn's) concepts about the self, based their assumptions on work with office patients. The patients that make up the clinical material of the Chicago school seem nearer to analyzability than do many of those about whom Bryce-Boyer (1971) or Giovacchini (1980) have described, who seem at the very edge of hospitalization[3] (or who have been briefly hospitalized) during the early phases of psychoanalytic psychotherapy.

To focus for the moment on the role of *empathy* in theoretical or therapeutic formulations about "schizophrenia," we must appraise these ideas not only in accordance with their surface reasonableness, but also in accordance with whether the theoretician in question is emphasizing empathy (as do Kohut, Szalita, and Searles) because his or her mind is especially well constructed for that quality. Furthermore, one must ask: is the *patient sample* of schizophrenic (or schizotypal borderline or schizoid) individuals, in relation to whom a certain theory was fashioned, one which could be reached via the average therapist's empathic skills? Or, do those writers who deemphasize the role of empathy, do so because the schizophrenic population with whom they are most familiar lies beyond the pale of empathy? It is probably fair to say that the more ill, and more continuously hospitalized, a schizophrenic patient is, the more time he will have spent making obscure utterances or gestures that defy ready interpretation by almost any therapist he is ever likely to encounter.

Comparisons among theories that we are attending to at the moment are rendered the more difficult owing to the unpleasant paradox that those who write about analytic psychotherapy of schizophrenic persons write, as Guntrip (1967) would say, in the *humanistic* mode. Those who describe best whatever categorical, diagnostic distinctions may exist between one patient and another are usually psychiatrists with no facility or experience in this

---

[3]Actually, Bryce-Boyer (1966) advocates the avoidance of hospitalization wherever possible.

kind of psychotherapy. It is owing to this unfortunate trend that we find it so unclear whether the patients Balint (see Morse, 1972) saw as exhibiting the severest degree of "basic fault" were schizophrenic in the DSM-III sense of the term, or were schizotypal persons functioning at Kernberg's borderline level, or what.

The Kleinians, in fact, hypothesize a paranoid/schizoid position as a normal stage early in infant development. Schizoid withdrawal can become exaggerated (Guntrip, 1962, 1967) if fear of the "bad" (maternal) object is intensified through maternal insensitivity or destructiveness. The British school envisions a continuum between normality, neurotic with schizoid tendencies (Balint's "philobat": see Sutherland, 1980), and the sicker forms of schizoid behavior (including, presumably, outright schizophrenia). There is a tendency here to analogize the normal infant's temporary withdrawal from its caretakers with the adult schizophrenic's repudiation of the external world. There is something ironic in this tendency, at least to my way of thinking, insofar as the Kleinians have been instrumental in broadening psychoanalytical theory through their emphasis on object relations, so as to encompass the deeper (schizophrenic) disturbances that classical theory deals with so awkwardly; yet the Kleinians pay so little attention to conventional diagnosis as to leave their readers bewildered as to how ill some of their "schizoid" patients really are. Their implied notion of a continuum from normality to schizoid regression is left as a matter of faith.

It may seem to many that our knowledge of the nature and of the optimal treatment for schizophrenics is still too meager to support a solid theory; in which case are we not open to the accusation of indulging in so much Talmudic *pilpul?* My personal view is that we are indeed rather far from establishing a solid theory about schizophrenia, but that we have come far enough in our understanding to justify model-building of some preliminary sort and to test some of the theories spawned by this kind of intellectual exercise. There is, after all, a dynamic equilibrium between therapy and theory. Effective therapy (initially relying on intuitive hunches) contributes to the formation of (better) theories. A good theory should improve therapy (if case B resembles case A, what benefitted case A may be helpful with B, etc.). There are pitfalls, however. Theories can be mistreated, and can lead to rigidification of approach. Theories represent simplifications. In psychiatry, this means certain clinical data are ignored while others are scrupulously attended to. Adherence to a theory carries with it the danger of inflexibility; this is the price we pay for the ease in therapeutic approach that the theory may promise. I have seen neophyte psychiatrists eschew medications in treating certain "borderline" patients, having learned the ABCs of Kernberg's formulations about the sufficiency of expressive psychotherapy for borderlines. But when these (usually, affectively ill, hospitalized) "borderlines" were seen in consultation by Kernberg—who knows the XYZs, as well as the ABCs—Kernberg would (in the eyes of the residents) depart from his own theory, and recommend antidepressants. Some borderline patients are simply exceptions to the rules that apply to the majority, no matter how that majority comes to be defined.

Before we examine in greater detail some of the psychoanalytical theories regarding schizophrenia, it is worth noting that even the best theoretician, equipped with the most comprehensive theory about schizophrenogenesis, will not always succeed in helping certain patients within the schizophrenic spectrum (even broadly defined), because of what one might call the human element. As the British school has reminded us, "To be able to love and enjoy, the baby has to be loved and enjoyed" (Sutherland, 1980, p. 857). But, as Dahl (1978) points out, "There is no consummatory act that the child can perform to satisfy his wish to be loved." Optimal human development depends on the nonrational factor of a mother's spontaneous and unteachable love for her baby. Most people are lucky enough to have been the recipients of this love. Some (though not all) schizophrenic persons appear to have started out in life seriously handicapped through not receiving such love. Others fail to integrate the love they receive from what probably are good-enough mothers, in Winnicott's (1965) terms, and end up starving amidst plenty.[4] Although improvement in schizophrenic patients is not contingent on their receiving the love they may not have been given as children, optimism, the ability to radiate hope, and a joyousness in one's work are probably important ingredients in therapists who do well with such patients (Stone, 1971). Yet these human qualities cannot be imbibed along with the ingestion of this or that theory. Some schizophrenic patients are lucky enough to find a therapist who truly enjoys working with them and who communicates hope with a conviction emanating from deep within his personality. Just as children sense genuine emotion so accurately, schizophrenic patients can usually tell genuine hopefulness and joyfulness in their therapists. This is not to say that the presence of these qualities guarantees success. But feigned joyfulness, affected hopefulness, will almost surely guarantee failure. The best theory about the psychotherapy of schizophrenia, in addition to knitting together all that is known about biological factors, developmental factors, early object relations, and the like, would have to pay homage to these irrational and indispensable human qualities.

[4]Clinicians who adhere strictly to purely psychological theories of schizophrenogenesis would dispute this claim, and would insist that the mothering *had* to have been defective. I believe the burden of proof is on them to demonstrate this convincingly.

A Note on the Evolution of Contemporary Psychoanalytical Theories of Schizophrenia

As London correctly observed, ''The schizophrenia problem is the best example of a tendency to overextend crucial psychoanalytic concepts in the service of maintaining a cohesive unified theory'' (1973, p. 190). London distinguishes between an earlier ''unitary'' theory, enunciated by Freud and elaborated by Arlow and Brenner (1969), in which schizophrenia is visualized as a disturbance more severe than neurosis, though on a continuum with the neuroses. The spotlight on schizophrenia, in the unitary theory, remains where it is in the neuroses—on conflicts and defenses. Certain unconscious purposive behavior characterizes schizophrenia, which can therefore be explained in psychodynamic terms. Even the productive signs, hallucinations and delusions, are dealt with in this fashion. Adherents of this theory are at pains to see other signs and symptoms of schizophrenia primarily as ''defenses,'' as well.

Despite Freud's preference for a unitary theory, some of his formulations suggested a different model where schizophrenia is concerned—which London refers to as the ''specific'' theory. According to the latter, schizophrenia is unique and separable from other forms of aberrant mental life or behavior. A central notion of this theory concerns the withdrawal of emotional investment (''cathexis'') from the mental representations of other persons (''objects''). To this extent, schizophrenia is understood as a *deficiency state,* a view with which Wexler (1971) is in agreement.

These two outgrowths of classical Freudian theory are incompatible. Though London feels neither can be proved or disproved, he inclines toward endorsement of the specific theory, inasmuch as the evidence (that intrapsychic conflict and defense are primary determiners of schizophrenia) for a unitary model is weak. London's point that some aspects of the schizophrenic's deficiency state can, via a kind of feedback mechanism, be later utilized defensively is well taken. Certain schizophrenic patients can, after a time, ''learn'' to block out emotion-laden memories just when they are being urged, in psychotherapy, to deal with an uncomfortable subject. The blocking they then demonstrate looks every bit like the blocking one might witness from time to time in any catatonic patient (including those with suspected ''organicity,'' where one feels more confident one is in the presence of damage rather than defense). Nevertheless, as is consistent with the specific theory, schizophrenics do often behave as though there is something innate missing in them—something that is present in ordinary people—that begs to be understood as the epiphenomenon of an inborn integrative defect of the central nervous system, not as the end product of defenses against

particular conflicts impinging upon a "weak" ego. The specific theory permits linkage to modern neurophysiological conceptions of schizophrenia,
and thus promises escape from the narrow, solipsistic cell within which proponents of the unitary theory have, as I see it, immured themselves.

• • • • •

As psychoanalysis reached out to more severely disturbed patients, the
applicability of Freudian theory, even as it was evolving into the tripartite
structural model (Freud, 1923), was questioned in relation to what we
would now consider borderline and psychotic levels. The tripartite model
requires as a substrate some kind of cohesive or integrated self (Singer,
1979), and it is just such an integrated self that is missing in these lower two
levels of personality organization (Kernberg, 1967). In patients ill enough
to be diagnosed as unequivocally schizophrenic, there is, in place of a
"self," a collection of fragments, some of which are of dubious ownership,
since they are replicas of other people's thoughts and attitudes, and not genuine, assimilated aspects of the patient himself. In the place of a superego,
one finds a set of harsh, primitive prohibitions that the schizophrenic may
experience at times not only as not part of his "self," but not even part of
his physical space: they come from *out there* (as hallucinations). Or one may
see the kind of shifting moral postures or chameleon-like values we associate
with the "as if" personality (Deutsch, 1942)—often a schizotypal borderline patient.

Despite the fragmentation of self in clear-cut schizophrenics—or even the
severe splitting of self and object representations into all-good or all-bad elements in borderline schizophrenics—these schizophrenic-spectrum patients
are often remarkably "self-centered" or narcissistic. As is well known,
Freud felt that those who suffered these "narcissistic neuroses" were unable
to form a transference; hence his pessimism about the utility of the psychoanalytic method.

A later generation of analysts who devoted themselves to the treatment of
such patients felt that what took place in the dyadic encounter could hardly
be characterized as "no transference," but was often a chaotic, intense
"psychotic" transference, in which, as Rosenfeld expresses it, the schizophrenic "puts his self so completely into objects that there is very little of the
self left outside the object" (1969, p. 628). This tendency to projective identification interferes with communication and leads to exaggerated reactions
of all kinds. Some analysts, nevertheless, become very adept at recognizing
these projections, "containing" them (as Winnicott might put it) and interpreting them for the patient in a nonhostile manner, fostering a measure of

psychic integration where chaos reigned before. Treatment oriented toward clearing up confusion between self and others via transference interpretation may lead, in time, to amelioration of the ego-boundary disturbance that is so characteristic of patients in this category (see Searles, 1965; Rosenfeld, 1965; Bryce-Boyer, 1971).

Analysts who, in conformity with the unitary theory, ascribed this highly pathological form of narcissism to failure of the caretakers to provide an adequate, nurturing environment, attempted to make up for these deficiencies (Fromm-Reichmann, 1939; Winnicott, 1965). Federn (1943), in a similar vein, felt it would be helpful to supply the desexualized, parental love that was (supposedly) missing; he also considered the schizophrenic too fragile to deal with negative transference themes and kept the transference atmosphere positive. Searles disagreed with this viewpoint, as did Eissler (1951); work with negative feelings was seen as both necessary and feasible.

Other analysts, also uncomfortable with the tripartite theory as a foundation for comprehending schizophrenic disorders, took note of the disordered self- and object representations in severely "regressed" patients. The object-relations theories of the Kleinian analysts were an outgrowth of this new focus. Parallels between certain aspects of schizophrenic thinking and the primary-process, all-or-none thinking infants and very young children seem to exhibit led the Kleinians to postulate fixation points in commenting on the etiology of psychotic patients, situated at these early periods of development. In this respect, the Kleinians are environmentalists in the same sense as are the more "classical" adherents of the unitary theory; they too speak of a deficiency state (namely, the "basic fault") engendered by parental failure. But the ego-boundary disturbances and the aberrant "self" of the schizophrenic are more easily conceptualized in the language and model of the object-relations theorists. The therapeutic styles that were developed by these theoreticians were not wholly congruent, however: whereas Winnicott sought to heal the deficiency state (pictured as a wider than usual rift between the *true self* and the *false self*) via a nurturing approach (being a new and better "mother" for that patient), others, such as Bion (1957) and Rosenfeld (1969), felt that psychoanalysis with very few modifications was adequate to the task, and that, furthermore, both negative and positive transference attitudes could be resolved through exclusive reliance on verbal interpretations.

Debate about the efficacy of verbal interpretations, difficult to resolve even in relation to well-integrated analysands, is particularly difficult to resolve where schizophrenics are concerned. Those who have elaborated psychoanalytic theories about schizophrenia have not necessarily limited their practice to "core" schizophrenic patients. Although Sullivan, Fromm-

Reichmann, Searles, Szalita, and Arieti worked with "deeply regressed," hospitalized patients throughout much of their careers, other investigators have devoted themselves mostly to ambulatory patients who might bear such diagnostic labels as "acute schizophrenic" (which may have only a remote connection to "process" schizophrenia; see Kety et al., 1968), "narcissistic," "borderline," and so on.[5] Americans of prominence in the object-relations approach include Jacobson (1953, 1967); Mahler (1971), whose psychoanalytic work with children has focused on early developmental stages of relevance to narcissistic and borderline states); Kernberg (1975), Masterson (1975), and Rinsley (1977). The theoretical positions adopted by these writers incorporated many elements of both classical Freudian developmental psychology and the Kleinian object-relational psychology. Jacobson noted that self- and object representations are not well demarcated during the early development of future schizophrenics. Instead, archaic self- and object images tend to fuse. There is a loss of self-boundary that may, in crisis, express itself in the schizophrenic's experience of "the end of the world," or the loss of his identity. Jacobson's view of delusion formation also integrated object-relations theory, insofar as she felt that, at times, primitive self- and object images could "find their way to consciousness,"—merge with certain elements of more realistic thought—and form a new and delusory train of thought (1953, p. 64). The desperate struggle to hold onto a sense of *sameness* by a schizophrenic who is rapidly becoming more panicky, may, according to Jacobson (1967, p. 18), help account for the last-ditch effort he may make to refashion the external world in line with his idiosyncratic needs and ideas; the outbreak of actual psychosis may supervene only after a failure in this "alloplastic" effort.[6]

Kernberg, Mahler, and Rinsley see borderline (including schizotypal borderline) conditions as stemming from the interaction of constitutional and pathogenic environmental factors. Masterson, as well as the British Kleinians, tend to lay predominant, if not exclusive, stress on abnormalities in the mother-infant relationship. Despite these differences in relation to etiology, the American object-relations school, if I may so designate it, con-

---

[5]It is easy to see why sharp distinctions are not always made between, say, the typical cases of Searles' early papers, of Bryce-Boyer's, or of Kohut's, since analysts concentrate on the ego-psychological and psychodynamical aspects of their patients, and it is in just these aspects that one can meaningfully speak of a *continuum*. One could even include manic-depression on this continuum (Carpenter et al., 1977), whereas study of hereditary factors would cause one to see schizophrenia and manic-depression as distinct.

[6]Further remarks on Jacobson's contribution to the understanding of schizophrenia are to be found in Pao's book (1979).

curs in a treatment approach advocated by Kernberg and Rinsley, emphasizing "confrontative and interpretive exposure of the split object-relations unit within the . . . transference," which, under optimal conditions, contributes to the restructuring of endopsychic representations as well as to the working through of mourning for the mother, from whom the borderline patient can now become psychologically more separate (Rinsley, 1977, p. 67).

Certain issues about technic, such as whether the couch is used with schizophrenia-spectrum patients, are not easily resolved by extrapolation from one's theory of preference, although it is probably accurate to say that theoreticians favoring the notion of a continuum between the better and worse integrated patients are more apt to use the couch (especially those trained a generation ago, e.g., Searles, Bryce-Boyer, Giovacchini). Even so, modifications are likely to be made, such as a limitation on how long a silence is permitted to continue, lest the borderline or clearly schizophrenic patient become acutely anxious. It need hardly be said that it is much easier to explain in psychodynamic terms a borderline patient's withholding of crucial information, or of his skipping two or three sessions without telephoning his therapist, than it is to fashion interventions that successfully interrupt behaviors of this sort. Here, theory and therapy are far enough apart that the cleverest theoretician will not always carry the day against an obstinate patient.

To return to the topic of interpretation, one may generalize that there exists a loose correlation between theoretical preference and therapeutic style. Those who envision schizophrenia on a continuum with the psychoneuroses tend to assign verbal interpretations a keystone position in their therapeutic edifice. This will be all the more true if clinical experience is confined to ambulatory schizophrenics, of whom the better functioning can blend in with other "quasi-analyzable" patients. A generation ago, the use of deep interpretations of id impulses (i.e., relating to cannibalistic, incestuous, and other primitive wishes) was resorted to with hospitalized schizophrenics, in a rather extreme fashion, by Rosen (1947) and his followers. Though some surprising short-term improvements were achieved through this technic, the long-term results were disappointing (Horwitz et al., 1958). Heavy reliance is still placed on verbal interpretations by Bryce-Boyer (1966, 1971), but the focus is more on linkages between transference phenomena and the events of the patient's current life, rather than predominantly on the events of childhood. Giovacchini (1969) similarly advocates such "linking" interpretations as helping to minimize the interminable "primary-process fantasizing" indulged in by many schizophrenic patients and, simultaneously, to heal the ego defects. In this respect Bryce-Boyer and Giovacchini are in agreement with earlier recommendations by Eissler (1951) and Margaret Little (1966), who warn against the meaninglessness of interpretations unless there has been some stabilization effected in the life and in the therapeutic relationship of the schizophrenic patient. One important aim of "linking" interpretations is to establish some rationale for the otherwise chaotic or "crazy" thoughts, so the patient can "begin to understand how his mind works" (Giovacchini, 1969, p. 180). In contrast to analytic work with neurotic patients, where interpretive remarks do often center on "genetic" (childhood) issues, the emphasis in interpretations with schizophrenics is on translation from primary-process language to conventional secondary-process language. Kernberg and Kohut, in line with the above-mentioned authors, warned against delving into certain primitive areas of conflict, lest one mobilize *fears* of irreversible regression (in a borderline patient) to a state of fragmentation. But in contrast to Bryce-Boyer and Giovacchini, Kernberg would underscore the defect—as opposed to continuum—aspect of clear-cut schizophrenia, and would be less inclined to employ a transference-oriented, interpretive (i.e., "expressive") technic with a schizophrenic patient, however much he would recommend this technic with a patient who functioned at the *borderline* level (even if some schizotypal features were present, phenomenologically).

A number of French psychoanalysts have also objected to the classical position that the healing effects of the analytic method are transmitted solely via interpretation. Nacht (1963), for example, saw the human condition as a struggle between two needs: one for *separateness;* the other (and earlier one) for *union.* The need for union, or fusion, plunges to a level below language—and may be mediated instead by the analyst's silence. In silence, subject/object duality ceases to exist. The nonverbal aspects of therapy may be of just as great (and at times of greater) importance as the verbal aspects. This seems particularly so with schizophrenic patients—with whom, as Nacht and Viderman (1960) mention, strict analytic neutrality "must at times be replaced by an attitude of *presence*" (the analyst's being watchfully and compassionately *there* for his patient). This presence, they feel, may help interrupt regression, while minimizing the pain of separateness. Emotional warmth of this kind may also be an antidote to the early deprivation the schizophrenic patient may have suffered. This would be in keeping with the theory that, apart from whatever conflicts the schizophrenic may be gripped by, something crucial was also missing from his early environment. As we have noted, however, most analytic commentators now concur that love by itself cannot compensate for what may have been missing, nor can every therapist generate this feeling in relation to every schizophrenic patient. The therapist-patient "fit" is personal, human, unpredictable. Logical understanding is easier to achieve—and to dispense in the form of verbal interpretation. Hence, the role of interpretation tends to be accented in our theory, in our therapy, and in our supervision of therapists; it is the element over which we have some control and which is teachable, however high or low interpretation may actually rank in the hierarchy of curative ingredients.

Perhaps the most sensible attitude we can adopt concerning the role of interpretation with schizophrenic patients is that interpretation as conveyor of *insight* has probably been overrated as the curative agent. There are few schizophrenics who can integrate the therapist's insights with such facility as to convince one that insight has been the prime agent in their improvement. Interpretation as (almost inadvertent) conveyor of certain emotions and positive kinds of interrelatedness (such as Nacht spoke of) may be the key factor. Interpretation is important, after all—but not in the way that was imagined by "classical" analysts, whose experience was derived chiefly from neurotic patients.

The feeling of being understood (Eagle and Wolitzky, 1981, p. 363) may count for more, with many schizophrenic patients, than analyses of childhood paradigms, transference, or other psychoanalytic elements.

· · · · ·

In recent years considerable attention has been devoted within the psychoanalytic community to the theme of narcissism. Kohut's psychology of the self (1971) spurred the creation of a separate school of thought, whose concern has been the examination and treatment of disorders of the self at all levels of psychic organization. The theories of Kohut and his collaborators (Kohut and Wolf, 1978; Goldberg, 1980, 1981) have a bearing on the particular forms of identity disturbances encountered among schizophrenic and borderline schizophrenic patients. Self psychology, which London (1980, 1981) sees as an advance in the clinical theory of psychoanalysis, and not a divergent movement, may also be viewed, at least in part, as an extension of Kleinian object-relations theory, or perhaps as a parallel development.[7] Both focus on self, object(s), and their internal representations; both emphasize environmental factors as causative of the ego-defect disturbances in the development of a sense of self, as would be encountered in less-integrated patients, though in one of his later papers, Kohut spoke of the nuclear self in schizophrenia as remaining "noncohesive . . . either because of an *inherent biological tendency* or because its . . . continuity [was] not

[7]See above, p. 38.

responded to with even minimally effective mirroring [on the parent's part] in early life'' (Kohut and Wolf, 1978, p. 415; italics mine). This broadening of Kohut's theoretical base to include inherited defects would suggest that he had begun to envision the ego splits and early ''defects'' of the ''primary disturbances of the self'' (i.e., the psychoses) and of the ''borderline states''[8] as arising at times or in part out of biological rather than purely environmental factors.

Gedo (1979) has spoken of the need, within psychoanalytic metapsychology, of an object-relations theory as an ''essential tool for the illumination of certain types of archaic mental functioning.'' Elsewhere Gedo credits Freud with the realization that ''a psychology of sexual love, even one that paid proper attention to one's own person, is not a sufficient explanation for the realm of mental life that [lies] beyond the pleasure principle'' (1979, p. 365). Both Kohut and Gedo express the need for other than classical psychoanalytic interventions if the self disorders of more deeply disturbed patients are to be rectified. We have noted that Kohut advised against tampering with the relatively vulnerable defenses of the borderline patient, though he felt that it is sometimes possible to make the patient's defenses more flexible through psychoanalytic reconstruction of the dynamic sources of this vulnerability. Interpretation would play a role in this process, of course, but so would identification with the analyst, as emphasized by Volkan:

> If the patient suffers an . . . ''ego-defect'' neurosis; i.e., has a psychotic or borderline . . . personality organization, . . . one may expect to see in the treatment the open and continued appearance of introjective-projective relatedness (1981, p. 162).

The course of therapy in such patients will tend to encompass the development and resolution of a therapeutic symbiosis (see also Searles, 1965), following which the patient's ego organization may mature in the direction of forming a more cohesive (integrated) self. If this level is reached, the transference takes on the qualities associated with classical neurotic analysands; the more primitive (introjective-projective) relatedness will be less and less manifest in the therapeutic encounter. Volkan does not give us a clear picture, however, no more than do the other theoreticians of the Chicago school, of how often one may expect this type of favorable resolution, nor of the precise level of psychopathology exhibited by the sickest (most near to unequivocal schizophrenia) patient who still made major

---

[8]''Where the central defect [is] covered by complex defenses'' (Kohut and Wolf, 1978, p. 415).

gains via this method. By the same token, similar lack of diagnostic clarity makes it difficult to assess some of Kohut's enthusiasm over the efficacy of interpretation, as when he claims that certain attitudes of irritability and suspiciousness in patients with narcissistic personality disorders have (1) a purely psychological cause, that is, a narcissistic injury stemming from an unempathic, overburdening response from an important other ("selfobject") and (2) a purely psychological cure: these manifestations "disappear speedily when an empathic bond with the selfobject has been reestablished, i.e., in therapy, when a correct interpretation has been made" (Kohut and Wolf, 1978, p. 420).

Gedo's criticism (1980) of Kohut's view of empathy as not only a tool of observation but also as an *agent of healing* may be apt within the realm of classical analysands, but as one descends to the lower levels of psychic organization, where schizophrenic and borderline schizophrenic patients mostly reside, Kohut's point about the healing properties of empathy may, as with Nacht's opinions about the nonverbal aspects of therapy, become increasingly appropriate. In other passages, Gedo has commented on what I take to be borderline-level patients from an ego-psychological rather than self-psychological viewpoint. He endorses Grinker's recommendation for a supportive technic, in working with patients who "do not have a realization of the need for their own responsibility and efforts in therapy," whose ego-integrative capacity is "insufficient to tolerate the anxiety generated by interpretations of derivatives from the unconscious," and whose object relations "consist predominantly of transferences whose irrationality they are unable to perceive and whose self-representation is that of a child lacking autonomy" (1964, p. 534). As mentioned above, Gedo has underlined the need for a therapy, in dealing with patients of this kind, directed toward the acquisition of ego skills, as when he mentions, in his critique of Goldberg's casebook on the psychology of the self, that a certain Mr. B. showed an "alarming disorganization," which was ameliorated "without dealing with any psychological content" (1980, p. 373). Instead this (borderline?) patient, who became helpless and disorganized without appropriate external assistance, improved gradually as he learned about the nature of his deficit, and acquired better ways of self-management through planning.

· · · · ·

André Green of the French psychoanalytic school notes a point of similarity among Searles, Giovacchini, and the Kleinians, in that all have striven to extend psychoanalysis beyond its traditional frontiers, in contrast to others (Greenson, Loewenstein, Sandler) who would limit the scope and variety of its interventions. The former group claims, nevertheless, to have preserved the basic spirit and methods of psychoanalysis: refusal of active manipulation, maintenance of neutrality, and major emphasis on transference. While not discussing schizophrenia per se, Green examines borderline states in some detail within the context of a continuum hypothesis: "Nowadays the analyst is less deterred by the presence of a psychotic kernel within a neurosis, provided it appears accessible, than by fixed and rigid defenses" (1975, p. 5).

Green makes an interesting distinction between analysis of the neuroses, which he sees largely as a deductive process, and analysis of borderline states, which is largely inductive. I see this as essentially correct, and suspect Green would agree that analytic work with psychotic persons, such as Searles and Fromm-Reichmann have carried out, relies even more on inductive processes. There has also been essential agreement, in Green's view, among writers from the various schools that borderline patients (1) experience considerable confusion between subject and object; (2) evolve a particular mode of symbolization derived from a "dual organization" of patient and analyst; and (3) demonstrate a need for structural integration through the "object" (here, the analyst).

One way in which borderline (and psychotic) psychopathology strain the limits of conventional analysis is through the primitive defensive styles the therapist is likely to encounter. Green mentions somatization and acting out, where (as in the latter) psychic reality is "expelled," leaving the analyst with the impression of being out of touch with the patient's reality. The analyst must somehow make an "imaginative construction" of this reality, relying on his storehouse of memories and his own empathic skills. The sicker the patient, the more we must play detective.[9] Other mechanisms seen repeatedly in this domain of patients include splitting and "decathexis," wherein the patient "seeks to attain a state of emptiness and aspires to non-being and nothingness" (ibid., p. 7). Reminiscent of Little's comment (1966) about the borderline or psychotic person struggling with fears of annihilation (in contrast to the milder fears of the neurotic), Green's formulation posits a fundamental dilemma for the sicker patient: the alternative between *delusion and death*. A related point concerns the nature of the primary anxiety in patients at the different structural levels: the neurotic is affected by castration anxiety; the borderline and psychotic, with separation (versus intrusion) anxiety. There are profound implications for therapy in another of Green's observations, reflected also in the writing of

---

[9]Green captures this notion in his comment that the analyst must often make an "intense effort of thought in order to try to think that which the patient cannot think" (ibid., p. 8).

Kernberg; namely, that sexuality and aggression are not well separated in patients at the two lower levels of organization, with the result that what should be pleasurable activity is often vitiated and permeated by aggressive components. Furthermore, these patients show an extreme sensitivity to loss, yet tend nevertheless to provoke separation—only, a little while later, to attempt desperately to reinstate the severed relationship. The analyst witnesses the degree to which he is alternately overvalued and undervalued, clung to and rejected. It is helpful for therapists of patients in the schizophrenic domain to be aware of these cyclical and extreme shifts in attitude, and to anticipate—when caught up in one polar attitude—that its opposite will not be long in manifesting itself.

Certain schizophrenic patients become entangled in intense sadomasochistic relationships, where the emotional atmosphere is at all times highly charged—either by blind adoration or by venomous hatred. Conflicting attitudes toward the other person remain unintegrated; tiny alterations in the emotional climate (the spouse came home with a frown; the child said "hello" in a cheerier than usual way) are amplified instantaneously into intense love or hatred, each shift accompanied by an erasure from memory of all previous feelings the schizophrenic person had toward the other. Here the therapist has a special task: to try to acquaint the patient with the nature of this chaotic life-style and of its dependence upon unintegrated perceptions of other person(s), and to try to smooth out the wide attitudinal swings and corresponding behavioral excesses through an integrative approach. Optimally, the schizophrenic patient comes to learn that the person he or she was vilifying yesterday is the same person that was cherished the day before and the week before that. This awareness, if it develops, generally leads to more modulated, tolerant responses, better designed to preserve than destroy a relationship. I have presented material on this subject in greater detail elsewhere (Stone, 1981b), along with data concerning the relative proportions of schizotypal patients in my practice who were able to make this kind of integrative growth.

· · · · ·

The concern with annihilation so common to schizophrenic patients is particularly noticeable among those with prominent paranoid features. The paranoid person comes to operate, as a result, on what might be called the survival-mode of existence. This mode is quite appropriate among soldiers in combat (shoot first, then ask questions), but it is wildly unsuited to the peaceful coexistence one strives for in ordinary human relationships. Schizophrenics often take comfort in a black-or-white view of life—an oversimplification to which they are driven by their constitutional inability to distinguish the subtle shades of grey that make up the major portion of life's picture. In the Rhadamanthine code to which the paranoid sub-scribes, distinctions are not made between a momentary lapse of attention and total rejection, or between an innocent glance and consummated infidelity. The paranoid must treat mild offenses like gross offenses, because, as would be true of the soldier, an oversight could be "fatal."

A paranoid man I have worked with for several years complains constantly about other men "noticing" him on the street. He feels many of these looks have homosexual overtones, though he realizes intellectually that only a small fraction of the men who "stare" at him would really be overt homosexuals. He knows that there is a continuum between men who have an exclusively homosexual life and those who are exclusively hetero-sexual; that in between there are those with an occasional homosexual interest, but who function almost entirely as heterosexuals, those with "unconscious" homoerotic wishes but no corresponding behavior, and so on. He cannot, however, even begin to distinguish one type from another. *To be on the safe side,* he must, therefore, avoid friendships with all men. For another set of reasons, he must also avoid women. This compels him to live as an isolate.

Psychoanalytic theory has little to tell us about the neurophysiological or-igins of a thought disorder of this sort, although the *psychodynamics,* such as set forth in the Schreber case (Freud, 1911) may have some applicability to certain paranoid cases. Knowledge of these dynamics may help therapists understand paranoid patients better. It is widely appreciated, however, that confrontation about delusionally misinterpreted material usually fails to penetrate the defense. Here again, the best theories we have devised have not facilitated therapy to any appreciable degree. From a practical stand-point, we can do little to prevent the paranoid from generating "paranoid" thoughts, just as we can do little to prevent the melancholiac from elaborating pessimistic thoughts. Sometimes we make better progress by encouraging the paranoid patient to develop a kind of distrust of his own paranoia. If we succeed in getting him to adopt this attitude, his social rela-tionships may improve appreciably. I think in this regard of a schizotypal and markedly paranoid woman I treated for a number of years, who was reluctant to permit her lovers access to her own apartment. She was afraid they would swipe something, even though they were honest men to whom such behavior would be unthinkable. She ruined one relationship when, having noticed one glove was "missing," she accused her friend of having taken it. The limited utility of pilfering just one glove did not make her sus-picion seem any the less likely to her. Needless to say, within a few days she

found the glove (under a desk). After some months of concentrating on issues of this kind, she was able to keep accusations unvoiced when similar
incidents occurred, and to say to herself, "I shouldn't let my suspicions run
away with me; I probably just misplaced the (missing article)." This led to
a salutary increase in the harmoniousness of her relationships.

. . . . .

There are a number of symptoms peculiar to *space, movement,* and *time* and
which in particular concern the body image. In Sechéhaye's description of
Renée, the autistic schizophrenic child with whom she worked for so many
years, she spoke of Renée's difficulty in realizing that a chair, when seen
from one perspective, was the same chair that she might see after walking to
the other side of it. Rey, who has written an excellent article on schizoid
phenomena integrating Freudian and Piagetian concepts, mentions, by
way of analogy, Swann's comment in the first book of Proust's *A la Recherche
du temps perdu:* "If one wakes up in the night in the dark, not knowing the
time or where one is, then one does not know *who* one is" (1979, p. 482).
The blurring between self and other, and the interdependence of the two in
schizophrenia, is expressed in certain patients by their reluctance to leave a
familiar setting because their sense of self—of their very existence—is inextricably bound up with a particular surrounding: continuity in their sense
of "I" cannot be preserved if "I" steps outside the picture. Dynamically,
the familiar setting becomes the equivalent of mother's body, closeness to
which alone creates comfort. In this sense the schizophrenic may be said to
perpetuate a state, highly abnormal even in a nursery-school child, of infancy, when security depended upon contact with, and psychological merger with, mother: self and object separated to their least possible extent.

One schizophrenic man, as an example, spent all his adult life in a room
two blocks away from his mother's apartment. Safe in his room, he conducted a modest business via telephone and wrote numerous letters to public officials about social injustices he learned of from TV broadcasts.
The room served simultaneously as "object" (surrogate mother) and
"self"—more accurately, as extension of self and, by its sameness, as cor-
roborator of the self's continuity and sameness. Rey (ibid, p. 474) mentions
that the persistence and distortions of self-space versus non–self-space experiences lie behind many typical schizoid phenomena. One may encounter
patients who feel that they live "in" the object, because part of oneself is
experienced as in the object. Or else, the schizoid person may insist on
never leaving the object out of his control. Or one may have a sense of im-

minent catastrophe through possible loss of the object (via separation, vacations of a therapist, etc.), since part of the self is felt to be in the departing object. Similarly if one's own greed, envy, or destructiveness are projected onto the "other," one feels simultaneously ennobled by the absence of those negative emotions, but also persecuted by the other, who is seen as the repository of what originally was one's own hostility.

Considering the abnormalities in the formation of self- and object representations characteristic of schizophrenia, it would be useful, as Rey advocates, to incorporate Piaget's stages of object formation into any psychoanalytical model of this condition. Rey stresses the importance, nevertheless, of differentiating between Piaget's notion of "objects" and the libidinal objects of psychoanalytical metapsychology. Objects (here, inanimate objects in particular) of the external world are understood as permanent, as existing whether one is looking at them or not, by toddlers at about 18 months (the end of Piaget's sensorimotor stage). The libidinal "object" (that is, mother) is meaningful to the infant long before the sensorimotor stage has been completed. In my view, awareness of the Piagetian stages may be useful in helping us pinpoint the developmental tasks any given schizophrenic patient has shown difficulty in negotiating. One must still be cautious, however, about assuming that the presence of one or another stage-related difficulty is a sign that some environmental failure or trauma must have occurred during this stage. The more severe the hereditary predisposition or perinatal C.N.S. damage, for example, the less one need invoke parental intrusion, deprivation, or the like as prime causative agents. In any large sample of schizophrenic persons—even with similar peculiarities in self- and object representations—one will confront many combinations of interacting biological and psychological factors. The utility of the Piagetian schema, where schizophrenia is concerned, resides not so much in providing a framework for understanding causes as in its therapeutic implications. Certain schizophrenic experiences and symptoms become less "uncanny" to the extent that they may be seen as phenomena comparable to the experiences and evolving thought patterns of very young children. A therapist familiar with these parallels will find it less anxiety-provoking to hear such material; this conduces to a more comprehending and reassuring attitude, which in turn ought to lessen the patient's anxiety. This familiarity will make it easier to provide verbal clarifications that are "on target," contributing further to making the schizophrenic patient feel understood, hence less alone and less anxious. Rey mentions a patient (ibid., p. 483) who "only had a sense of existence when he drove his motor bike so long as there was a car in front of him or if his engine was going." Presumably he relied, after the manner of infants whose sense of object permanency has not yet become solidified, on visual or auditory cues *in the here and now* to reassure himself that he was not alone in the universe.

. . . . .

Apropos the uncanny feeling of the motorcyclist, the theories of Harry Stack Sullivan were directed, to a large extent, toward explaining in rational terms what lay behind the peculiar and irrational feeling states to which the schizophrenic is prone. Sullivan did so within the context of his *interpersonal* theory—a theory that underscores the impossibility of disentangling the "personality" of one person from the "complex of interpersonal relations in which the person lives and has his being" (1940, p. 4). Because of Sullivan's repudiation of classical psychoanalytical drive theory, and perhaps also because of his penchant for prolix thought couched in phrases of his own coinage, Sullivanian theory has existed, where schizophrenia is concerned, as an island close to the mainland of Freudian theory, with very few bridges between them. *Anxiety,* for Sullivan, was not the signal anxiety of Freud's 1926 paper, but rather a state of discomfort evoked, originally, by the emotional disturbances of the mother, whose discomfort the child senses (Sullivan, 1953, p. 9). According to Sullivan, the infant comes to experience three special feeling states: *good-me, bad-me,* and *not-me.* The *bad-me* experience may relate to an inchoate awareness of mother's disapproval or rejection, as the child concludes it "deserved" this rejection (mother knows best), even if an outside observer might feel that the child was blameless. The *bad-me* feeling is a manifestation of what classical theory would label "anxiety." Of relevance to schizophrenia, the *not-me* experience accompanies extreme dread, loathing, or terror. This panic-like state, in which the "self" is about to be annihilated, or where the *sense* of self is suddenly exploded into fragments, may occur during the nightmares of normal people but is a frequent counterpart of the acute schizophrenic episode. Sullivan assumed that the schizophrenic adult began life with an excessively anxious mother who stirred up excessive *not-me* experiences in the child. The reawakening of this *not-me* feeling state in the adult schizophrenic, Sullivan felt, was accompanied by "uncanny" emotions. Sullivan's view that the schizophrenic became ill owing to destructive mothering apparently applied to those who underwent "acute" schizophrenic episodes, but who were otherwise for the most part in contact with reality and amenable to psychotherapy. The chronic, deteriorating forms of "nuclear" or "process" schizophrenia, even Sullivan, despite his strong environmentalist bias, saw as the end product of some hereditary condition (1956a, p. 309).[10]

Corresponding to Sullivan's interpersonal theory was an interpersonal mode of psychotherapy, as it evolved during and after his years administering a special research unit at the Sheppard and Enoch Pratt Hospital. One expression of this mode was an emphasis on the therapist's function as participant-observer. In the observer role the therapist attended to correspondences between current behavior and the behavior of the patient in his past relations with the important figures of his life. In the participant role the therapist paid special attention, in addition to noting transference distortions, to the nuances of countertransference feelings. The respectful distance Sullivan advocated in the therapist-patient relationship was also to be accompanied by a measure of candor—which would, when deemed appropriate, include revelation of the therapist's reaction to the encounter with his patient. Sullivan himself was much given to a bantering style of confrontation in his demonstration-interviews with schizophrenic patients. This highly personal and active approach was designed to goad the patient into accepting a more realistic view of some situation, by pointing up, with good humor, the absurdity of the patient's denial or delusory views (see also Chapter 12). The following example, provided by Clarence Schulz (1980), shows the translation of Sullivan's theoretical stance into the therapeutic encounter: A schizophrenic patient felt that a tooth-chip he had inadvertently swallowed was "eating away at his stomach." Sullivan retorted: "Well, prizefighters swallow teeth without ill effect. So why should just *part* of a tooth eat up your stomach!? Isn't that far-fetched—when a *whole tooth* won't do any harm to a prizefighter?!''

Summary

In the preceding section we reviewed a number of psychoanalytic theories bearing on schizophrenia, both from an etiological and therapeutic standpoint. The review can have no pretensions of completeness, since the literature on the topic is enormous. Some analytic theories have enjoyed wide but temporary popularity, in a manner reminiscent of the wide but temporary popularity of certain biochemical theories of schizophrenogenesis over the past thirty years. The formulations of Jackson (1960), Haley,

[10]Sometimes chronic schizophrenia is heralded by an acute schizophrenic episode. Of interest with respect to Sullivan's teaching is Kurt Eissler's opinion that the therapist of the acute phase ought not to go on to treat the chronic phase. Frieda Fromm-Reichmann, who, along with Otto Will, Alfred Stanton, Jarl Dyrud and Harold Searles, was much influenced by Sullivan, opposed this view (C. Schulz, 1980).

and others regarding the role of the "double-binding" mother underlie one popular theory, the validity of which has, in my opinion, not withstood the test of time. The theories of Lidz (1963) and his coworkers concerning the role of skewed family communications as the key schizophrenogenic factor have also failed to be validated as carrying primary *etiological* significance, although adverse familial factors do appear to contribute to the intensification of schizophrenic symptomatology in predisposed individuals.

What are we left with? Do the theories we have—some overlapping others, some in sharp disagreement with others, some dealing with different phases or different levels of severity than others—constitute a crazy-quilt as fragmented as the schizophrenic mentation they are supposed to explain? Perhaps the situation is not quite so dispiriting. What we currently have may, I think, be seen as making up an unfinished quilt containing about two-thirds the patches it would need, along with a small number of patches that do not fit anywhere and should be discarded. The incompleteness of our analytic theory is a reflection of its failure to have incorporated sufficiently into its framework, data from genetic and neurophysiological sources. To be sure, psychoanalytic theory has traditionally been a psychological theory. But no theory about schizophrenia can claim any pretension to completeness unless biological factors are taken into consideration. *Severity* of clinical manifestation becomes a key issue. The more severe the case, the more likely one is dealing with a "deficiency state" as alluded to in Freud's specific theory (see London, 1973). Here, the deficiency state is more than can be accounted for solely on the basis of faulty input from the psychosocial environment. Neither the British object-relations school nor the family-interaction school of Lidz (1960) and Wynne (1974) can provide a satisfactory explanation of certain peculiarities of schizophrenic speech. Children who later become schizophrenic were not "taught" to confuse self-object boundaries in such a way as to claim, with conviction, "I am growing my father's hair"—to cite the paradigmatic example of Arieti (1970).

Some schizophrenic patients, on the other hand, do appear to suffer the kinds of parental deprivation that Winnicott and others had in mind when speaking of a "psychological" deficiency state. Gedo's emphasis on the need to teach ego skills in working with borderline and psychotic patients is appropriate to that very large segment of patients within the schizophrenia spectrum who require such teaching. Their need will not always be a reflection of poor parental instruction, however: in some instances, an inherited integrative deficit will render the future schizophrenic slower to assimilate the norms of social interaction even when parental input has been adequate. As we have seen, almost all patients to whom the schizophrenic label could apply have sufficient difficulties in self-object differentiation as to require revisions of classical psychoanalytic theory along the lines proposed by Klein, Fairbairn, Mahler, Kernberg, and others. Kleinian emphasis on a paranoid/schizoid position in normal infancy, however, probably represents a stretching of psychological theory to cover a territory (insofar as schizophrenics are concerned) best accounted for in biological terms; this is a piece that can be omitted from our patchwork. One also encounters, occasionally, relatively well functioning schizoid persons—some of whom are in the schizophrenia spectrum, if viewed from a biological vantage-point (they may have many clear-cut schizophrenic relatives, for example)—who show very little in the way of identity problems. They may function at the *neurotic* level (in Kernberg's psychostructural language), and thus be comprehensible in terms of Freud's triparite model, in which the focus will be on intersystemic conflicts rather than on ego deficiencies or, in Kohut's term, self-pathology.

In Table 2–2 I have attempted to portray the many theories we have been examining, in such a way as to show some of the lines of influence among the prominent theoreticians. The mere array of these names and schools of thought cannot of course recreate even the incomplete quilt psychoanalytic theoreticians have thus far sewn together. Indeed, most of the contributors whose work we have been surveying have been preoccupied with one or a few topics of relevance to any general statement about either the causes or treatment of schizophrenia.

Table 2–3 represents my attempt to show the interrelationships between the various theoretical and therapeutic positions we have outlined, with the stages or subtypes encountered clinically within the schizophrenic spectrum of disorders. Ping-Nie Pao (1979) has offered a useful schema, unifying theory and therapy within a largely Sullivanian context. Pao divides schizophrenia into four types (I and II, the more acute; III and IV, the more severe), emphasizing family psychopathology as part of his diagnostic subtyping. I question the validity of that approach, since I am unconvinced there is a particularly great correlation between severity of family pathology and the type or severity of clinical schizophrenia one sees, apart from the probability that severely ill parents tend to beget severely ill offspring (McCabe, Fowler, et al., 1971). Wender (1977) has also shown that the adopted-away children of schizophrenic parents succumb to manifest schizophrenia in approximately the same proportion as would be expected in a population of children reared with their schizophrenic parents. Pao's schema concentrates on the less well integrated side of the schizophrenia spectrum, whereas, in Table 2–3 I have included schizotypal and schizoid uses as well. This broader approach permits one to see the regions of the

TABLE 2 – 2 THEORIES OF SCHIZOPHRENIA: LINES OF INFLUENCE

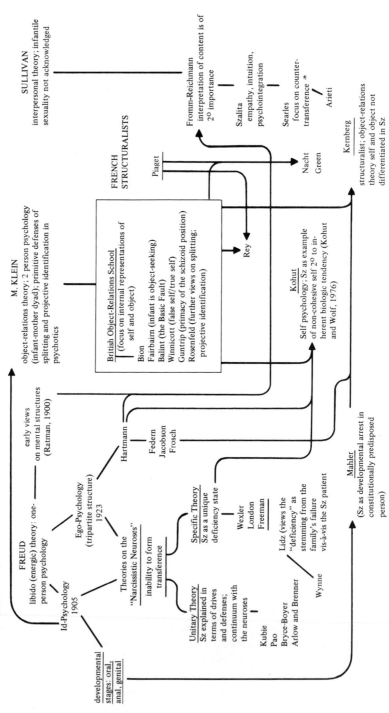

TABLE 2–3

Position along Schizophrenia Spectrum	SCHIZOPHRENIC PATIENT, OUT OF CONTACT		SCHIZOPHRENIC PATIENT IN SOME CONTACT; HALLUCINATIONS AND DELUSIONS LESS INTENSE AND PROTRACTED	SCHIZOTYPAL BY PATIENT	
	Chronic Schizophrenia (Pao type III, IV)	Acute Schizophrenic (Pao type I, II)			
Relevant Theory	Tausk (ego-boundary Disturbances) Fromm-Reichmann: Sz can form transferences Uncanny Feelings: Sullivan, Rey Little; fear of annihilation Inherited factors: (Kety, Rosenthal, Wender); attention deficit (Cancro); dominant hemisphere abnormality (Flor-Henry)	Freud Schreber case, 1911	A. Green (inductive aspects of psychoanalysis) British Object Relations School (Schiz. as emotional deficiency state); Wexler Jacobson (emergence of primitive self- and object representations) Mahler (Schiz. as developmental arrest in constitutionally predisposed persons) Rosenfeld (proj. identification)	Kernberg (various functions of splitting) Kohut (self psychology) Rinsley (position developmental path Gedo (ego-psych viewpoint)	A. Green (deductive aspects of psychoanalysis) Freud (1923 tripartite model) Kernberg (assessment of reality testing) Guntrip (primacy of schizoid position) Balint (basic fault)
Relevant Psycho-therapy	Sullivan (interpersonal approach) Fromm-Reichmann (compassion, empathy, attention to countertransference Sechehaye (transference; symbolic realization as means of gratifying needs) Rey; Piaget (problems in space, time, motion, self/object confusion) use of hospital staff, data from relatives, to supply gaps in history	Sullivan (confrontation to decrease denial) Arieti (cognitive approach to enhance recognition of the psychological antecedants of hallucinations and delusions) Fromm-Reichmann (less reliance on insight)	Reality testing poor, but dialogue possible; intuition and supportive techics more important than insight Nacht (the analyst's presence; neutral love) Szalita (psychointegration; reliance on intuition and empathy) Searles (work with countertransference) Bychowski (active interventions) Winnicott (therapist's neutral love as compensation for parental deprivations) Eissler, Searles, Rosenfeld (important to work with negative as well as with positive transference)	Kohut (role of empathy) Kernberg (less and more cautious use of transference) Boyce-Boyer, Giovacchini (here-and-now "linkage" interpretations; avoidance of hospital) Rosenfeld; Bion (analysis with few parameters) Eissler, Little (stability takes precedence over content interpretation) Gedo (teaching of ego-skills) Green (dilemma over delusion vs. death)	Rey (use of Piagetian stages as guide to interpretations) Gill (transference) insight: oriented toward dynamics, correlations between past and present

clinical spectrum where the various analytic theories have their greatest utility. I have purposely omitted from Table 2–3 reference, on the theoretical side, to some of the earlier Kleinian formulations (where formal thought disorders are envisioned as resulting from "regression" to a paranoid/schizoid position),[11] the doublebind theory, Arlow and Brenner's unitary theory, and, on the clinical side, such once popular but now largely discredited approaches as Rosen's "direct analysis."

Cursory inspection of Table 2–3 will be helpful in alerting the reader to important differences in the average patients described by one or another author. The unequivocally and chronically schizophrenic patients about whom Fromm-Reichmann was writing so compassionately in her 1939 paper seem distinctly more ill, for example, than those who figure in the descriptions of Bryce-Boyer (1971) and Giovacchini (1980); the latter, in turn, are roughly comparable to the "latent" schizophrenics mentioned in Bychowski's paper (1953). These patients will generally exhibit a psychotic structure (as defined by Kernberg) and thus appear less integrated than Kernberg's "borderline" patients, some of whom show schizotypal features. The patients of Guntrip's clinical vignettes, or of Balint's, probably inhabit the healthier regions of the schizophrenia spectrum: borderline schizophrenia ("schizotypal borderline") or schizoid personality.

. . . . .

Table 2–3 also highlights the interplay between the intuitive versus deductive faculties of the therapist in dealing with patients at different loci within the spectrum. Schizophrenic patients in relatively poor contact with reality and with their environment will call upon our intuition, including our ability to sense the moment-to-moment shifts in our countertransference attitudes. The patient may be largely uncommunicative, placing himself, as a result, quite far away from amenability to an insight-oriented therapy. At this end of the spectrum, what Fromm-Reichmann said over forty years ago is still appropriate:

> It is certainly not an intellectual comprehension of the schizophrenic but the sympathetic understanding and skillful handling of the patient's and physician's mutual relationship that are the decisive therapeutic factors. (1939, p. 423)

[11]As examplified in a paper of Bion, who speaks of a patient who, as he regresses, "turns destructively on his embryonic capacity for verbal thought as one of the elements which have led to his pain" (1954, p. 118).

Apropos this comment of Fromm-Reichmann is the matter of therapist-patient "fit," not reflected in Table 2-3, but of considerable importance throughout the schizophrenia spectrum, especially at the sicker end. Even though diagnosis in the strictest sense of the term is a function of anamnesis and current observation—not of "reachability" or prognosis—clinicians who are able to effect emotional rapport with schizophrenic patients will tend to see them as less ill and place them in a correspondingly less "severe" diagnostic category, than will those who fail to effect such rapport. No doubt, in the era of phenothiazine and other neuroleptic drugs, many have come to regard some of the extraordinary efforts expended by Fromm-Reichmann, Sechèhaye, and Searles to establish contact with deeply regressed schizophrenics as unnecessary, quixotic, and in any case, beyond the capacities of the average psychotherapist. Nevertheless, contact can often be established with such patients—but to a degree that depends largely on the patience, adroitness, and compassion of the therapist. No Thorazine® was available to Fromm-Reichmann when, confronted with a schizophrenic man who sat "naked and masturbating on the floor of his room, talking for the first time, yet so softly that I could not understand him," she chose to sit down on the floor next to him, whereupon he said, "You can't do that for me; you will get too involved." Subsequently he pulled a blanket around himself, saying, "Even though I have sunk as low as an animal, I still know how to behave in front of a lady." He then "opened up" to Fromm-Reichmann, talking to her for several hours about his problems and his history (1939, p. 420).

Schizophrenic patients who are in some degree of contact with reality and who can enter into conversation, if not into dialogue, with their therapists occupy a level one step higher in overall function than those we have just been discussing. The balance between intuition and deduction will still swing to the side of intuition, although "rational" processes in verbal therapy can be used more often. Because the discourse of the schizophrenic who is in poor contact will often be elliptical, indirect, and full of obscure allusions, more reliance will have to be placed upon intuition and upon a more direct style of intervention (namely the "active" approach of Bychowski, 1928). Our conceptual framework will still rely heavily upon those patches of our analytic "quilt" that deal with merger phenomena, ego boundary, self-object differentiation and Kohutian self psychology, although attention to specific conflicts will become more and more relevant.

Much use will also be made of countertransference phenomena as indices of what the schizophrenic patient is, from moment to moment, projecting onto us. Many passages in this book touch on this theme; countertransference, indeed, held the center of the stage in psychoanalytical writing on schizophrenia throughout much of the 1950s and 1960s (see Savage, 1961; Bryce-Boyer, 1961; Searles, 1958, 1979; Grinberg, 1962; Reich, 1960; Little, 1957; Sechèhaye, 1956). Here, I will let one example from supervision with Harold Searles suffice to illustrate the importance of the therapist's aliveness to countertransference nuances. A resident therapist was describing to Searles some recent sessions with a schizophrenic woman who spoke on and on, and rather glowingly, about her boyfriend. There was not much that was either new or conflict-laden in her monologue; the resident felt he had "nothing to pick up on." The material was "boring." If a therapist kept struggling to find something in the *content* of what this patient was saying, he would no doubt feel bored or stranded. He might even take an ego-psychological view of the form created by the apparently meaningless talk and interpret a *resistance* (to the effect that the patient must be covering up something of emotional significance underneath the empty chatter). But Searles' reaction was quite different. He sensed that if A speaks endlessly and lovingly about B in the presence of C (who is, to that extent, left in the role of mere witness), A does not much care about C. C (in this case, the therapist) would have to feel "left out." Jealousy of B would be C's natural countertransference reaction. The question then becomes: why has the patient found it necessary (albeit unconsciously so) to make the therapist jealous? Often, schizophrenic patients will fall into this kind of pattern when they themselves are jealous about someone of importance in their lives, but are still too out of touch with their feelings, or too embarrassed to admit jealousy, or whatever. So their unacceptable feeling state is communicated in a highly indirect way, by behaving in such a way that the *other* person is compelled to feel what the patient cannot even identify within himself, much less express.

. . . . .

As we move toward more integrated states within the schizophrenia spectrum, we encounter patients who never exhibit a formal thought disorder. They may experience occasions of referentiality and magical thinking, but will in general be more "reachable" by a modified psychoanalytic treatment. Therapists will find themselves drawing upon object-relations theory and classical analytic tripartite-structural theory in equal measure. Classical theory will be of even greater applicability with schizoid personalities who function at or near the neurotic level, although even in these instances, abnormalities in the "narcissistic" path of development will almost invariably have been present. The works of Kernberg (1975) and Kohut (1971,

1977) will facilitate the conceptual and therapeutic approaches to these abnormalities.

Psychoactive medications—which may play a vital role in acute or severe forms of schizophrenia, often taking precedence over verbal technics during phases in which delusions, hallucinations, or panic states dominate the clinical picture—will be less often necessary in schizotypal borderline patients. In those with schizoid personalities, medication is of limited usefulness (Stone, 1981a).

. . . . .

It is both a virtue and a shortcoming of psychoanalytic metapsychology that meaning can be found within this theoretical framework for symptoms and syndromes of any sort—including every variety of schizophrenic manifestation. The virtue lies in the rationale we can provide for the often bizarre and superficially "meaningless" verbalizations our schizophrenic patients will utter. Our translations, as we have noted, eventually have a reassuring effect, since they help the schizophrenic patient appreciate that his craziness is not so crazy after all, when viewed as symbolic of otherwise quite ordinary human conflicts and emotions. The shortcoming of this handy rationale lies in the degree to which it can mislead fledgling therapists into thinking that because psychoanalysis can provide an *explanation* for schizophrenic symptoms (we are putting to one side for the moment the issue of plausability versus validity) it can also provide an effective therapy. The schizophrenic process in its fully developed forms interferes grossly with the assimilation of the very explanations we hoped would be curative. Other nonspecific factors, including personality type, introspectiveness, intelligence, and motivation, will enter the equation as either facilitators or impediments to therapy.

There is much debate about the implications of being paranoid in addition to being schizophrenic (Ritzler, 1981). Paranoid personality, which appears to be a dimension separate from schizophrenia (Meissner, 1981; Megaro, 1981), despite their often traveling together, is felt by some to augur well for psychotherapy, especially when present in "spectrum" conditions that fall short of obvious paranoid schizophrenia (Frost, 1969). In other respects, however, the suspiciousness and fear of emotional closeness, so characteristic of paranoid individuals, operate against the success of an analytically oriented approach. Awareness of psychodynamic issues may, nevertheless, make the therapist's task easier as he attempts to get past paranoid defenses. One highly paranoid engineer, for example, would become preoccupied, during some of our sessions, over food adulterants, supposedly excessive amounts of radiation exposure from his annual dental x-rays, and the like. Counterarguments about the harmlessness of the various foods and medical procedures he was so sedulously avoiding were of no avail. What was helpful was to turn the conversation to his very exaggerated fear of death that served dynamically as the foundation for these paranoid elaborations. His life had thus far been unfulfilled in many important ways; he feared death as the malign agent that would rob him once and for all of the joys ordinary folk experienced. Premature death—from chemicals, x-rays, or whatever—had to be avoided at all costs.

The paranoid disposition may be seen as one of many personality types encountered amongst patients within the schizophrenia spectrum, and it may manifest itself in a variety of ways. Religious/philosophical preoccupations, general suspiciousness, delusional jealousy, food faddism, overzealousness for certain political or social reforms are but some of these manifestations. Although many schizophrenic patients with paranoid tendencies are free of formal thought disorder and function fairly well occupationally (especially if the *paranoid system* is well encapsulated and hidden from coworkers and acquaintances), analytic therapy will seldom succeed in dispelling the "system." What we may accomplish is a salutary reduction in the degree to which the paranoid patient experiences the world as hostile.

Other personality types may predominate: schizoid (perhaps a fourth of schizophrenics show a "schizoid" personality; Bellak, 1976), narcissistic, histrionic (as in some cases of "hysterical psychosis"; Hollander and Hirsch, 1964), obsessional (e.g., some cases of handwashing compulsion), antisocial (e.g., Bender's "pseudopsychopathic schizophrenia," 1959), and so on. Personality type may, in fact, be said to constitute another important patch in any total psychoanalytic/psychobiologic theory of schizophrenia—one that has not thus far received sufficient attention. This may be related to the greater applicability of the personality dimension to clinical issues and prognosis than to the more abstract concerns of analytic theoreticians, having to do with etiology and psychodynamics. My own impressions on the prognostic implications of the different personality types have been presented in some detail elsewhere (Stone, 1981b).

3

The History of the Psychoanalytic Treatment of Schizophrenia:

THE EARLY PERIOD

Michael H. Stone, M.D.

Psychoanalysis, having developed primarily out of efforts to reach hitherto untreatable ambulatory patients, did not at first concern itself with the more deeply disturbed hospitalized patients. The application of psychoanalysis to schizophrenia represented an extension, a later development, of the psychoanalytic movement. For the *beginning* of psychoanalysis it may be appropriate to select as the date 1893, the year Breuer and Freud published their epoch-making papers on a new method for treating cases of hysteria. Their patients were considered "psychoneurotic," as against "psychotic," though review of the cases by contempory diagnostic standards suggests that many were "borderline" patients—rather sicker than the kinds of patients for whom psychoanalysis, in the strict sense of the word, would be reserved nowadays.

There was at first little impetus to translate Freud's discoveries into the realm of traditional hospital psychiatry. Freud was not granted access in those times to the higher academic ranks of organized psychiatry, yet it was from within these ranks that hospital cases were managed. Freud had hoped to make a bridge between the realm of ambulatory patients where, perforce, he worked, and that of the sanatorium, where, for example, Kraepelin and Bleuler worked. Professionally this gap remained unbridged, although by the end of the first decade of our century Bleuler and Freud were familiar enough with one another's works that some degree of academic cross-fertilization may be said to have taken place. Bleuler was profoundly influenced by Freud's writings; Freud, less so by Bleuler's. A few analysts in Freud's entourage, however, were quite impressed with Bleuler's research among the hospitalized patients in the Burghölzli and near Zürich. It is these analysts, as we shall see, who became in effect the first to apply the "talking cure" to schizophrenics.

Freud's inner circle was accustomed to meet Wednesday evenings in the Professor's home to discuss new articles of interest. It was at such a meeting in October of 1906 that Bleuler's book on affectivity, suggestibility, and paranoia was reviewed (Nunberg and Federn, 1962).

Adler felt the book was "not too impressive." Freud, nonetheless, gave credit to Bleuler's notion that an *affect* can give rise to an illness—an idea, as he put it, "of great originality." Stekel commented later that "in paranoia, the unconscious spreads itself over the waking life of the patient." Schizophrenia was, in other words, seen then as an invasion of id content (not then so described) into waking life. This resembled Freud's own comment about psychosis as being similar to a dream.

In the following year Paul Federn was to suggest that psychotics could form a transference, after all, despite Freud's conviction that this was unlikely. Jung expressed the opinion, also in 1907, that the apparently senseless answers of psychotic patients were nevertheless strictly determined. With respect to causation, Jung felt, as did many German-speaking psychiatrists of the late nineteenth century, that these patients were afflicted with some form of toxin.

In 1908 Abraham was to suggest that patients with "dementia praecox" differed from the hysterical psychoneurotic in that the latter exhibited increased resistance to the analytic process, whereas the psychotic patient succumbed to his illness specifically because of a "lowered" resistance. Here he is presumably alluding to the relative ease with which the conscious mind is flooded with primitive ideas and feelings in dementia praecox, compared to the situation with healthier patients. The term "complex" had recently been introduced by Jung. Freud now expressed the belief that the dementia praecox patient must "be confronted directly with our awareness of his complexes," rather than be allowed to work alone in the relative silence of the analytic mode (until the patient himself discovered these complexes). This was a forerunner of comments Bychowski, Reich, and many others were to make in the 1920s about "active" therapy.

An inchoate awareness on Freud's part of the more deep-seated disturbances present in some of his "neurotic" patients becomes manifest in his caveat about the difficulty in detecting underlying psychosis in certain cases of "hysteria" who go on to exhibit transient delusions and hallucinations (see, for example, the "hysterical psychosis" described by Hollender and Hirsch, 1964).

These more serious cases were described by Freud under the rubric "narcissistic neuroses." He was very pessimistic about these conditions, having expressed the belief (1908, 1914) that "these patients form no transference neurosis." The special kind of relationship on the part of the analysand, in which he systematically, though unwittingly, endows his analyst with all the various distortions and misperceptions from the past about other people, Freud felt did *not* develop in the "narcissistic" patients.

The year 1911 saw the publication of Bleuler's magnum opus, "The Group of Schizophrenias," which he had written some three years earlier. It was he who coined the term "schizophrenia" to denote the prominent split between affect and thinking so characteristic of the patients he was describing. The term replaced Kraepelin's "dementia praecox," now seen by Bleuler and others as no longer apt, inasmuch as not all patients with kindred mental disorders break down in mid-adolescence, nor do all deteriorate further. In fact, it may well have been Bleuler's more optimistic impressions that inspired a determination in others to try new methods, with renewed vigor, on behalf of this hitherto "untouchable" class of patients. Many analysts in Freud's circle became fascinated now with the prospect of working with schizophrenics, as they now came more and more to be called, although Freud himself restricted his therapeutic efforts to rather healthier patients. Bleuler, it should be mentioned, was a man of unusual perseverance and assiduity, seeing his patients at the Burghölzli for several minutes each, sometimes longer, six days out of seven, with a clock-like regularity well befitting a Swiss. He did not appear to appreciate the impact this devotion and predictability made upon those whom he saw, but from our vantage point, the success Bleuler enjoyed with schizophrenics must in no small measure be related to this felicitous combination of attitudes.

One of the first psychoanalysts to work *intensively* with a schizophrenic patient was Poul Bjerre, of Swedish origin, who published in the fall of 1912 a long paper in Freud's journal about his treatment of a paranoid woman.

Interesting here are hints in Bjerre's observations of the same psychodynamics that Adler had already postulated for certain male paranoid patients in 1908, and which Freud was soon to elaborate in his monograph on Schreber (1911). Adler had spoken of the use of projection, as well as of detachment of homosexual affection from father onto the analyst. Bjerre's patient was a 52-year-old spinster who developed the delusion that men in the street were lasciviously protruding their tongues at her. This woman also exhibited a close attachment to and an inability to separate from important female figures in her life. Bjerre's tact at going around her referential system, his cautiously worded suggestions regarding more likely interpretations of her misperceptions are models that hold up well even by today's standards. Consider the following example, as he gently confronts her about her idea of reference:

> "Well, it could be just as you say, I can't deny it. . . . But it seems also possible that you've been the innocent dupe of a peculiar misperception; life is full of illusions—sometimes people get stuck in them. You for instance had a crush on Mr._ and he rejected you. You then try to bury the pain—you are, after all, a sensitive person. But perhaps you inadvertently were then *thinking* with your feelings (i.e., confused thought with reality [ed.]). When that happens all sorts of discrepancies become possible!" (1912, p. 816; my translation).

After many months of such encounters, Bjerre was able to nudge her from her psychosis and she returned to her rather good premorbid level of functioning.

Freud's famous commentary (1911) on the case of the jurist Schreber concerns a man who underwent a paranoid psychosis in middle life, probably in response to the increased responsibility of a new promotion. In the diary he kept in the asylum to which he was committed, Schreber gave many hints of preoccupation with homosexual conflicts. Freud postulated that a conflict over such impulses is central to the genesis of paranoid disturbances, an idea to which he gave the most coherent and forceful expression up to that time, although he was by no means the first to suspect a connection. Indeed, as Zilboorg mentions in his history of psychiatry, Johann Weyer described a similar connection in 1563:

> "And I have known of a [priest who was a] sodomite[1] who complained of always hearing in his ears the noises made by people passing him in the street, or even by those closely related to him. He wrote to me about this situation in a very discreet manner, asking if I had not some advice I might proffer him, inasmuch as everyone else kept telling him there was something the matter with his ears. . . . Whenever this preacher's spirit was troubled, he claimed he could command the angels Gabriel and Michael to come and speak with him and to answer his questions. But when the Cardinal of Tournon requested that he make this happen in the

[1]"masculorum concubitor"

Cardinal's presence, the priest said he could not do so, unless he first prepared his body by various fasts and prayers, and then only if it were on behalf of some business of paramount importance to the church'' (Zilboorg, 1941, p. 307; my translation).

The important effect, for our purposes, of Freud's synthesis was that it gave a rationale, and by that very fact, encouragement to other psychoanalysts to work with psychotic patients they might otherwise avoid. Ferenczi wrote a confirmatory paper, for example, in 1911–12, concerning the latent homosexual conflict in cases of paranoia.

Meantime, Adolph Meyer, who had recently come to America, was helping rid the psychiatric community of its pessimism regarding schizophrenia through his influential teaching that this condition is not so much a disease as a "reaction": a reaction, that is, to a multitude of factors, as much psychological as constitutional, environmental as well as genetic. Not himself an analyst, Meyer was nonetheless an admirer of Freud and of the new movement, which was now beginning to take root in America as well as on the continent.

One prominent figure among the analytic pioneers in America was Isador Coriat, the first president of the American Psychoanalytic Association, who, in 1917, expressed great optimism about treating cases of "dementia praecox." He mentioned how little space Kraepelin and Bleuler devoted to issues of treatment, then cited Meyer, who felt that "many cases are reactive, i.e., develop on the basis of abnormal personality—and can be prevented by combatting any shut-in tendencies they exhibit." Coriat went so far as to say that *hope* in such cases actually "depended on our view of dementia praecox as purely psychologic" (1917, p. 327).

Kempf introduced a note of caution into Coriat's enthusiasm by his assertion, in 1919, that more was necessary to the treatment of schizophrenics than the new verbal technic itself: good hygienic measures, playful exercises, and crafts were also important. He emphasized, in other words, an analytic approach supported by what we would call an "appropriate milieu" therapy as well. Without the latter, Kempf felt these patients would too easily succeed in slipping away from reality, as they so often wished to do.

At about the same time, Victor Tausk (1918) wrote his famous paper on the influencing machine. In this monograph about a paranoid psychosis, he introduced a new concept into the body of analytic theory concerning schizophrenia and its causation; namely, the loss of ego boundaries.

The first two decades of psychoanalytic work with patients of psychotic potential were characterized by uncritical enthusiasm for the new method (which may have reached its peak when A. A. Brill claimed that five or six schizophrenics he analyzed in 1911-12 were still "cured" in 1930), along with a focus almost exclusively upon drives and content.

To be sure, the emphasis on content was quite apparent in the psychoanalytic literature on healthier (neurotic) patients up to the late 1920s. One would expect this among the pioneers of a new "language" whose "words" (content) would of necessity have to be mastered before their underlying "grammar" (form or structure) could be perceived. Id analysis, as part of a natural evolution, had to proceed the analysis of ego, for the latter addressed itself to the patient's characteristic defenses, habits, and overall life-plans—in which matrix his impulses and their verbal expressions (content) were embedded.

However this may have been, Freud was not to elaborate his structural theory of the mind until 1923. Before this compartmentalization of psyche into id, ego, and superego, pathological mental states had to be explained within the context of the earlier topographic theory, emphasizing what was *conscious* versus what was *unconscious*. Attention was also paid to basic drives (similar to what was later subsumed under "id") and the defenses erected (by the "ego") against them. But the notion of an intersystemic conflict involving superego and ego appeared only with Freud's 1923 paper; the extend to which such conflicts might play a role in schizophrenia could not, before this time, be conceptualized or evaluated.

· · · · ·

By the late teens and early 1920s, a number of notable developments had taken place in analytic psychotherapy. To begin with, many practitioners took Freud's tenets about analytic silence and the analyst-as-mirror too literally, so that many analyses stagnated and stalemated. Paradoxically, Freud himself, as we know from a number of his former patients' accounts, could be by turns warm, chatty, contentious, or exhortatory, as well as "silent" (Ruitenbeck, 1973). Adler, Ferenczi, and others proposed modifications involving greater activity on the part of the analyst, at least for certain difficult patients. Alongside this change in therapeutic posture was a growing dissatisfaction with analyses directed solely at content, and a growing awareness of the importance of *form*, a transformation spurred by Freud's new structural theory. Finally, some analysts had begun to realize more fully that many of their sicker (i.e., "schizophrenic"—though it is often unclear to readers fifty years later whether we would always diagnose their cases as they did) patients were all too well in touch with their "id"—and yet were none the better for it. Although Freud thought in the 1890s that cure depended on making the unconscious conscious, he and others began to see that some patients, for all their surface insight about "content," were still the servants, not the masters, of their drives.

For all this, the days of systematic approach to psychodiagnosis were still years away—decades actually—so that it is next to impossible to assess the claims of the first generation who treated schizophrenics by an analytic approach. Perhaps it is necessary to the evolution of a new mode of therapy that a phase of uncritical enthusiasm precede sober reflection and meticulous appraisal, lest the new method die in its crib. It is probably no accident that the analysts, in the main, treated office patients whose assets both social and financial allowed them the luxury of such treatment. The importance of social class as a factor in the outcome of the analytic method was appreciated by the early writers (see Ruitenbeck, 1973, pp. 495–503). Freud was certainly aware of it. Yet this factor tended to be glossed over. There is little question that the "schizophrenics" treated so successfully by the founding fathers of psychoanalysis enjoyed tremendous advantages over those treated by, say, Philip May's psychiatrist residents in the Camarillo inpatient study (1968). Much of the current criticism about the efficacy of modified analytic methods in schizophrenia is based on work with patient populations so very different from the more fortunate cases treated by the analysts of the 1920s (or even of our own day) that proponent and critic are as two ships passing in the night (Stone, 1973).

· · · · ·

As we enter the decade of the 1920s we see a much more widespread acceptance within the analytic community regarding the capacity of the more deeply disturbed patients—by whatever name they were to be called—to form a transference relationship. Abraham (1927) came to feel, along with Federn (1928) that even patients engulfed in melancholia could be reached via transference analysis.

But alongside this greater optimism came the growing realization that the analytic method needed extensive modifications, to become accessible to, let alone able to benefit, such patients. In addition, the analytic community was openly acknowledging that its treatment had hitherto been confined to a narrow segment of the population, and that a vast *terra incognita* stretched out beyond it, containing not only the majority of humanity but also a large array of clinical conditions rarely encountered by the analysts of that era.

Freud was certainly aware of this in 1918, when he addressed the International Psychoanalytic Congress in Budapest. He said, at one point:

"It is very probable . . . that the application of our therapy to numbers will compel us to alloy the pure gold of analysis plentifully with the copper of direct suggestion. . . . But whatever the elements out of which it is compounded its most effective and most important ingredients will assuredly remain those borrowed from strict psychoanalysis which serves no ulterior purpose."

One of the first who tried to expand the analytic method to psychopathological conditions, and to social levels not ordinarily within the purview of analysis, was Wilhelm Reich, whose monograph on the "impulsive character" (*Der triebhafte Charakter*) was published in 1925. Reich, only 28 at the time, was very interested in extending psychoanalysis to working-class people, and helped set up a clinic for this purpose in Vienna in the mid-twenties. Many of the patients he saw there exhibited serious disorders of character and were described as "driven," "acting out," "sociopathic," and the like. Many resembled patients we now tend to classify as functioning at a borderline level; others seemed distinctly schizophrenic. In not a few cases diagnostic distinctions remained blurred, as in our own day:

"In the histories of schizophrenic patients we see rather often grotesque drive-manifestations; later on we will see in connection with a certain case how difficult it can be even after months-long psychoanalytic treatment to distinguish between a schizophrenic diagnosis and one of transference-neurosis" (1925, p. 17).

Or again:

"The boundaries of schizophrenia, especially paranoid and catatonic forms, are sometimes so blurred that schizophrenia can only be discerned because of the lack—in the schizophrenic cases—of a lively relationship with the outside world. At times some, who were at first called 'psychopathic inferior cases' at the Vienna Psychoanalytic Clinic, turned out later to have megalomanic and persecutory ideation" (ibid., p. 24).

All throughout the 1920s articles appeared advocating greater therapist activity in order to reach certain patients who otherwise proved highly resistive to effective analysis. Since sharp distinctions between the different ego-function levels at which patients characteristically led their lives were not being made at this time, the kinds of cases that seemed to require special activity were classified not so much along lines of diagnosis (as we tend to do nowadays), but along lines of certain symptom clusters or character traits.

Ferenczi (1926), for example, began to modify standard technique on behalf of a particular "hysteric" young woman who had led an apparently deprived childhood and who now demanded "love" from all those around her, including her analyst. When the classical approach did not seem to reach her, Ferenczi took for a time to allowing her to sit on his lap, hoping to make up vicariously for some of the love of which she had felt cheated. But this seemed to provoke storms of affect just as uncontrollable as those unleashed earlier by her sense of deprivation. He abandoned this technical manuever shortly thereafter, as he described at length to Freud, in a paper that marks, almost inadvertently, the beginning of the era of preoccupation with "countertransference."

In general, Ferenczi was reacting to what he termed the excessive "passivity" of his contemporaries, and advocated working always "against the grain; that is, against the Pleasure-Principle" (1926, p. 208). For example, a female patient with many tics and onanistic gestures was asked to stop these, whereupon new memories surfaced and became accessible. He cautioned that this technic required a stable transference, because until it developed, the patient might quit. In a follow-up paper on contraindications, Ferenczi spoke indirectly about the temptations and hazards inhering to "active therapy," and gives a hint that psychotic patients would be particularly at risk:

> "Occasionally the patient attempts to express early infantile desires to exhibit or, naturally without result, to provoke the disapproval of the physician by craving to perform onanism or incontinence. In cases that are not psychotic, one may be sure that they did not carry out any act that could be dangerous to the physician or themselves. In general an active technic is to be allowed. . . . so long as the role of the physician does not exceed that of the friendly observer and advisor" (ibid., p. 224).

In the latter part of the 1920s Reich and his supervisee at the Vienna Psychoanalytic Clinic seminars on treatment, Gustav Bychowski, addressed themselves to the psychoses per se, schizophrenia in particular. Reich began to urge a more active technic with schizophrenics, one that paid particularly close attention to the patient's gestures. A compelling example of Reich's prowess in this area is contained in a letter to Liebeck, written in 1935, in which he describes having helped a very resistive patient open up about her anxiety concerning death, through his intuition about her "corpselike" posture. Reich often became an active participant in the therapeutic encounter, shaking up certain otherwise heavily "armored" (characterologically resistant) patients by screaming, yelling, and on occasion punching—all to draw them out of their shells. Bychowski (1928), a milder man than his teacher, was content to advocate less forceful measures, largely of an exhortatory nature, to help overcome the strong resistances of many schizophrenic patients. He was much opposed to the tenets of the Polish psychiatric school in which he had his early training, for this school taught that schizophrenia was an organic brain disease. To Bychowski such a notion conveyed a sense of hopelessness; as he put it: "How could you then find a place for psychoanalytic therapy?"

It should be mentioned that the authors we have so far encountered offer little demographic data about their patients, nor do they provide much material concerning "mental status." Hence, a reviewer, fifty years later, cannot easily locate these patients with any precision on a map of psychodiagnoses. Even their social class is not always obvious; neither is the length of time spent in analytic therapy. The very first descriptions (Bjerre, 1912; Maeder, 1910) came from physicians still steeped in nineteenth century traditions of the medical model, and they accord us detailed information about family background, occupational and educational level, degree of contact with reality, and so on. But those whose chief identity was as analyst, rather than alienist, were as stingy with these details as they were bounteous in the presentation of their patient's inner life. Speculation about psychodynamics tends to replace the mere humble delineation of clinical observations. At our remove in time, we cannot often even hazard a guess as to whether a given patient was schizophrenic or not.

· · · · ·

The active therapies developed by Ferenczi, Reich, Bychowski, and others paved the way for more effective applications of analytic technic to the schizophrenias. It is of interest that Freud was less intimately concerned with these disorders, the "narcissistic neuroses" in his terminology, than some of his pupils, but all the same, he let it be known that their ideas by and large originated with him. Already in 1914 he had suggested that the treatment of phobic cases ultimately required pushing the patient into the region of dread. And he advocated introducing into the analysis of certain patients (most notably, the "Wolf Man") an arbitrary termination date. Similarly, some of Ferenczi's ideas on active therapy were, as Balint (1967) has detailed, crumbs from the master's table. Reich could perhaps claim more originality for his views on character disorders. As Brown (1961) points out, Reich felt they should be regarded as a specific form of "neurosis'' even though they may be unaccompanied by symptoms (in the ordinary sense of the word), and that all neuroses have their root in *character*. Reich's methods of pointing out to patients the essence of their character deformations was often bold and sometimes aggressive, but they helped provide the foundation for later work with borderline and psychotic patients by Sullivan and his followers.

One of the first psychoanalysts to concentrate on work with hospitalized schizophrenics was Ernst Simmel, whose important paper on analytic treatment in a sanatorium[2] was published in 1929. This article was an expanded version of a paper read at the Innsbruck Congress two years before. In it, Simmel discusses the need for hospital confinement of certain patients whose symptoms, particularly behavior manifestations, either interfered markedly with their overall function, or affected the survival capacity of the family of which they were a part. He gives as an example of the first instance the case history of a woman both of whose lower legs were deformed as if afflicted with elephantiasis, because ''for two years she had felt that she must never assume a horizontal position'' (1929, p. 71). As an example of the second kind Simmel described a case concerning a man whose high social position and professional reputation were constantly being jeopardized by his wife's ''dipsomania.''

Simmel was aware that the patient's illness is often only ''one symptom of a collective illness.'' Parents, siblings, spouses, children often have ''complementary neuroses,'' as he called them, sometimes arising out of homologous needs in the other family members, or sometimes induced by the powerful influence of the patient's more dramatic symptoms. In modern family therapy theory one speaks of the ''designated'' patient, nestled amongst other interacting members of a poorly functioning family. Simmel's ideas presaged these modern conceptions. He was likewise one of the first to realize how (1) patients tend to express their neurosis through behavior and (2) how this tendency is repeated predictably and faithfully before the eyes of the hospital staff, once the neurosis is carried over into the arena of the sanatorium. Simmel was also well aware how threatening the recovery of the hospitalized patient could be to the network of relatives remaining at home. He referred to their efforts to hinder recovery by any means at hand (in order to preserve the status quo) as a ''negative therapeutic reaction'' on their part. To counter this, a long period of analysis often needed to be conducted in isolation (from the relatives), or at least under strict medical regulation regarding visits, if therapy were to thrive.

While living within the institution the patient was offered a ''new real-

[2]The sanatorium, called ''Tegelsee,'' was opened in the fall of 1926, with Freud's enthusiastic endorsement (Jones, 1957, III, p. 129).

ity" more effective in adapting to the world outside than the faulty "reality" the patient brought with him. Life inside was to serve as a "prosthesis" until the patient could "get on his feet *extra muros*" (ibid., p. 77). As adjuncts to therapy, artistically decorated rooms, beautiful country surroundings, and kindly attendants were all to be a part of the hospital environment.

The sanatorium drew much of its power, in Simmel's view, from its capacity to nourish powerful womb-fantasies in its inmates; this capacity may be of great significance in the opening phase of treatment, since it fosters the kind of satisfaction and optimism that enables the recovering schizophrenic to endure the rigors of the subsequent stages. The latter, of course, require acceptance of the outside world as it is, along with the renunciation of magical wishes—wishes the "ideal" intramural environment could, partially and briefly, gratify. Simmel also advocated paying close attention to the observations of the attendants, which then, at the proper time, are brought into the analysis proper. The nursing staff in general acted as an extra "sense organ" for the analyst, who could also turn his attention to aspects of the patients' conflicts that were projected onto the nurses. All this represented a departure from the strict confidentiality of classical analysis, a departure made necessary by the seriousness of the disorders requiring institutional treatment. Perhaps the main rationale for this hinged on the use, by these more disturbed patients, of strong denial and projection. Both these mechanisms involve total nonacceptance of responsibility for the behavior and feelings underlying them; hence the necessity of forceful measures to break through such defenses.

Structurally, Simmel's sanatorium consisted of analyst plus groups of ancillary personnel who fed information about patients' behavior to the analyst; this enabled the analyst to deal with "our patients' constant endeavors to draw *others* into the magic circle of their neurosis," and to reveal these endeavors as manifestations of the transference. Apropos the transference, the institution, with its set of rules and regulations, was designed specifically to close off to the patient all avenues of evasion, so that he soon found himself "in the midst of that primary, infantile reality where he originally came to grief" (ibid., p. 81).

Conceptually Simmel's psychodynamics partook of Freud's structural theory, and although aware of the pregenital regression points of the typical inpatients, Simmel saw their psychopathology primarily as deformations of Oedipal conflicts and castration anxiety. The patient with an addictive problem (e.g., alcoholism) was viewed as a "melancholic" who makes his "superego drunk with the poison with which he murders the object(s) in the ego" (ibid., p. 84).

During the tense years of prewar Hitlerian Germany, the sanatorium fell upon hard times and had to be closed in 1931, to Freud's keen regret as well as Simmel's (Jones, 1957, III, p. 161). Simmel himself emigrated to America, where he founded the Los Angeles Psychoanalytic Institute, directing it until his death in 1947.

Simmel's technic of sanatorium management remained the model for analytically oriented treatment of inpatient schizophrenics for years to come. The prevailing methods practiced at the New York Psychiatric Institute, for example, were until the 1970s very much in keeping with Simmel's precepts. Even then, his precepts were not abrogated, but rather embellished with newer concepts, including minute attention to intrastaff conflicts, and increased psychotherapeutic responsibility for ancillary personnel.

The one-to-one encounter is the hallmark of the psychoanalytic technic; as such, a bias existed among analysts that had to be overcome if many borderline and psychotic patients were to be accessible to therapy. For many of the latter, group, family, and other supra-individual combinations are needed, if not throughout the entire process of their recovery, at least for some distinct phases of it. The patients in Simmel's sanatorium were not, for example, gathered in various groups for the purpose of dynamic or task-oriented group psychotherapy as would be routine in treatment centers of our day. But the fact that Simmel made a systematic effort to include the impressions of his nonmedical staff into the analytic therapy establishes him as having taken a crucial step in overcoming the barrier of the hallowed "one-to-one."

Although Simmel was one of the very few who, in the 1920s, were applying Freud's teachings in so integrated a way to the treatment of hospitalized patients, he was not the only one. Georg Groddeck introduced Freudian principles into the management of patients at his sanatorium in Baden-Baden. He had become a member of the Berlin Psychoanalytic Society in 1920, as a man of 54, having been preoccupied with medical (but nonpsychiatric) and philosophical and literary interests before. Freud, whom he had met three years before, was much impressed by him and had tried to "tame" his "demonic" spirit (Grotjahn, 1977, p. 315). Groddeck was a remarkable intuitive clinician who effected miraculous recoveries in his sanatorium. He influenced many of the great figures in the psychotherapy of schizophrenia through his interest in symbolic thinking and in the strong *mother* transferences of his patients, which had been rather ignored by his predecessors. His 1921 publication of the *Book of the It* (*Das Buch vom Es*) was concerned with symbols and innate human drives, and contributed (along with Nietzsche's use of the term) to Freud's metaphor of the "id" in his forthcoming paper on structural theory. Groddeck wrote little on schizophrenia or psychotherapy per se, but impressed Fromm-Reichmann, who gave him credit for her method of treating schizophrenics. Others indebted to Groddeck in this way include John Rosen, Marguerite Sechèhaye, Melanie Klein, Jacob Moreno (the founder of psychodrama), and René Spitz. During the mid-twenties Groddeck wrote about himself with a candor not to be seen again in analytic circles until the sixties, when a number of psychoanalytic writers, intrigued with countertransference issues, were to walk the thin fence between enlightening self-revelation and morbid "true confession." The contributions of these authors, including the better ones (Searles, Bryce-Boyer, Savage) were foreshadowed nonetheless by Groddeck's spirit a generation earlier.

Toward the end of the 1920s the application of the analytic method to the psychoses was pursued further by Ruth Mack Brunswick. The daughter of a Harvard judge, she received training with Freud in Vienna, and it was to her care that Freud entrusted the continued treatment of his former patient, the "Wolf Man." This famous émigré from the Russian aristocracy was analyzed briefly on two occasions by Freud, beginning in 1910, for a severe "neurosis" that had left him in a state of near-abject dependency. For twelve years he enjoyed reasonably good health, only to succumb again in 1927 to a disorder then characterized by paranoid ideation and homosexual conflicts. The illness was precipitated by his coming to learn of Freud's facial cancer. Brunswick treated the Wolf Man on and off until 1940.

Brunswick, whose chief interests lay in the clinical as opposed to the theoretical area, gave us a detailed account in 1929 of her analytic work with a young married woman who suffered a circumscribed delusion of jealousy. Her description is particularly instructive, inasmuch as she does not fail to include material relating to her patient's family and socioeconomic background, and to the length of analysis.

The case, a 29-year-old housewife, depicted as a "small, poorly developed, intelligent, not unattractive proletarian woman . . . who seemed habitually shy and distrustful," consented to see Dr. Brunswick "only under pressure." There had been a violent scene of jealousy at home, in which she threatened suicide after upbraiding her husband for his supposed infidelity. She was about to have been committed to an institution, but her reluctance to enter one led to the compromise of a consultation with the analyst. Brunswick proposed a diagnosis of "paranoia," ruling out, after much difficulty, hysteria and paranoid schizophrenia. The couch was used straightaway, after the manner of the times, and although the patient was hesitant at first, she settled down soon and came faithfully for her daily sessions. Brunswick at first unearthed scenes of infantile seduction by her older, mentally retarded sister, and proceeded to analyze the patient's infantile masturbation, penis envy, and castration fears, and finally, the layer of homosexual jealousy. During the analysis, which spanned a scant $2^{1}/_{2}$ months, the patient experienced three brief paranoid episodes. The last one occurred in the pretermination phase of treatment: One day the patient missed her session, offering a flimsy excuse about ''having some sewing to do'' for an acquaintance of the analyst's. Brunswick reasoned: ''Only the wish to insult me could have made her put her sewing work ahead of her analytic work with me. Is she perhaps trying to make me jealous?'' She then remarked, ''Is this perhaps your old anger at your sister that you have always denied?'' The patient acknowledged this was so (1929, p. 166), and confirmed this interpretation with a flood of relevant memories about the sister. By this point the patient's function had improved in both the spheres of symptoms and object relations. Formerly frigid with her husband, she now enjoyed intercourse; she became cheerful and confident. Two years later, Brunswick noted she was still well, having become ''a little more common and fitting to her environment.''

Diagnostically, the patient was particularly challenging. There were features resembling both paranoid schizophrenia and hysteria. Yet, as the author pointed out, there were no speech mannerisms, no hallucinations, no delusions save transitory ones of jealousy, and no deterioration of a sort that might support more fully the schizophrenic label. Furthermore, Brunswick felt that the patient's attachment to the seductive sister began so early in life as to constitute a primitive fixation point, rather than a manifestation of severe ''regression.'' Yet schizophrenia was conceptualized among analysts of this era as an end product of profound regression of the libido. Therapeutically, according to Brunswick, it would be easier to ameliorate a condition arising out of primary fixation than out of regression (ibid., p. 713). However this may be debated, she used this argument to account for the surprisingly good result she obtained in merely $2^{1}/_{2}$ months of analysis. With respect to hysteria, on the other hand, there were too many paranoid manifestations present to resemble typical hysterical cases, as well as a type of transference more feeble in nature, arising out of a certain tenuousness in the patient's ''reality power,'' than would be characteristic of hysteria. I mention these points to show more vividly the mental processes of Dr. Brunswick, one of the eminent psychoanalysts of her day, as she grappled with a case that defied the diagnostic classifications available to her. Today we would see such a case as exemplifying a borderline state, perhaps founded on a genetic predisposition to a schizophrenia, which was not otherwise so apparent at a *clinical* level as to permit the unequivocal diagnosis of schizophrenia also.

''Borderline states,'' which were to occupy so much space in the analytic literature—as well as in analysts' offices—in the decades that followed, were not yet comfortably dealt with by the analysts of the twenties, for whom the psychodiagnostic world remained bipartite: either "neurotic" or "psychotic."

It is of interest that the same constellation of symptoms in the jealous housewife that so bedeviled Brunswick diagnostically were present in the Wolf Man also. Here I am referring to the fixities of thought, obsessional in their recurrence and paranoid in their coloring. In neither did this pattern reach frank delusional proportions; hence, the diagnosis of "schizophrenia" seemed unsupportable. As Muriel Gardiner notes in her commentary on the Wolf Man (1971, p. 364): "The patient himself, as Dr. Brunswick tells us, while insisting that [a certain minor] injury to his nose was all too noticeable, nevertheless realized that his attitude to it was abnormal." Yet, this ideational pattern was regarded—and rightly so—as too intensely paranoid to be altogether in keeping with an ordinary obsessional neurosis. Kernberg would categorize this pattern as an overvalued idea in keeping with borderline pathology. I would agree, adding that such patterns are often seen in those who are schizotypal constitutionally (such as the borderline schizophrenics noted among the close relatives of some unequivocal schizophrenic persons; Kety et al., 1968).

Having mentioned the metapsychological views of Ruth Brunswick and how these influenced her appraisal and treatment of schizophrenic or "almost" schizophrenic patients, it would be appropriate to become more acquainted with the views of her colleague, Hermann Nunberg. Though the bulk of his writing concerned the neuroses, he contributed several long articles on schizophrenia during this period. Nunberg was not as innovative in his handling of schizophrenics as some of his Vienna colleagues (e.g., Bychowski and Reich), concentrating instead on the translation into the realm of schizophrenia of Freud's theoretical statements about psychoneuroses. Nunberg is also known for his having advocated a personal analysis for all those undertaking to practice psychoanalysis, a position he put forward at the 1918 Budapest convention, and which soon became standard procedure at analytic institutes (see F. Alexander, 1966, p. 54).

In a paper he presented at the Vienna Psychoanalytic Society in 1920 on the "catatonic attack" (1961, ch. 1), he expostulated on the precipitating events and dynamic mechanisms in an acute schizophrenic episode. There are not many clues in this densely written material as to the method of treatment per se, but it would appear that Nunberg's technic was "classical" in his use of the couch, concentration on dreams, and (apparent) avoidance of "active" maneuvers such as Ferenczi had been advocating. Nunberg acknowledges a debt to Tausk, whose ideas about paranoia and ego boundaries (see, for example, "The Influencing Machine") Nunberg incorporated into his schema. Nunberg was well aware that schizophrenics can manifest a transference, but he cautioned that such patients may experience "frequent regressions to a phase so far back, that actions replace speech as a means of expression." The patient who formed the basis of his 1920 paper was a well-educated engineer of 32, who had functioned as an "obsessional neurotic" before his break, and who had always struggled against homosexual impulses. His breakdown was precipitated by his attempt to commit incest with his sister. He became violent, excited, voluble, and began to smear feces and other excreta. While the patients Ruth Brunswick described were only "questionably" schizophrenic in her eyes, the diagnosis in Nunberg's patient seems certain. He experienced thought insertion, thought removal, and various other boundary disturbances of an unmistakably schizophrenic stamp.

In the first phase of analysis it became clear to Nunberg that the patient's "love" of his sister represented a narcissistic object-choice. (He had moved in with this older, unmarried sister two years earlier.) He felt he could not find a wife for himself because his genitals were too "small, ugly and mutilated"—but this is also how he regarded those of his (in fantasy, "castrated") sister. The arrangement with his sister seemed like the fulfillment of his old dream of being "married," and for a time his self-confidence grew, even to the point of his coming to feel invincible.

The analytic work then concentrated upon the patient's florid somatic delusions, which began with a wish to regenerate himself via special "breathing exercises." During one round of these exercises, he felt a "tear inside," and imagined a fatal abscess forming near his navel. While the meanings of these fantastic notions were being explored, he began to elaborate a "womb fantasy," imagining that his breakdown was the equivalent of his having "died," from which point it would require "nine months for me to become hardened again . . . the same time as it takes for a child to be born." Nunberg interpreted this as a wish to be reborn, via impregnation of the sister, but since the latter was telescoped into a projected image of himself, the fundamental dynamic was one of rebirth via *self*-impregnation (ibid., p. 8).

In another passage Nunberg relates certain symptoms whose nature foreshadows what a subsequent generation of analysts would designate as "splitting." At the height of his illness, the patient had the impression, as he walked along the street, that people were of two kinds: "the real ones of 1917 and others, with gray garments, languid, as if from a time thirty or forty years ago." Nunberg conceived of this phenomenon as arising from a "*detaching* of libido from the outside world, in which process the objects lose the vivid tinge of a world endowed with libido."

It is my own impression that in these, and in the many similarly worded explanations of Nunberg, he confuses metaphor with "cause," and comes to regard what is basically an *analogy* ("the world becoming dead and gray" is *as though* "one's emotional interest in the world suddenly diminished") as some kind of *causal* explanation belonging to a different and more abstract frame of reference: the "libido" (emotional interest) became "detached," as if one had unlocked the secret of a mysterious, hitherto unnoticed, neurophysiological process. In all likelihood, there *is* some strange neurophysiological process that accompanies, even underlies, schizophrenic withdrawal of this sort, but most modern theoreticians (whether in psychology or neurophysiology) would agree that the kinds of explanations Nunberg (and other proponents of libido theory) proffer do not put the finger on this "process." These explanations are thus more to be seen as metaphors (usually of Freud's) that hardened into concretisms in the hands of his pupils. I have permitted myself this digression here to illustrate an important point regarding the theory and therapy—the two are of course interrelated—of this epoch. Many of Freud's students were, as acolytes, more pious than their mentor: while Freud retained the principles of his neurologic apprenticeship, and along with it his belief in the importance of a constitutional factor in the "narcissistic neuroses," some of his disciples, though paying lip service to these principles, began to evolve wholly psychological explanations for the mental phenomena they encountered. In the case of the healthier, "neurotic" patients, this tendency did less violence to certain biologic data. But in the case of psychotic patients, this generation of analysts was often willing to look aside fairly strong evidence of constitutional and other factors. Many, in fact, felt that to acknowledge the latter was to abandon hope, because what was "done" psychologically to their patients could be "undone" with their new method. But what was "done" *in utero*, or worse still, *in ovo,* seemed insuperable. Schizophrenia was thus constantly analogized to neurosis; what seemed fundamentally different about the two states at the turn of the century, now seemed like matters of a similar nature differing only in degree. The serious boundary confusion of Nunberg's patient was conceptualized as a marked withdrawal of libido from objects (outside) onto the ego itself, to the point where "world outside" and "self" were no longer distinguished. (In fact they weren't—but was that the "reason," or merely a translation into a different universe of discourse?)

More convincing are Nunberg's translations of certain otherwise incomprehensible acts to a symbolic level. Here the analytic method can apply itself with great force to the schizophrenic's dilemma. During the analysis of the oral-sadistic component of the patient's dynamics, Nunberg recounts an episode in which the still hospitalized man was about to be visited by his sister. She used to bring him his favorite foods, and he could scarcely contain himself in anticipation of her coming. He would then masturbate, in order, as he explained it, to precipitate her appearance, for "the penis is a magic flute, and when I do that, sister comes sooner!" (ibid., p. 11). No one who understands that the Magic Flute of the legend (and the opera) is symbolically a penis should cavil at his notion!

In the hypochondriacal phase of the engineer's illness, various parts of his body seemed to take on attributes formerly inhering to things or people of importance in the outside world. Defecation, for instance, was experienced as a special "sacrifice" with which he would "repay his debt to humanity." His delusional system was seen, along the lines of Freud's metapsychological views as expressed in the Schreber case, as a *restorative* attempt, an "attempt to cathect anew the objects of the outside world with the overflow of narcissistic libido" (i.e., overflow arising from excessive detachment of libido-to-outside-objects onto ego, at an earlier phase of illness): "The endeavor to regain the objects [of the external world] is realized through the *body.*"

Nunberg noted that many schizophrenics exhibit unusual degrees of recollection from early childhood, and of self-observation in general. The engineer, for example, was a "compulsive rememberer." This phenomenon Numberg attributed to a marked regression of "attention" onto internal perception. This was different from what obtained in the neuroses, but still explicable within the accepted framework: "In analysis we have to force the psychoneurotic to turn his attention to the internal processes and to relate his associations without discrimination. . . . By these means we artificially call forth a state that exists *a priori* in the schizophrenic." This ironic situation Nunberg ascribed to a peculiarity of the schizophrenic's mental censorship: the severe ego regression causes the institution of censorship to lose the component of reality testing, likewise of conscience. This faulty "censor" permits the flooding of consciousness with "perverse" ideas emanating from the drives, and also the regression of outward-directed attention back to "that stage of ego development when the internal world was the exclusive object of perception" (ibid., p. 22). Here one sees, in Nunberg's theoretical formulations, hints of Melanie Klein's attention to the very earliest stage of infant development as crucial for the understanding of schizophrenia. In fact, Nunberg invokes Rank's idea of birth trauma in his own formulation, as he compares "the climactic catatonic attack with the first great eruption of affect in the human being, namely birth anxiety" (ibid.,

p. 23). As he put it, "The most important experience for the individual is his birth"—but he makes it clear that this is *literally* an experience inchoately recalled by each individual, and potent, under certain circumstances, as an activator of neurotic (or psychotic) disturbances.

Elsewhere in his discussion of this same case, Nunberg offers another "irony" in the theoretical approach to mental disorders: "In psychoanalytically treated neuroses . . . recovery begins after removal of the repression, recovery begins in schizophrenia after repression has been restored" (ibid., p. 58). Hence, he suggests, in one's therapeutic endeavors, effecting the proper degree of repression of over-remembered painful connections and memories—in cases of schizophrenia.

As a last point, Nunberg deserves credit for beginning to understand what is now referred to as the mechanism of "projective identification" as a powerful operator in the dynamics of schizophrenic patients. He speaks of phases of illness during which the (external) object(s) become "lost," with a concomitant accumulation of libido back onto (internal) organs. Some of this, then, gets projected back onto objects—and the object becomes endowed with the subject's own aggressive and sadistic impulses. This abstract and impersonal description would take on flesh and assume great importance in the metapsychological formulations of the Kleinian and Sullivanian schools of the generation that was to follow.

While Brunswick's and Nunberg's experiences were largely of ambulatory patients seen in their private offices, Leland Hinsie's (1929) experience was primarily with institutionalized patients. The then-associate director of the New York State Psychiatric Institute, he can serve as a spokesman for American hospital psychiatry of that time. His background, like Adolph Meyer's, was psychobiological rather than psychoanalytic. His survey on the treatment of schizophrenia is of special interest for this reason, because it represents the view of an enlightened but traditional psychiatrist, familiar with the analytic approach but not steeped in it, writing in the era that preceded the great advances of Sullivan and Klein in the intensive therapy of schizophrenics.

Hinsie credits Paul Hoch with noticing, along with Freud, Jung, and Bleuler, that the symptoms of dementia praecox were "not to be regarded as scattered and bizarre productions, but rather as representations of definite meaning to the individual." Still, one had best not ignore constitutional factors, "in the sense that when demands for adaptation arise, the [schizophrenic] individual is found unfit to meet them, unfit through inherent weakness, but also . . . through false attitudes which have developed through lack of proper training" (1929, p. 10). As Hoch added, it was in this last direction that hope lay for modifying such defects. Hinsie took a position midway between the pessimism that Freud was still expressing about the application of psychoanalysis to the "narcissistic neuroses," and the tremendous optimism of Coriat or Kirby. The analytic method required the use of the couch; the schizophrenic patient, much like the one described above by Ruth Brunswick, would trace step by step the successive orders of repressions. Finally, it was hoped, the patient could reconstruct a true picture of his dilemma, which he could then act on, as soon as his insight was "deep enough to release the repressions and fixations" (ibid., p. 12). Well aware that for many schizophrenic patients (especially hospitalized ones, presumably) the analytic method was not strictly applicable, or might even prove harmful, Hinsie advised that this group of patients was "entirely too complex in its symptomatology to warrant any but an individualistic method of therapy. . . . Sometimes psychoanalysis alone may be sufficient to induce improvement; sometimes reeducation may obtain the same results; still again, removal from the usual environment to the less stressful hospital life may help to achieve a more peaceful adjustment" (ibid., p. 16).

The proper boundaries for the analytic treatment were, in Hinsie's time, constantly tested and renegotiated. Since alternative therapies were scarcely available (there were no phenothiazines or ECT in that era), these boundaries were often pushed further than might seem reasonable to the generation of the 1980s.

. . . . .

Psychoanalysis began as a psychology of the individual, with the focus always on inner structures. It is not that the early analytic writers necessarily underestimated the impact of other people on the life of the individual; far from it. But in their efforts to encompass the phenomena of mental life (as well as of one person's interaction with another) within a scientific system and language, the emphasis remained on what was simplest: the individual, essentially a one-person system. Even the then-prevalent use of the term "objects," to denote significant others, serves to underline how life beyond the confines of the individual's skin were seen only with "peripheral vision." With respect to the parents in a family, father's importance seemed to overshadow mother's for Freud and his pupils—at least until the mid-1920s.

This metapsychological stance had its bearing on how schizophrenia and its treatment were viewed. Freud's analysis of Schreber makes much mention of a father-figure—in the person of Dr. Flechsig—but, as Searles (1965) pointed out, little or no mention of Schreber's mother. There was little awareness of how many of Schreber's conflicts may have centered around the mother-son relationship, and consequently of how the *sun* imagery in Schreber's delusional productions may have reflected that, rather than the father (+ "sun")-son relationship.

In Nunberg's papers of the twenties we begin to see a shift in emphasis; we see, in effect, interest in the mother-child relationship and in the interpersonal generally, *in statu nascendi*. By the thirties mother and the interpersonal are given their full due, as has been mentioned, in the works of Melanie Klein, Sullivan, and their followers. Even so, the newer metapsychologies enlarged mostly from one-person to two-person systems: mother-child, therapist-patient, and so on. The still more complex systems of whole families, i.e., three and more persons, were not to receive widespread attention until sometime later.

Awareness of the therapist's personality as it influenced treatment, especially with the schizophrenic, was a by-product of the emerging two-person psychologies of the thirties and forties. The interest in "countertransference" was not so apparent in the earlier literature. There would seem to be at least three reasons for this. First, the emphasis was initially on the free-association productions of the patient, revealed to a relatively silent and unobtrusive analyst. Second, psychotherapists as a rule were treating fairly disturbed but not grossly psychotic patients until the late twenties (Sullivan, for example, at the Sheppard and Enoch Pratt Hospital in Maryland). I think it is fair to say that less disturbed patients, as a group, induce less uncomfortable feelings in analysts, than do the most disturbed patients. Hence, even though the best integrated analysands induce a wide range of feelings in their analysts, these feelings are not so often of an intensity or discomfort as to push the countertransference to the center of the stage. And finally, the interaction between "neutral" analyst and the "neurotic" patient was not at first viewed as a two-way interaction between near equals. Rather the view was more along the lines of the "medical model": a "healthy" physician observing a "sick" patient, and ignoring the influence of his personality on what he "observed." As psychoanalysis progressed, especially into work with the schizophrenic, the Heisenberg principle of the observer affecting the observed became more and more relevant in the psychotherapeutic situation.

· · · · ·

The special impact of the schizophrenic upon his therapist (specifically, the way in which this tends to differ from the "classical" situation of well-integrated analysand and analyst) became an important challenge to the adequacy of Freudian theory, especially in regard to the treatment of highly disturbed persons. In a similar vein, Freudian structural theory, even in its elegant reformulation in *The Ego and the Id* (1923), met with difficulty when stretched to encompass borderline and psychotic conditions, as well as the neurotic conditions that served as the foundation for this theory. Schizophrenic patients, especially during acute episodes of psychosis, do not exhibit patterns of thought and behavior that are easily compartmentalized into "id" and "ego." The dreaming-while-awake quality of thought makes it seem as though "id" has overrun "ego" completely; the self-observational and synthetic functions attributed to ego seem lacking or seriously compromised. The values and ideals ordinarily subsumed under the notion of "superego" are so often in a fluid or alien (as if belonging to someone else) state in the schizophrenic, that structural theory again encounters a stumbling block.

In the sphere of personal relations, schizophrenics, whether acutely psychotic or not, were noted by many observers to perceive and to experience others as either impossibly good or bad. Or, again, the same person might be viewed in a highly idealized "good" way one moment and as the devil incarnate the next—and in such a manner that the schizophrenic patient while engulfed in one distorted viewpoint had no access whatsoever to the opposite sentiments he harbored a short while before. Nunberg was aware of these primitive defensive postures exhibited so often by schizophrenics. But it was the British psychoanalytic community that was to delineate these mechanisms more fully, weaving them into a more coherent theory of psychic function (with respect to schizophrenia) than had thus far evolved among the classical Freudians.

Moving away from their preoccupation with libidinal stages (oral, anal, genital) and the psychological deformations peculiar to each, the British school placed its emphasis on *object relations*. Particular attention was paid to internalized object relations, as the latter are experienced and recorded in the mind, over time, to serve as the basis for subsequent goal-oriented behavior. It is not that the strict Freudians had no intimation of what object relations signified: prelibations of an object-relations theory are already to be found in Freud's *Mourning and Melancholia* (1917). Likewise, in Abraham's paper on pregenital levels of the libido, he mentions that, at the onset of illness, the depressive patient "has completely broken off all object-relations" (1924, p. 431). It is rather that object relations remained in the background with Freud, Abraham, and Nunberg, but were put centerstage by Melanie Klein, Fairbairn, Winnicott, Guntrip, Rosenfeld, and other psychoanalysts active in England in the decades before and after World War II.

It was Fairbairn who proposed, in voicing his objection to the narrowness of the libido theory, and its reliance on a simple pleasure/pain principle, that "libido is not primarily pleasure-seeking, but object-seeking" (1946, p. 30). The bodily organs (including mouth, anus, and genitals, as focused on in the libido theory) are better viewed as "channels whereby personal aims may be achieved" (ibid., p. 31). Mere release of tension may occupy a prominent place in the psychology of the newborn, but object seeking acquires an ever more prominent place in the development even of the young child. In adults, exclusive preoccupation with simple tension relieving implies, in Fairbairn's view, a failure of object relationships: not a means of achieving libidinal aims, but a means of mitigating the failure of these aims.

Psychosexual maturity, according to Fairbairn's object-relational amplification of libido theory, rests not merely on an orientation to the genitals of the opposite sex, but upon a "mature dependence," characterized by "the capacity on the part of a differentiated individual for cooperative relationships with differentiated objects" (ibid., p. 34). The (ideal) relationship involves evenly matched giving and taking between two individuals who, though mutually dependent—we might say "interdependent"—show no disparity in their levels of dependence.

In depicting both normal development and psychopathological states, the object-relations school dwells extensively on such issues as the psychological internalization of objects (analogous to the physical incorporation of mother's milk), whose inner representations may be viewed as psychical "structures." Good and bad aspects of mother and significant other persons are kept separate by infants and very young children—a "splitting" process that, up to a certain age, is universal, perhaps inevitable.

Object-relations theory has considerable importance in the history of the psychoanalytic treatment of schizophrenia. By virtue of the close comparisons between the normal infantile predisposition to split objects into all-good and all-bad representations, and similar tendencies in schizophrenic adults, Kleinian metapsychology seems to enjoy greater explanatory power in dealing with schizophrenic (and indeed with other psychotic) manifestations than inheres to traditional libido theory. Klein was to write, in relation to melancholia, for example, that "the manic-depressive and the person who fails in the work of mourning . . . have been unable in early childhood to establish their internal 'good' objects and to feel secure in their inner world" (1940, p. 153). Klein went so far as to express the opinion that "every infant experiences anxieties which are psychotic in content" (ibid., p. 129). These anxieties are dealt with, by the infant, via the "infantile neurosis" centering around conflicts that relate to what Klein termed the "infantile depressive position"—a "melancholia in statu nascendi" (ibid., p. 126). In this situation, weaning mobilizes depressive feelings that express a mourning of the no longer available maternal breast. The depressive state is further characterized, in Kleinian metapsychology, by the infant's "uncontrollable greedy and destructive fantasies" directed against the mother. The retaliatory fantasies appear to invoke similar expectations of retaliatory behavior from mother (or from other caretakers), so that pining for the lost supplies and persecutory feelings exist side by side. They exist in a split fashion, however, at least during early infancy: the good and bad internalized images of mother are kept, as it were, in separate mental compartments.

Much space could be devoted to arguments for and against Klein's metapsychological views; much of her theorizing about the state of mind in very young infants strikes the modern reader as highly speculative. It is also an open question whether it is legitimate to ascribe *etiological* significance to some of Klein's observations and impressions. To note points of comparison between the psychological concomitants of normal weaning and adult manic-depressive psychosis does not justify the claim that the adult psychosis necessarily stemmed from traumata occurring precisely at the weaning phase. Indeed, contemporary genetic and psychobiological research pertaining to both schizophrenia and manic-depression suggest that, in certain persons at least, strong hereditary or constitutional factors may trigger psychotic illness at some stage of life, irrespective of how the weaning or the separation-individuation phases of childhood were handled by the parents. It may well be, then, that Klein overread and overestimated the etiological significance of a number of typical childhood mental phenomena. But she and her followers deserve considerable credit in drawing our attention to these analogies between adult psychosis and primitive mental states in childhood and, more especially, to the similarities that exist between the modes of thought in psychosis and in early childhood.

Schizophrenics do behave, and do provide us evidence from their verbalizations, as if good and bad images of self and others are split and unintegrated. Object-relations psychology, with its focus on internalized representations, provides a useful instrument for conceptualizing the otherwise bewildering, primitive mental states of adult psychotic patients. To the extent that Sullivan's interpersonal concepts provide what may, according to some, be an even more useful instrument, Fairbairn's object-relations theory marks, as Fromm-Reichmann mentions (1950, p. 83), an interesting transition from Freud to Sullivan. Winnicott, carrying forward the Kleinian object-relations viewpoint, considered schizophrenic illness the "negative" of processes that "can be traced in detail as the *positive* processes of maturation in the infancy and early childhood of the individual" (1965, p. 9). Specifically, he postulated that the "good enough mother" enables her baby to stifle the "unthinkable anxieties" (of annihilation) to which infants are prone and to develop a personality built on the pattern of continuity, in contrast to discontinuity and fragmentation of self. In the absence of good enough mothering, the infant will tend to develop a pattern of fragmentation, leaving him with a developmental task that is "almost from the beginning, loaded in the direction of psychopathology" (ibid., p. 61), particularly schizoid psychopathology.

Guntrip goes a step further in emphasizing the significance of the *schizoid position* in infancy, which, the Kleinian school asserts, antedates by some months the depressive position. According to Guntrip, "mankind's universal preference for feeling bad but strong, rather than feeling weak and afraid" (1962, p. 99) has contributed to excessive attention to the depressive position, at the expense of the (in his eyes) earlier and more important schizoid position, upon which the former may be said to rest: "schizoid trends can always be seen pushing through the depressive overlay" (ibid., p. 104).

Extrapolating from his analytic work with a schizophrenic patient, Rosenfeld, in a paper written originally in 1947, hypothesized that schizoid processes can be used as a defense mechanism during later stages of development. These processes, which can include depersonalization, may, however, adversely affect the structure of the ego, "causing varying degrees of splitting and projection" (1965, p. 33). Schizoid splitting mechanisms would appear to underlie both schizophrenia (allied states) and depersonalization, in Rosenfeld's view. The patient Rosenfeld described in this paper exhibited "rigid detachment and denial of all feelings," along with feelings of "dimness and half-consciousness": there was something like a blanket separating her from the world; she felt dead, "not here," and cut off from herself (ibid., p. 17). The depersonalized state seemed to serve as a defense against impulses of all kinds in a patient who struggled against full-blown insanity.

Again, it is important to side-step casuistical discussions of whether schizoid phenomena in patients derive solely from traumata at the analogous "schizoid" phase in early infancy. One must instead come to recognize the therapeutic applications of the Kleinian school to the psychological treatment of borderline and of unequivocally schizophrenic patients. The delineation of primitive "schizoid" states in early life, as set forth by analysts of this object-relations orientation, has helped those who work intensively with such patients to comprehend better the verbal and behavioral counterparts of these primitive states, as they unfold over the course of treatment. Therapists have, as a result, learned to become more familiar with, and correspondingly less afraid of, these phenomena. This contributes to the capacity, on the part of the therapist, to attune himself to the moment-to-moment manifestations of schizoid processes. Presumably, the fashioning of appropriate, healing responses is facilitated by this enhanced awareness. Not all schizotypal persons can achieve symptomatic recoveries through verbal interventions alone, but insofar as interpersonal processes between therapist and patient can be effective, they will be the more effective to the extent that one has assimilated the object-relations literature devoted to schizoid mechanisms.

4

Stages in the Course of Intensive Psychotherapy with Schizophrenic Patients

Michael H. Stone, M.D.

"Intensive psychotherapy" with schizophrenic persons customarily refers to a method of treatment in which the major emphasis is on the verbal interchanges between therapist and patient, conducted within a format involving frequent visits (two to five times per week) of "standard" length (three-quarters of an hour to an hour), in order that the patient's central conflicts and defects can be brought to light and explored via a modified psychoanalytic technic (see Fromm-Reichmann, 1950; Searles; 1965; Rosenfeld, 1965; H. Segal, 1975). Work with dreams, attempts to translate the patient's obscure symbolic expressions into the language of everyday life, clarifications about unrecognized feeling-states—are all a part of this process. Interspersed with these psychoanalytic interventions will be efforts at education concerning nuances of feeling, the meanings behind other people's gestures, etc., since schizophrenics often need specific help in these areas (see Schulz, 1976). One does not always have the opportunity, in doing intensive psychotherapy with schizophrenic patients, to begin at the beginning. Schizophrenic patients are not always comfortable with the first consultant to whom they are referred, so that, in many instances, no one therapist will be privileged to witness the unfolding of treatment from beginning to end. Another factor militating against *one* therapist beginning and completing intensive therapy with all his schizophrenic patients is its very length: one or another participant may move to a different city; illness may cause a premature interruption in the work; and so forth. In such cases the new clinician will see the patient at some point in the middle of the evolutionary process toward recovery, and may never, or only briefly, see the patient grossly out of contact with reality.

Still, those who dedicate themselves to this branch of psychotherapy will, after they have been in practice a number of years, have come to recognize the stages of which we shall speak here, though the experiences on which this recognition rests will not necessarily be derived from the treatment of any one particular patient.

In the midst of, or in the immediate aftermath of, an acute psychotic break, the schizophrenic patient will most likely be in poor contact with reality in a number of important sectors of his personality. Ego-boundary disturbances may be quite blatant and may take on any of the dozen forms alluded to in Schneider's (1959) description of the schizophrenic's "first-rank symptoms." The following vignette from my experience will illustrate this point:

> During residency, one of my colleagues at the Psychiatric Institute was struggling with the task of treating a grossly psychotic young woman, whose chief symptom consisted of a curious thought-insertion or delusion of influence. She would speak, whenever her parents visited, of their "thinking me" or, at other times, of their "chunking me."
>
> Eventually it became clear that she was talking about the frightening experience of having the ideas, expressions, attitudes etc., of her parents' lodge somehow in her brain during the course of a visit—as though these aspects of her parents' personalities got forcibly injected into her conscious life without her having any capacity either to assimilate such material nor yet again to distinguish it from what might be manifestations of her own unique self. Like the little chunks we see in vegetable soup, her parents' thoughts became part of the soup, while remaining at the same time readily separable. The only way in which she could preserve any sense of differentiation from the rest of the family was by insisting they not visit her at all.

In other schizophrenic patients, the onset of psychosis may not be accompanied by the kind of bizarre ego-boundary disturbance of the previous example, but, rather, by a more logical-seeming delusion or *idée fixe* whose most prominent features are not so much loss of boundary as misinterpretation and oversimplification. One manifestation of this may be seen in the schizophrenic patient who "protests too much," in a self-deprecatory fashion, about some fault or imaginary condition. Some schizophrenics will begin, for example, with the complaint that they are homosexual. They may profess this loudly, as if to say: "This is my problem, doctor." When one probes further into the matter, one discovers that although that identity would be genuinely uncomfortable for the patient, two other things are true. One is that such an identity may represent some secretly longed-for wishes that the patient cannot fully accept. This is the dynamic Freud spoke about in relation to the Schreber case. The other is, that to have any kind of label—even an unpopular and disagreeable label—can be much more comfortable a state to be in, than to exist continually in a state of total undifferentiatedness. In the latter situation, the individual feels as if he were merging or floating and—worst of all—as if he had no predictable, reliable identity. Paradoxically, it may be more comfortable—a refuge, in fact—for the schizophrenic to think of himself as a "fag" than as a "nothing." I am speaking here of an unusual dynamic that would be germane, I think, only to the world of schizophrenia. Those who work with schizophrenic patients have to be aware of unusual reactions of this sort if they are to fully understand some of their patients.

Example

A chronically schizophrenic man of about 25 had to be hospitalized because of progressive deterioration in his personal hygiene and in his capacity for autonomous function. Though no clear-cut precipitant was discernible, he would make frequent allusions to how his (much better functioning) brothers had "made him ill" by playing pool with him in such a way that, as he put it, "the 8-ball was always behind the cue-ball, whenever it would be my turn." Or else, "the balls would be lined up in a way where I wouldn't get off a straight shot." His brothers seemed to be "ganging on me." His speech was full of veiled allusions of this sort to homosexuality, and he was later able to admit his apprehension that he turn out to "be" a homosexual. But still further along in the course of his therapy it developed that, beneath his fear of being a homosexual—in actuality he was still a virgin—was the still more paralyzing fear of being found out by others as a "nothing."

This man, who had never worked on his own, never completed school, and never had any close friends, saw himself for many years as little more than a collocation of atoms—which had coalesced through some freak accident some 25 years before into a creature bearing such-and-such a name, but which was destined to decompose not many years hence into a similar number of no longer tightly bound atoms, to scatter hither, thither, and yon throughout the solar system.

· · · · ·

Our purpose in this chapter is to describe the stages of intensive psychotherapy rather than to outline the ideal program of treatment for helping schizophrenic patients progress through these stages. Some approaches to the delusional patient or to those who are actively hallucinating have already been delineated by Arieti and Forrest (see Chapters 1, 11); the role of psychotropic medication in abridging the out-of-contact phase of the acute psychotic episode has been outlined by Albert (see Chapter 16).

Once we succeed in winning the patient away from the autistic withdrawal in which he may be locked in the early phase of therapy, he may be seen to pass into a different stage or, as it usually happens, a new and orderly sequence of stages. These may be characterized by a variety of feeling states occurring in both the patient and the therapist. These feeling states, like the stages to which they correspond, tend to appear in a particular sequence. It is fair to say, however, that the phenomena in question, and an awareness of the *sequential* emergence of these feeling states, are seldom identifiable to the therapist as he is going through them—much less to the patient. Their presence is often recapturable only in retrospect.

The schizophrenic patient and his therapist may be ready, once the patient is in good contact, to embark on the last and often very long phase of therapy. Now established in what we hope is analogous to the therapeutic alliance between analyst and neurotic analysand, the patient is ready to explore sequentially the various important conflicts in his personality organization as they may relate to the classical Freudian developmental stages—oral, anal, and genital. This work tends to be preceded by a stage characterized, ordinarily, by womb fantasies and rebirth fantasies. These may be not unlike what neurotic patients bring to the surface at the beginning of analysis.

Such fantasies in schizophrenics tend, however, to be much more intense, more poignant in their expression, and a good deal more primitive. For example, when I was a resident, I worked with a patient who, after the initial psychological skirmishes were over between us and she was beginning to get ensconced in therapy, had a dream in which she saw me as a Thorazine® tablet. This she then ingested, enabling her to retain me, as she thought, totally inside her, rather like Jonah in the whale. Sometimes, after our sessions, she would run·down to the restaurant around the corner and wolf down two hamburgers, which to her mind also represented the incorporation of myself within her body.

Although both schizophrenic and well-integrated psychoneurotic patients often express rebirth fantasies in the beginning of therapy, the degree of emotional involvement in the fantasy tends to be quite different. The neurotic patient usually does not need to be literally reborn or remade: much of his personality is all right the way it is. So the typical rebirth dream—say, at the beginning of analysis—expresses a kind of parenthetical assumption that one is about to have a fresh start in some important segment of his life. Ordinarily only one or two dreams—during one or two sessions—will be spent on such material. Typically the dream(s) will involve an archeological expedition in the company of a stranger (the analyst) or a shopping trip to the sub-sub-basement of a large store; that is, some image representing the exploration of the deepest strata of one's personality. Thereafter, the neurotic patient may launch rather directly into the main business at hand, which usually concerns some problem in intimate relationships. What follows has been analogized by Freud to the peeling of an onion, the outer (more recent) layers coming off first, as one progresses to the "core" (the earlier layers of experience). This means that one progresses from the more recent "genital" layer through the "anal" layer (having to do with separation and individuation) and on down to the "oral" layer (having to do with one's earliest identifications, earliest feelings about mother, and the like).

With the schizophrenic patient, however, the evolution may at times be just the opposite. There may be a rather extended period—weeks or a few months—of womb and rebirth fantasies. The patient will then tend to progress in his psychosexual development from the ground up—starting with "oral" conflicts and progressing gradually toward conflicts centered around intimate relationships. And whereas the neurotic patient may give voice to a rebirth fantasy as a mere *façon de parler,* without much more intensity of feeling than is attached to our quipping that "life begins at forty" when we happen to approach that birthday, the schizophrenic patient may have the deepest longing to erase his actual past and begin over as a baby of the therapist. In no other way does it seem to him that he has a chance of becoming an autonomous and comfortable human being. At times the achievement of self-sufficiency may seem so remote that the patient acknowledges no more ambitious a hope than to curl up beside the therapist—to the extent that the latter can come to be seen as unambivalently warm and giving—for the remainder of his life. Thus, a young schizophrenic woman admitted to the Psychiatric Institute after a shattering romantic disappointment, would take to wrapping herself in a large blanket and sleeping, in this woolen cocoon, under the grand piano of the patients' lounge for several months on end. This infuriated the nursing staff, who were convinced she would never come out of this phase on her own and who berated the therapist, accordingly, for what they saw as wholesale indulgence. Eventually this patient did emerge from her cocoon, did adopt a less obscure manner of speaking, and did substitute conventional female attire for the monk's garb she insisted on wearing initially—but not before she gratified for a sufficient length of time this powerful wish to return to the womb. Happily she did not consume the whole nine months in the process, but even so she exhausted the patience of nearly all those concerned with her treatment.

· · · · ·

Although it is often possible to characterize the sequence of conflictual areas spontaneously dwelt on by the recovering schizophrenic as "oral," "anal," and so on, one can also place the focus on the shifts occurring within the therapist-patient relationship. Writing in a purely psychological framework, Bryce-Boyer (1980, p. 133) emphasizes disturbances in the *symbiotic* and *separation-individuation* phases (as outlined by Mahler) as crucial to the development of functional psychoses, including schizophrenia. Searles (1961) speaks of these stages in the following manner: once beyond the out-of-contact phase, the patient enters a phase of ambivalent symbiosis. This is followed by pre-ambivalent symbiosis, next by resolution (of the symbiosis), and finally by a phase, often lengthy in duration, whose main tasks are the establishment and elaboration of the patient's "newly won individuation." It should be apparent that we are speaking here of a genuine and mature individuation—one rooted, finally, in conventional reality—and not of the delusional "self" so often adopted by the schizophrenic patient initially in his pathetic struggle to distinguish himself from the rest of his human (or even, as Searles [1960] has emphasized, *non*-human) environment.

Before we show the usefulness of these evolutionary subdivisions through clinical examples, it will be well to digress for a moment about the matter of etiology. The Sullivanian school saw in the vicissitudes of the mother-child dyad the main causative element behind schizophrenic decompensation. Specifically, ambivalence on the mother's part, if sufficiently profound, was viewed as grossly hindering the child's ego integration and paving the way for the kind of faulty ego-boundary sense and fragmented conception of self and others that are the hallmarks of the illness we call schizophrenia. This is a purely psychological explanation of the genesis of schizophrenia and one that tends to lay particular blame upon the mother.

I personally adhere to a viewpoint, such as that of Arieti (1977), which stresses biological (hereditary, constitutional, neurological . . .) components as well, and draws attention to the interaction among all relevant factors. Elsewhere, I have gone so far as to say that inherited factors, probably on a polygenic basis in most instances (see Shields, 1976, p. 64), constitute a necessary, though not in and of themselves sufficient, precondition to eventual schizophrenic breakdown (Stone, 1978). A similar opinion is reflected in the work of Erlenmeyer-Kimling (1975) and Kety (1977). According to this viewpoint, the schizophrenic-to-be comes into the world with such faulty integrative equipment that he would have trouble mastering many of the tasks of infancy (e.g., differentiating himself from inanimate objects, animals, other members of the family), even in the company of nurturing and empathic parents. An intrusive, insensitive, and markedly ambivalent mother may highlight or exaggerate these difficulties, but probably cannot bring them into being except in already vulnerable children (see Anthony, 1971; Garmezy, 1974; Shapiro, 1981).

What are the implications of this theory for psychotherapy? Simply this: that we must be on guard not to side too much with the schizophrenic patient—and then only when the evidence of his having really been victimized is overwhelming—as he recounts horror stories from the past about his parents. It will be more accurate to view the patient as having been driven to regard his parents in extreme ways—as ogres, witches, monsters or (occasionally) as saints—out of his constitutional handicap in what Bellak et al. (1973) and others refer to as the "synthetic function." If a neurotic patient happens to have had a cruel or neglectful parent, his perceptions of the parent are usually fairly accurate; his trouble derives from his assumption that other figures in his life, including the analyst, will treat him in a similar way. Transference distortions of this sort are relatively easy to sort out and correct, especially with a patient who has a good synthetic capacity to begin with. Far different, the situation in psychotherapy with the schizophrenic, for here we must determine whether the patient's recollections are convincing or quite otherwise, and whether the subsequent transference distortions with which we become familiar are based on realistic perceptions of, say, a truly terrifying mother, or on a delusory perception of a mother who would actually pass muster according to Winnicott's (1965) criteria.

Correcting the schizophrenic patient's distortions is all the more laborious—if not Sisyphean—a task, precisely because (1) we cannot at the outset take for granted the patient's recollections about what his mother and father were really like; (2) we are dealing with someone whose "reality organ" is impaired to begin with; and (3) we are struggling to modify distortions often clung to with tiger-like ferocity because they are shoring up a view of the world—as unstable and unpleasant as it may be—that the schizophrenic patient has come to regard as vital to his continuing existence. To cast doubt on some small aspect of this world-view, before the patient has been given something more workable in its place, is to shake this world to its foundations. Rather than risk being left with nothing, the patient will defend his house of cards with vigorous denial. The therapist will be experienced as a destroyer rather than as a potential savior; hence, the vociferous repudiation of our attempts, in the beginning, to challenge his perceptions.

At all events, the phases Searles speaks of are encountered with regularity in the course of intensive therapy with schizophrenics: they occur, irrespective of the theoretical position favored by the therapist. If, as I am advocating, we espouse a more complex, interactive model of schizophrenogenesis, we will be inclined to make more neutral remarks, such as "you seemed to see your mother as a heartless witch," rather than to agree prematurely that she *was* a heartless witch. This approach has the advantage of permitting us, potentially—if we have patience—to disentangle truth from fiction in the schizophrenic's remembrance of things past.

The Phase of Ambivalent Symbiosis

When the grossly psychotic symptoms—delusions or hallucinations or incoherent speech—have subsided, and when the translational work of the middle stage has largely been accomplished, so that the patient is talking about real issues rather than their obscure, symbolic equivalents, the *first* phase of the late stage has begun—the one Searles has called "ambivalent symbiosis." In this ordinarily stormy and uncomfortable phase, patient and therapist are locked into a tight relationship, in which feelings on both their parts are intense, contradictory, and rapidly shifting. The therapist is alternatingly seen as engulfing and abandoning, lovable and murderous; in the therapist himself are registered, in quick succession, compassion and contempt, lust and hatred. The still undifferentiated feeling states of the patient get projected onto the therapist who, at first unwittingly, reacts toward the patient with the same inchoate and unalloyed feelings that are buffeting the patient. The slightest gesture or shift in intonation by the therapist may suffice to evoke the most sweeping, at times grotesque, display of emotion in the patient. Half a minute later, another slight gesture—a change in the position of one's legs, a stifled yawn, a smile—may elicit, with the same suddenness, a totally opposite emotional state. A young schizophrenic man, enmeshed in this phase of treatment, was once showering me with compliments on my intellect and depth of understanding, when I interrupted our session momentarily to answer the telephone. As soon as I finished saying, "I'm with someone now" (the complete text of my part in that conversation), his expression changed to one of withering scorn, as he began to vilify me for caring about his distress so little as to answer the telephone.

The stage of ambivalent symbiosis is oftentimes punctuated by long silences. Searles speaks of how such silences foster the weakening of ego boundaries between therapist and patient, also of how they intensify projections and introjections of various aspects of both participants' personalities (see also Chapter 16 on silences). I still recall very vividly several examples of such phenomena from my residency days—more dramatic and disturbing than similar experiences in my more recent work because of their unfamiliarity. After eleven months of intensive therapy with a chronic schizophrenic woman—the one who regularly "ingested" me via her hamburgers and Thorazine® tablets—there occurred a session in which her pronunciation and tone of voice suddenly became quite childlike. She said, for example, "widdle" for "little." The theme of the session was her intractable insomnia. Somewhere in the middle of the session I began to get the distinct impression she was reenacting for me some period in her infancy when she was especially prone to night terrors. I asked whether the childlike quality I was noticing in her voice was perhaps telegraphing to me some hitherto unexpressed preoccupation with these painful experiences of her childhood. At first she was very distressed at this suggestion: "Don't tell me it has to do with a time that far back!" she protested. "I couldn't stand that! It'd mean I was hopeless!" She nonetheless recalled at that moment a dream the night before in which a doctor was giving her "sleeping injections," while her mother sat nearby, looking rather bored. The patient then recalled: "I was on my knees, crawling," and immediately exclaimed—as though I already knew this dream fragment—"Oh! You were thinking it has to do with my childhood, because I was *crawling!*" I reminded her that she had mentioned the crawling, not I, but she retorted, "No, it was *your* thought!" For a minute or so we got into a kind of argument about where that notion had originated—in her mind or in mine. I began to feel uncomfortable—as though sucked up, somehow, into her crazy, boundaryless world where thoughts, feelings, experiences were mutually interchangeable and of dubious parentage. Our minds seemed connected as if by a bridge upon which our thoughts were free to scamper back and forth. I had not felt such a blurring of identity before, and shared with her the nature of my discomfort. She nodded understandingly and said, "It's awful, isn't it?" I asked her whether that was the sort of thing she had in mind when she spoke of constantly "merging" with the people around her. She readily agreed.

Several years later I had similar feelings of boundary blurring while working with a borderline schizophrenic woman whose speech was so peppered with allusions, unfamiliar phrases, or else familiar words used in idiosyncratic ways as to render her barely comprehensible. After two or three months, I had begun to grasp these obscure references and secret meanings to the point where I could pretty much follow what she was saying. There were magical moments of closeness and of being transported outside one's customary self, as happens when one has mastered just enough of a foreign language to understand it immediately and without strain.

As time went on, experiences of this sort grew less frightening; they might be accompanied instead, as in the last instance, by a sense of satisfaction at having overcome nearly insuperable obstacles in the path of communication with another human being. In other situations these moments of boundarylessness may be accompanied by less welcome feelings, such as bewilderment or embarrassment. For a male therapist, it may be disconcerting at first to feel intensely "maternal" in relation to one of his schizophrenic patients. More disconcerting still, especially in relation to one's family and private life, are feelings of erotic preoccupation with such a patient. One will be in a quandary, for some time, about whether such feelings constitute a necessary step in the therapeutic venture, or a serious impediment. Is this countertransference in the most pathologic sense? Or the manifestation of empathic resonance stemming from the healthier facets of the patient's personality? Many questions of this sort arise during the ambivalent symbiotic phase of treatment. They are particularly hard questions to resolve because they are accompanied by such powerful feelings of guilt, disloyalty, and at times, doubt about one's very integrity as a human being—to be kept from rather than shared with supervisors, colleagues, or even one's analyst.

In recent years I have experienced moments of boundary blurring much less often in my work with schizophrenic patients than was customary during my training. It is not easy to say whether this is a reflection of a certain solidification that takes place over the years in one's professional and personal identity or of having grown more choosy in the selection of patients with whom I am willing to become emotionally entwined to this degree.

However this may be, I have noted that time seems to have exerted an opposite effect with regard to the acknowledgment of tender, even of lustful, feelings. It is one of the more curious paradoxes of our ostensibly peace-loving, Judeo-Christian culture that hostility is easier to confess than love. Patients who for months on end sing what Henriette Klein likes to call "hymns of hate" to their therapists, suddenly become awkward and diffident when their predominant affect toward us is one of gratitude, friendship, or sexual yearning. It is not much different with us. We are taught that erotic feelings toward our patients are manifestations of pathologic countertransference—something to be analyzed *away,* as it were, not merely analyzed. But it is only when we become confident that our own thoughts toward our patients will not become transformed into deeds, that we can confront with comfort the full range of emotions of which we will sooner or later be the target.

The experience of parenthood, besides fostering a degree of wisdom in human affairs not easily acquired from books or teachers, also strengthens one's identity, at the same time providing opportunities for dealing with unrealistic (though to one's child, temporarily quite normal) feelings of idealization and adoration. Partly for this reason, it has become less embarrassing and less threatening for me to find myself the object of a schizophrenic patient's admiration or love or to notice in myself feelings of a similar kind toward the patient. It is less embarrassing to admit to myself that I may actually have deserved at least some portion of that idealization, nor is it too crushing to admit that my actual worth and place in the world are much less awesome than they appear to be, for the time being, in the eyes of the patient.

To an extent that I suspect is greater than what is necessary for effective work with neurotic patients, it is the integrity of one's personal life (and not necessarily its outward success) that permits one to withstand the tempestuous feelings of schizophrenic patients in this ambivalent-symbiotic phase. This ability, in turn, becomes an object lesson for the patient, whose parents or acquaintances are often unable to tolerate these intense and highly polarized feelings without exploding into irrational behavior. After the schizophrenic patient has tested us to our very limits and has seen for himself that we are neither crushed nor corrupted, he may begin little by little to identify with our greater integration and strength. It is this process that allows the patient to advance to the next phase, and if I am correct, technic can never be the sole ingredient here, no matter how excellent. The *person* of the therapist is a critical factor—as Kurt Eissler (1951) pointed out years ago. And the French psychoanalyst Sacha Nacht (1962) drew attention to an even more elusive and unteachable factor: a nonexploitative love for the patient. Nacht was referring to a kind of neutralized, or at least behaviorally nonsexual love, such as might typify parental love in its most mature form. This love is not always present from the beginning nor, when it does develop, is it always sufficiently uncontaminated to permit us to do our best work. The range of schizophrenic patients whom we can guide successfully through this ambivalent phase is probably fairly narrow for each therapist and will itself depend in many instances on irrational and unresolved elements of the therapist's personality. The latter seem to provide the fuel energizing the long and arduous work, the final outcome of which is then affected by the degree to which technic has been mastered.

Think of the soldier in battle: his ability to assemble his rifle in the dark is of little use without the "irrational" factors of patriotism and courage; patriotism without skill is not effective, either.

One may well ask, when excellent neuroleptic drugs and improved behavioral methods are now available—why bother to develop the therapeutic skills and personality attributes necessary to deal with this phase of a schizophrenic patient's recompensation? Why, particularly, when controlled studies of psychotherapy in schizophrenia thus far fail to show much difference between those treated with intensive psychotherapy (with or without drugs) and those treated with drugs alone (May, 1968; Grinspoon and Ewalt, 1967; Gunderson, 1977)? To begin with the latter objection: the controlled studies thus far reported in the literature are few in number and have been based on patient samples in which good results from intensive psychotherapy would hardly have been expected in the first place. The May Study patients (at Camarillo State Hospital) were mostly from lower socioeconomic circumstances, of average to below average intelligence, and had received therapy for relatively brief periods (several months, 70 or 80 sessions). Given the nature of the group it is not surprising that psychotherapy seemed to add very little to standard hospital care. The Boston Study (Grinspoon and Ewalt) used more seasoned therapists than the Camarillo study, but here the patients were very chronic schizophrenics; again, not too surprising that psychotherapy did not surpass thioridazine in effectiveness. More optimistic results emerge from the work of Bryce-Boyer (1980, p. 170) with a small group of schizophrenic office patients "of average to superior intelligence," whose symptom picture was characterized by "strong depressive tendencies" and the absence of chronicity or withdrawal. In this admittedly uncontrolled study, analytically oriented therapy yielded satisfactory or striking improvement in fourteen of seventeen cases. A study is now in progress that involves young schizophrenic patients who fulfil more of the criteria of suitability we spoke of earlier. This is the project headed by Drs. Stanton and Gunderson at the McLean Hospital in Belmont, Massachusetts, and is the only project thus far whose patients are representative of those who we feel would most likely benefit from the addition of intensive therapy to their regimen.

So we should not be too discouraged at the few negative reports (based only on hospitalized patients, by the way); their findings need not cast doubt on the efficacy of this form of treatment for a more carefully selected group of patients. If we are willing to trust our intuition where rigorous proof is lacking, I think an excellent case can be made that intensive psychotherapy lifts certain schizophrenic patients to levels of function, especially in the interpersonal sphere, that could scarcely have been achieved through any other method. Learning to cope with the emotional storms of the ambivalent-symbiotic phase, is, as a corollary to this, a crucial task in mastering this technic.

As for the former objection—why become adept at intensive psychotherapy with schizophrenic patients, now that such excellent psychopharmocologic agents are available—a number of points should be made. To begin with, the drugs do their best work on specific "target" symptoms, such as anxiety of panic proportion, or the productve signs. Schizophrenic patients who would be considered the best candidates for "expressive" psychotherapy customarily fail to demonstrate these target symptoms (except during brief "acute" episodes), and in fact benefit rather little from the phenothiazine or related drugs. Perhaps more importantly, *schizotypal* persons (the more generic term includes borderline as well as chronically psychotic patients) experience considerable difficulty in everyday life, just from their failure to integrate, and to apply in the appropriate situations, the ordinary ground rules for comfortable coexistence. Hence, a great deal of social reeducation must go on in psychotherapy, alongside the unraveling of psychodynamic factors and alongside interpretations of the latter-day revivifications of these old "dynamics" as they assert themselves in the transference.

I recall from my residency days, in this connection, a schizotypal borderline patient who had been hospitalized in her early twenties following an outbreak of bizarre and incapacitating symptoms (including globus hystericus) during her second year in a college. Although she came from a family that was highly placed socially, and that prided itself on elegant form and manners, she was shockingly wanting in tact. She thought nothing of barging in on friends at all hours (her supply of "friends" dwindling in direct proportion to this tendency) and could be predicted not to phone someone who was waiting for her if she missed her train. As she began to reintegrate and to go to work outside the hospital, that person was often enough myself—who felt constrained to wait the whole length of her appointment on the occasions she failed either to show up or to phone concerning a delay. At that phase of my training, I was still intent upon treating such lapses through further exploration of as yet untapped dynamics—one of which, I felt certain, would, being brought to light, unlock the secret of her cavalier social behavior and liberate her from her tactless ways. The supervisor guiding me in this case, a wise and seasoned psychoanalyst, kept urging me to take an entirely different tack. She suggested I confront my patient with a pointedly educative (and not at all psychodynamic) approach, with a comment like, "I find myself wanting to ask you, 'didn't your mother ever teach you to knock before coming in the room, or to phone if you'd be staying out late'?!'' Such an approach seemed to me hopelessly pedestrian—a betrayal, almost, of the psychoanalytic foundation on which, I assumed, my supervisor's treatment method was modeled. But only when I finally adopted this approach myself was I able to nudge my patient toward compliance with the sensible rules we adhere to in social interaction. Her acceptance of these rules, finally, could even be said to mark the end of the ambivalent-symbiotic phase in her treatment: she no longer behaved in such a way as to induce the so anguishing mixture of concern, fury, affection, and exasperation that characterizes, from the therapist's vantage point, that phase of the work.

Accompanying her improvement, brought about initially through reeducative efforts, was a "bellwether" dream of the sort that at once lays bare and conveys vividly whatever dynamic components may have contributed to the central problems of a particular phase of treatment. It was as though the gains recently made through the more behaviorally oriented technics increased her ego strength and self-assurance to the point where self-revelations on a deeper level became possible. There was more to her tactlessness, after all, than mere lack of training. Nor had her parents and nurses been as neglectful as one might have supposed. This patient was also highly narcissistic, scornfully disrespectful of the feelings of others, for reasons that had, as far as one could tell, a strong psychodynamic component. Hints of this component were revealed in her dream:

> "I was hungry and poor. To earn a bit of money for food, I posed nude for pictures, for some woman. She was my dormitory manager at college. She had a big penis that seemed to point toward me, but which doubled back on itself and ended up going into her own mouth."

It was through this grotesque—and at the same time rather transparent—- dream that she could begin to grasp the essence of her central dynamic: the primordial, overwhelming feeling of *deprivation* by a highly self-centered mother, who only pretended to give nurturance to her child. In the imagery of her dream, breast and penis seem interchangeable: mother's nurturance-giving organ is bent back to feed mother and not the baby. The patient had never been courageous enough before this dream to acknowledge the (in this case, truly) depriving and rejecting qualities of her mother, on whom she had become so slavishly dependent that she had, for her own survival, to extol and justify her. The daughter's dog-eat-dog brand of disregard for others could now be seen, in part, as an identification with her intensely narcissistic mother. During the months of therapy that followed the dream, and the new phase of treatment it ushered in, there was a salutary lessening, though by no means a disappearance, of the egocentric trends in her relations with others.

Schizophrenic patients often have what seems like an uncanny ability to strip us of our professional facade down to our elemental humanity, of whatever this may consist. They have been betrayed too many times by people behind whose pleasant social exterior lay cruelty, exploitativeness, or indifference. In addition, their own integrative defect makes it difficult for them to appreciate ordinary decency in others, unless the good qualities can be displayed in a much more dramatic form than one's good qualities usually are. In this respect I would agree wholeheartedly with Hans Strupp's (1978) position that the "blank-screen" model of therapeutic superneutrality is not relevant—and probably quite destructive—to the treatment of such ill patients. One's simple humanity must be much more exposed; one must be much more "real," especially when the patient is still too ill to grasp the subtleties of human interaction. And the humanity we expose must, as Strupp also mentions, contain empathy, perseverance, candor, self-control, and a wholesome set of values—all of which must be genuine and none of which can be acquired out of whole cloth in analytic school or in one's residency. A healing attitude, if already present, can be refined through training.

The Stage of Pre-ambivalent Symbiosis

Some time—usually measured in months—after the storminess of the ambivalent stage has crested, the symbiotic relatedness between therapist and patient begins to take on a new emotional tone. Feelings of rage, hatred, scorn—what Rado (1956) used to call the "emergency emotions" —have been largely shorn of the disruptive lust and exploitativeness of the earlier phase. As Searles mentions, this does not ordinarily happen in such an abrupt way as to leave clearly recognizable lines of demarcation between one and the other; rather, one notices a distinct shift in the prevailing tone of current sessions, compared with those preceding.

Therapist and patient now find their affection for one another less problematical, less sexually tinged, less urgent, and less menacing to the close relationships already present in the external lives of each participant. The therapist's love for his patient now takes on qualities we might find in the most relaxed and selfless mother toward a still small infant: genuine regard, admiration, and a mental life devoted, to the point of exclusive preoccupation, to plans and thoughts about the welfare and growth of the child.

Silences may be as common as before, and as long, but the tension is much reduced. During the ambivalent phase, long silences often induce in the therapist concern that the patient is consumed with hostile feelings and is about to do something rash—like storming out of the office, quitting treatment, throwing an ashtray, or mutilating himself. In the pre-ambivalent phase, prolonged silence may arise from the patient's need to absorb or to become absorbed in the therapist—but in a more positive and loving way, no longer in a destructively cannibalistic way.

There is often an air of relaxation in the sessions. Partly this stems from a sense of relief that each has survived the other's most consuming feelings *intact*. Partly this reflects genuine enjoyment of one another. Searles speaks of a "childlike playfulness" that now pervades the hours. Certainly there are many sessions in which the atmosphere is disconcertingly unprofessional. There may be an exchange of jokes like those each shares ordinarily only with friends. The jokes typically center around themes whose content was too painful to acknowledge in the earlier phase. With the patient who once fantasied making me part of her forever by turning me into a Thorazine® tablet, I could now quip that, after all, I might have had a different fate: I could have made a rapid tour of her digestive passages and then be *lost* to her forever. This struck us as quite hilarious at the time, whereas such a re-mark only a few weeks before—when she was still deeply concerned about the possibility I might cease to exist when she closed the office door behind her—would have been pointless and cruel.

The two-against-the-world nature of therapist-patient togetherness dur-ing this phase has its source no doubt in the early mother-child relationship, though it probably represents a grossly exaggerated, if not pathological, version of this otherwise normal state. Searles makes the point, in writing about the reactions of the hospital staff to such a twosome, that the others often become impatient and resentful. The situation of the father and older children to a mother and her newborn provides a convenient analogy. Just *when* this exclusive relationship is "normal" and about to usher in a still healthier stage of widened capacity for human relatedness, and when it is a pathological development from which neither party can extricate himself, cannot always be determined, except in retrospect. I think this applies equally well to the same phase of an office patient, though instead of a vocal hospital staff there will be a silent chorus of (often disapproving) spouse, colleague, supervisor in one's mental life.

It happens with some regularity as the pre-ambivalent phase draws to a close that enough fragments of the patient's hitherto alarmingly undifferen-tiated and shattered self come together to create a clearly recongnizable per-sonality. One may not have a stable and richly detailed picture of the inner self, but certainly a good outline.

I think it is this development that permits the therapist to cherish the patient for his "specialness," much as one's love of a child may become enhanced as he or she does and says certain things, acquires particular talents, particular ways of relating. One is no longer in the precarious position of having to love the patient simply because he *is*. Sometimes one is fortunate enough to witness—and to foster—this development, from the chrysalis stage to nascent individuality, over a matter of a few months or perhaps a year or two.

Our initial regard for a particular schizophrenic patient may be professional and empty, like a stewardess's welcome. The coming into view of a unique personality not only evokes a special affection in the therapist, but accounts for our capacity to care deeply about more than one such patient at a time. It now becomes possible to love one patient for his trenchant insights into other people's behavior, another for an ironic sense of humor, and a third for his gutsiness in trying to rebuild a life from the ruins of his schizophrenic decompensation.

Resolution of the Symbiosis

In normal development the mother-infant symbiosis becomes modified, after a long-enough period, into a relationship of two separate persons interdependent in many ways but by now distinctly individual as well. Searles has emphasized how marriage reintroduces a mixed interdependent-autonomous existence—something to be viewed as a healthy adaptation and not as a pathological deviation or as a halfway stage to "perfect" separateness. Complete independence is not an ideal state we approach asymptotically; it is, rather, a particular brand of sickness—to be encountered most frequently, I suppose, in certain schizophrenic hermits.

To the extent that the phase of pre- (or perhaps non-) ambivalent symbiosis is cherished by both participants, whether mother with her infant or therapist with his schizophrenic patient, their natural evolution into a more individuated and autonomous pair is by no means experienced with any regularity as a "natural evolution," but often as a painful disruption. Such growth is as much an occasion for mourning—over the never-to-be recaptured closeness that was—as for joy.

One important difference in the therapist-patient symbiosis that is not a counterpart of the mother-child analog resides in the chronic illness of the patient. The child is expected to achieve, one day, a high degree of self-sufficiency. The mother who continues to treat her child as frail and in constant need of her watchful eye long after his age-mates have established their separateness with some comfort becomes recognized herself as deviant. She is the "sick one." This distinction is much more difficult to make when dealing with recuperating schizophrenic patients, who will retain, in the majority of cases, enough intolerance of everyday stress as to justify at least some of his therapist's reluctance to let him try his wings. As therapists we are always having to measure how needy is our no longer so dependent schizophrenic patient; this measure must then be compared with the measure of our own need for the more primitive symbiotic relatedness of the preceding phase.

In this connection I recall some moments in the treatment of a phobic young woman with whom, like her father before me, I had for so many months remained locked in a mute and ambivalent symbiosis. Once she had begun to improve, she made such rapid strides that I found myself, paradoxically, resenting the rapidity of her progress—which, I realized, would soon culminate in marriage and the establishment of a new life too far from New York City for us to continue our work. At a certain level it had become clear to both of us that she was ready for this move, but outwardly for some weeks this readiness was denied on both our parts: she affected in her sessions to be more anxious about the future and more dependent on me than was actually the case; I became preoccupied with a variety of unexplored conflicts, for want of whose resolution treatment seemed dangerously incomplete. I was particularly fretful over the lack of attention to problems centering around the mother relationship, which I assumed, now that she had resolved the "superficial" issues concerning her father, would lie in wait, ready to push her back into illness were she to avoid probing these deeper layers.

To the extent that therapists are ordinarily better integrated than their schizophrenic patients, it more often happens that we, who have usually had some gratifying moments of reasonably autonomous existence, take the initiative in nudging our patients out of symbiotic relatedness. Only exceptionally will they, who have usually found independent life so unrewarding, be the first to leave us. But not only did this patient interrupt on her own this all too brief period of symbiotic togetherness, she went on, in seeming defiance of my retaliatory pessimism, to improve dramatically without me. We have exchanged letters every Christmas in the fifteen years since she left the hospital and have had "follow-up" meetings on a few occasions. From these it has been clear that her recovery has been both substantial and solid. Happily, it has also become clear that my original concern about "unfinished work" was more a reflection of sadness at the passing of this nonambivalent—i.e., predominantly loving—phase of our work, than it was an appropriate response to her, as I then saw it, continuing neediness.

Where the therapist is the first to make the shift away from symbiotic relatedness, the patient is either improving but still reluctant to take the initiative, or is in such a state of stagnation as to have grown tiresome to the therapist. Strong loyalty to the therapist, still viewed transferentially as a weak and needy parent, may inhibit the recovering patient from asserting his independence. Similarly, a lifelong difficulty in breaking away from a seductive and jealous parent may provoke intense guilt, magnified in the case of a schizophrenic patient to truly awesome proportions. A schizoaffective woman who had been caught up for many years in a highly ambivalent relationship with an alternatingly seductive and cruel father began to confront, in the third year of her treatment, her own powerful and ambivalent feelings toward him. These included lustful feelings of a most embarrassing sort, coupled with a fear that she could free herself from his clutches only by her own death—or by his. But death wishes toward him stirred up a guilt just as pervasive as had the lustful feelings, and which could, again, be expiated only by her own death. No longer so suicidal at the behavioral level as she had once been, she was beginning to see the role suicide had played for so many years—as the "natural" finale to her life drama. With the inevitable emergence of warm feelings toward me in the transference situation, the same mixture of lust, murderousness, and guilt rose to the surface. The revelation of these feelings was no longer accompanied by the kind of terror that characterized the ambivalent-symbiotic phase of our work, during which time these emotions had remained literally unspeakable. The prospect of separating from me and choosing a mate of her own, without my sending out hired killers to do her in, no longer seemed so remote.

Changes in the therapist's life may have significant and unanticipated effects upon his tolerance for relating symbiotically with certain schizophrenic patients. The therapeutic relationship, instead of undergoing resolution, undergoes dissolution. Even if the therapist has access to excellent supervision, the relationship cannot always be salvaged. As an example, I once treated a very dependent schizophrenic woman who had been hospitalized for over three years, largely because of a series of suicide attempts. During the long ambivalent phase of our work, I felt quite drained emotionally. She had a habit of not quitting her chair when it was time to end the session, necessitating repeated verbal reminders from me—each of which evoked more piteous, tearful expressions on her part—and more guilt on mine. After a while I grew courageous enough to suggest to her that this tragic scene at the end of each meeting was something she cleverly staged to test whether I cared more for her or for the next patient—whose allotted time with me she seemed so eager to obliterate. Interpretations of this sort elicited, as might have been expected, even more piteous stares than before—to the point where, on the two or three occasions when she instead screamed at the top of her lungs and slammed the door behind her, I experienced the tantrum as a welcome sign of progress, rather than as the infuriatingly childish display that it was.

But it would be giving only one side of the picture were I not to admit at many other moments—in between the tears and fireworks—there was a sweetness about this patient, and a shyness, that would put one in mind of an injured madonna—and made her uncommonly endearing. So much so, that between her insatiable claims upon my time, and my naiveté as a therapist-in-training, I once promised that I would continue treating her as long as she had any need of a psychiatrist.

After three years of arduous work, during which time she used up most of her "nine lives" in various manipulative suicide gestures, she made enough gains that she was able to leave the hospital, fill a demanding position, and maintain an apartment. Exploitativeness had given way to cooperativeness; she came and left on time, and no longer begrudged me my small success with her—as she herself acknowledged—"difficult case." (Earlier, she saw me as narcissistically exploiting her, as though her recovery was valuable to me only as a trophy to show off to my colleagues, and she refused for many months to "gratify" me by getting better. Projective identifications of this sort are of course quite common in patients at this primitive level of functioning [see Rosenfeld, 1965; Bryce-Boyer, 1978].)

She seemed well on the road to recovery and had graduated, as far as I could tell, from her previously suicidal view of the world, when my wife, who shared my office, became quite visibly pregnant. The envy aroused by this event rapidly reached psychotic proportions. The patient found it impossible to concentrate on her work and experienced feelings of profound helplessness, prompting her to call me at all hours with such demands as, "You've got to see me or do something for me. . . . I can't manage. . . . I can't even make a peanut-butter-and-jelly sandwich." All capacity for objectivity vanished. Interpretations (about her feeling lost unless she could be more baby-like than the baby) and exhortations (you do know how to make your own food, and you have to make that sandwich no matter how left out you feel) were useless. I was able to tolerate these phone calls with a minimum of irritability until the baby was actually born. At the moment my feelings shifted dramatically: I now had a sweet and presumably normal baby of my own, what did I need this grotesque caricature of a baby for? Having once given this patient a lifetime guarantee of help, it was particularly embarrassing to admit to her now that I could no longer give her the kind of care she needed, let alone the kind of boundless attention she craved. This symbiotic relationship thus ended by severance rather than by evolution to maturer forms of therapist-patient interaction.

Unsuccessful symbiotic relationships with schizophrenic patients often end with one partner wishing to be rid of the other but unaware of this impulse at the conscious level. In place of candor, one sees a maneuvering to drive the other person—through impatience, boredom, shabby behavior, etc.—to take the initiative in ending the relationship, thus freeing the true protagonist from any responsibility in the matter.

Intense relationships, whatever their predominant feeling tone, cause a blurring of boundaries and a loss of objectivity. This is true for our schizophrenic patients particularly, but the strong emotions they so regularly induce in us create a similar impairment in our own critical faculty. Alberta Szalita (1958) has taught how the schizophrenic patient tends, at any moment in treatment, to be either objective (but also excessively aloof) *or* emotionally involved (but to the point of losing boundaries). The therapist, Szalita added, has a greater capacity to be objective and involved simultaneously. One of the major goals in the intensive psychotherapy of schizophrenics is the expansion of the patient's capacity to be rational, and reflective, about his own emotions. Under optimal circumstances the resolution of the symbiotic phase will be accompanied by a knitting together of these otherwise unconnected elements in the patient's mental life. One can speak about this task in theoretical terms, as we are doing here to a certain extent; the process itself remains an art—a very human art, whose product has been aptly labeled by Szalita, "psychosynthesis."

After Resolution of the Symbiosis: The Late Phase

Successful resolution of the symbiotic relationship between the schizophrenic patient and his therapist usually brings with it a major shift in the attitude of the patient. There will be less pressure now to "actualize the transference"; i.e., fewer attempts to maneuver the therapist into direct gratification of the patient's wishes. The patient will by now have acquired better tactics for dealing with his environment, and a better sense of reality. He does not need the therapist so much as protector, avenger, or lover, and can begin to take advantage of the therapist's roles as adviser and interpreter.

The patient feels more like a "whole person" and can, as a result, more easily give the therapist the benefit of the doubt—picturing him, too, as a whole person. So long as the patient's mental life was characterized by fragmentation, the small inconsistencies of behavior and thought in the therapist were experienced as disjointed and unassimilable—in other words, "crazy." The world of everyday reality in which the therapist is ensconced was also viewed, because it is so discordant with the "reality" of manifest schizophrenia, as "crazy." This mutual sense of strangeness begins to wear off in the pre-ambivalent-symbiotic phase. By the late or postresolution phase, the patient's cooperativeness and enthusiasm for discovery will often have advanced to the point of being quite analogous to the "therapeutic alliance" between analyst and analysand. The patient will usually be ambulatory, even if therapy had begun in the hospital.

It is in the long "late phase" of treatment that intensive psychotherapy can focus on contradictions in the patient's sense of self as well as on his love relationships, including those as marriage partner and parent. Schizophrenic patients who enter this late phase of psychotherapy will be preoccupied, like their neurotic counterparts, with sexual relationships, conflicts involving "triangular" situations, and the like. The recurrent themes during the sessions are, outwardly at least, on a "genital" level, although the intensity of emotion and the polarization of attitudes are much greater than what one ordinarily sees with one's neurotic patients. The schizophrenic patient, even after having advanced to this point, will tend to perceive others in extreme terms and to operate as if still quite deficient in any buffering mechanism.

One female patient with whom I have worked for some years will, for example, meet a man at a party, become enraptured with him after five minutes' conversation, and elaborate fantasies of marriage and a blissful life thereafter—before even finding out his name. Later, on their first date, if he throws a sidelong glance at some other woman in their vicinity, the patient upbraids him, at least in her mind, as a perfidious Don Juan—totally untrustworthy and certainly undeserving of continuing interest on her part. Mere interpretation of the childhood antecedents of such reaction patterns usually fails to set her on a more realistic course. A reeducative approach becomes necessary. To pursue this example a bit further, it had never occurred to her that a man could be emotionally and behaviorally faithful to her—even on a lifelong basis—and still derive pleasure from the sight of other women, from fantasies of other women, and so on. Sometimes, as in the case of this particular patient, the parents really did an inadequate job of instructing their child in the subtleties of human relations. But, as was also true of this woman, a serious integrative disturbance may also be present, of a sort that seems to confine the patient to an all-or-none view of the world. Years of repetitive clarifications from the therapist may be necessary before the patient is enabled—and emboldened—to trust our more complex picture of interpersonal reality.

· · · · ·

Thus far we have concentrated on a pattern of improvement characterized by the patient's orderly progression through stages. If everything goes well, one may begin with a schizophrenic patient who is out of contact and who trusts no one, and end up, after having dealt with problems in separation and individuation, with a patient preoccupied with higher-level problems related to intimacy.

In some instances improvement during the course of psychotherapy proceeds along a different line. Certain schizophrenic patients exhibit a curious transference distortion, in which the therapist is perceived as a carbon copy of some important figure from the patient's past. This figure is often the mother, but it may also possess an amalgam of qualities belonging to both mother and father. What is special about such a transference distortion— after all, neurotics also see qualities of each parent "reduplicated" in their analysts—is its sweeping nature. The therapist is seen as having *no* features uniquely his own, but instead as merely a stick figure papered over with the image of, say, the mother. Schizophrenic patients of this sort may actually regard the whole world as peopled with *doppelgängers* (doubles) of the mother, spewed forth, it seems to them, from some cloning machine out of *Brave New World*. With such patients the work of psychotherapy does not proceed so much by the methodical analysis of conflicts pertaining to successive stages of development; instead, the work proceeds by making the patient aware of the differences between the therapist and the figure from his early life with whom the therapist is constantly being confused. It is as though the picture of, say, the mother, superimposed on the picture of the therapist, is scraped away patch by patch, as with the uncovering of a palimpsest, until the true image of the therapist comes into view.

One patient with whom I have worked for approximately ten years frequently switches into a state, during a session, in which I am experienced not "like" her mother (who has been dead some twenty years); I become the mother. I will hear comments like, "Your eyes are heavy and too wide apart . . . you're my mother! You don't love me!" The patient is not grossly deluded in this matter; the conviction that I am, or change into, her mother is transitory. She can be nudged away from confused perceptions of this kind by replies like, "You see me now as her, perhaps because we started the session a minute late, which you took as a rejection on my part—similar to the rejection you felt from her." The faulty logic here, one that partakes of the syllogism with the undistributed middle, is considered a classic example of schizophrenic thought disorder (see Matte-Blanco, 1977): *Mother always rejected me—you reject me—therefore, you are mother.*

The therapeutic approach to this kind of confusion depends first on pointing out the error in assuming that, to continue with the preceding example, keeping the patient waiting one minute arose out of a wish to humiliate or inconvenience. One explains how the delay arose out of much more banal causes—a telephone call, an improperly set clock, or an innocent misjudgment of the time. One can see in this example the sweeping egocentricity of the patient: all external acts are understood in highly personalized terms (i.e., referred to the self). We are of course not speaking here of vanity, as one might encounter in highly narcissistic individuals, but of an involuntary egocentricity, imposed upon the patient by the underlying schizophrenic integrative defect.

Implicit in the statement "You seem to be seeing me as a copy of so-and-so" is the notion "But in reality I am *not.*" Each clarification of this type helps dispel another element of confusion in the schizophrenic patient's attempt to establish boundaries between himself and others, or between one person and another person.

Once the patient has succeeded in scraping away enough patches of, say, mother's image from his perception of the therapist, not only will he begin to accept the therapist as a distinct entity in his personal universe, but he will find it less incredible to suppose that still other individuals, situated in the periphery of his everyday life, also have unique qualities that stamp them as different from himself and from the members of his original family. As he now learns to appreciate the differentness of everyone else around him, to the extent the patient once regarded the important "other" in his life as menacing or rejecting, the less nightmarish it becomes for him to reenter the world of others. This "peeling away" is a tedious job for the therapist, the more so as the patients most in need of it are those with the more chronic ego-boundary distortions (such as one encounters in those nearer the "process" that to the "reactive" pole of schizophrenic nosology). By the same token, the therapist will seldom experience the gratification that accompanies his having helped a patient make a quantum leap from one stage of development to another. The gradual and continuous business of peeling away does not seem to proceed by quantum leaps of awareness on the part of the patient; to return to the analogy of the palimpsest: it is difficult to specify the precise moment when one washes away enough of the outer superimposed layer that the original figure becomes recognizable.

The final phase of psychotherapy with schizophrenic patients will last in some instances most of their adult life. There will not be a natural termination as occurs spontaneously with classically psychoneurotic analysands. Instead, there will be an ever-continuing series of minor life crises (the major ones having been brought under control) because of the life-long vulnerability that stems from the central integrative disturbance. But not every patient whose diagnosis is "schizophrenic," and especially not every "schizoaffective" patient, manifests the same sort of integrative defect. Clinically there will be a profound difference between the childhood-schizo-phrenic-grown-up whose family was rather normal, and a schizoaffective patient whose family was chaotic. The former may exhibit the peculiar gaucherie in social situations—even an awkwardness of gait—that telegraphs the nature of his illness to the most casual observer. Yet he may have absorbed from his family a conventionality of values, decency of character, and trustfulness that allows the rapid formation of a therapeutic alliance. There may not be much need, in the late phase, to undo transference distortions, because these may not have been very marked to begin with. Instead, the late phase will be dominated by lengthy reeducative work related to the patient's maladresse in ordinary social situations, job interviews, and the like. It may be useful to let the patient see himself on videotape so that he can grasp something of the nature of this awkwardness, if not to modify it (sometimes this is scarcely possible), then at least to understand more fully the impact his behavior may have on others.

The schizoaffective patient with the pleasant social facade but the chaotic background may, in contrast, require greater attention—and time—in earlier phases of therapy, and less in the final phase. Transference distortions may be severe and the ambivalent-symbiotic phase stormy and nearly unendurable to one or both parties. Yet, if the patient progresses past that stage, one may see a person emerging with little in the way of odd speech, not much eccentricity of behavior, and a good capacity to make gratifying (though somewhat stormier than average) relationships. A patient of this sort does not stick out like a sore thumb socially, and we do not find it necessary to socialize him via special behavioral methods.

5

The Criteria of Suitability for Intensive Psychotherapy

Michael H. Stone, M.D.

In this section I will be concentrating on the criteria of selecting schizophrenic patients for intensive psychotherapy. Because of its length and the frequency of visits, analytically oriented psychotherapy is never a light undertaking even with better integrated patients. The need for careful selection is all the more important when one is evaluating a patient within the schizophrenic spectrum of disorders. The latter includes frankly psychotic schizophrenic patients as well as those with "schizophrenic" signs and symptoms (e.g., odd or eccentric communication, along with exquisite sensitivity to criticism, shyness, social isolation, autistic thought) who happen to be free of delusions or hallucinations. With respect to intensive psychotherapy, one should also enlarge this spectrum to include certain schizoaffective patients who function, at least when they are being seen in consultation, at a *borderline* level (as defined by Kernberg, 1967). Patients in all these categories are prone to disorganization not only under the impact of classical psychoanalysis, but even when in a more supportive therapeutic atmosphere certain highly conflictual material is unearthed or explored.

It is worth stating at this point that because of the many treatment modalities available—or more highly developed—in the 1980s, we are well beyond the situation confronting the therapists of the 1940s or 1950s, for whom intensive psychotherapy was, for schizophrenic patients, often the only alternative to chronic institutionalization and neglect.

With chemotherapy, behavior-modification technics, and better methods of group therapy now accessible to most patients, we must be more discriminating about the "whether" and "when" of intensive psychotherapy.

As a first step in selecting a schizophrenia-spectrum patient whom we think intensive therapy will benefit—over and beyond what help he may derive from the other modalities—we appraise the patient according to the criteria used in evaluating neurotic patients being considered for classical psychoanalysis.

Some of the criteria remain the same whether the patient is ambulatory or hospitalized; others relate more specifically to the patient's status when first seen.

General Criteria of Suitability

As with the prospective analysand, one looks for the presence of (1) a capacity for relatedness, (2) a character structure free of all but the slightest measure of antisocial features, (3) psychological mindedness and (4) average to better than average intelligence.

CAPACITY FOR RELATEDNESS

This feature constitutes a better criterion for exclusion than inclusion; a good capacity for relatedness certainly augurs well for psychotherapy (as for good outcome in general) but unless buttressed by other favorable attributes it will not suffice for a prediction of good suitability. A poor capacity for relatedness, on the other hand, will almost surely militate against a successful psychotherapeutic venture. One is speaking here of the degree of relatedness seen in the relatively quiescent phases of illness, of course, since at the height of a psychotic episode, a schizophrenic patient who otherwise has the ability to enter into a close relationship may suddenly lose this ability until the acute symptoms have subsided.

A commonly used indicator of this capacity for relatedness is the patient's history of friendships. Schizophrenic patients who have been able to retain at least one good friend during adolescence have, other factors being equal, a better prognosis than those who have been friendless. Occasionally it works out that, in treating a previously friendless schizophrenic patient, the therapist becomes the first "real friend," upon which template other gratifying friendships are then fashioned in the outside world. It happens more often, however, that the friendless schizophrenic has not merely been the victim of a hostile, rejecting world, and therefore never had the experience of friendship; rather, the patient has exhibited some socially alienating character trait that has kept others very much at a distance: one such patient may not bathe, another makes insulting remarks to all and sundry, a third drones on endlessly in a robot-like voice, and so forth. To like, let alone love, such individuals has been quite beyond the capacities of most of the ordinary folk who have rubbed shoulders with them before they sought help in psychotherapy. It is not so easy for the therapist to like them either—even within the context of the patient-therapist relationship. Obnoxious social traits, when present, constitute a serious impediment to the course of psychotherapy; how one may deal effectively with such traits will be discussed at some length by Dr. Albert.

At the other end of the patient spectrum are those schizophrenics who, even in the face of severe integrative disturbances, frequent breaks with reality, etc., have such a good capacity for relatedness and are so appealing as individuals, that family members and friends rush to their support in times of crisis.

Example

Two sisters, born to an upper-class family consisting of a paranoid schizophrenic mother and an alcoholic father, themselves succumbed to schizophrenic illnesses in early adult life. One of the sisters was extremely grandiose, narcissistic, manipulative, and intrusive. She had no insight into her illness, and blamed her academic failures and broken marriages on others. The other sister was shy, artistic, self-effacing, and extremely empathic. Both led chaotic lives during their twenties and thirties. Both entered psychotherapy in their early thirties. The sister who was scheming and intrusive, despite having considerable poise in social situations, eventually alienated everyone she knew and led an aimless, lonely existence, moving from one town to another, always with great "plans" that never materialized. The shy sister who, despite her lack of self-confidence, got along well with others, found a supportive husband with whom she had a gratifying relationship and surrounded herself with a small number of devoted friends. She was also able to utilize psychotherapy well and in a manner that lent further stability to her life, whereas her sister repudiated any help that was offered, so that her life became all the more unstable as she grew older.

CHARACTEROLOGICAL ASPECTS

To appreciate the impact of character type upon suitability for intensive psychotherapy in schizophrenia, it will be helpful first to enumerate the characterological subtypes in current use. Some are used by psychiatrists in general and are to be found in the standard manual of diagnosis (the DSM-III). Others reflect the vocabulary of the psychoanalytic community. In the first group are included the hysteric (or "histrionic"), the obsessive, the phobic, the passive-aggressive, the schizoid, the paranoid, the explosive, the inadequate, and the antisocial. In the latter, one encounters the terms infantile, narcissistic, and depressive-masochistic. If one wished to include the temperaments, alluded to by Kraepelin, commonly found in association with manic-depressive illness, one would add the hypomanic and cyclothymic. These temperaments are, however, seldom, if ever, noted in a schizophrenic population.

We need to be aware that, however customary it has become to assign only one such term to each patient, we rarely confront a "pure" type in actual practice. Instead we find in one patient a "paranoid personality with obsessive and narcissistic features," or a "schizoid personality with antisocial features," and so on. The label we use designates the predominant, not the exclusive, character type. It is possible, and quite helpful, to make a character "profile" for each patient, in which we record the degree to which the patient demonstrates the features of the dozen or so main subtypes (see Stone, 1980).

With this profile in mind, we can begin to compare which constellations of subtypes have been associated with successful psychotherapy of schizophrenic and other fairly seriously ill patients, and which with unsuccessful therapy. Although it has not yet been possible to do this in a rigorous and systematic fashion, a number of prominent analysts (e.g., Kernberg) who have worked with patients in the sicker range of psychopathology have expressed the opinion that certain subtypes predict therapeutic success; others, failure. The better-prognosis subtypes emerge as the hysteric, infantile, obsessive, and depressive-masochistic. At the other end of the spectrum are the hypomanic, the inadequate, and the antisocial—all associated with a low likelihood of benefit from intensive psychotherapy. The intermediate group contains the phobic, the narcissistic, the paranoid, and the schizoid. Where these subtypes predominate, successful intervention will tend to depend on the overall level of personality assets and liabilities as well as on the *intensity* of the predominant type and on the *balance* between this type and the accompanying features. For example, the extremely paranoid schizophrenic patient with obsessional features may keep the therapist perpetually at great distance and have little access to his emotions. With such a clinical picture, intensive psychotherapy, even the most skillful, may fail to work any significant change in the patient. Where paranoid features overshadow others, yet are not so intense, and where there is an admixture of depressive or hysteric traits, the patient may be much more reachable.

Prognostically, the most ominous features are the antisocial. Even here one must distinguish between the basically honest and respectful individual showing the barest trace of antisocial proclivity versus the ruthless and contemptuous psychopath. I assume the "pseudopsychopathic schizophrenic" of Bender (1959) was simply a schizophrenic patient with marked antisocial character traits; I also assume that the prognosis in this group was uniformly grave, at least with respect to social recovery.

Example

Both the following patients were referred as good candidates for analytically oriented psychotherapy.

A chronic schizophrenic woman in her middle thirties had a predominantly schizoid personality with depressive-masochistic features. Antisocial features were almost negligible, as were the narcissistic. On one occasion, shortly after she began intensive psychotherapy as an office patient, and during a time in her life when she was feeling particularly lonely and deprived, she engaged in an act of shoplifting. She was very sheepish about the incident, which she regarded as highly discrepant with her usual character. The next day she returned the article and felt immensely relieved. This patient was highly motivated for treatment and ultimately made an excellent social recovery.

In contrast, another chronically schizophrenic woman, in her late twenties, exhibited a predominately paranoid personality, also with depressive-masochistic features. She was very suspicious of others and had numerous ideas of reference in relation to people in the street (who she imagined were calling her "ugly" or "lesbian"), but at other times could be tearful and quite self-defeating in her relations with men. But in addition, antisocial features were prominent. Thus, in the course of intensive outpatient psychotherapy, she would grow markedly resentful of the therapist whenever the monthly bill was presented. To her way of thinking, so misunderstood and unfortunate a person as herself should be showered with love and attention free of charge. A pattern developed where she would pay the bill the session following its presentation, but only after having pilfered a precisely equivalent amount of sweaters and dresses from a large department store. Far from feeling remorseful, she could not even acknowledge having done anything wrong. This patient also persisted in taking hallucinogenic drugs, which aggravated her condition. Unable to comply with admonitions against both the antisocial and self-destructive behavior, she broke off treatment, continuing to lead a marginal existence.

PSYCHOLOGICAL-MINDEDNESS

This quality is seldom found in the absence of average to better than average intelligence, but by no means do all intelligent patients show good psychological-mindedness. A related term from the field of psychology is *intraception*, implying a capacity for taking things "in" (ideas, memories, stimuli of whatever source and sort) and for reflecting on them in such a way that creative solutions and syntheses emerge.

The mere presence of psychological-mindedness does not guarantee success with intensive psychotherapy. Some schizophrenic patients are keenly aware of their own psychodynamics and are unusually self-reflective in their cognitive style. Yet they are so overwhelmed by their conflicts that they remain helpless, despite all their intellectual insight. But without psychological-mindedness, intensive psychotherapy will be of little benefit even in a patient with reasonably good functioning and personality assets.

Carpenter has recently devised a scale for assessing this attribute. There are nine items, each to be scored from one to seven. Included are the level of awareness of one's fantasies and emotions, the level of the ability to look at oneself from a distance, and the level of curiosity about the influence of the past on the present. The ability to express thoughts and feelings in words is scored in a similar fashion.

A related concept centers around the issue of "integration" versus "sealing over," studied in a schizophrenic population by McGlashan and Carpenter (1976) and others. Many schizophrenic patients, as they recover from an acute psychotic episode, push back the memories of the episode itself, and along with it, the various early recollections, disturbing fantasies and other, usually painful, mental accompaniments. These patients, who are said to "seal over" as they improve, become highly intolerant of their past "craziness" and wish to forget it completely. Since intensive psychotherapy aims at bringing such material to the surface, therapist and patient will find themselves in a tense struggle, from which the patient will generally emerge the "victor." Only victory, in this case, means to succeed in obliterating the past and learning nothing from it.

The "integrator," the patient with high psychological-mindedness, finds it more congenial to expand his grasp of his own psychological make-up by including more and more erstwhile taboo material in his consciousness. Patients of this sort feel that developing the ability to see their conflicts and fantasies in perspective allows them later on to make sense out of the otherwise irrational-seeming psychotic material. From this stems a greater mastery over the same conflictual material that previously exerted such a pathogenic impact on their lives.

As one may readily imagine, so simple a schema as "sealing over versus integration'' cannot do justice to the many varieties of schizophrenic patients with whom we come in contact. One would, for example, have to admit that there are "integrators" who profit little from their penchant for delving into their own dynamics. There are numerous schizophrenic patients who operate as though there is little censorship of normally forbidden material; they will talk readily and after only brief acquaintance of the most repugnant and embarrassing aspects of their life history, and will make the most convincing correlations between these memories and various interpersonal events of the past—all without the slightest trace of affective involvement, let alone improvement. Here we are dealing with a kind of intellectual integration gone haywire, one effect of which is to make a mockery of our aim to effect genuine insight. This is not integration so much as empty psychologizing; the therapist must be on the alert not to mistake the one for the other.

Examples

Sealing-over

A flagrantly psychotic young woman was admitted to a psychiatric hospital because of an anorectic syndrome following a schizophrenic breakdown on the part of her mother. The latter event left her willy-nilly in the position of "little wife" to her father; her guilt over finding herself an Oedipal winner, along with the sexual excitement stirred up by her father's excessive attentions to her, precipitated an acute psychotic episode. At the height of her psychosis she groveled about in the halls of the hospital, eating dirt, lint, and various small objects lying about on the floor. She was monomanic in her preoccupation with the theme of worthlessness, feeling that she was evil and must purge herself of her sexuality. She ate dirt because, in her eyes, she "was" dirt. No amount of confrontation made the slightest dent in her delusional system.

She was placed on phenothiazines, and quickly made an excellent recovery. After 2 1/2 months she was feeling fit enough to try living outside the hospital and to look for work. Interviewed at this time, she had almost no recollection of her psychosis, apart from knowing that she had somehow "gone crazy" some three months before, and had been doing some "funny things" around the hospital. She felt "the past was the past," expressing no interest in the possible meanings of her symptoms nor in the antecedent life-events that may have precipitated the breakdown. Her recovery has, however, been stable for at least a year and a half.

Pseudointegration (Psychologizing)

A 21-year-old male college student was referred for intensive psychotherapy upon his release from a psychiatric facility where he had been admitted—ostensibly—for a "borderline" condition, but actually for a paranoid schizophrenic psychosis. His mental life was dominated by openly incestuous fantasies concerning his mother. Even after high-dosage phenothiazines and eventual release from the hospital, these fantasies continued at the same intensity. He would spend two hours each morning "doing the images"—which consisted of lying on the floor and conjuring up the image of his naked mother—all in an effort to "work through," as he put it, this stage of his psychosexual development. He was intent upon seeing his analyst as often as possible: four to five times a week, but there was little dialogue, just the endless recitation of what he saw before his mind's eye while "doing the images." When a second analyst, whom he saw because of a change of locale, tried to make cautious interpretations about his using this pseudoanalytic method to prevent rather than promote genuine improvement, he precipitously quit treatment. There was, during all this time, no change in his outward appearance or life-situation: he remained an isolated, eccentric, and poorly groomed student who, though he came from a wealthy family, shunned bathing and thus reinforced his isolation.

The first therapist of this patient appears to have fostered the kind of "deep interpretation" to which the patient later became so addicted. The example illustrates the need for careful appraisal of which patients one selects for such a technic. One is reminded of the young schizophrenic housewife, described by Robert Knight (1954), whose analyst told her, after she admitted taking an occasional nip of whiskey to bolster her spirits, "you are symbolically taking your father's penis into your mouth in order to steal his strength." In this situation, a second analyst needed actually to help her "seal over" the effects of the frightening interpretation—once it became obvious there was no way she could "integrate" those remarks to her advantage.

Genuine Integration

This example concerns a divorced engineer in his mid-thirties. He had made a hasty marriage during his graduate school years to a woman with whom he soon fell out of love. They parted after two years—shortly after she bore a child, which they decided to give up for adoption. He functioned well occupationally after this experience but suffered a paranoid psychosis following the death of both his parents not long thereafter. Exquisitely shy and awkward premorbidly, he now became more isolated than ever, was rather eccentric in social situations, and seldom maintained friendships for any length of time. His speech was so mechanical and tangential as to be at times hard to follow. Despite these handicaps he was highly gifted in his field and had considerable psychological aptitude. He enjoyed working in psychotherapy—which he had kept up for a number of years after the acute episode—especially with his dreams, and was quite adept at unraveling symbolism. There was tremendous concern about "getting better," especially about learning how to prolong relationships with friends. For some time he had had the habit of wearing dark glasses, even during his sessions, whether the sky was bright or overcast. He expressed a discomfort at the sun's beating down on him, and after a while grew to dislike bright lights of any sort. Therapy had been conducted under reduced lighting for some time to accommodate this peculiarity. During the sixth year of intensive therapy it chanced that the subject of the adopted-away boy came up in conversation with a new girlfriend. In this context a number of dreams were reported that clearly reflected preoccupation with this child; in fact, he was struggling with intense remorse over having insisted the baby be given away, even though this had seemed the only reasonable alternative at the time. As these issues emerged in therapy, there occurred a session in which both he and the therapist were suddenly struck by the pun on the word "son"; concretistically, he had been avoiding the celestial *sun* for years, as an insurance measure against thinking about his own *son,* now lost to him because of the adoption. Following this piece of integrative work, he grew rapidly more tolerant of the sun and bright lights, and relinquished the odd habit of wearing dark glasses. The loss of the baby was still capable of evoking strong feeling, but was no longer literally *unthinkable.*

It is a matter of some debate whether and how the outcome of intensive therapy with schizophrenics is modified by the presence of affective symptoms. Many have agreed that the prognosis is better the more access the patient has to his emotions, even within the context of a symptomatically mixed illness, one where schizophrenic and affective symptoms are both present. The truth of the matter is not easy to determine. Controlled studies of intensive therapy of schizophrenics have been few in number; the May study (1968) from Camarillo Hospital was based on a patient sample for whom intensive, analytically oriented treatment would probably not have been initiated by most practicing analysts who work in this area. Nor were sharp distinctions drawn regarding the degree of "affectivity" among the different patients. The term "schizoaffective" (see Kasanin, 1933) is often used to describe patients with a mix of schizophrenic and affective symptoms, but the term is usually used loosely and covers a wide range of patients. In fact the stricter the criteria in common use of schizophrenia and manic-depression, the more patients there are who seem to fall in between; i.e., into the schizoaffective range, loosely defined. Much of the acrimonious dispute (see Procci, 1976) about terminology and outcome in this in-between area hinges, in my opinion, on the degree to which the average patient in a particular sample happens to lean toward the schizophrenic end of the spectrum, how much toward the manic-depressive end. As an example, the "schizoaffectives" in the outcome study of Amos Welner and his collaborators (1974) are nearer the schizophrenic pole than are the "schizoaffectives" of Clayton's 1968 family study. There is an apparent contradiction; namely, that "schizoaffectives" should "really" be included in any definition of schizophrenia, because they have a deteriorating course (Welner's conclusion); yet "schizoaffectives" "really" have a type of affective disorder (Clayton's conclusion), because the ill family members in her study were themselves manic-depressive. The paradox, I believe, can be resolved by taking into account the different positions occupied by these patient samples on a continuum of clinical types, stretching between the two extreme conditions. Where intensive therapy is concerned, there is no hard data to help settle the question. I have only my own clinical impressions and those of my colleagues to rely on—but these suggest rather strongly that, other variables held constant, intensive psychotherapy is more likely to benefit those schizophrenic patients who show an admixture of affective—in particular depressive—symptoms (Stone, 1981). The admixture of predominantly manic symptoms is another matter entirely: this would tend to render intensive psychotherapy less useful. In real life, of course, we cannot hold other variables constant. The suicide rate is high in schizoaffectives in whom the symptom mix is quite even (De Alarcon, 1975; Helmchen, 1975)—higher probably than in "pure" bipolar patients. From the standpoint of life versus death, then, it may be advantageous to be schizophrenic without any tendency to depression. But from the standpoint of intensive psychotherapy, the admixture of depressive symptoms may be associated with greater ease of access to the psychotherapeutic process. The schizoaffective patient may form a clinging attachment that binds him to the therapist strongly enough to make him willing to endure the rigors of intensive treatment. Some "pure type" schizophrenics may be so aloof or withdrawn or paranoid as to keep the therapist at bay interminably: attempts to work with the transference may fall flat, motivation to relate to the therapist and to enter the world of other people may be too low to permit intensive treatment. The patient with depressive signs, on the other hand, is ordinarily more eager to make relationships, since he is so dependent on them. This does not mean that a schizoaffective patient with poor psychological-mindedness and meager intellectual assets will outperform a "pure type" schizophrenic patient who has those assets. Nevertheless, all but a few of the patients, originally diagnosed as schizophrenic, whom I have seen make remarkable improvements after several years of intensive psychotherapy have exhibited at least some admixture of signs and symptoms that we have come to associate more with affective illness.

Examples

The first example concerns a 27-year-old married lawyer who suffered a schizophrenic decompensation during the course of severe marital strife. He was hospitalized and admitted to a unit specializing in intensive psychotherapy. Initially he was floridly psychotic, with persecutory delusions and frightening illusions. At times he experienced his therapist as a persecutor who had, in his eyes, assumed the shape of an "outer-space monster." Never, throughout the long course of his hospitalization (18 months), were any affective symptoms displayed, apart from a transient forlornness associated with the therapist's vacations.

Characterologically his most prominent features were passive-dependent and obsessional. He showed excellent psychological-mindedness and was also remarkably sensitive to the feelings of other people. Neuroleptic medication was given, initially in high doses, later at maintenance levels; delusional symptoms rapidly subsided, but what surfaced in their place were violent, sadistic fantasies in which either he was killed or maimed by others, or others maimed by him. He experienced these fantasies as quite frightening, the more so as they seemed to him out of keeping with his ordinarily gentle, self-effacing nature. At first he tended to disown such sadistic fantasies. Focus on the transference—which was stormy and chaotic in the beginning—led to greater acceptance of his own hostile feelings, especially when the interpretation was made to him that it was in no way out of the ordinary that he might experience anger toward a vacationing therapist, alongside a sense of loss and helplessness. His therapist was a woman, and he began, in the middle phase of treatment, to express feelings of "love" for her, including what he described as strong sexual feelings. On closer inspection these turned out to be predominantly aggressive: his fantasies included, for example, transfixing his therapist to the floor with an elongated spear-like penis. He needed little prompting at this stage of treatment to appreciate some of the nuances of this image: the therapist was both punished (for leaving) and held fast to the spot (and therefore unable to leave). There was no tenderness in this "love," only a kill-or-be-killed attitude about separation. This patient happened to be able to utilize material of this sort—which poured out of him in abundance—and eventually made enough progress with his longstanding fear of separation that he could endure absences of various important people in his life without panic. He also became more capable of genuinely tender feelings.

The kind of success noted in the preceding example was not obtained with another "pure type" schizophrenic patient, an unmarried student of 23, referred for intensive therapy because of difficulty concentrating on his schoolwork. He had never been hospitalized. Paranoid and narcissistic features were both prominent. Several observers had regarded him as "Machiavellian." All problems were externalized; he felt victimized by malicious neighbors and incompetent psychiatrists, and took great delight in maligning the latter. Though he had worked with one psychiatrist for a year and a half, there had been many others whom he had quit seeing after three or four meetings. There were no close attachments in his current life. He had had only one close friend during adolescence, but now imagined that this fellow—who lived on the other side of the country—was somehow "spying" on him through a network of agents. The patient, an intelligent young man, was aware that other people regarded this notion as highly unlikely, if not altogether crazy; still, he could not relinquish it. Remarkably supercilious and sarcastic, he would spend most of his sessions in berating the therapist. Well aware of the homosexual implications of his paranoid ideas about his old friend, he nevertheless failed to progress beyond the point of intellectual pseudoinsight, and after several months moved on to a new therapist, who, he imagined, would "give in" to his demands (for advice, reassurance, etc.). This patient exemplifies the old diagnosis of "pure paranoia," a rare variant of schizophrenia seen for the most part in intellectually gifted males.

· · · · ·

The following patient shows a small admixture of symptoms ordinarily considered affective (tearfulness, suicidal ruminations). She was originally diagnosed as a "pseudoneurotic schizophrenic" and could also be visualized as a "predominantly schizophrenic schizoaffective" patient.

This patient was the only child of an obsessional but otherwise well-functioning mother and a paranoid schizophrenic father from a socially prominent family. He had never been able to work throughout the marriage and had such a gross thinking disorder that communication was rendered almost impossible. Temperamentally he was quite irascible. The parents divorced when the patient was 13. This event appeared to precipitate her breakdown; in any event, she spent the next seven years in a succession of psychiatric facilities. For many months at a time she would be mute, and she developed agoraphobia, which in time became so severe that she could scarcely venture out of her room in the hospital. By the time she was twenty she had "gone through" a succession of psychiatrists and had a trial of half a dozen psychoactive drugs, with no apparent benefit.

My own work with her began in the middle of my psychiatric residency. Although she said almost nothing to me in the beginning, it was clear her main feeling states, where I was concerned, were hostility and contemptuousness: therapists had come and gone; all had failed her. After a brief period of history-taking, the sessions dried up; whole months passed without a word being spoken between us, except for an occasional interpretive and rather academic remark on my part ("you must be churning with a lot of contradictory feelings today, that you remain so silent"), which, needless to say, always fell flat. During the fifth month of this absurd and fruitless exercise, by which time I had become at least as hostile and discouraged toward her as I sensed she had felt toward me, I acquired a new supervisor—one widely known for his work with hard-to-reach schizophrenic patients. I presented the case to him in a lengthy and garbled fashion, to which he remarked, "I find it hard to follow your remarks about this patient or to think of anything genuinely helpful to say to you. This occurs about 20 percent of the time in my experience with supervisees, so I find myself wondering—is there something about the patient you cherish just the way she is!?"

I immediately began to think of how the patient and her father would sometimes sit together in silence for hours on the porch of her old house. Her father, a lonely and himself quite phobic man, could neither bear to part with her nor admit how much he hoped she would remain. Our sessions had come to reduplicate this pattern. It occurred to me that, despite my annoyance at being stuck with so ungratifying a patient, there were qualities about her I "cherished." There was something restful, even pleasant, about staring at this attractive and childlike woman three hours a week—but this was a secret pleasure of which I had not been aware until the supervisor made his comment. This awareness proved liberating for me, in the sense I could now more freely admit my irritation at her—since it was no longer a matter of my feeling *only* fury. To criticize a child, by analogy, toward whom one feels only hostility is withering; to criticize the same child within the context of a—for the most part—loving relationship is not experienced as a total rejection. The child can therefore accept the criticism and make a change for the better. Our patients can in a similar fashion bear up well and even improve when we tell them something that is painful to hear—so long as they sense in us a fundamental and genuine regard.

In the session that followed my meeting with the supervisor, I told her, after about ten minutes of total silence, that if another minute of silence had to be endured, I would feel like exploding. Her response, "Jesus, you too!?" was followed by a long recitation of all the fears she had been struggling with over the months—that I would dislike her as she was, that I would resent her trying to get better, that lightning would somehow strike were she to walk a few steps beyond the entrance of the hospital. After this "turning point" session, she emerged not only as a talkative patient, but one with considerable psychological-mindedness and curiosity about the psychological roots of her misperceptions of other people. She now began to make rapid strides, successfully working through the two important paradigms that lay at the foundation of her misperceptions: (1) the belief that the "other person" in her life (father, therapist . . .) was terribly dependent on *her* and (2) the fear that, as a retaliation against any move on her part toward independence, she would be killed.

This patient had the capacity to deal effectively with her dreams and also with the transference. These qualities were not apparent at the outset. As the psychosis lifted and she became communicative, her level of personality organization rose to the borderline level (as defined by Kernberg, 1967). The ability of a schizophrenic patient to reach and maintain this level may itself be considered a criterion for suitability of intensive psychotherapy.

. . . . .

The next patient I would like to mention showed a still greater degree of affective symptoms than the preceding one. On the schizophrenic side of the ledger, she manifested disorganized thought, mutism, blunting of affect, persecutory delusions, and chronicity. On the affective side: self-depreciation, tearfulness (at times), severe suicide attempts, and depressed facies (usually only before separations from her therapist). This symptom mix established her as a mid-range schizoaffective patient (on Cohen's scale [1972], 57/43 was the score of schizophrenic to affective symptoms). The family, upper-middle-class socioeconomically, consisted of a father and brother, both well, and her mother, who was considered a "latent" or borderline schizophrenic (never hospitalized).

The patient had been ill since age 15 (suicide attempt), and spent the next six years in hospitals. She was self-effacing, often lost in autistic reverie, and never spoke above a whisper. At the same time she was unusually attractive and had been a straight-A student—both of which qualities served to bolster some hope in those concerned with her care, despite the chronicity of her illness. She was transferred to the Psychiatric Institute after she had failed to respond to the therapy and medications of the previous six years. Her care was entrusted to a colleague of mine, highly gifted in the intensive psychotherapy of schizophrenic patients.

The gravity of her illness may be gauged from the following anecdote, stemming from the second month after her transfer. Her therapist was away on a brief vacation. As the covering physician I made an arrangement to visit her one afternoon, only to discover that a patient of my own—a girl of 15—was locked in what appeared to be mortal combat with my colleague's patient: my patient, I thought, was pushing the other patient's head against the wall. I ran over to intercede and in the process knocked my patient to the floor to save the other, only to discover that the older girl was hitting her *own* head against the wall quite forcibly—a grotesque suicide attempt.

So far there was not much to inspire optimism. Yet she showed great curiosity about her inner life and her incapacities, and tended to form "anaclitic" relationships.

As with many schizophrenic patients who become dependent, and who also suppress angry feelings in a wholesale fashion, she developed a strong bond to her therapist, that did not snap during times of frustration. Overtly paranoid patients, as I mentioned above, will often react to disappointments, separations, and the like by breaking off treatment. When this happens there is usually no possibility of seeing the patient again so that the underlying resentment can be brought to light and resolved. The depressive patient, on the other hand, clings even in the face of resentment—thereby offering himself and the therapist the opportunity of dealing with the negative feelings. This is a much healthier situation because, given two schizophrenic patients with roughly equal personality assets, the depressive one may ultimately become less dependent yet still capable of intimacy. The paranoid patient may remain as ill at ease with human closeness as he was before. Psychological-mindedness is also more apt to be present in the depressive patient (who tends to take blame onto himself for everything, to look inward into his own feelings, and so on), whereas the paranoid patient externalizes and is not often disposed toward introspection and cooperation with the spirit of insight-oriented psychotherapy.

The patient in this example satisfied many of the criteria for suitability we have been speaking of and eventually made an excellent recovery. Some of the technics employed in effecting this unexpected result will be detailed later on.

. . . . .

The last two cases also illustrate a point relating to suitability for psychotherapy that does not inhere to the nature of the patient so much as the nature of the therapist. The favorable mix of qualities—a capacity for relatedness, more "depressiveness" than paranoia, good psychological-mindedness, and good intellectual endowment—was present throughout their long illnesses. Nevertheless, years went by before these assets could be mobilized for the benefit of the patient. Why?

The reason, I think, is to be found in the peculiar chemistry that seems to be necessary between doctor and patient before intensive psychotherapy can take hold and progress. It is perhaps not too extravagant a claim to assert that most competent psychoanalysts can do good work with most "classical" psychoneurotic analysands. The neurotic patient usually has a social facade that is agreeable to most people, including potential analysts; his comportment is not too challenging; heroics are not required; the analyst can easily get by without revealing much of himself, and so forth. Not so in the realm of schizophrenic patients. Many of the latter are quite difficult, or eccentric, or demanding; one must be prepared also to deal with stormy sessions, life-threatening gestures, calls at odd hours, and all the rest. One must be professional, always, with the schizophrenic patient, and yet not hide behind a mask of "professionalism." Not every therapist can like, or work successfully—even comfortably—with every schizophrenic patient. Certain patients are forced, as it were, to search for the therapist whose personality is attuned to his own and who can, often because of some quirk in the therapist's make-up, work well with the patient where others have failed.

Sometimes, as I have spoken of in an earlier article (Stone, 1971), the factor that allows the therapist to enjoy what for others has been drudgery is a more curious fit between patient and doctor: the patient may resemble a younger sibling of the therapist, or a former sweetheart, or a parent. Certain therapists have, for example, been the "Oedipal winners" in their original families, beating out a sibling for the affection of one of the parents. The guilt engendered by this sort of victory may get put to rest not so much through resolving conflicts with the sibling, as through "rescuing" the schizophrenic patient who shares, unwittingly, various attributes of that sibling. Obviously these are chance matters. But it is for reasons of this sort one cannot reduce to neat formulas the business of intensive therapy with schizophrenics, or even the business of their *selection*. A patient who satisfies abundantly all the criteria I have mentioned will still be found irksome, boring, or threatening to one set of therapists, no matter how well trained, while a few of their colleagues will, for reasons they might not recognize or might not readily admit, find the same schizophrenic patient interesting to work with. The young woman my colleague eventually rescued seemed eminently salvageable to him even when she was mute and suicidal, whereas the psychiatrists who had struggled with her before had come to regard her as a hopeless case.

Differences of this sort in the ability of one therapist to succeed with a certain schizophrenic patient where others have failed highlight what Margaret Little has called the "positive contribution of countertransference" (1981, p. 129). Sudden and wild reactions on the part of the patient may engender in the therapist a momentary state of panic; his anxiety will tend to replicate the "psychotic" anxiety to which the schizophrenic patient is so vulnerable: anxiety about *survival*, as opposed to mere anxiety about acceptance—with which the neurotic is preoccupied. With no time available to mull over the patient's response—delay would be disastrous—the therapist must do or say something straight from the shoulder. The response must be spontaneous, direct, human, and intense, in headline type the schizophrenic patient can read easily, not in the footnote size most human interchanges are cast in. Little gives an example concerning an impulsive and seriously disturbed woman who one day looked around Dr. Little's office in a frenzy and said, "I *must* smash something; what about your sham ink pot!?" Little, aware at that moment only of her anger at the patient (but dimly in touch with concern she might hurt herself) blurted out, "I'll just about kill you if you smash my pot!" later adding, after a prolonged silence, "I think you thought I really would kill you, or perhaps that I had done so." The patient replied, "Yes, it felt like that, it was frightful, but it was also very good. *I knew you really felt something, and I so often thought you didn't feel anything at all*" [italics mine] (1981, p. 131). About the healing effect of this interchange—for it did seem to constitute a turning point in therapy—Little offers the following:

> "She came to see that something she had despised had a value not only for me but in the outside world as well [upon closer inspection, it was really valuable]; . . . her judgment was not infallible; I would defend something I cared about and that included *her*; her feelings and mine about the same thing could be different, [but] we could both survive the separateness that this involved" (1981, p. 131).

Others who work with transference and countertransference issues in the analytically oriented therapy of schizophrenics are quick to point out that such therapy does not seek to stir the patient up intentionally: rather, when stormy feelings are mobilized in the patient (and subsequently in the therapist), it is the therapist's ability to stand his ground—to be honest and compassionate about the emotions unleashed in *both* participants—that can be integrative and curative. Wynne mentions, for example, that "a fully psychotic regressive transference is not sought by most psychotherapists today with individual schizophrenics" (1980, p. 193). This reflects in part the respect (and fear) within the therapeutic community of the schizophrenic's extraordinary vulnerability, often to the most ordinary of social stresses, such that, as Wing (1978) has put it, "the therapist [would be] foolhardy, if not irresponsible, who allows or encourages amplification of any of the problems." Within the limits of what the patient can tolerate, however, occasional revelation of certain countertransference emotions may be appropriate and helpful—the more so because of their memorable and dramatic quality (see also, Searles, 1974).

INTELLIGENCE

At least average intelligence is a prerequisite in schizophrenic patients one is evaluating for intensive psychotherapy. Usually, the patients in whom we effect the best levels of improvement have better—in many instances, decidedly better—than average intelligence. By itself, of course, the presence of this factor does not ensure success. One can, for example, have high intelligence and poor psychological-mindedness. It has been mentioned by a number of authors that schizophrenics favored with high intelligence show a milder clinical picture (see, for example, Weingarten and Korn, 1967)—more like Hoch and Polatin's (1949) descriptions of the "pseudoneurotic" schizophrenic than of the patient who satisfies Feighner's (1972) research criteria. Schizophrenic patients who are brighter than average often overcome the tendency to delusory ideation more readily than less endowed patients, who often remain mired in their psychotic perceptions. It is as though high intelligence permits a better degree of reality-testing, even in the midst of an acute breakdown, so that the patient soon recuperates to a level of function more in keeping with borderline than with psychotic organization.

There are exceptions to this rule. I saw one hebephrenic young woman—the most dilapidated and flamboyantly psychotic schizophrenic person I have encountered thus far in my clinical work—who I imagined must have shown subnormal intelligence. Neuroleptics, ECT, psychotherapy—nothing made the slightest dent in her illness. But her IQ was in the "very superior" range (137); I suppose one must ascribe the unrelenting nature of her illness to extremely high genetic liability (her father and brother were both chronic paranoid schizophrenics). I have also seen, in my work at the Psychiatric Institute, a small number of brilliant but deeply schizophrenic mathematicians whose personalities were markedly schizoid. These young men seemed to have no access at all to their emotional life, were extremely isolated, and were unable to make contact with their therapists.

But for every unfortunate case of this sort, there are a dozen patients whose combination of intelligence and introspectiveness permit them to gain important insights into the sources of their disordered interaction with others and into the subtleties of their own current and maladaptive behavior, so that they are able in time to integrate at a distinctly higher level than they have ever functioned at before.

6

Psychotherapy of Schizophrenia:

THE EARLY PHASE OF TREATMENT

Harry D. Albert, M.D.

One of the most difficult challenges in psychiatry is the treatment of schizophrenic patients. The severe and sometimes frightening symptoms of the condition and the frustrations of treatment may lead the therapist through a thicket of uncomfortable reactions: boredom, fatigue, real countertransference feelings, helplessness, perhaps even hopelessness and withdrawal. There are several reasons for these feelings, apart from the difficulties inherent in work with schizophrenic persons.

Much of our training in psychotherapy is derived from experience with other, often nonpsychotic disorders and is of doubtful help in work with schizophrenic patients. Too much emphasis is placed on nosology and theory; too little on phenomenology and treatment technique. Even during supervision, the senior supervisor is often years away from the last schizophrenic patient that he himself actually treated.

It is commonplace to denigrate the teaching of therapy technique, as if in some way a knowledge of therapeutic strategies would interfere with the intuitive and empathic capacities of the therapist. The opposite is actually true. It is the therapist with little knowledge of such strategies or of the phenomenology of schizophrenia who becomes anxious the most readily. Only when the therapist has the technical means of dealing with the manifestations of this disorder will he have sufficient freedom to use his intuitive and empathic skills to some advantage.

I shall illustrate an integrated strategy of treatment that I have found useful in office practice. All these patients described have had at least one psychotic break requiring hospitalization. They form a mixed group of diagnostic subtypes and range in age from the early teens through late forties. Some of these patients were practicing professional careers while others were in junior high school at the time of treatment. Some met with me as often as three times weekly, though most were seen once or twice weekly (well within the range of conventional office practice with nonschizophrenic patients). This point is worth noting, because one frequently encounters the idea that intensive therapy requires daily meetings, whereas in fact this may be necessary only during times of crisis. With some patients, meeting so frequently may even be harmful. Powerful transference feelings may be so overwhelming that they spill into the patient's daily life with socially disastrous consequences. The framework of this treatment has been designed around the expectable recurrent problems of intensive work with schizophrenic patients. I would like to begin by discussing certain problems arising from common preconceptions and then proceed to discuss problems inherent in the work itself.

Polarization of Ideas

Any theory, model, or concept has the power to imprison the mind. Yet all therapists must have a construct around which to organize data. The danger in this work, particularly where competing theories abound, is to become so enamored of one construct as to forfeit the benefits of contrasting views. As therapists, we should also beware of a tendency to fit the data to the theory. It is essential to distinguish clearly between the data of observation and of nonobservation, the latter being inferred from one or another theoretical construct. Mudd (1978) discusses the problem of reification at some length, in this connection.

Some current models are the Social, the Family, the Biological, and the Psychodynamic. No single model is adequate to explain or predict the phenomenology of schizophrenia, though all have some pragmatic utility.

Theoretical bias and rigidity may prevent the therapist from integrating different viewpoints into a more comprehensive technic. This bias may, for example, prevent the therapist from employing medication effectively. Or it may lead to overreliance on drugs to the exclusion of other modes. Similarly, the therapist may use—where it is inappropriate—an unstructured approach derived from psychoanalysis. He may not structure the therapeutic situation sufficiently or he may fail to gather specific details about the social situation of his schizophrenic patient.

Phenothiazines and related medications can be a crucial element of treatment, provided the therapist titrates dosages appropriately, ensures adherence, and avoids medication in specific situations (which I will discuss at greater length further on).

Learning theory offers effective modes of training social skills, altering habits, and modifying certain behavioral patterns (especially those related to rituals and avoidances). This set of constructs also emphasizes the value of pursuing a precise knowledge of life factors that sustain psychotic thinking and behavior. Arieti's use of the patient's "expectant attitude" in making a direct attack on hallucinations is an example of this precise knowledge at work.

Psychodynamic theory holds out the hope of our being able to explain and understand the bizarre and symbolic expressions of our schizophrenic patients. Searles and Fromm-Reichman, among others, offer elegant examples of the use of psychoanalytic theory and psychoanalytic technique much modified for the treatment of schizophrenics. For the therapist just learning to do this work, however, and who may already be familiar with psychoanalytic technique, many of the technical devices he knows for intensifying transference, eliciting free associations, and maintaining therapeutic distance may be counterproductive.

The Social model offers guidance in helping these patients gain order and support for institutions, friends, and relatives. This model is especially important when working with families, and within an institutional framework.[1]

The therapist need not become expert in the theory and practice of all these areas. It is important, rather, to maintain humility and scientific integrity in recognizing the need for flexibility.

Overall Conception of Therapy

The treatment of schizophrenic patients ought to rest on careful planning, with interventions derived both from theoretical propositions and from our observations of the patient's assets and liabilities. A careful appraisal of defects that need to be improved, and of assets that can be utilized, may lead to any of several possible treatment approaches. I have seen no convincing evidence that any *one* approach, from classical analysis through network therapy to psychopharmacology, can be the method of choice for all schizophrenics. Therapy must be shaped for each specific patient.

This does not mean a "cookbook" approach. The overall approach

[1]Goffman (1961), Wynne (1974), Jackson (1967).

taken here relies heavily on psychoanalytically informed understanding, which implies a familiarity with the phenomena of transference and countertransference. This understanding may be used, at times, more as a guide for the timing and choice of *other* techniques (e.g., from the realm of cognitive treatment or supportive psychotherapy) than for a strictly interpretive, psychoanalytic therapy.

A textbook cannot substitute for an experienced supervisor, but clinical illustrations can flesh out the bare text and can supply, to some extent, the answer to the perennial question one addresses to psychotherapeutic technique: when, and why, is this done?

The patients who are encompassed in my recommendations are primarily outpatients. The therapist I am addressing has a base of hospital support, but functions primarily in an office setting. He should be aware at the outset that some of the suggestions I shall be making are in conflict with a purely psychoanalytic treatment. Though I believe the work of many eminent psychoanalysts has been of a pioneering and, indeed, heroic nature, it is not always suitable for the "average" therapist treating the "average" schizophrenic person. For this therapist and this person, the therapist may have to be teacher, counselor, exhorter; indeed he may have to be a family adviser. He can do these tasks effectively, I believe, if informed by psychoanalytic understanding, particularly regarding the timing of events and the psychodynamic meaning of seemingly unrelated issues, without using the *technical* maneuvers of formal psychoanalysis.

Countertransference

The term has acquired multiple meanings with the passage of time. We ought to speak of two countertransferences. The first, "objective" countertransference as described by Winnicott (1949, 1960), concerns the natural reaction of the therapist to rather extreme manifestations of the patient's behavior. We are all familiar with examples of incessant telephoning, vitriolic denunciations, and persistent assertions about our harmful or evil personalities as therapists.

These so-called objective countertransference experiences tell us that issues of management need to be addressed and that in some fashion the patient is overstepping our limits of tolerance. It is imperative not to let such a situation continue. It could lead to abandonment of the patient or, even worse, a mutual abrasion that may persist for years. Situations of this sort arise generally because the therapist lacks techniques for managing the patient's actual behavior. Somewhat less often, the therapist may believe that bizarre, provocative behavior is somehow therapeutically useful. "Letting feelings out" is a term commonly heard among trainees and in slightly different form among experienced therapists who confuse theoretical issues of expressive psychotherapy with the phenomenology of disturbed ego function. The therapist must of course come to learn about the patient's maladaptive responses. Witnessing the reenactment of these behaviors provides valuable clues to the early genesis of these activities, the current distorted perceptions that support them, and the situations these tactics are designed to deal with. To permit, however, the stereotyped repetition of maladaptive behavior, once these goals have been reached, is harmful rather than useful.

The second type of countertransference (and this is countertransference as we usually use the term) refers to an unconscious process in the therapist. Here we mean specifically the reappearance of unresolved conflicts and archaic identifications under the stress of work with schizophrenic patients. Kernberg speaks in this connection of how the therapist confronts several dangers within himself that may interfere with the treatment (1975, p. 254ff).

The therapist may, for example, experience anxiety connected with his own primitive aggressive impulses toward the patient. With certain other patients anxiety and dread may arise from experiences of a relative loss of ego boundaries.

The therapist may experience powerful but unrealistic wishes to control the patient. This may arise, for example, if the therapist senses a correspondence in some aspect of the patient and some poorly controlled, archaic object representation in himself.

Masochism may be reactivated in the therapist in the form of permitting himself to be ill-used or in the form of fantasies of rescue or superhuman effort on behalf of specific patients.

Countertransference of the second kind is an inevitable occurrence in working with people who operate frequently on the level of the therapist's archaic experience. This experience is dangerous to the therapy only when not recognized and understood. Evidence of this countertransference lies in the affective experience of the therapist as it pertains specifically to one patient. Fatigue, boredom, reluctance to begin a particular hour, or the reverse—heightened interest, intrusive fantasies during nonworking hours, and the like—all signal this phenomenon in regard to a particular patient in a particular phase of the treatment. As such, any appearance of a constellation of special feelings ought to be considered useful as observer signs.

Observer signs, despite their subjectivity, are a useful instrumentation of the therapist, no less than the cloud-chamber of the physicist. To work with schizophrenic persons successfully a therapist must become familiar with the meaning in himself of these predictable and recurrent experiences. One begins simply by establishing a routine of treatment. Without a routine, the appearance of countertransference is less likely to be noticed; or if noticed, less likely to yield useful data.

The most useful piece of information to be derived from the sudden appearance of countertransference phenomena is that some transition is occurring in the patient and presumably also in the dyadic relationship. Determining the nature of this transition requires scrutiny. The scrutiny may require reviewing the patient's current social setting, levels of medication, events of the previous several therapy hours, or intercurrent events in the therapist's personal life or health. If further observation and review are not helpful, a consultation with a colleague may be in order, as discussed below. The following example illustrates the use one may make of a mixture of neurotic countertransference and objective countertransference.

A young schizophrenic woman offered me a cigarette during our first meeting. I declined, indicating that I do not smoke. She continued to offer me a cigarette each time she smoked one herself, during this and succeeding hours. I asked her about this, since each hour brought twenty or more offers. As far as she was concerned, she was merely being polite. As she said this I felt profound unease. My inordinate fear was clearly a countertransference to an archaic experience in the patient. This internal experience alerted me to treat this as an important issue, and no mere habit. We were also dealing here with *objective* countertransference, since the frequent interruptions were quite exasperating.

Once alerted to this issue I could introduce the experimental method into the history taking (described below). First I underlined the behavior, by suggesting that it had meaning; second, we reviewed the role that repetition had in her life; third, I suggested that we might conduct an experiment to discover why this behavior persisted. Later on we would be able to chart a more useful substitute. She reiterated the idea that the offers were meaningless, habitual acts.

I shared my reasoning with her. "If there is no meaning in your offers beyond habit, then it should not matter whether I accept or refuse. Let us see together. I will accept one of your offers in the course of this meeting."

At the next offer I accepted, lit the cigarette, and smoked it. The patient began literally to shake with terror. She said that her heart was pounding, her stomach was churning, and she felt a headache suddenly beginning. We agreed to label this experience "fear." This in itself was a step forward for this person, who was ostensibly without feelings. As we spoke further she said that I had visually melted as I lit the cigarette, as if changing into another person. We both realized that her repetitive offers were therefore checks, to be sure that "I," smoking, was the same as the nonsmoking therapist of a few moments earlier (i.e., that I had continuity in time). This concerns a common ego defect in schizophrenic persons. The demonstration provided an opportunity to explore other ways in which this person tried to bridge her deficient sense of continuity (or identity).

Our exploration remained on the level of actual interactions with other people. Discussions of the angry and controlling aspects of this psychotic behavior were not appropriate to this early moment in the treatment (nor was the later, admitted fact that she *wished* me to smoke, so that I would get cancer as punishment for "mistreating" her).

This example illustrates the use of countertransference as an indicator of hidden feelings in the patient and as a signal of an appropriate time to bring such material to the attention of the patient.

It is imperative for therapists working intensively with schizophrenic persons that they become aware of the various forms countertransference feelings may assume. To facilitate this process, therapists should become familiar with a wide variety of patients (in terms of age, sex, and degree or type of disturbance).

A particular time ought to be set aside before and after an hour for preview and review. If this is done, certain countertransference wishes (e.g., to dwell inordinately on a particular patient or to avoid considering one) quickly become evident. There should also be a comfortable routine of greeting and leave-taking. Even with due preparation, the treatment of schizophrenic patients is difficult enough; to see patients one after another introduces an unnecessary handicap (Greenson, 1974).

The therapist may do well to utilize audiotapes or, even better, videotape playback of treatment hours. Berger makes clear how much we can learn about our own inner states, and about the form in which we communicate these states by observing how patients respond to our nonverbal communications (Berger, 1970). Often the so-called hyperacute awareness of our schizophrenic patients is really a learned, early warning signal which they develop by way of navigating through the more difficult passages of their family lives. These skills are now misapplied upon ourselves. A tape playback allows us to hear what we might otherwise overlook.

Our missing these data may, of course, be motivated by the ordinary forces of repression (for countertransference reasons), or it may be material we are not attuned to in our ordinary practice. In this sense, a poker face and little movement is also communication, but a communication open to a wide variety of interpretations.

Example

A 27-year-old schizophrenic artist made repeated references to being overwhelmed, dominated, and controlled by me. She offered pictures and diagrams of a giant towering over a figure diminished almost to invisibility. Our interviews were taped for later use in a resident teaching exercise. On viewing them with my class, we were all impressed by the physical reality that this frail woman *was* overshadowed by my height and expansive gestures. In a following session, I offered the observation that I was large, and she was small, and it was understandable that she felt herself reduced in size (and potential power). At once the fantastic elaborations about rays emanating from my eyes and the thoughts locked in my desk were replaced by more conventional concerns about our relationship.

The paraphernalia of recording, in my experience, do not provoke undue concern in patients. The contrary is true—they provoke undue concern in therapists.

Empathic Communication versus Countertransference

Apart from the therapist's reactions to his own archaic experience and to the current overt behavior of the patient, there exists also an *empathic* kind of communication with which experienced therapists are familiar. Hearing and seeing tapes of one's interviews help confirm the accuracy and therefore the usefulness of these feelings. While learning to do therapy with schizophrenic persons, the therapist may find it difficult to empathize with the patient, especially at the outset. He may not trust the feelings evoked in himself. Yet, a meaningful interview must produce affectually significant interchange between the two participants. Some therapists use vivid dramatic techniques for stirring an affect-laden interchange (e.g., Rosen or Searles). They use surprise, coupled with a thorough understanding of schizophrenic unconscious process. They may say, "You wish to fuck me," or "I find in myself wishes to strangle you," often with dramatic and useful effect. These techniques, however, if they can be taught at all, clearly depend on unusually good empathic skills. Not everyone has the opportunity for apprenticeship with a therapist who has this ability. A charismatic personality helps, in this regard, but of course charisma cannot be acquired even by the best teaching. For the majority of therapists the parodying of these techniques, possibly witnessed at a public presentation, is inadvisable and is best termed "wild interpretation."

If we recognize the difficulty in achieving empathic understanding, we may then proceed in a reasonable way to develop and use evocative material.

First, then, why do we not experience these patients as we do other people?

For one thing, the schizophrenic may appear emotionally dead, or else completely out of touch with emotions that are obviously present: he out-obsesses the obsessive with respect to isolation of affect. Even weeping may be passed off as "something flew into my eye." So, it is useful to observe, and to have the patient report, bodily experiences—cues for therapist and patient that something, as yet unnamed, is occurring.

The patient's affect may be "inappropriate," a somewhat unfortunate term. Actually, the patient's feelings are "appropriate" to his *inner* vision and understanding, though not to ours. Thus a bland recital of the events of the death of the patient's father may overlay many feelings, including triumph, guilt, sexual arousal, and incestuous fear. The therapist who is set on loss or on some largely sympathetic response will not attend to these other possibilities. A patient in treatment with me once announced the completion of his doctoral thesis. I expressed congratulations. He berated me for hypocrisy, convinced that I knew he regarded his work as excrement and was therefore mocking him (just as his thesis adviser had done). He also berated me for not "realizing" that his inadequacies would now be on public view.

The patient should always be asked *his* reactions to reported material. The therapist should use his inner response as a guide to further questions. This he can do more forcefully as his confidence in the accuracy of his impressions grows. Even so, the therapist is bound to be in error often enough. The errors of understanding may nonetheless be pressed into service as reminders that the therapist is not omniscient, that the burden of communication goes both ways.

Again, I emphasize that the technique of passive neutrality, borrowed from psychoanalysis, will allow the patient's distortions all too much play. A passive technique will fail to promote affectually laden communication. Therapists tend to fall back on neutrality out of fear of unduly exposing themselves. The point of this section is to encourage the therapist to use his own feeling—as a key to the patient's hidden feelings. The presentation of the therapist's feelings should be to help acquaint the patient with himself—not to acquaint the patient with the therapist's self.

The Early Phase of Treatment:
The Initial Interview

The first meeting with a schizophrenic person will, to a large degree, set the tone of later meetings, and it is often recalled by patients quite late on in treatment. This meeting should therefore be designed to accomplish more than simply the accumulation of factual data as might be gathered in the familiar mental status examination format. The meeting should also set a tone of collaboration and respect that will, one hopes, continue in the sessions that follow. Learning the rules of treatment may even be more important for patients with much prior therapy than for those new to treatment. It is not rare for a patient to see me after long treatment elsewhere and to open the hour by talking of their wishes to have sex with mother, of their "father transference," and so on, and to be genuinely puzzled by my simple inquiries as to what work they do, or what their living arrangements are.

It is well to have a conceptual framework for the purpose of this meeting so that the details of it can be organized to fit the individual needs, experience, and talents of the therapist. Ideally, the interview is a situation in which patient and therapist can observe each other with the minimum arousal of anxiety. The therapist must be aware that the patient's anxiety will stem from perceptual distortions, transference phenomena, and from the repeated experience that entering a relationship has led mostly to his being revealed as "inadequate" or as an object of disgust. This conceptualization helps chart our course through the sometimes conflicting recommendations in the literature about the management of the initial interview.

The importance of mutual observation suggests that the interview be done without interruptions from the telephone or other sources. If assaultive behavior seems at all likely, attendants should be present to mitigate the therapist's fear. Likewise, if it is known that the patient fears attack from the therapist, security must be established through the therapist's empathic comments. For patients with no prior therapy the purpose of the interview should be briefly explained. Any questions the patient may have should be answered directly (unless they are bizarre or incomprehensible, in which case the therapist should indicate his lack of understanding). Concerns about whether the therapist has a family, is Irish, or whatever, are generally related to "security operations." Along with his answer, the therapist should inquire what the patient has made of the answer. It is to be emphasized that at this point a secrecy modeled on psychoanalytic anonymity is likely to produce only suspicion. The patient's genuine need for information (because of his faulty reality testing) should have primacy. The use he makes of the information he receives can always be examined later. The interview should be long enough (one may have to set aside two or three hours) to allow the initial surge of anticipatory anxiety to diminish. Patients often experience note-taking as an invasion or as a withdrawal on the part of the therapist. Notes should be recorded *after* the meeting, not only for these reasons, but also to allow the therapist fuller use of his faculties. It is well to have an office arrangement in which the therapist and patient are seated relatively far apart, with chairs either mobile or not directly facing one another. Many schizophrenic persons, especially those on a paranoid axis, are deeply concerned about eye contact. Mobile chairs will allow the patient to select both his comfortable viewing angle, and his best distance from the therapist. If the office arrangement does not permit this, Sullivan's suggestion of a 45-degree angling of the chairs (rather than vis-à-vis) is useful.

If chairs are mobile, the therapist will have the chance to appreciate, each meeting, the shifting balance between fears of abandonment and fears of engulfment—just by noticing what the patient does with this chair, even before a word has been spoken.

If possible, the patient should be seated nearer the door to minimize feelings of entrapment.

Example

A 20-year-old schizophrenic woman law student was comfortable in classes only when sheltering herself behind enormous, mirrored sunglasses. This defense of distantiation did not prove sufficient in my office. She suggested moving a small end table between us. I encouraged her to do what was needed for her comfort. Finally, it became clear that her fears of me were of sexual attack. The only way she could be comfortable with me was across an open doorway, with herself in the hall.

With the reduction in anxiety, we could talk of her ways of "managing" male classmates by mannishness, anorexic thinness, and isolation. Once "safe from me" she could, in time, venture to talk of the sibling sexuality which underlay her transferential and projected fears.

In her prior therapy with a woman she had been unable to mention the sex with her brother (as being too disgusting); with a previous male therapist, she feared arousing him. Sitting in a hall outside my office she felt safe from attack, and also comforted that she could flee at the first sign of my disgust without a humiliating explanation of her departure.

The patient's concerns about being revealed as a failure or repulsive object suggest the form and course of eliciting historical material.

If the patient is mute or profoundly withdrawn, the therapist will do well to sit quietly for a time, and then to describe some of the aims, techniques, and purposes of treatment. He may go on to discuss some of the fears people commonly have of the process, and express his willingness to discuss any issues the patient is curious about. The therapist should indicate that he is willing to allow the patient to proceed from his defensively withdrawn position in however gradual a rate he requires. Obviously this is a taxing experience, and many therapists will find that they do not do well in this situation. Still, if the therapist can endure this, he and the patient may be able to form a useful working relationship in which the waiting time actually serves as a shared experiential base for more active aspects of the treatment.

If the therapist bears in mind that the patient fears rebuff he will not ask pointed questions about the patient's disability. Rather the patient should be asked his reasons for coming to the interview, and what he hopes to get from it. The patient will proceed then to give an account of some hopes, aspirations, assets, talents, and (carefully edited) fears and failures. He should be interrupted only to clarify obscure meanings. This is not to be construed as a psychoanalytic interview in which the patient is to say whatever his associations bring forth. It is also not to be done as a relatively mechanical process following some prescribed path.

The standard interview, in contrast, often brings up the most damaging and disturbing material at the outset (that is, the immediate aspects and causes of the patient's decompensation). The standard "why have you come" also tends to evoke the complaints of others about the patient's conduct and may fail to elicit the patient's own view of "what hurts."

After the patient has had expressed himself reasonably fully he should be asked to reconsider what he has said and whether he wishes to add or clarify anything. Patients are usually surprised and gratified at being taken seriously. This approach also preserves a spirit of mutual exploration rather than one of interrogation. After the patient provides emendations and additions the therapist may ask the patient for his theory of how he has become the person he is. This allows an assessment of the patient's psychological-mindedness.

At the conclusion of this part of the interview the therapist should possess a relatively clear picture of the patient's view of himself, of his origins, his assets and liabilities. The patient has meanwhile participated in a mutual endeavor, free of humiliation, whose focus has been his own experiential world.

The therapist may then inquire into the patient's own recommendations for what should be done to help him in attaining his goals, making use of his assets, and alleviating his difficulties, in that order.

Schizophrenic patients are not accustomed to having their opinions solicited! It is enhancing to their self-esteem to have the therapist do so. This is an implicit communication that they will be regarded as full-fledged persons, to be taken seriously in the collaborative venture of psychotherapy.

This rather long initial consultation should obviously be divided into segments so that it does not become fatiguing to either party. Some authors recommend that the patient be asked to speak about his own reaction to the therapist. This is a useful question. The patient, however, may hesitate to express antipathy, doubtfulness, or other negative feeling at the very outset. Such a question is therefore likely to be evaded or to provoke severe anxiety. It is best asked in some later session so that the patient may have the comfort of voicing his complaints in a more distant fashion (e.g.: "A *week ago* you hurt my feelings . . ."). The patient should be reminded that the therapist is asking for these reactions to minimize the patient's discomfort, not as a sneaky way of courting praise. Of course the therapist should expect to be disbelieved in these disclaimers, at least initially. Eventually, if the therapist's comments are seen as genuine, the patient will begin to realize that the therapist was not being exploitative, after all.

Relations with the Patient's Family

The relationship between the therapist and the family of a schizophrenic patient is generally rather difficult. The question often arises even before the patient is actually seen, how and under what circumstances one should meet with the relatives. Ordinarily one wishes to do so for the purpose of gaining historical material, or of communicating certain instructions the patient may not yet be ready to act on responsibly, or perhaps to provide some prognostic information. Problems attending this seemingly straightforward beginning are legion.

At an initial interview the patient's parents or relatives may be heavily burdened by feelings of guilt and responsibility for the patient's illness. They fear, and often rightly so, the therapist's hostility or blamefulness. It is not surprising that they may exhibit, besides a self-exculpatory attitude, an angry defensiveness toward the therapist and some hostility toward the patient, all apart from whatever personal difficulties they may already be experiencing in everyday life.

The patient may feel the presence of his relatives to be protection against the unknown and feared doctor. More likely he will be concerned that the therapist will adopt the views of his relatives or that his confidentiality will be breached.

The therapist often will have acquired, consciously or not, angry and blameful feelings toward the relatives. Additionally he may have residual difficulties with his own parents, the more so if he is relatively young. The therapist may fear showing his hostility, particularly in the face of defensive maneuvers on the part of the relatives.

In spite of these potential difficulties it is recommended that one meet with the patient's family at the beginning of treatment. If family members are excluded, they will almost invariably take this as a criticism. They may then disparage the therapist, play down changes in the patient, or otherwise sabotage the treatment. Some parents, as Lidz and Lidz (1952) describe, are so convinced that their understanding and support are vital to the patient's very survival that they cannot, and ought not, be expected to tolerate an abrupt displacement from their accustomed role.

This meeting ought, therefore, to be constructed with guidelines to deal with these feelings. If it is, it should facilitate transition into conjoint family therapy, if this appears desirable at some later time.

Usually the family should be seen toward the end of the first interview. A useful explanation for them is that the therapist is confronted with a difficult task and will do best by hearing the patient's view of his situation first. The patient should be told that he has absolute confidentiality vis-à-vis the relatives except in the overriding circumstances of potential suicide or harm to others.

Toward the last third of the interview the patient should be given the option of inviting his relatives in. In keeping with the spirit of collaboration, the patient ought to be asked what help *he* feels his relatives may be able to provide—in the form of information, outside living arrangements, financial help, etc. He ought also to be asked what his concerns are regarding negative attitudes on their part.

Once the relatives are in the office, they should be told forthrightly that the therapist is aware, from meetings with other relatives, that they probably have concerns about being interviewed. These concerns should, of course, be aired, and will likely center on the issue of how responsible they feel for the patient' plight.

We will also want to hear from them their hopes for the patient's future and their assessment of his achievements and strengths. Talk of the present difficulties should be limited to those the family considers of immediate importance. One wishes to avoid the all too common experience of hearing the patient described, within earshot and in the very earliest sessions, as (to cite an example from one particular family): "He's been strange since the first time he kicked in my womb!'' Such a comment, overheard so early in treatment, can only contribute to the patient's demoralization.

Families customarily respond with surprise and pleasure when they realize their aid is being sought. Often they have become despondent about the patient. Because of this they will respond all the more warmly upon seeing they have something positive to offer. Frequently relatives can, within the extended family, create opportunities for jobs, housing arrangements, and social support systems, all of which can be pressed into service during the rehabilitative process. Sometimes these resources exceed what even the best network of day hospitals, halfway houses, etc., can provide. Younger patients in particular may well need to return to their home of origin for greater or lesser periods. In any case the patient and his family are likely to remain in contact of some sort. Ample evidence now exists that better prognosis is associated with improved family relationships (Brown, Birley, and Wing, 1972; Linn, 1980; Langsley et al., 1969; Vaughn and Leff, 1976).

One family presented their 18-year-old son with the despairing comment that his only ''resource'' seemed to be his propensity to walk around the streets like a Bowery bum. They contrasted this with his range of interests, hobbies, and intellectual pursuits of two years past (prior to his psychotic break) as though he were now a completely different person. Apart from his seemingly aimless walks, he spent the remainder of his waking life, according to his parents, virtually motionless in bed.

During our meeting I encouraged this young man to share his experiences during these trips and to talk of what he derived from them. To his family's amazement, he spoke of ''keeping healthy'' by being out in all kinds of weather, of having contact with other ''street people,'' and of the idea that one could learn much as a wanderer. The patient's father spontaneously offered to accompany him on one of these walks, and afterward reported that his son was not so crazy in what he actually did, even though his ideas still sounded crazy.

MacKinnon and Michels (1971) have described the use of telephone interviews in various situations. It has been my experience that the telephone is quite useful as an adjunct in managing the relationship with relatives of the patient. A routine call schedule should be set up by appointment, and billed as any other treatment time. If no such arrangement is made, calls will often be made anyway by certain patients, under the pretext of ''emergencies.'' Such calls may be quite frequent and may come at inconvenient times. This, in turn, may provoke the development of a retaliatory ''countertransference'' in which the therapist may return the calls unduly late or ''forget'' them altogether.

It should be understood at the beginning that the gist of these and all other contacts with relatives will be shared with the patient and that, however well intentioned, imparting information with the intention of its being kept secret from the patient is (with rare exceptions) inadmissable.

In hospital-based treatment a social worker or other member of a therapeutic team may work as an intermediary between the patient and the family. It is crucial that contact be maintained with the family, as outlined here. The technical management of that contact deserves serious consideration.

The "team" approach ordinarily appropriate to the hospital setting may be duplicated in a loose way using halfway houses, day treatment programs, and the like. If an intermediary is to be used between family and therapist, the following variables must be weighed:

1. How will the *patient* understand the therapist's not meeting with his family? He may conclude that the therapist is firmly on his side (which carries the connotation, as well, that the family is in the wrong). He may conclude that the therapist fears his family. He may conclude that the therapist cannot be trusted to meet the family and is openly declaring this. The point to be made is that this arrangement, as with other arrangements of the treatment, must be understood from a patient's eye view.

2. How will the *family* understand this? Will they see themselves receiving special attention? Will they feel the therapist is denigrating them? Will they perceive a continuing connection to their relative even through one more "layer" of personnel?

3. As a therapist, one should understand one's *own* reasons for this arrangement. The therapist should work with a familiar colleague with whom a past contact assures the possibility of frequent, open communication to resolve the (to my mind) inevitable personal and professional rivalries, and enhanced possibilities for countertransference complications.

The positive outcome of this arrangement assures the patient of his privacy and of having a "therapist of his own." For the therapist, it means the family, too, can have the stabilizing and supportive advantages of a therapist of "their own." This may spare him the unpleasantness of having a patient snatched from treatment just as it verges on success.

At times, perplexing interrelationships in the family will be mirrored in the relationship between the therapists (in a form, one hopes, which will now permit understanding and resolution). As Kernberg (1977), mentions, "The therapist and the hospital management team, through its team leader need to communicate with each other while remaining autonomous, so that unconscious fights for power can be diagnosed and resolved in time.'' If this is true in a hospital setting, with all the support of the institutional structure, how much more true for a therapist and colleague working in an office setting.

Depending on the considerations outlined above, a therapist may be able, with selected patients and their families, to function as both therapist and intermediary. It may be useful for some family meetings to include both therapist and social worker, to provide a sharing of viewpoints and to avoid, as much as possible, the development of factions. This is particularly true in those families where the patient is felt to be so special or fragile that catastrophe is ''likely'' unless contact is maintained through a family member. These families can often remain relatively reassured if they can maintain contact with their child at one remove through the therapist. When this is denied, it is not unusual for the family to disrupt the treatment, often at just the moment the hospital staff are congratulating themselves about some move toward individuation on the part of the patient.

The mother of one of my patients would regularly present herself at the ward door with food she had prepared. Almost invariably, this would be something he was forbidden while on a trial of MAO-inhibiting drugs. She, on the other hand, was certain her son would become sick without it, and even threatened to sign him out, then and there, if she were not permitted to feed him. I complimented her on her concern and effort, and wondered if she might share some of the food with me while we discussed the problem. As she fed me, her agitation diminished markedly, and she began a process of accepting reassurance, happy that I, at least, did not see her as a witch. She continued to bring some food—cookies at least—to each meeting, evidently as a necessary test of the current attitude the social worker and I had toward her.

Diagnostic Issues

Issues regarding the differential diagnosis of schizophrenia must be considered from the first interview. Therapists may become too immersed in the day-to-day aspects of treatment to see that a condition may actually demand a quite different approach. Bellak (1976), Schneider (1959), Feighner et al. (1972) and Spitzer (1978) have described systems for diagnosing schizophrenia. The point to be made is not simply to differentiate among the schizophrenic subtypes, but to maintain suspicion that one may be seeing a condition other than schizophrenia.

An acute psychotic reaction with primary-process thought, hallucinations, ideas of reference, or even mutism and posturing may well not be schizophrenia. One must remain aware that the initial diagnosis is subject to modification, depending on the patient's course. Some patients are diagnosed as suffering "schizoaffective schizophrenia" whose condition more properly belongs in the realm of affective disorders (Spitzer, Endicott and Gibbon, 1979).

One should also consider toxic delirium, especially in younger patients. Abuse of amphetamines, for example, may counterfeit paranoid states; LSD ingestion may mimic acute schizophrenia. More recently, we have begun to see abuse of phencyclidine ("angel dust"), which may present with many of the features of catatonia. This last also presents the hazard of the "whack attack," in which extremely violent behavior may erupt suddenly and without provocation.

Still other, less common situations must be kept in mind. Cerebral tumors, especially slow-growing forms, may produce a picture consistent with simple schizophrenia (Belfer, 1971). Petit mal epilepsy may, especially in adolescents of schizoid personality type, produce the apparent lack of concentration, tangentiality of thought, blunting of feeling, and withdrawal suggestive of undifferentiated schizophrenic states. Particularly in these latter two situations patients develop psychological defenses to foster their denial of deficit, all of which can make for a very complicated clinical picture.

Example

A 17-year-old girl was seen in consultation after 18 months of fruitless psychological therapy and phenothiazines in high dosage. During the interview I noted, every quarter of an hour or so, half-minute periods of seeming inattention. The patient denied hallucinations vigorously, and even more vigorously denied that she ever suffered "absences" (momentary lapses). She worked herself into a fury about the direction these questions took. It happened that she was interrupted in mid-course by just such an "absence." Eventually, on appropriate antiseizure medication, with remedial schooling, and no further formal psychotherapy, this young woman did quite well.

Morrison (1979) has described a condition of adolescence and early adult life that he terms "adult minimal brain dysfunction," which appears to be responsive to amphetamines. David Olds has kindly shared with me the details of two such cases, both originally diagnosed as "chronic undifferentiated schizophrenia.'' The major signs were distractability, concreteness of thought, seclusiveness, easily provoked rage, and autistic thought productions (see Huey et al., 1978).

There is an extensive literature on sources of misdiagnosis in schizophrenia (Procci, 1976; Pope and Lipinski 1978; and Spitzer et al., 1979). A number of these sources are discussed by Dr. Stone elsewhere including the so-called schizophreniform or ''atypical'' psychoses, schizoaffective disorders, frank affective psychoses posing as ''pseudoneurotic schizophrenia,'' etc.

The Middle Phase of Treatment: The Setting of the Treatment Contract

The treatment contract is discussed extensively and elegantly by Menninger and Holtzman (1973) as it applies within a psychoanalytic context. What they have to say is of particular relevance to individuals with whom the ordinary concerns of human relatedness are already (and implicitly) understood. With schizophrenic persons, generally speaking, the less left implicit, the better. The contract as I shall present it specifically includes mutual agreements about the handling of some of the more problematical aspects of the patient's actual past experience with other people and, most particularly, with other therapists. The patient will know, more or less, a number of ways I may be hurtful to him. Our contract is a quid pro quo that, at the outset, will spell out our mutual responsibilities to each other. We get down to the concrete aspects of our relationship, usually focussing on how to avoid the predictable kinds of hurt the patient fears. Avoidance of hurt may be said to constitute the patient's motivation for entering into this contract.

The therapist, similarily, needs some kind of protection. The patient may or may not know this. If he knows it, he may fear being too open with his awareness. In experiences with other people he may have gotten into arguments about time, or money, or about the handling of phone contacts.

Early in the course of therapy the patient and I work out these basic issues. We specify how time, money, missed sessions, vacations, and the like are to be handled. We also discuss how to handle disagreements, and just which sort of disagreements are the most likely to arise. One woman patient let me know that she was likely to call me ten or more times daily. She ascribed them to mounting panic about whether or not I would go on living. She knew she was ''evil'' and had worried about causing the illness or death of her previous therapists. I made no attempt to interpret the wishful aspects of this complex, but rather focused on how such telephoning might affect me. She agreed that contact with my answering secretary might suffice during the day. For night-time reassurance we talked of a number of alternatives, finally settling on her tape-recording our sessions so that she might hear my "voice" under her control at these moments of panic. In this way, right at the outset we avoided the battle over control that had disrupted her earlier treatment (amid recriminations by her therapists about her insatiability). In my contract it was explicit that I would not answer evening phone calls under any circumstances.

The reader may wonder why so much is made of protecting the therapist. For the answer one need only look at one's colleagues to see how few manage any large number of psychotic patients, and how disproportionately stressful they feel this part of their practice to be. Many therapists treat psychotic persons in the beginning phases of their careers and then stop. Others never begin, fearing that they probably lack what they assume to be some special intuition that constitutes a minimum requirement for this work. But more often the stumbling block will concern not intuition but skill in management. Specifically, the therapist's otherwise laudable wish to be available to his patient may backfire owing to the extreme demands put on him by a "devouring" patient of this type. The therapist, trapped by his own kindliness, experiences the therapeutic encounter as a malignant one. The problem here—and one sees it again and again in work with young psychiatric residents—is in the area of limit setting; the therapist not only fails to impose proper limits on the patient but on himself as well.

It is imperative for the therapist to resist the temptation to align himself with the patient's idealizing transference (when this is present) and likewise to resist the impulse to prove himself all-loving in the face of strong negative transference. In no way can the therapist make up to the patient the losses and failures of a deprived or chaotic childhood. Fromm-Reichmann tried to help her patients realize that their symptoms were ways of dealing with current life experience in terms of a thwarted past (1950). She wanted each patient to become aware of the losses he sustained early in life, but aware of them on a realistic level. The patient must strive, that is, not to transform the losses symbolically, but to accept the fact that they can never be made up, meantime acknowledging that many gratifications are still possible to him as an adult. The concreteness of a contract can help the patient see these issues in perspective, and may be especially useful in getting the patient to recognize how hostile he often becomes when caught in intense and conflicting needs for both gratification and emotional distance.

Examples

A 26-year-old architect told me of his abrupt terminations with three previous therapists. In each case they had disagreed over some relatively minor issue. The patient, for reasons unclear to himself, would feel backed into a corner. After leaving the therapist's office he would ruminate for days on the impossibility of healing what would seem to him an irreconcilable rift. On two occasions he had simply left a message with the therapist's answering service that he was no longer going to his sessions. He had spoken by telephone with the third therapist. The patient found this call humiliating, since the therapist merely reiterated his offer that the patient come in and talk the problem over. The patient took this as a hypocritical suggestion that he come in to "eat crow."

I said that this was upsetting news, because it was my experience that disagreements between people were inevitable, I now expected that the patient would leave with me helpless to effect a reconciliation. He was amazed by the idea that a "pathetic" figure like himself could defeat a powerful man like me. I asked him to consider how I might possibly get to see him if we had a disagreement to which he reacted in the usual manner. He could think of no way, and discussed at some length his extreme carefulness in avoiding "disagreements" with clients and colleagues. He now registered some surprise as he related how this wish to avoid being cornered affected even trivial issues. He always parked his car in a parking lot, for example, to avoid parking disputes, and he was overly concerned about his place in movie lines.

In discussing the impasse I anticipated were we to continue, he suggested that a conciliatory attitude on my part might make a difference. I would be the one to "eat crow" instead of him. Earlier in his life, his father had make him proffer virtually endless apologies before allowing the patient back into the family. I indicated that I would probably feel much the way he had felt as a boy when this happened. The patient responded by talking of how there were good aspects to cultivating humility and began to discuss some of the abstract philosophical concerns with which he had been preoccupied. I brought him back to our present reality, implicitly indicating that the withdrawal into such speculation would not work any better now than it had in his adolescence. He made me aware, however, that this tendency to immerse himself in speculations had probably kept him from physically harming his father years before. We extended our work, for this reason, to include some concern for methods of handling angry feelings, though the patient, at a conscious level, had not experienced even mild irritation for more than ten years.

I suggested that the patient make a point of observing the methods other people use to resolve difficulties. I also recommended his reading some popular books on conflict strategy, on conventional behavior (Emily Post), and literary works that dealt with these themes.

A young woman with catatonic symptoms was recovering from a psychotic episode. She warned me that she was likely to become "frozen" if I answered the phone during our sessions. Nevertheless, she made it clear that if she were ever to call me from outside, even if I were with another patient, I was to pick the telephone up. I raised the question of becoming "frozen" myself, either with concern about people who could not reach me in emergencies or with anger at having someone dictate to me how my attention was to be centered.

As we discussed the matter further, two lessons were brought home to the patient. First, that alternatives existed. In her rigid view, things either *were* or *were not*. I proposed, for example, that my secretary screen calls henceforth, and ring only for urgent ones. This left her nonplussed. Second, she experienced surprise that I would actually change my routine as a result of our discussion. Her idea of treatment was that it provided "insight," which in some mysterious way changed things. The idea that changes could come about in other ways as well seemed to her preposterous. Regarding the interpersonal aspects of our situation, this patient knew the dynamics all too well, even though she would not admit the true situation for seven months. She knew she had wanted to interfere with my life, much as she had with her parents' life, to control me as she had controlled them, and to prevent me from having private aspects to my life that were not shared with her.

The simple rules of conduct we had begun to develop in the meantime went a long way toward minimizing the kind of acting-out to which she was prone.

How should the therapist deal with problems of this kind? How much should we gratify the patient's wish to be regarded unique? These are matters requiring a refined clinical judgment, depending, as they do, on our total view of the patient, on his stage of treatment, etc. Very early on in the therapeutic relationship, however, we can begin to teach the patient something about the nature of the treatment *partnership* and about the possibility of negotiation when conflicting needs are present between the two parties.

In the latter example, our hammering out a contract of mutually permissible behaviors helped to highlight the more pathological aspects of the patient's interaction, helped outline perceptual and cognitive distortions—without tacking onto the patient some pejorative label for disagreeable conduct. We begin by getting the patient to reflect on his behavior and to describe it to us with some objectivity. We get him to make a prediction about the social consequences of his usual way of doing things. We then point up, when it seems he would be receptive to hearing it, the practicality of changing his pattern. Finally, we discuss various alternatives. Most of these will seem very new to him; some, we hope, will require only minor adjustments on his part and thus will lie within his capabilities.

This deliberate structuring of the therapeutic situation, with active measures to minimize acting-out, should begin early in treatment, for the therapist's sake as well as for the patient's. With regard to the patient, our fostering more appropriate expressions (in the outside world) of his underlying conflicts helps prevent demoralization. And the social gains that will stem from his more appropriate behavior help set up a positive feedback mechanism that rewards his efforts at socialization and spurs him on to still greater efforts. The patient will, of course, experience difficulties in making such changes, and I believe there is an advantage in these difficulties: they help hold in check his tendency toward grandiose fantasies of magical transformation.

The contract negotiations also provide a model for dealing with some of the intense conflicts that arise in the midcourse of treatment. A number of these are described later on by my colleagues.

The concreteness of this experience is also useful for maintaining a balance toward reality in those therapists who experience an undue fascination with the primary-process material his schizophrenic patient makes so readily available.

The flow of talk between past and present, perceived and real, symbolized and abstract, is illustrated in the vignette with the architect. This is the conversational mode I maintain from the beginning of the treatment to its end. I concentrate on behavior and its consequences (whether it is adaptive or "functional," or whether it is self-defeating, and so on). Choosing this as our reference point helps free us from the tendency to categorize behavior as "normal" or "crazy." The patient can participate with us in the inspection of conventional behavior—as it is encountered in books and films and in everyday life—without our imposing on him some standard for "correct" behavior. The patient will be encouraged to make corrections in perception and in an evolving strategy for adaptation, where, in a similar positive feedback mechanism, refinements in the one lead to improvements in the other. We help the patient *choose* to get better, whereas often enough the important figures of his past tried, in desperation, to *force* him to get better.

The contractual mode of therapy that I have been advocating will encourage the patient to see himself as *actor* rather than merely *acted upon*. The patient will come to understand something about predictability and reciprocity in human relations. For many schizophrenic patients these concepts have never formed or solidified properly at any point in their development. Entering into "contracts" with the therapist can correct these deficiencies, the more so as learning by doing often works better than learning by talking about.

Contracts emphasize structure and attention to details. The meticulous spelling out of certain details about how therapist and patient are to get along together helps to sharpen the patient's observational skills, which are often poorly developed in schizophrenic persons. The young woman in the clinical vignette had, for example, to begin paying close attention—which she had never bothered to do before—to the time of day, since we now had rules that called for separating phone calls into day calls, night calls, office hour calls, etc. It is not as though schizophrenic individuals are inherently deficient in observational skills, incidentally; indeed, as Searles and others have observed, schizophrenics may be inordinately acute observers of certain cues and gestures. Their problem is more one of unevenness—paying too much attention to some (including socially trivial) cues and too little to others that may be more important.

7

Therapeutic Adaptations to the Cognitive Features of Schizophrenia

David V. Forrest, M.D.

Early in the course of schizophrenia, affects tend to be inaccessible. Meantime, the patient's prominent cognitive features require special understanding and adaptations of therapeutic technique. I believe that while most of us are familiar with these features (they have been extensively studied and reported in the psychiatric literature) we tend not to take the next step, which is to change our approach to schizophrenic patients accordingly. Perhaps this is because we sense that what the cognitive states of schizophrenia require of us is more than attention to what we say; it is a broader adaptation of our manner, our style, and our underlying theories and strategy of therapy. Mostly it is a case of the medium largely being the message. Because our personalities and self-presentation are that medium, we may dislike the thought of such revisions, which seem difficult and perhaps too personal in prospect. Personal analysis and preparation for intensive psychotherapy of neurotic persons, extensive as these may have been, have not usually concerned themselves with the adaptations that are necessary for schizophrenic persons. It is true, of course, that the empathic comprehension of psychological development, defense mechanisms, and psychic representation that are learned in analysis and analytic supervision provide a structure for the psychotherapy of schizophrenia, especially in the later stages.

I have compiled a list of cognitive features of schizophrenic patients along with corresponding suggestions for modifications of the therapeutic approach. I wish to emphasize that this is not to be construed as a standard profile, as there are many forms of schizophrenia and each patient is cognitively unique, perhaps to a greater degree than people in general are individual. To illustrate this point, and also for its intrinsic practical value, I would first cite Silverman's classification (1964) of schizophrenic cognition, resembling radar in its functions of scanning and field discrimination of relevant from irrelevant stimuli:

	Scanning	Field Discrimination
Acute reactive schizophrenia	Extensive	Diffuse
Acute process schizophrenia	Minimal	Diffuse
Paranoid schizophrenia	Extensive	Highly differentiated
Nonparanoid schizophrenia	Minimal	Diffuse
Normal controls	Intermediate	Differentiated

From such observations one already has a guide to the vicissitudes of scope and resolution of schizophrenic cognition that would have implications for such different aspects as the impact of the decoration of the therapist's office and the advisability or inadvisability of certain work environments in job placement.

Cognitive Features of Schizophrenia, Found in Variable Degrees in Individuals, with Suggestions for Therapy

1. PASSIVITY

Perhaps the most basic feature of schizophrenic cognition is passivity of volition, underlying such symptoms of diminished cognitive ability as thought insertion or removal, "made volition," ideas of reference and, compensatorily, ideas of influence. Many things follow from this, but the primary implication is that one's mere presence in the room may seem, to the schizophrenic person, to do violence: to violate boundaries of the self and intrude with heavy step. Not only all one's interventions, but one's personal style should also be considered from this standpoint. When tempted to be dramatic or flamboyant, perhaps to catch the attention of a diffusely distracted, seemingly sleepy patient, for example, one might recall beforehand that, for passive patients, playing possum is a frequent defense against violation. By coming on strong or being "noisy" in the informational sense, one may merely increase the need for inattention. Therapists who exercise great personal charisma, with a few exceptions, may be better suited to family or group therapy, where the attention-riveting force of their personalities may be diluted by the number of persons present. It is especially because one must so often strive to get the patient's attention that one must learn to soft-pedal oneself and not be abrasive.

2. VULNERABILITY

In a cognitive as well as affective sense, the schizophrenic person is open to being impressed, deeply changed on a moment-to-moment basis, and sometimes harmed. Related to passivity, "vulnerability" is here meant to specify the *impact* that the passively experienced stimuli have; the *depths* of penetration of the person by stimuli; the *pain* of baredness. One implication of passivity is the possibility of foisting constructions of reality and theories on the patient's pliant process, at least for a while, before all disapears in the Bermuda Triangle of his or her vagueness. Another implication is the schizophrenic person's compulsion to obey, which may take forms that are less dramatic than the instantaneous echolalia or echopraxia that we usually associate with those terms. Compelled, but not genuine (and even outraged) obedience may take the form of mocking, clowning, and bizarre twisting and parodying of the therapist's words, or carrying out treatment plans that are forced upon one in letter only and not spirit, or without an obvious ingredient. Or there may be an imitation of the therapist that seems at once touchingly childlike and embarrassingly flattering in its particularity and depth, resembling idolatry or fetishism. All attributes of the therapist are commands to be followed; the patient may resist or comply, but there will always be a degree of passive experiencing and awareness of the therapist's manner, words, style, and dress.

3. ATTENTION (OVERATTENTION AND UNDERATTENTION)

Problems in attending properly to ongoing significant events surrounding the individual are so typical of schizophrenia that the psychologist Brendan Maher (1966,1968), for one, has chosen this cognitive feature as central to his theory of schizophrenia and of schizophrenic language. The question that has been posed in a number of studies of schizophrenic attention is whether this is a static cognitive feature present across the board in schizophrenic processing of experience, or whether it is a dynamic defense more in evidence in conflictual subjects. While some studies have shown deviant processing of presumably unconflicted as well as conflicted cognitive areas, it is difficult to design experiments that remove response biases, and in view of clear evidence of evasive inattention in any given patient,[1] I would prefer to view attentional difficulties as a fundamental psychophysiological tendency that is then often used or capitalized upon.

The attentional difficulties are quite variable, as Silverman's table, previously noted, suggests. Paranoid schizophrenic patients are overattentive to selective stimuli (e.g., the grease on the doorknob has great importance and is worth dwelling on), but this is still a kind of inattention to the main configuration of significant human reality surrounding the patient. With

---

[1](See, for example, my videotape "Schizophrenic Language," ER 4 in *The Electronic Textbook of Psychiatry*, Educational Research, N.Y.S. Psychiatric Institute, N.Y., 1973)

paranoid overattention the therapist needs to explain and make safe the larger and more humanly relevant contexts that the patient is avoiding through his overly narrow focus. Also the therapist should simplify information about emotional contexts, leaving no uncertain spaces where fear and suspiciousness might arise. The need for vigilance and visibility should be respected. During my emergency room service as a first-year psychiatric resident, I had the task of interviewing a very paranoid young black woman who had said she was carrying a knife in the pocketbook she clutched. A patrolman stood nearby to protect me. The decision *not* to try to remove the pocketbook was a marvel of practical empathy on his part. Meantime, I had yet to benefit from the then-still-unwritten experience of Kinzel (1971) with violent prisoners who needed to carry a knife to *avoid* becoming violent. The patient began to tell me of her fears that someone had been tampering with the electricity in the walls of her home. It was beginning to happen here at the hospital too, she said, and almost as soon as she had said that, the lights in the examination room indeed seemed to flicker. "I told you!" she said, and a moment later, the lights went out in earnest. The patrolman was gone from the door, and outside there was chaos, with the sounds of people running back and forth. We didn't know it yet, but it was the night of the great Northeastern blackout of 1965. The patient repeated, more shrilly, "I told you!" and I remembered her and the knife. A hospital guard happened to come by with a flashlight. I called to him, "In here!" and grabbed his flashlight, illuminating the girl's terrified face to show him the problem. He left the light with me and I had to decide whether to shine it at her face, effectively blinding an anxious paranoid, or at her purse, possibly focussing her attention on the knife. But the solution in psychiatry lies always in empathy, and it occurred to me that she would most of all want to reassure herself visually. So I gave *her* the flashlight, which she held with both hands straight at my face until the low light of the auxiliary power supply came on. I regained considerable composure myself, since I could see that she was occupied with the flashlight rather than with the knife.

In the less perceptual, more cognitive realm of language, the patient should not be faced with communicative unclarity on the part of the therapist, which is analogous to poor visibility in being threatening. Unclear therapists might preferably work in the burgeoning field of psychopolitics, not treating paranoid schizophrenia.

The more disorganized acute schizophrenic patient, often anxious but not focally wary, is aided by simplification of a concrete sort and, as Arieti (1955) had pointed out in his first edition of *Interpretation of Schizophrenia*, is desperately in search of signposts. In one case a young woman had lost all sense of will and felt there was nothing in the world she knew for sure. I found it helpful to begin in a gentle way to suggest she name colors around us in the room. It was diagnostic of her schizophrenic cognitive state that she did not smile or hesitate in beginning to do so.

As part of the difficulty with attention, we might include one of Norman Cameron's (1944) four features of schizophrenic language, *overinclusion* (the others, *metonymy, asyndesis* and *interpenetration of fantasy*, will be subsumed under other headings). One might argue whether the overinclusive categorizations to which schizophrenic persons are prone originate in ''primitive'' undifferentiated perception, but the result is this: signals become confused with noise, the irrelevant and the relevant are commingled, as are the nonhuman and human emotional contexts (the person of the therapist included among the latter). To a greater extent than in most people, schizophrenic persons see the therapist as imbedded in his style, clothing, office furnishings, etc., and may give as much attention to these appurtenances as to the therapist's personality, which is harder for them to grasp and, at the same time, more difficult for them to free up and perceive separately from other categories of perception. Overinclusion also ''dirties'' the line of thought and language with other matter, clutters the spaces for feelings and attitudes. But the therapist ought not to be so negative about the overinclusions as this. A clean, pure line of linear reasoning is a modern Aristotelian concept and we may rely on cultural and historical relativity for an alternative view of a more reticulated form of pretechnological thought.

We might consider that while we use language in many useful ways, the schizophrenic person also uses language in different, but natural, ways.

With our Western approach to thinking as linear, cause-and-effect sequences that proceed by Aristotelian logic, we have become conditioned to ignore the more netlike, simultaneous processes that are most natural to our brain function and differ from the processes of computers, according to Von Neumann in his book, *The Computer and the Brain* (1958). In parallel with the logical sequences of word-symbols are the rich associations provided by our languages: The metaphorical images attached to words, the sounds of the words, and the many fail-safe redundancies that we layer on to get a message across emphatically.

The most socialized individuals in our society—which in a technology means to be in harmony with technical and mechanical things, and would include such folk as astronauts, pilots, engineers, and neurologists, with their checklists and procedures—are the most sequential in their disciplined, linear thought trains.

Those who have escaped socialization through improper exposure or incapacity such as some schizophrenic persons, or the young child learning a language and who is as yet unsocialized, are most free to reticulate.

Still others, such as poets, who explore these sidewise slipperinesses and stickinesses in language, tend to be in low repute in technological societies and poorly paid, if at all, whereas in pretechnological societies the poet may be among the most esteemed. In medieval times the poet was given the choicest cuts of meat and sat by the side of the king; the linear historian got the foulest cut and sat farthest away.

Diffusion of attention, while roughly descriptive, is too simple a concept to explain the broad reticulated swath (or holographic waves, to borrow Pribram's description [1971] of cortical processes) of schizophrenic thought. If we consider there to be a first tier of human meaning, the target of sequential logical operations, and a series of from 2nd to nth concentric peripheral tiers of associated images, sounds, synonyms and partially relevant concepts and perceptions, then we can list a series of processes that may interfere with the first-tier targeting by pushing or repelling away from it:

A. Aphasia, especially anomia
B. Recall impairment; short-term memory loss
C. Attention diffusion (e.g., from anxiety)
D. Conflict; the need to confound oneself

A and B are usually not problems in scizophrenia.

There are also processes that are conducive or attractive to the 2nd to nth tiers of peripheral association:

A. Exploiting of 2nd to nth imprecision

   (1) Need to disappoint or to confound the auditor, or to drive him or her crazy (Bateson et al., 1956; Searles, 1965)

   (2) Need to elevate and remove oneself from ordinary meanings, to express scorn, be obscure or mysterious, or keep expectation at bay (as was said of the surrealist painter Max Ernst)

B. Recruitment of 2nd-tier resources

   (1) Need to reinforce first-tier meaning and import (normal and abnormal rhetoric)

   (2) Need to overcome the conclusions of first tier (poiesis) (Forrest, 1965) (see Chapter 17)

Awareness of the complexity and simultaneity of such processes can aid the therapist in gauging the trends and the degree of intentionality of schizophrenic patients' thought and their choices of language to convey it.

The therapist will, despite all, tend to be the one who keeps track of the direction, if not line, of thought; but in so doing he may choose to regard and include the more illuminating "irrelevancies" as proper embellishments or metaphors that are just unidentified, as Bateson described them. A plodding, literal following of the patient's words would be misleading because of this, but so would an exclusively "transparent" analysis based on *seeing through* the manifest level of words and references to the grand structures and configurations above. To a greater extent the meaning is skin-deep in schizophrenic persons, as their "skin" is so thin and revelatory. Even where the underlying psychodynamic structures seem to loom obvious, the patient can seldom embrace them with affective ownership.

4. DISORIENTATION

The absence of confusion and delirium in most cases weighs toward schizophrenia in differential diagnosis, though there are exceptions to this and some acute cases may look quite "organic" for a while in terms of cortical dysfunction. Also, many schizophrenic patients may have stable cognitive disabilities such as learning deficits and may inhabit the more "neurological" end of the spectrum of schizophrenia, with soft neurological signs. So it is important to allow for degrees of disorientation that are subtler than the gross disorientation to time, place, and person that is more frequent in cortical disease and delirium. As a correlative to difficultes with rod-and-frame orientation tasks, schizophrenic persons may seem to lack fixed axes for their mental viewfinder or a gyroscope with which to navigate; they may seem to have the mental analogue of astasia-abasia; i.e., a disorder of finding the upright in all manner of behavior.

I choose metaphors because so much of the difficulty is cognitively elaborated rather than of such primary origin as actual difficulties of balance. I think of Nijinsky in this regard, and of a profoundly schizophrenic young man who frequently had difficulty orienting himself to situations, who yet would be found standing on one hand on the edge of the coffee table in the patients' lounge. One patient in my videotape, "Schizophrenic Language," (op. cit.) illustrates schizophrenic disorientation as he enters the room to be interviewed by Dr. Robert Spitzer. Manifesting extensive scanning and diffuse field articulation (as well as overinclusion later in the same interview), he does not head for the obvious target of the two chairs and microphone, and instead winds up part of the way across the room until directed to the chair. On sitting down he "discovers" the floor below and asks, "Where did you get this rug?" It is not orientation to up and down that he needs, but orientation to the interview situation, which Dr. Spitzer, uninterested in rugs, readily provides. But we are thereby forewarned of his needs for our anxiety-relieving directions as to what we are about. A useful rule is to avoid indirection in what we say to schizophrenic persons. We may introduce themes with topic sentences, much as we learned to do in the beginning of paragraphs in freshman composition, and we may profitably summarize at the end. Speaking in Basic English is best, but the goal is clarity, not harshness, bluntness, or lack of tact. Furthermore, the "topic sentence" should serve a parenthetic function, as it provides a boundary between our statements and the often amorphous soup of the rest of existence for the schizophrenic person. We should not say, for example, "It seems you blame your parents a lot," but rather, "I want to talk with you about how you blame your parents."

5. NEOPHOBIA

Neophobia and the next four features (segmentalization, probabilistic incapacity, de-automatization, and poor habituation) are emphasized by David Shakow (1967), whose valuable papers on the psychology of schizophrenia warrant clinical application in the psychotherapy of most schizophrenic persons. "Intolerance of novelty and change" would probably be a better term than "neophobia" for this schizophrenic feature of inelasticity of adaptation. Practically it amounts to our avoiding underestimating the impact of any contemplated change upon the schizophrenic person and our helping him to take his "neophobia" into account also. In my experience, few schizophrenic patients have observed about themselves that the first few days in a new work situation are much worse for them than subsequently, or that the first minutes in an unfamiliar room are accompanied by anxiety and some disorganization. Perhaps it is their tendency not to integrate the preadapted and postadapted experiences into a whole (see Segmentalization below), or a more general lack of self observation in various situations. But the result is that much of what appears to be panphobia and avoidance is based on the fear of facing novelty and mastering new situations. Perceiving time and sequences in fragments, the schizophrenic person sees the initial anxiety as permanent and reacts appropriately to this erroneous conceptualization. The therapist can help by explaining this tendency to the patient (always as an individual trait, never categorizing the patient; i.e., not "All schizophrenic patients have this," but "Have you noticed about yourself that it's easy to underestimate your ability at first in a new situation, compared to a little later when things fall into place?"). I am fond of teaching them a form of passive relaxation that I find is well accepted, encouraging them to put off worrying about being confused because anxiety makes it worse and relief is coming soon. I use the Chinese proverb from the *Tao Te Ching*: "When the water is roiled and muddy, the unwise man struggles in vain to separate mud from clear water; the wise man merely waits for the sediment to settle." In this and all use of metaphor, the patient must have regained metaphorical capacity (see below) or the point will be lost and one will truly be muddying the waters of therapy.

The therapist should describe neophobia in his patient according to its manifestations in the microcosm of the consulting room, pointing out for example that the patient probably felt more uncomfortable about the therapist (and the room) at first and may have had some first impressions that were discarded later. One hopes that this principle may then be applied and learned on the larger scale of adaptation to the initial phases of new social and occupational challenges.

Neophobia dictates the pace at which the therapist should let things happen in therapy, insofar as they can be under control.

This would include allowing for a latency period between assisted adaptations to social realities: advance warning in regard to changes in hours or days of appointment, therapist's vacations and conventions, daylight savings time, and redecoration of the office. (Raising the fee, however, often has little impact as schizophrenic patients are subfinancial in their orientation, much as they are subsocial and subpolitical.) If there is a possibility that the therapist might miss an appointment (for example, if the therapist commutes to the office and the appointment is an early one), specific instructions should be provided for this contingency. I tell the patient to wait 15 minutes (as far as I would wish to wait unexpectedly) and to go get coffee and a paper. The idea is to provide a specific replacement for oneself, much as one provides another psychiatrist in one's absence and has the patient meet the covering doctor well in advance of one's departure.

A corollary of neophobia is the proper handling of what one might describe as *tests of surprise*. While most patients test their therapists to see, in an unguarded moment, the therapist's spontaneous reaction to what troubles them, schizophrenic patients seem to do this more regularly and severely. Often they do so with an uncanny depth that in all likelihood reflects the ease of escape of their mental contents. Thus the proper reaction is not to reply in kind by trying to top the patient with a rapid comeback or startling witticism; it is not a competition, however much one may be put off balance; it's a test the patient wants one to pass. One memorable test of surprise from a quite paranoid man with much affective blockade occurred when he came into the office one day with a portable record player, which he plugged in and played a Beethoven symphony at top volume while reading passages from his diaries. My job was clearly not to react; he was much relieved that I did not and specifically said he now felt I could help him. In some ways, in addition to testing my reaction to surprise, he seemed to be testing my reaction to input overload. *Vulnerability to overload* could be considered a separate cognitive feature of schizophrenia but I feel it is most useful to include it under neophobia and encourage the therapist to tease out the new elements in the input and help the patient the better to specify factors that will ameliorate with time. Intolerance of confusing, noisy surroundings with many simultaneous activities tends to be a persistent difficulty—not surprisingly so, in view of such other features as diffuse attention, slow habituation, and abnormalities of integration.

Finally, neophobia leads both to overestimation of the patient's pathology at the beginning of treatment at a time when the patient is adapting to the therapist, and to underestimation at the termination (or phasing out, as few schizophrenic patients should be abruptly terminated). The latter is true because the patient becomes so well accommodated to the therapist that one may fail to realize the neophobic difficulties that would still appear in future interpersonal situations.

6. SEGMENTALIZATION

Instead of integrated perceptions, thoughts, emotions, gestures, and actions, schizophrenic persons experience and enact these totalities piecemeal or, as Shakow puts it, they have difficulty in maintaining major psychological sets. Instead, they *segmentalize*. Often they omit a crucial component or step so that they do not realize the totality, either through inability or defensive avoidance. Psychotherapy of schizophrenia demands great skill in synthesizing from fragments, akin to paleontological reconstruction or code breaking. There is not always the redundancy and great overdetermination of neurotic mental products; often one seems to have pieces not of the same, but of an endless succession of different puzzles.

In one's interventions, too, one must spell out complex interactions into component parts—a knack one may acquire, perhaps analogously to the way one simplifies syntax in conversing with a person not fluent in English. A simplified presentation of components in sequence can also become automatic in the empathic therapist with experience.

As schizophrenia often first manifests itself in high school and college-age students, there are many opportunities to be helpful in organizing work. Segmentalization can be a defensive operation, an ordering of chaotic experience, and the schizophrenic student may be helped not only to perceive wholes, but to subdivide work into manageable parts. For example, in examination periods, we help him concentrate only on the next exam in the exam period. Schizophrenic students are the last to learn to use college outline books as study aid and become lost in the volume of assignments; they have trouble paying attention to lectures and "psyching out" exam questions from the professors' lectures. Poor relations with other students make the sharing of lecture notes difficult and, withal, the schizophrenic students have difficulty discerning the main important point in a given topic. They often have no difficulty conveying the links and transitions between their ideas, a feature of schizophrenic language that Cameron called "asyndesis." In these situations I become actively involved in discussing schoolwork, especially where a more unstructured assignment allows the mental processes more free play to manifest themselves.

7. PROBABILISTIC INCAPACITY

A poor ability to evaluate the statistical or common-sensical likelihood of events is characteristic of schizophrenia and seems all the more pronounced in paranoids, standing out in sharp contrast with their logical facility (the problem being premises). Nonparanoid schizophrenic persons have trouble too, but it is more difficult to see against the background of their generally more vague misapprehension. Probabilistic incapacity occurs especially, as might be expected, when evaluating *human* behavior. But it is not limited to human intentionality, perhaps because so much of the nonhuman environment is perceived projectively—as having conscious purpose, according to the stage of reasoning that Piaget (1930) called "animistic" in young children. It may do little good to point out the astronomical improbability of the patients' ideas of reference, but it is worth bringing up the idea of statistical evaluation in the brighter patients to help them doubt their worst fears. One especially intelligent paranoid patient turned the whole argument around, saying, "It is the very astronomical improbability that all these books, magazines and television programs would be referring to me that *convinces* me that there is a huge plot. It is flattering, but I am puzzled why I should be singled out for such special attention."

Another patient, suspecting his therapist was linked to the CIA, wished to find another therapist to cover for him during a vacation. As a precaution the patient saw a new internist and obtained a new referral for the purpose of randomizing the selection of a covering doctor (to guard against more unwanted CIA influence). Ironically, had the patient asked the new psychiatrist directly, he would have found that this doctor and his usual doctor were quite closely associated in their hospital work (I am indebted to Dr. Ira Silverstein for the anecdote)!

In regard to paranoid fears, I find it useful, as with phobic fears, to assure the patient that events will, for all practical purposes, not happen. This simplifies the set of probabilities with which the patient is struggling—especially when the event in question is, in my estimation, outlandishly unlikely. The patients tend to offer exceptions and complicated rationalizations to argue why they can't be sure; nevertheless, they also are comforted. One must recall in therapy that one is dealing with emotional reality first and foremost. One ought not to care whether one is "right" or not as long as one makes emotional headway. All therapists are called upon to offer *plausible closure* at times to reassure sicker patients.

8. DE-AUTOMATIZATION

Akin to segmentalization, this fittingly awkward term denotes the breakdown of previously automatic, integrated social actions into awkward remnants. As one patient remarked (on the "Schizophrenic Language" videotape previously mentioned), "just saying 'hello' became a major problem." One may learn to marvel at the complexity of an ordinary greeting upon learning the ways in which a schizophrenic person can fail to bring it off (or succeed in not bringing it off, if such capitalizing on de-automatization is the case). De-automatization is more properly a lack of coordination of the expressive and emotional significances of actions rather than any soft sign of motor incoordination, and does not gainsay the presence of physical grace. The young male patient who walked like a mechanical soldier had conflicts that led to a simultaneous obeying and mocking of parental directives to "straighten up and be a soldier" about things.

The therapist will have many occasions to be tolerant of de-automatization and to aid the patient to reassemble, or in many cases assemble himself for the first time—if rearing or schizophrenic inattentiveness has led to missing instructions in the assembly kit of the self. Much modeling may be done, and practice on the order of aphasia rehabilitation, which I see as a fruitful analogy if one is willing to see schizophrenia as an emotional aphasia (more on this later). When modeling social actions for schizophrenic patients, one must act out sequences slowly and (one would hope) appropriately.

9. SLOW HABITUATION AND EXTINCTION

Whether out of disorganizing degrees of anxiety or out of inattentiveness to specific cues, schizophrenic persons acquire slowly and incompletely the most common normal mental mechanism for dealing with the incessant anxieties, challenges, and choices of life. Here I refer to *habituation,* or the acquisition of habitual modes, the standard operating procedures of everyday lives, that permit us to place ourselves on "automatic pilot," for example, after we have driven a few times to a new work location. The schizophrenic person, in the lab or in life, does not readily adapt to new stimuli and continues to react as though they were fresh intrusions. Reactions are not as readily extinguished as in normal persons, when the stimulus is removed. This "inertia" can be explained to the patient.

The implication for therapy is the need for patience and a willingness to repeat all interventions and corrective emotional interactions, at times seemingly endlessly. The need for repetition can be decreased, as in all therapeutic work, by careful attention to whether the window of receptiveness (to borrow a term from the launching of space vehicles) is open.

10. METAPHORICAL INCAPACITY

Schizophrenic persons often have difficulty with metaphor. They do not only miss the point by interpreting the metaphor concretely, they may also miss the point by being overly abstract and overgeneralizing beyond the immediate interpersonal situation that is the referent of the metaphor (the *metaphicand*). They also get involved in the literal details because these are safer than constructs about human emotional reality. I have reviewed the problems with metaphor elsewhere (Forrest, 1969a and 1976) and Searles has written movingly about experiencing with a patient the regaining of a metaphorical capacity previously lost (1965, p. 560ff).

One must consider the degree of metaphorical capacity in all that one says to schizophrenic patients. Even then one is likely to be misinterpreted frequently. A good example is the young man, who, when I used the metaphor of a woman he had a distant crush on as "looming (in his great isolation) as the only mountain to climb," responded by going off on a tangent about a camping and boating trip with kayaks. Yet the transition from mountain climbing to boating trips was typically not totally irrelevant—no schizophrenic association approaches total randomness—he had gone on the kayak trip "with a guy" for purposes of "killing time" and "escapism" but said he couldn't "appreciate being with a guy—a void has to be filled." But the example illustrates the perils (in terms of distracting and derailing the patient) of metaphorical excess on the part of the therapist. The more the manifest content of the metaphor attracts attention to itself, the more difficulty the schizophrenic patient will have integrating the metaphor into a human context or subordinating the metaphor to its meaning.

Rarely one may be able to fight fire with fire, and answer metaphorical concreteness with more metaphorical concreteness. A youngish man of great but incompletely integrated technical and philosophic knowledge produced complex manuscripts with advanced mathematical formulas to explain problems of emotion and perception, and was greatly concerned with the vulnerability of the brain to toxic agents and electromagnetic irradiation. Although my contact with him was marginal (he would occasionally show up without appointments at a neurological clinic at which I consulted), I established a relationship based on my accepting and reading his work. One day I photocopied the first page of an old article by Abel Lajtha entitled "The Brain Barrier System" and gave it to him, saying, "The brain is protected, even though our feelings may be vulnerable." Although he correctly pointed out that the blood-brain barrier was variable, he seemed to appreciate my interest and to derive some emotional reassurance, which was the thrust of my gesture.[2] I do not generally recommend this technique for more paranoid patients unless there is a very good rapport, as it is easy to miss the mark and introduce material that makes the patient feel you are poking fun or not taking the schizophrenic productions seriously. Patients are prone to feel thus anyway, as they often have remnants of insight that permit them to doubt the import of their productions and suspect that they are indeed defensive mazes they have constructed around their own feelings.

Schoolwork, as mentioned earlier, frequently provides a playing field of metaphorical language on which to practice with the patient and be of help, particularly in eliminating overinclusive ramifications of metaphorical reference.

The undesirable metaphorical proliferation that a glib schizophrenic patient may associate to the names of medication should also be considered. I once polled a group of hospitalized adolescents and young adults and was astonished to find what they thought the names of their medications might represent. Stelazine ®, for example, frequently reminded patients of the stegasaurus or other dinosaurs, although Mellaril ® sounded "nice" to one young woman taking it, who confessed that she "used to play with words," to categorize everyone as alligators or crocodiles, and also every word by its sound. "Alligators" included more diffuse and scattered people with small and isolated features on their faces, and also included words such as birds, trees, sails, and lids, all of which had a short "i" in them; whereas "crocodiles" included solid and whole people with round eyes and words that are full, such as bananas, frogs, shoes (maybe not shoes; yes, shoes), clouds, moon, and turtle. I quote this example partly as excess of metaphorical extension and partly to demonstrate the plausible, artistic flavor in much schizophrenic metaphor. I think any poet would agree there is something to the patient's classifications by sounds and her synesthetic association of small and isolated versus round and full features. But what can be made to work in poetry will not necessarily pass for general communication.

To return to medications, the importance of what I. A. Richards used to call the "image-bodies" of words (in *Science and Poetry*), as idiosyncratically elaborated by schizophrenic persons, is that their somewhat weaker self-concept (also to some extent a metaphor, as argued by Julian Jaynes, 1976) is more forcefully affected by the addition of a new outside entity with an unfamiliar name than the average person's would be. One is adding a defi-

[2]Elliott, Page, and Quastel, *Neurochemistry.* 2nd ed. Springfield, Ill., C. C. Thomas, 1962, ch. 18, p. 399ff.

nite entity to a more than usually indefinite entity, and the impact is greater, particularly when the schizophrenic individual experiences the taking of a drug as the literal incorporation of the metaphorical associations to its name. I have even chosen drugs on this basis, where I had no other particular rationale in choosing between roughly equivalent congeners, and I have switched to generic prescribing where the nonproprietary name had less disturbing "vibes" for a particular patient.

11. IDIOSYNCRASY

Many names could be applied to the one-of-a kind features of each schizophrenic person's cognition, from Bleuler's autism to a more-than-British eccentricity, a more-than-Yankee individualism, or a more-than-artistic originality. Solipsism may be an appropriate description. Even though certain persecutory themes may attain a certain currency in a given time (e.g., the CIA or the Mafia are now more current than the Communists), close acquaintance with the patient reveals a more specific oddity. Dealing with this requires not so much a series of techniques as it does an attitude of acceptance of differences. A therapist for schizophrenic persons ought or perhaps has to offer appreciation, imagination, and tolerance of a broader spectrum of possibilities of being human than an acquaintance with most other categories of people would demand. Part of this idiosyncrasy may derive from *process*, from the unique constellation of these cognitive features in each schizophrenic individual. But the *content* of thinking lends the most original flavor to every schizophrenic person. Certainly a tolerance, if not a fondness, for unconventionality will aid the therapist in maintaining sympathetic interest; a rigid dedication to unconventionality may stand in the way of helping the patient to participate more in conventional and communal life. Some schizophrenic patients are more like "conformists manqué" anyway, desperately wanting to be like everyone else and, with therapeutic assistance, making a fetish of conforming (thereby remaining deviant). But most, in my experience, however aware they may become of the sadness and loneliness to which their "being different" relegates them, nonetheless have a strong allegiance to their differentness.

12. INTERPENETRATION OF FANTASY

"Interpenetration of fantasy" is Cameron's term for a feature of schizophrenic language that reflects the multilevelled cognitive-emotional process. Since language is largely sequential and linear, aside from its more poetic dimensions of sound and metaphor, it must represent multiple levels by interrupting itself. Discrepant facial affects could be considered an interruption from another channel of expression, but gesture cannot render story (try a TV newscast without the sound), and the basis of all complex human motivation is fantasy. Thus, much of what seems interruption because of inattention is simply attention to other levels than the one on the surface—the schizophrenic person having greater access, willy-nilly, to these levels. One patient, an unmarried man in his early thirties, still living with his parents but desirous of overcoming his difficulties with socialization, could not make small talk (a common failing among schizophrenics). This was not, as one may imagine, abetted by his reading Descartes each evening. As I often do, I prescribed *The National Enquirer* and *People* as a source of material for small talk and what is called by linguists the "phatic" level of communication (maintaining social relations and emotional bonds rather than conveying information). Leafing through a *People* magazine he had just bought, the patient said, "I like all these pretty girls, Stay-Free Minipads, this woman reporter looks nice." "Stay-Free Minipads?" I inquired. He flipped back and turned the page around to show me he had been looking at the girls featured in the ad for the feminine hygiene pad; the overinclusiveness here represents the interpenetration of sexual fantasies into speech and failure to exclude them. He also selected for small talk an article in *People* on the dangers of escaping propane gas in the event of train wrecks. Later I had encouraged him to join the congregation of some church, again a standard procedure of mine for the second phase of treatment, as I shall discuss later. He negotiated this well, and was invited to small-group Bible study classes at the home of a devout and evangelical married woman in her early forties, about the age of the patient's mother, with whom he still lived. He developed a deep crush on her, and discussed this in treatment as unrealistic in view of her devotion to her husband, family, and religion. Yet the fantasy helped orient him toward a better self presentation, and I encouraged him to view it as a *bridging fantasy* until he could find a woman of his own. He accepted this, but upon the happy event of his obtaining a job, he impulsively called her up and asked her to live with him. The woman, understandably appalled that anyone could so misunderstand her passion for religion, rejected his advances. He called me up to report that "Life is harder than I thought." Needless to say, the therapist cannot try to stamp out all fantasy, as fantasy is trial emotion and trial action, but the patient may be helped to stay on his bridges and not leap off them.

13. Inconstancy of Object Identification

Drawing both from Piagetian developmental psychology and object-relations analysis, this concept and the phenomena it describes remind us that the patient may have difficulties perceiving us as the same individual if we are not rather constant and predictable in our self presentations. Wide variations in dress, style of hair and facial hair, and moodiness on the part of the therapist disturb the patient's fragile integration of various experiences with the therapist into a single person and one who can be trusted. The patient has difficulty anyway, because of the inner state of inconstancy of cognitive and affective benchmarks.

8

Procedural Matters in the Therapy of Schizophrenics

David V. Forrest, M.D.

Early Work on the Latency Phase

Almost all schizophrenics have serious problems corresponding to the life tasks ordinarily associated with, and mastered during, the so-called latency phase. This would appear to be true even to a greater extent than is the case for the schizophrenic's "adolescent phase" problems—which have nevertheless received more attention. While it is true that many schizophrenics have great trouble managing the heightened intensity of pubescent drives and manifest strong conflicts of identity around this time, the typical late-adolescent onset of overt schizophrenia is more often, on the psychological plane, a crisis of separation from the family. Associated with this is the inability, so commonly encountered in schizophrenia, to envision life as an independent adult, as a partner in forming a new family or as a worker cooperating with fellow workers.

But peer relations, being one of the gang, competing, relating to others on the same level, or *looking others in the eye,* which is the facial gestural counterpart of directness and consensuality of equals—have been impaired almost without exception in my schizophrenic patients.

This is not to say that schizophrenia is a disorder of latency alone or that earlier problems with self and others are not the preexisting substrate for latency-level disturbances; but it is surely a fallacy to think that one must begin therapy with the earliest and hypothetically causal phases of development. This would be to peel the onion from the inside out, even to assume that the core of the fruit will provide the most rewarding meat.

The underemphasis of latency problems would seem to me to be evident in Ping-Nie Pao's description of his classification of schizophrenic patients according to their developmental record. Pao, who was director of psychotherapy at Chestnut Lodge, describes his subtype schizophrenia I as those who do not become psychotic until their late teens, when they are faced with the final steps of the second separation-individuation process; schizophrenia II are those whose symptoms appear in mid-adolescence after a "relatively uneventful" latency, but who have had a more disturbed infancy and a childhood with developmental lags. Schizophrenia III are those who "may flourish during latency" but who had a very disturbed infancy and childhood, and whose symptoms appear at "the slightest drive intensification" at the "dawn of puberty."

Type IV (which Bertrand Russell would have called another Logical Type), is a type I, II, or III who has been repeatedly or long hospitalized and who is resigned to sickness as a way of life (but whose prognosis is "not always poor").

The subtypes are defined so that early pathology and an earlier onset of psychosis in adolescence equal more severe pathology, assumptions of psychoanalysis that eminently lend themselves to testing. Prospective data from studies of children at risk are likely to clarify this assumption.

My own feeling about such a classification is that I would not say a schizophrenic patient had "flourished" in latency or had negotiated that stage well merely because the psychosis was not overt symptomatically. If an individual cannot deal with peers and remains monistic (or Momistic) about object relations (whether symptomatically schizophrenic or severely phobic), then there surely were not green signals by which to "highball" through latency.

Thus I find it strangely put, and somewhat to ignore the interpersonal dimension, when Pao says that:

> No matter how badly they were traumatized, most adult schizophrenics seem to have been clinically asymptomatic during latency. The absence of symptoms does not mean that an active process was not covertly operating, e.g., the person might have been overburdened by guilt feelings, unable to identify with his father, unable to enter peer relations comfortably, etc. But it does mean that he successfully kept his conflict in check — so successfully that he had enough energy left to develop some new skills, including the concrete operations type of thinking.

It has seemed to me, in fact, that the presence of latency pathology in schizophrenia has not been sufficiently appreciated in our psychoanalytic formulations. The symptoms that only appear in adolescence can be seen as betraying a specific failure in the capacity for peer relations and the establishment of consensual validation by peers, or in other words, a failed main task of latency.

Furthermore I have grown increasingly convinced of the difficulty of getting the patient to relinquish the cherished monistic theories about his own pathogenesis when he continues to live them out as the satellite of his mother or of, yes, the therapist. Until he has the choice of at least a semblance of peer-level relatedness, he is unlikely to budge. The same is true to a lesser extent of depressives.

Other cognitive features of latency (see Sarnoff's book, *Latency*) with which schizophrenic patients have difficulty are abiding by rules (subsuming motivations to social contracts) and sharing of conventional fantasies (around which individuals organize into cultures).

The Several Levels of Speaking Attitudes that Coexist in the Treatment of the Schizophrenic Patient and Family

Seldom recognized in the treatment planning is the fact that a recovering patient may need to be angry with and rather censorious toward the parents as a first approach to his problems of autonomous functioning and differentiation of the personality. This is akin to the initial oppositional phase of child development. Parents will of course experience it as ''not fair.''

The treating doctors may erroneously overidentify with this emotional attitude in their desire to find and extirpate the ''cause'' of the patient's illness. But imagos, the archaic representations of the parents in one's mind, can never be extirpated. They may be seen in a new light, but the priority of early experience in psychological layering assures that they will be retained in some form. Doctors nonetheless wish to annihilate pathogens. As such the parents become specimens scrutinized for their peculiarities and abnormalities, and these may rather uncritically and pejoratively be taken as the cause of the problems or as contributory to them. This would be acceptable as a speculative hypothesis for exploration, if the ''witness'' were not led and if the process of pathologic influence were conceptualized according to developmental stages (rather than in some simple model such as a template or die). All too often the patient is coaxed, as he experiences these transient hostile attitudes, into an enduring resentment toward the parents. This is compounded of projected self-blame, dependency, and delegated omnipotence. Such an attitude, if unduly prolonged, helps no one, is cruelly unfair to the parents, and inconsistent with the patient's real situation, in the majority of cases, of being largely or totally dependent on them for financial and personal support.

Meanwhile the parents must sustain the liability of sharing and enacting their children's conflicts. In any case the parents, just like our patients, are the product of their own rearing, traumata, and socioeconomic factors, and deserve the same consideration as the patient—perhaps even more when their potential guilt about contributing to their child's psychosis is taken into account. And from a purely practical standpoint they can, if their feelings are ignored, undermine the treatment at will or even take the patient away if they are too hurt. Therapy, like politics, is an art of the possible.

These then, are some levels of attitudes that may coexist:

1. *The scientific attitude*—suspicious, tentative, hypothetical—in which the parents are scrutinized for any possible pathology or pathogenic motives. This attitude is heuristic only, and may, in the case of a hospitalized patient, be expressed conditionally among the staff, but it should not develop into an air of conspiracy about the parents.

2. *The patient's early attitude* of anger at the parents, a projective, oppositional, autonomy-anger necessary for the maintenance of a poorly differentiated sense of ego separateness at a time when his object relatedness is characterized by cardboard stereotyping, splitting, black and white thinking, and Manichaean dichotomization.

3. *The patient's more mature attitude,* associated with recovery but present to some degree all along, of ownership of the pathology and forgiveness of all, including the self, for having been a party to the illness. This is based on the growing ability to understand the parents' imbeddedness in their own determining factors, while maintaining toward them an attitude of empathy and consideration; or any approximation or way station to this. By virtue of being a generation younger, the patient generally has greater future opportunities for growth and change than the parents. We should encourage him to stop longing to change his parents via some alloplastic (rather than autoplastic) solution. All theorizing and reconstruction of parent-child relations tends to hold back developing peer relatedness.

4. *The physician's attitude* of nonjudgmental appreciation of pathology and the ways of aiding the patient and family to strive for better health. This attitude should be transmitted to both patient and parents at all times. The patient may be "helped to be angry" if this fosters the emergence of the person, but the doctor should at no time convey personal anger or judgment. The doctor should instead stand for the

eventual understanding of the parents (and their representations within the patient) and take the position that, while anger is permissible, undying hatred is more poisonous to the bearer than to his enemy and, in any case, forgiveness is the most mature and nondefensive outcome to be wished for. They may be vivid characters in the patient's mind, but not unlovable in any final sense.

A FURTHER WORD ON DEALING WITH THE FAMILY

The family will prefer any approach or theory that exempts them from the terrible burden of guilt that they may have caused or contributed to their child's schizophrenia. One of the most useful contributions to the understanding of parental guilt comes to us from work with the families of children with terminal cancer. In such situations, unbearably sad in the present day because of the smallness of families and because of medical triumphs over infectious diseases that in our grandparents' day made the loss of children a common event (though still sad), it has been found that the parents regularly feel *guilty* about their child developing cancer, even though there was, of course, nothing that they could have done to prevent it. The American attitude has been that parents take total responsibility for their children's welfare even to the extent of ensuring success in adulthood and happiness in marriage. Mere ills of the flesh are just problems to be surmounted. This guilt is not based on the classical psychodynamic of ambivalent rage at the child, appearing after the child's death, but rather as failure in what is perceived by both parents and child to be the normal social contract (something akin to the "implied warranty" we come to expect from manufacturers of automobiles and radios). In several years' experience developing a course on American societal institutions, both explicit and implicit, for foreign-born psychiatric residents from a number of countries, I found the American concept of *unqualified* responsibility for the welfare of one's children most difficult to convey to my incredulous classes of foreign-born doctors, who puzzled over our propensity to guilt in situations where obviously nothing could have been done. I gained the impression that the American concept of parental responsibility is perhaps the most extreme in the "civilized" world as represented by my class, which was a veritable United Nations in miniature. One of the advantages of talking with foreign people is that one slowly gains a perspective on one's own culture and, in this respect, I began to look at unqualified parental responsibility as both encouraging higher and higher standards of child care and also promoting a steady state of overabundant guilt. As world child-rearing standards go, ours constitute cruel and unusual punishment to the parents. Part of the dropping birthrate among our most educated and (in the anthropological sense) socialized potential parents may be the successful incorporation of this extremely demanding standard and the refusal to face it, or to face it so many times. The news from the psychiatrist that one's daughter or son is schizophrenic should be examined against the backdrop of this social expectancy. Generations of psychoanalytic and family theorists have found the parents of schizophrenic patients so willing to assume the burden of guilt that excesses in blaming them have been easy to fall into. Those parents who deny their complicity and seek purely biological explanations are often, in my experience, the parents with the most severe and unassimilable guilt, which does not prove complicity in pathogenesis, but is suggestive of it.

Departures from the Psychoanalytic Reconstruction of the Past

One of the reasons standard psychoanalytic technique does not work in profoundly ill and especially schizophrenic persons is that the *actual* ontogeny of the individual may be so engulfingly painful, for a variety of reasons, that the patient in reexperiencing it has no vantage point to view it from. It is as Archimedes said: "But for want of a fulcrum, I could move the world."

I wish to propose a departure from the pursuit of truth in the treatment of schizophrenia and hope that those of my teachers who have condemned schizophrenogenic parents for falsifying reality and feelings will not be scandalized. Facing the truth may not always be best for us humans and, perhaps mercifully, we seldom know what it is anyway.

If we were to think practically for a moment and, like Russian historians, eschew the search for truth about the past in exchange for propaganda to serve the needs of the present, the ideal fantasy with which the schizophrenic patient might replace the fantasy of being a victim—whatever an "impartial" observer continuously on the scene might have found to have been true—is the fantasy of having had autonomous choice about how things were experienced. If this fantasy could be accepted, the patient could then strive to relinquish passive and helpless images of himself and preserve a sense (or illusion) of mastery, of captaincy of his own soul. The parents, being omitted from the pathogenesis, would then be omitted automatically from the fantasy of the curative process, and ongoing dependency would be undercut. To make this version stick and work as an improved myth of the self, certain objections will have to be overcome.

1. *The problem of the pain.* The patient will ask, or should be helped to ask, why then do I hurt so much if I have not been hurt to a like degree? The reality of the pain should be emphasized as it, like any proto-

affect, is part of the real psychological truth of the moment. But as with depressives who must overcome their proneness to see in retrospect only moods of similar dejection, the patient should be encouraged as much as possible to see some of the pain as acute and transient and, as soon as possible, attempt to recover awareness of happier and less crazy previous experiences, rather than to collect and catalogue injustices. I have tried this at conferences with patients in usual psychodynamic therapy with residents and have been struck by their astonishment at being asked to recall positive things rather than to rehearse woes. They appeared to derive benefit from this, for them, fresh and unusual approach! Many somewhat begrudgingly admitted small, intercurrent satisfactions and kindnesses in their experiences with parents who were otherwise described as of the very worst stripe. In regard to blaming of the parents, I am reminded of a human interest news story (WINS, April 27, 1978) about a son who was suing his parents for "malpractice of parenting" to the tune of $350,000 for the lifetime of psychiatric care he felt he would need. (This is at the other pole from *Erewhon,* Samuel Butler's imaginary society, in which children were obligated to compensate their parents for the disappointment they caused them in getting sick.) The simple point is, both patients and their parents are hurt by the patient's illness and both need support and consolation.

2. *Passive fatalism: "Why me, God?"* The ideas that a pathological course was inevitable is often linked with the passive idea of unfair victimization by fate, luck, God, or the firmament of stars. Both are philosophically moot and, even if true in some ultimate sense, both are obstacles to the development of more favorable self-myths. Fatalism may be mitigated by suggesting other courses that could have been taken and still can. Many schizophrenic patients (and for that matter, patients with other incapacitating illnesses that hampered psychological growth and promoted overdependent reliance on parents) do not begin to address adolescent developmental issues until they are in their thirties. "Better late than never" is therapeutically more productive than counting up experiences missed forever.

The question "Why me?" cannot be approached by denying the seemingly singular distress of the schizophrenic person or by suggesting that the syndrome is, after all, quite common, affecting at least 1 percent of humankind and possibly more. Schizophrenic persons have so much trouble feeling a part of a group that they can derive little satisfaction from membership or identification with a large pathological minority. Also, if there ever was a condition that was *sui generis* in every individual, it is schizophrenia. Instead the singularity should be examined for what few good points can be gleaned from it. In psychotherapy, we should emphasize the patient's sensitivity rather than his vulnerability, his originality rather than his oddity, and so on. Usually there are a number of derivatives, such as occupational skills and interests, of which the patient may be encouraged justifiably to be proud. The further usefulness of giving these "advantages of being schizophrenic" their due is that the patient may be freer *not* to pursue them, to cultivate more calm and conventionality. A frequent area of appreciation of the schizophrenic sensitivity to things is estheticism, where at times an ecstatic perceptiveness can be found. Another is the capacity for fresh observations of the human situation.

3. *Obviously atrocious treatment at the hands of parents and others through development, or undeniable severe losses during childhood.* Again, there should be no lack of empathic appreciation of terrible experiences or sorrows, but the patient should be encouraged to feel that endless sickness is not a necessary result. Others with the same or similar bad experiences did not become schizophrenic.

Biological Factors and Depersonalization

In seeking a safe explanation of the patient's illness, the family in conjunction with experts may emphasize biological factors in such a way that the patient comes to believe that he or she *is* a "bad gene" or an endocrine abnormality per se. A recent example from my practice concerned a college junior whose family had had sufficient psychological sophistication to remove her from purely pharmacological treatment while her schizophrenia was still acute. They nevertheless treated minor side effects such as fine tremor as the major interest and, simultaneously with the beginning of psychotherapy, initiated an endocrine workup for her moderate obesity. A slightly abnormal adrenal androgen level gave the family the pretext to "kidnap" her from college, where she was managing to keep up her schoolwork, and to observe her 24-hour urine collections at home lest she "forget" and urinate during the day. The endocrinologist, until I spoke with him, allowed the family the fantasy that the key to all the patient's problems lay in the results of this endocrine workup. The family became excited and almost conspiratorial about this new hope. Despite, or perhaps because of, a scientific background in another field, the father favored a unicausal theory that temporarily protected him from guilt about his shallow, rage-bound relatedness that the rest of the family had previously emphasized. Also forgotten for the nonce was the history of persecution and loss of both the father's and mother's families in Europe and the appearance of the patient's severe problems when the mother's mother (who had raised the patient while the mother worked) died soon after the patient's menarche. The patient's close identification with this bizarre, narcissistic woman, the sole survivor of her generation of her family, had led to the patient's schizophrenic identity as a "dead person," a prominent part of her initial symptom picture. Now in the context of the biological workup the patient became more convinced she *was* (psychologically) dead already. She abruptly stopped her phenothiazine and tricyclic regimen and threatened suicide. It is important to note that all this occurred *before* the endocrine workup came out negative. Her suicidal preoccupation was the result, I feel, of the way her workup was handled: a schizophrenic person became convinced she was a thing—at best a biosystem—and not a person. A crisis was averted through consultations with both family and patient, as well as with the endocrinologist, before the tests were completed. The patient accepted a modification of emphasis concerning her hormone state, which permitted psychotherapy to resume. Eventually she made excellent progress.

I feel this principle will be of increasing importance as we continue to elucidate biological mechanisms that may contribute to symptom formation in some of the schizophrenias.

Reverse Gravitational Drift in Those with Paranoid Features

The paranoid schizophrenic patient tends more than most paranoid patients to drift away from other people. I embellished that simple idea with the term "reverse gravitational drift" to convey how constant, insidious, and therefore unfortunately often unnoticed this tendency is, until the patient drifts so far into solitude as to become vulnerable to minor upsets that, appropriately enough, may be of a "gravitational" sort. The paranoid woman whose initial breakdown had included an unrequited crush on a coworker (see Chapter 10), had been able slowly to decrease both the frequency of her visits to once every few months and her medication to 25 mg. of chlorpromazine a day. She had also, under readily forthcoming work pressure of a noninteractive sort, gravitated away from the superstructure of less than intimate social activities I had helped her establish. When her coworker returned from an out-of-town assignment and she again saw him daily in her sanctuary of work, she had a recurrence of unrealistic ideas that "rumors" were circulating about her and him, which she then struggled to deny. She recognized she was upset and consulted me immediately. After two weeks of twice-a-week therapy and a temporary increase in her level of medication, she began to feel quite herself again. She was amazed to see how she had let her social involvement slip and immediately began to resume these protective activities.

Retrodictive Explanations and the Need for Meaning

I would hasten to add that, in cases such as this, the level of medication may be a crucial factor. Even when the patient seems to have been stable for some months, the stability may be undermined by too little medication, regardless of the social situation. Here, we should be critical minded and honest with ourselves as therapists. Social and psychological factors are often clearly operative and should be emphasized—our explorations of them offer the best opportunities for the patient to take an active role in sustaining psychological health. Patients as well as therapists search for psychological causative factors retrodictively, and somehow always find them, even when it seems obvious that pharmacological factors were the most prominent cause of an episode or illness. Psychosocial factors are more amenable to incorporation into one's system of meaning than are biological theories. The latter are difficult for laymen to grasp and far from intuitively natural. Perhaps most significantly, biologic theories depersonalize and decrease one's sense of autonomous control, whether or not they are of scientific value. Central amine theories of schizophrenia and of phenothiazine effect are more difficult to ''sell'' to patients than is the relation of insulin to diabetes. The statement that ''nobody dies by accident in Africa'' (reflecting the usual explanation of sympathetic magic) should also remind us that ''nobody becomes schizophrenic by accident in America'': causation by human intent and under human control is everywhere prized, because it supports the illusion of being *completely* controllable; hence, curable.

On Being Funny

The French philosopher Henri Bergson wrote that we laugh when we are confronted by a rigidity of momentum, a mechanical elasticity of character, mind, or body, that reminds us of a mere machine. For Bergson laughter has a social function, and

> society will therefore be suspicious of all *inelasticity* of character, of mind and even body, because it is the possible sign of a slumbering activity as well as of an activity with separatist tendencies, that inclines to swerve from the common centre round which the society gravitates: In short because it is the sign of an eccentricity (1900, p. 254).

Furthermore, *a deformity that may become comic* (and here we may extrapolate from the physical to the behavioral) *is a deformity that a normally built person could successfully imitate.*

By Bergson's criteria, the schizophrenic person must surely be among the most laughable of people. At one time schizophrenic persons were actually incarcerated in what was called the Fool's Tower (*Narrenturm*) at the General Hospital of Vienna. Despite the sanctimony or the changed criteria of compassion in our society, we must not forget that for the majority of people, the sayings and shenanigans of schizophrenics are *funny.* We must not forget this lest we, too, are caught unexpecting and then led to laugh rather than to understand. Many of the surprises by which schizophrenic persons may test the therapist are, at first flush, risible.

One hospitalized schizophrenic youth in his late teens walked in a wooden, rigid way exactly like a toy soldier; another ambulatory young man walked on the balls of his toes in an odd, stiff gait, leaning forward with his arms rigidly at his sides and his fingers twitching madly, looking for all the world as if he were being walked by a wire attached to the top of his head. A young woman who had had many schizoid features as an adolescent (short of overt psychosis) recalled that she had often felt as if her limbs were controlled by strings as she walked down the street, so dependent had she been on external guidance at the time. Such oddly mannered bodily movement tempts ridicule. But many schizophrenic persons are extremely graceful or athletic, able to pursue solitary sports, dance with uncanny attractiveness or emanation of feeling or, as in one case of severe process schizophrenia in another young man in his late teens, capable of extraordinary agility and balance in the physical sphere. This patient had developed a standing back flip and a one-hand stand that he used to practice on the edges of the subway platforms and building ledges, along with a complicated ritual system with "flash insight" around the high bar.

Most schizophrenics, by means of their truly absurd and laughable ideas, sorely test our capacity *not* to laugh. For instance (and here I am avoiding cases in which there is a manic element or the manic's *intention* of making another person laugh), there is the invention I mentioned elsewhere (Forrest, 1976) as an example of the interference of schizophrenia with creativity. The inventor, who was in his mid-thirties and hospitalized, announced his invention completely deadpan in the course of an interview as "a new shaving device." As I have always been interested in new inventions and in fact have had some (unsuccessful) dealings with the patent office myself, I was eagerly sucked in and not ready for his elaboration: His machine consisted of whirling razor blades in a concave arrangement, into which one would insert one's face! I need not point out that my unfortunate and involuntary laughter betrayed an element of having been threatened and revolted as much as amused. Schizophrenic humor is often sardonic, cruel, satiric, or ironic, more travesty or lampoon than gentle wit or funny comedy. The less experienced the therapist, the harder it is to avoid laughing or adopting a tone of sarcasm with the patient. Young therapists feel themselves to be a sham and are more vulnerable to ridicule because of inexperience. But as Bergson points out, an *absence* of feeling usually accompanies laughter.

> It seems as if the comic could not produce its disturbing effect unless it fell, so to say, on the surface of a soul that is thoroughly calm and unruffled. Indifference is its natural environment, for laughter has no greater foe than emotion: I do not mean that we could not laugh at a person who inspires us with pity, for instance, or even with affection, but in such a case we must, for the moment, put our affection out of court and impose silence upon our pity. In a society composed of pure intelligences there would probably be no more tears, though perhaps there would still be laughter; whereas highly emotional souls, in tune and unison with life, in whom every event would be sentimentally prolonged and re-echoed, would neither know nor understand laughter (1900, p. 249).

The psychoanalytic view that laughter is the direct escape or venting of drives helps explain the fact that laughter is generally a healthy thing to do with one's drives in appropriate situations and is probably a sign of a strong ego. Schizophrenics, in contrast, rarely laugh with any consensuality or appropriateness. Many kinds of disordered laughter reflect the involuntary access to expression of the drives in schizophrenia. These include hebephrenic laughter and the forced or exaggerated laughter in humorless paranoiacs when they do laugh. Arieti has described the typical lack of a sense of humor (1974, p. 110) and sensitivity to the mild element of hostility in a joke made at their expense. Arieti remarks that: "For the schizoid, a joke is a serious rebuff. For the same reasons, schizoids are poor losers at play. Defeat is another proof of their inadequacy and increases their already strong reluctance to do things with others or to share experiences."

The social power of laughter is not to be underestimated. On a recent show (aired May 7, 1976), Johnny Carson attempted to break out of his usual role of comedian briefly to recite seriously Hamlet's soliloquy, "To be or not to be." It was clear that he was not clowning, but the audience would not permit him to do it, controlling the situation with laughter.

In my tendency to avoid laughter and humor in the therapy of schizophrenia, I am much in accord with Kubie's (1971) position on the destructive potential of humor in psychotherapy. But the potential of *laughing with* the patient in response to things that are funny in a sense that is not cruel, must be included among the most desirable goals of therapy, comparable to the sharing of consensually validated metaphor in the recovering schizophrenic person, which Searles has described as "about as intimate a psychological contact as human beings can have with one another" (1965, p. 583).

Discretion in Becoming Involved with Psychotic Content

Kolb (1956), in addition to recommending that the psychotherapy of schizophrenia avoid dream analysis—because it fosters withdrawal into fantasy and adds little when primitive impulses are already overt— recommends also that the content of delusions be avoided. Instead of obtaining associations to the content, Kolb suggests the therapist should establish the temporal relation of the occurrences of the delusional material "to the train of interpersonal events taking place in the therapy, and their relation to similar disturbing experiences in the past." Once learned, these correlations with circumstances can be fed back to the patient and are more useful than explaining to him the symbolic dimension of their meaning.

This does not imply asking the rather offensive question, "How long have you been feeling this way?" To such questions patients react, justifiably, as if the content of their thinking had been rejected as insignificant. The matter of the patient's metaphors—their content—is most informative, but much of the time the psychiatrist should merely listen to it and respond inwardly.

9

Symptoms Peculiar
to the Schizophrenic Condition:
SOME APPROACHES TO THEIR RESOLUTION

Michael H. Stone, M.D.

A number of clinical symptoms in the therapy of schizophrenic patients have special importance by virtue of their being only rarely encountered in patients bearing other diagnostic labels—symptoms that are, in effect, peculiar to schizophrenia. If we become adept at comprehending them, if we are then able to make the patient who exhibits them feel understood, we will enhance communication, and more importantly, we will help him feel less strange, less cut off from his fellow man. The most important trait in this category is eccentricity (or bizarreness). Throughout the centuries this is a trait that has distinguished the schizophrenic (by whatever name he was called) from other kinds of individuals and patients.

Another such symptom is distractability. One does of course see distractability during acute manic episodes. There is, as Ollerenshaw (1973) has mentioned, an overlap of symptoms in acute psychotic phases of both manic-depression and schizophrenia. Here, I am alluding to certain schizophrenic patients who, through sitting calmly in one's office, attend compulsively to all kinds of irrelevant details. It is this disorder of attention that constitutes the special schizophrenic brand of distractability. A number of authors, including Spohn, Thetford, and Cancro (1970) and Broen (1968) consider impairment in the capacity for focused attention to be one of the key qualities that distinguish schizophrenia from nonschizophrenia.

Many schizophrenic patients, particularly in the beginning, have difficulty in recognizing ordinary human emotions.[1] This may be more of a problem with those who are sick enough to warrant hospitalization than with the office patient. One may, for example, notice tears streaming down the patient's face while he is describing something. Yet when you ask, "What are you feeling?" he may reply, "Nothing," or "I don't know." At first this seems baffling. After a while you come to believe that he really doesn't know. At this point you may have to intervene—as is rarely necessary with a neurotic patient—to fill in the emotion and say, "I'm really convinced that you must be feeling sad," or "I've never seen anyone with tears flowing down his face, who was talking about a death in the family, when it didn't reflect genuine sadness. . . ." In that way we teach the patient the vocabulary of human emotions and help lift him out of what may be a kind of affectual undifferentiatedness. Generally these kinds of remarks will never come from the patient first. One almost always has to take the initiative. This, in turn, may be a bit jarring for those who are schooled in an orthodox psychoanalytic mode and who would tend to wait for the patient to recognize his emotions by himself.

Another important set of abnormal mental experience peculiar to schizophrenia are those we subsume under the rubric "fragmentation." Patients may experience fragmentation in the sense of *self* or in their internalization of other persons. Another and closely related manifestation of this fragmentation concerns a sense of discontinuity about the flow of *time*. This may be particularly severe in the more acute forms of schizophrenic illness or in the early phases of the more chronic forms. The type of time distortions schizophrenic patients sometimes exhibit resemble the condensations of past and present events encountered in dreams—where linkages are made according to similarity of emotions felt—rather than according to chronological sequence (see Matte-Blanco, 1976), to which the "logical" adult pays exclusive attention. This kind of "primary process" thinking is considered the preserve of the nondominant cerebral hemisphere (Stone, 1977; B. Wexler, 1980). Evidence has been accumulating that schizophrenics have abnormal patterns of cerebral lateralization: the old psychoanalytic adage about such patients "dreaming while awake" seems more valid than Freud or Jung, who espoused this view, could have known at the time. Taylor et al. (1981) have shown, for example, that on tests designed to discriminate between

---

[1]This difficulty is similar to the "alexithymia" described by Sifneos (1973) as occurring in many patients with psychosomatic disorders. Referring to their meager capacity to recognize feeling states, the term alludes to something very real in the eyes of the clinician. Derived half from Latin (*lexi-*) and half from Greek (*thūmos*), the term is an unfortunate hybrid and should be replaced either by a phrase that is correct (anoidothymia) or, failing that, by a phrase that is immediately meaningful ("affect blindness").

dominant and nondominant hemispheres, schizophrenics performed significantly worse on dominant hemisphere-related tasks than did affectively ill patients. Similar findings have been reported by Gur (1978), Schweitzer (1979), and Watson (1965). *Mutatis mutandis,* right (nondominant) hemisphere-related tasks, tend to be performed relatively poorly by *affectively* ill (manic or depressed) patients, as noted by Flor-Henry (1976) and Yozawitz et al. (1979). It is of interest to recall, in the light of this contemporary research, that "imagination" (which goes awry in affective disorders) and "reason" (which goes haywire in schizophrenia) have, for centuries, been identified as our two overarchingly important, and separable, mental faculties (see R. Bacon, 1640)—long before it was suspected that these faculties might be mediated, preponderantly, by the two separable, though (at times) cooperatively functioning, halves of our brain.

With respect to fragmentation about internalized images of others, I vividly recall one patient who, whenever the session ended, would close the door behind her and have the peculiar feeling that I suddenly ceased to exist. She would be quite surprised to discover that someone resembling me would be in the room were she to open the door again or to come for the next visit a day later. Little by little, however, we were able to help her knit together these very separate and discordant experiences. She began to realize that I was "there," whether she was in the room or whether she wasn't, that I had a continuity in existence and so did she.

One may regard this as helping the schizophrenic patient to master the Peek-A-Boo Game that mothers teach their children at around six or seven months of age. Mothers, at this stage, typically duck behind a screen or a piece of furniture and then let their faces be seen again. Babies will giggle and smile, delighted that mother hasn't disappeared. In working with schizophrenic patients whose time sense still shows severe discontinuity, the sessions need to be very regular. One should try not to go over the customary time, or under. The therapist should strive to be always on time; if any deviation has to be made, one has to be even more than ordinarily respectful of the patient's needs. I have called patients to say that I might be delayed two minutes. By so doing I allay anxiety and also let the patient know I care enough about his time and feelings to inform him about what, for better integrated persons, would be only a minor inconvenience. Ultimately this kind of respect and predictability has a healing influence.

A well-known example of fragmentation concerns the patient described by Marguerite Sechèhaye (1951) at the Burghölzli Clinic in Switzerland: a patient whom she called Renée and whom she treated for many years in intensive psychotherapy. This was a young woman who had a childhood schizophrenic reaction involving, among other things, an incapacity to comprehend that a certain chair, when viewed in the profile, was the same chair that she might look at later from the front. In other words, as she would walk around various objects, the slightly different appearances that they would take from position to position could not—in her mind—be assimilated and integrated. She could not grasp the "sameness" of objects seen in different perspectives.

Those who have worked intensively with schizophrenic persons over many years will have had several patients who react to the therapist's vacations—or, indeed, any absences—with about equal severity year in and year out. The abject state into which they are plunged with each separation seems, at least transitorily, to wipe away the memory of how each previous leave-taking was followed by a return. The seventh vacation is as upsetting (or almost so) as the first. This would appear to reflect an innate, central integrative defect peculiar to schizophrenia. Improvement tends to be very slow and, in some patients, incomplete. It is important for therapists to realize this, so they do not become discouraged and countertransferentially hostile to those among their schizophrenic patients who prove particularly slow in acquiring a sense of continuity about the therapist's existence (and of trust in his promise to resume work on the day earmarked for his return). The fact that our consistency and our interventions often do succeed in establishing the desired sense of continuity in our schizophrenic patients, despite their constitutional handicap, should encourage us about the power of the psychological forces we can marshall to combat an inborn and what once seemed, for that very reason, "hopeless" impediment.

There is another difficulty to be noted in many schizophrenic patients in that they cannot readily apply lessons learned in *one* situation to some other but analogous situation. This often accounts for a kind of tactlessness that one sees in some schizophrenic patients. One young woman, for instance, would go over to her parents' house unbidden. She never bothered to call them in advance and once got a rude shock when she was turned away at the door. But when she would visit a friend, maybe a week later, again unbidden, she was dumbfounded at being turned away again. As she expressed it, "You told me my *parents* might resent my visit as an intrusion or something . . . but you didn't tell me my *friend* would." The schizophrenic patient often functions as though "lateral communication" of this sort does not occur in his brain the way it does in other people's. Although this kind of difficulty at first seems so bewildering, each of us probably has a similar difficulty at least in some circumscribed area of life. Those of us who are tone-deaf would be no less exasperating to a singing coach than our more concretistic schizophrenic patients are to us whenever we struggle to initiate them into the world of tact and discretion. The analogy of the color-blind person, to whom the idea of matching his socks to his suit must seem equally incomprehensible, is often used in describing the concrete patient's dilemma.

Odd communication is considered a hallmark of schizotypal psychopathology (Spitzer, Endicott, and Gibbon, 1979). Schizophrenic patients who exhibit at the outset speech that is hard to follow are especially challenging to our efforts, though they need not be thought of, necessarily, as poor candidates for intensive psychotherapy. It will, of course, be easier to establish superficial relatedness with patients whose speech is relatively undisturbed. There is a tendency for therapists early in their careers to be quite fascinated with the highly allusive speech of certain schizophrenics. Such therapists may be misled into the belief that patients of this sort will respond well to intensive psychotherapy just because they are so interesting. My own impression is that, if the patient with highly allusive speech can be led fairly rapidly and without extraordinary effort into a more everyday mode of verbal interchange, this augurs well, other factors being favorable, for intensive treatment. But if the patient holds fast to his tendency to use autistic, solipsistic speech patterns, meaningful interchange will not take place. Here the patient will really be making a mockery of our efforts to reach him.

I remember once, early in my practice, a patient came for a consultation—a chronic paranoid schizophrenic woman who opened the door and said, "I'm petrified." She would make this remark over and over, in the meantime telling me very little about herself. On my note pad, I had nothing to show for an hour's effort except her name and age. It was only after she said "I'm petrified" for the third or fourth time that I got a brainstorm: maybe she was saying "petrified" (in the sense of turning to stone) to signify that she was turning to Dr. Stone for help! I made an interpretation to this effect, not without some pride, expecting now that she would feel understood and that it would be smooth sailing thereafter. As it turned out, however, my remark made no impression on her at all. She just went on to make other solipsistic and incomprehensible comments of that type, so that I never did learn what was troubling the woman. This experience taught me not to get caught up in communicational dead ends of that sort. Instead of relying on virtuoso mental leaps (in this case, into the void!), it would have been much more to the point had I challenged her with some remark like, "I really don't understand what you're getting at—although I think I half understand. Is there another way of putting it that might make it more comprehensible for me, so that I know what's troubling you?" In the process of evaluation for therapy, one should place some reliance on the ease with which verbal interchange can be steered into the direction of ordinary everyday language.

Much has been said of disturbances in attention exhibited by schizophrenic patients (Broen, 1968; Spohn and Cancro, 1970; Wild et al., 1978). Psychological testing aimed at assessing measures of attention often reveal abnormalities in distinguishing "figure" from "ground," as well as other abnormalities in the capacity to attend to the most relevant stimuli in any interaction with the (human or nonhuman) environment. Clinically, these disturbances crop up in a wide variety of situations. Neurotic patients usually know *what* is bothering them; they simply lack an awareness of *why* they came to experience certain difficulties in everyday life, or of how to deal with these difficulties more effectively. In contrast, schizophrenic patients often do *not* know what is bothering them, and may either exhibit blatant denial because they are unaware anything is the matter (despite horrendous problems apparent to any neutral observer), or else may "hurt" in some unspecifiable way, about which they have no clue at all, or may perhaps search through a variety of clues, valueless to them because of an inability to sort out the important from the trivial.

I have in mind in this connection a patient who, for some years now, regularly begins each session with a rapid-fire recitation of seven or eight troubles in her daily life, from which she hopes, I shall immediately select the *one* trouble most responsible for the depression, irritability, or whatever, besetting her the day of our session. Hitting me like shrapnel are staccato references to her fiance's rudeness, an ethnic slur from her boss, the neighbor's television booming through the wall of her apartment, her mother's untimely demise (fifteen years ago), my having started our last session two minutes late, and the approach of the holiday season (in relation to which she anticipates feeling "left out"). The attentional deficit in this patient does not permit her to choose in advance of our meeting which of the myriad possibilities will prove the most likely source of her discomfort, hence the most profitable avenue for exploration. Instead we must use much of the remainder of the session in searching for other clues and listening for subtle signs of extra "affect" related to one of the topics—which point the way to the important topic we ought to have been attending to all along.

Inattention to ordinary social cues will land certain schizophrenic patients in perpetual difficulties whenever they are out among people or are attempting to achieve some measure of closeness in an intimate relationship. The patient from the preceding example has long exhibited an inability to attune herself to the subtle but, to persons with normal patterns of attention, by no means invisible, cues signifying the end of a session. Closing the notebook, replacing the pen in my coat pocket, glancing in the direction of the clock—these cues either fail to register or make no impact. Internal cues, which announce to the majority of patients when three-quarters of an hour are more or less up, also appear not to be elaborated by her idiosyncratic neurophysiological machinery. These failures of attention compel me to remind her out loud or even to get up from my chair while she is in mid-sentence—bits of behavior I ordinarily would find repugnant in a therapist—if I am to preserve the proper time boundaries of our meetings. Naturally enough, this patient experiences my boundary-setting behavior as a personal rejection, even though it is engendered by her attentional handicap. This in turn necessitates further discussion directed at helping her differentiate true personal rejection from neutral and nonrejecting interventions arising out of her inadvertent neglect of social convention.

Closely allied with the difficulty in attention is the tendency in certain schizophrenic patients to assign roughly equal likelihood to all possible outcomes in a given situation. If a patient can think of five things that could go wrong during a planned vacation, he will take *equal* precautions against each of these eventualities, even though one might generally be regarded as "likely" (the weather could be unpleasant) and the remainder as rare. One shy and socially gauche patient with whom I worked for a number of years found it next to impossible to prepare for vacations. Weeks instead of hours were consumed in mental and physical preparations. Every conceivable danger and mishap was anticipated and was countered with the same degree of preparedness as might be summoned up to meet a certain calamity. Lisbon was known to rest on a fault, vulnerable to earthquakes; therefore he felt it necessary to pack a hat lined with metal, lest fragments from rooftops fall on his head during seismic disturbances. He packed similar outfits of suits, ties, shoes, etc., in two separate pieces of luggage—lest one be stolen, especially when he was to be in Morocco, where "everyone is a thief." Naturally these precautions weighed him down (literally) to the point where vacations promised more burden than pleasure. Many sessions were spent in my urging him to pay closer attention to the real probabilities of the various accidents he feared, but, as with Hydra's head, cutting down one source of apprehension only led to the sprouting of three more. Even though such activity seems perfectly logical to the schizophrenic—if not downright clever—we regard it as a manifestation of primary-process thinking, where, as in dreams, thoughts and impressions of every kind are accorded equal value; a thought is a thought.

At the very least, we would have to say that the schizophrenic person operates with seeming disregard for the (admittedly unprovable) statistics of everyday life: it could rain tomorrow (a 1 in 10 chance), therefore I'd best carry an umbrella—side by side with—it could snow here in Dallas, as it once did thirteen years ago, hence I'd best carry an overcoat. I once had a patient who illustrated this anomaly by carrying his umbrella with him into my office, resting it against his chair. On rainy days this was not only eccentric but inconvenient besides, since the umbrella dripped into areas I would just as soon have left dry. The problem here was not one of rudeness, as I had been imagining (on the basis of what I initially considered the most likely explanation). It was rather that the patient could not distinguish between the likelihood of an umbrella's being stolen from a public rack in a bad neighborhood from the likelihood of a similar theft in my waiting room—located in a less crime-infested part of town—which could be entered only after giving his name to a guard and announcing himself to me through an intercom from the outside door.

One can begin to see how the attentional abnormality we have been sketching, and the related tendency to treat the rare and the likely in the same fashion, contributes to the trait of *eccentricity*, mentioned earlier in the chapter. Someone wearing a toga in the middle of Fifth Avenue, prompted by the belief he is Julius Caesar, is eccentric because of a delusion. But eccentricity may be noted in persons whose inclination is to dress conventionally, but who carry a fur coat in July on the infinitesimally small chance there might be a sudden cold spell. When schizophrenic patients exhibit eccentric habits, of dress or behavior, that are socially alienating, behavioral-modification methods must often be introduced into the treatment. These methods, which may at times make use of videotape playback of segments of the patient's behavior, may help compensate for the apparent lack of a social feedback mechanism from which so many schizophrenic persons suffer. They may need literally to see, in order to believe, that they dress in a manner that would elicit uncomplimentary remarks, discourage prospective employers, and so forth. Dr. Albert provides several clinical vignettes illustrating the adjunctive use of behavioral techniques alongside more conventional psychotherapy. Inasmuch as slovenly or otherwise bizarre dress habits arise, in certain schizophrenic patients, more out of an inability to assess accurately what is conventional or appropriate than out of psychodynamic conflict, one cannot look to verbal therapy, geared as it is to conflict resolution, for amelioration of the maladaptive pattern. I have relied, in several instances of this kind, on a ''charm'' school in which the patient could enroll, at the same time psychotherapy was in an active phase, to learn the details of dress and comportment that could never be adequately communicated in the therapeutic encounter. It is a matter of judgment as to whether, and when, separate attention to behavior may be helpful during the course of an otherwise unmodified analytically oriented approach. Similarly the tolerance and respect for any eccentricities in speech, judgment, or behavior that we as therapists always owe to our schizophrenic patients need not limit us to an exclusively verbal technic where our clinical intuition tells us that temporary addition of a behavioral approach might greatly accelerate the correction of certain maladaptive tendencies. Interpretations may, in other words, have to be amplified by teaching—sometimes of the most elementary kind.

At all events, it is important to keep in mind that these eccentricities are clinical characteristics about which the schizophrenic really has little choice. Unlike those who seek attention through mannered speech, attire, and gesture—consciously adopted—most eccentric schizophrenics have not been striving for effect. They are, instead, inwardly driven to behave in ways that seem normal to them, but odd to us, because of their gross miscalculations about other people and events, or because of their chronic lack of attention to the norms of dress and social intercourse.

To the extent that persecutory and certain other types of delusion are characteristic, though not exclusively so, of schizophrenia, such symptoms also have a place in this chapter, but because other contributors to this volume deal with these phenomena more extensively, we shall allude to them here only briefly. With certain schizophrenic patients we find ourselves grappling with a distinctly delusory idea that expresses poignantly the dilemma with which the patient is preoccupied. Often enough, the delusion may express one aspect of a pair of highly important but conflicting feelings. The patient starts out reluctant to speak of his feelings except through the medium of the delusion—where the conflict is alluded to only *symbolically*. As therapists, we feel constrained to do battle with the patient, to drag him—by force, if necessary—from his precious but irrational and unserviceable ideas to a more workable, if also more pedestrian and humdrum, view of the world. The schizophrenic patient, by the time he comes to us, has much reason, either through mistreatment by others or an inability to relate comfortably to others, to be terrified of the world conventional folk inhabit; he does not come easily or willingly to our side.

By way of example, I have in mind a young man of 22 or 23, admitted to a psychiatric hospital because of markedly delusional ideation, which so tormented and distracted him that he was unable to work or maintain his few social contacts. He had become increasingly aggressive toward his mother and sister; as a result, they could no longer contain him at home. His father had died earlier in the year. The patient's central delusion concerned "The Force," as he called it, which he took to be a manifestation of the Divine Presence (though at other times, he assumed it was an emanation from Lucifer). The Force controlled his thoughts, feelings, actions, and in particular commanded him at various—to him unpredictable—moments, to trip women walking near him in the street or to pinch their breasts. It may easily be imagined that when The Force exerted itself in relation to his mother and sister, the two women were rather slow to accept the patient's conviction about the divine origins of such commands.

This patient, who received the customary phenothiazine regimen during his hospitalization, was assigned to a resident gifted in expressive psycho-therapy. She spent months in getting him to realize, despite the most vehe-ment denial, that the abstract and rather bewildering Force to which his dis-course was monomanically devoted could be much better understood as a concretization of two strong feelings: *hostility* at his bossy mother and sister, and ordinary lustful feelings toward them and toward attractive women in general.

As counterpoint to the delusion of a Force was, as might be anticipated, a feeling of powerlessness and impotence on the part of the patient. The idea of having to succumb to a supreme Force was not so unpleasant for this man: such submission freed him, as it were, of any responsibility for his ac-tions. Also it spared him from having to deal with the more painful issue of his own little-boy feelings of helplessness. The therapist had to spend many months in building up the patient's inner sense of strength; other members of the hospital staff had to help him understand that he really could travel downtown without getting lost, really could manage a simple job, and so forth, before he was emboldened enough to accept the idea of his former weakness. The weakness, in other words, had to be *behind* him a bit, before it became safe to acknowledge the fact of it. By the time a year had gone by, he seldom spoke any more of the Force; instead of *delusion*, there was, as is so often the case with resolving psychoses, *obsessional* worries; namely, about his therapist's regard for him, about the extent of his anger, about the sinfulness of his no longer repudiated sexuality, etc.

Clinically, he now appeared to harbor an obsessional neurosis—albeit one of unusual severity and rigidity. The classic positive signs (hallucina-tions, delusion) of overt schizophrenia were no longer discernible.[2] In inten-sive therapy with schizophrenic patients we try very hard to convert clas-sical delusory ideas into less disruptive obsessional (or other more neurotic-like) symptoms. In the latter state, it is possible to communicate with the patient; the patient is no longer out of contact with the world.

[2]Of course, the schizophrenia per se did not go away, because "schizophrenia" is a state of vulnerability that persists throughout life in predisposed individuals. It is only when this vul-nerability gets exercised by various life stresses that certain symptoms begin to appear—which we label "schizophrenic."

It may be useful at this juncture to remark on certain verbal interventions that may have to be called into play in dealing with the particularly primitive defenses (of which denial is the prototype) erected by schizophrenic patients. The gentle hints and soft-spoken interpretations that usually suffice in classical psychoanalysis will fall flat before the denial or projection of the schizophrenic. Confrontational technics of various types are often required. By these I am not referring to the often blunt and unnecessarily painful verbal slings in which the followers of "direct analysis" (see J. Rosen, 1947) placed such great stock throughout the 1950s. I am referring to the compassionate but firm, at times strongly worded, interventions of the sort described by Buie and Adler as "specific technics for dealing with avoidance defenses" (1973, p. 144).

A confrontational intervention, if it succeeds in breaking through some measure of denial, may of course unleash storms of scarcely controllable affect. In office practice, confrontational technics will for this reason tend to be used more sparingly and couched in less dramatic terms than might be acceptable within the safer environment of the hospital.

With a patient already hospitalized, I feel much freer to use a moderately confrontational approach in an effort to evoke genuine feeling from the patient. I strive for a poignant interpretation—a comment that captures in a few words the schizophrenic patient's central conflict—some comment that will bring recognition, and sometimes tears. And if I succeed in this, I feel I am in the presence of a patient who can be reached, who wants to be reached, and who is now ready to be reached.

The following clinical vignette illustrates how unexpected confrontations in the course of the interview may suddenly expose to the patient the absurdity of some cherished opinion, so that he has no alternative but to repudiate the "statement" of his own delusion. In so doing he is compelled to step closer to ordinary reality. The example concerns an adolescent of 18, a young man who was admitted because of inability to function at school and because of the persistent somatic delusions about the blood in his heart and brain (which he insisted had somehow come to a halt). All this had occurred not long after the sudden death of his father from a heart attack. During my interview with him, he got to describing his breakdown in college. He took to lying motionless on his bed for hours and hours on end, just staring at the ceiling. Later in the interview, he kept me at arm's length, mouthing one dry intellectualization after another. When he spoke of the episode in the dormitory room—staring at the ceiling—I interjected, "You were, of course, imitating a corpse." Here I was acting on the assumption that instead of being able to mourn his father in an ordinary way (I was told he showed no emotion at the funeral at all), he was reduced to identifying with his stricken father, whom he must have come to resemble rather closely—stretched out on that bed, rigid and glassy-eyed. But the comment was so pungent and challenging that the patient could scarcely ignore it. He was no longer able to deny that, indeed, that *was* what was on his mind at the time. It was at this moment in the interview that he turned towards me for the first time. He now spoke in a direct and audible tone, later becoming tearful. He was able finally to speak about having missed his father, an emotion he had never been able to acknowledge before, let alone give vent to.

10

Intensive Psychotherapy with a Patient with Paranoid Schizophrenia

David V. Forrest, M.D.

The case of an attractive and highly competent female biostatistician in her late forties who developed a brief decompensation will illustrate the approach in stages to the treatment of a more paranoid variety of ambulatory schizophrenia.

EARLY PHASE

My first contact with the patient was dramatic. She had withdrawn to her apartment and was found crouching, terrified, brandishing a hammer, when close work-associates (concerned that something might have happened to her) had forcibly entered with the help of police. As I happened to be nearby, I was called on a Good Samaritan basis. My mere arrival greatly decompressed the entire situation. In retrospect I believe that my familiarity with severe paranoia from a year as a military psychiatrist in Vietnam helped me to project a manner that was direct and assured amidst an atmosphere of tentativeness, and the patient was quite willing to put down her hammer and talk with me.

I arranged immediate hospitalization and began her initially on 400 mg. of Thorazine® a day.

The patient began to talk about her infatuation with a handsome and flirtatious but married younger coworker, and about her concern over "insinuations" linking them. It became clear that, because of her social isolation, she had immensely overvalued this largely unrequited interest. In her referential thinking she was expressing a wish for signs of affection from him, the cognitive distortion replacing the feelings she wished he had been feeling. Her history included the loss of her father when she was 14 and a brief marriage in her twenties to an artistic man, a failure who died young of a coronary, to whose support in isolation she had become totally devoted in a *folie à deux*. An older brother remained unmarried in an apparently neuter bachelor existence close to their aged mother.

During her six days' hospital stay the patient exhibited several cognitive traits that were clues to treatment in the early phase: (1) She was projective and referential, fearing people's spying through windows and thinking she was a "sex maniac and wife stealer" (sic). In sessions through the early and middle phase, she frequently began by perceiving her own affects in me, thereby announcing, for example, "You look worried." These were gently reflected back to her. (2) She had an illusion, reminiscent of the nineteenth century Capgras syndrome, concerning imposters. She doubted, for example, that one other female patient was really a patient or that the internist I had chosen as a medical consultant was really a doctor. This suggested confusion about the doctor-patient relationship and ultimately defects in trust and in the constancy of objects. These defects required firm role definitions and limits, a warm but restrained, straightforward, and formal relationship on my part, and no presumption of ready trust or cooperation. (3) She was easily distracted, tending to preoccupy herself with irrelevant details, such as the edelweiss pattern on a chair in her apartment. Often she would stare vacantly, inattentive to what was going on around her. This inattentiveness required much patience with repetition and reorientation. In our sessions my emotional tone with her expressed optimism and affection, as well as a respect for her person and the boundaries between us.

MIDDLE PHASE

The therapeutic alliance was now well established and the patient's implicit question about her differentness had been implicitly answered. I had explained, for example, that she had for a long time become overly isolated. Inwardly I hoped she would begin to move toward and ultimately rejoin the human race emotionally. The middle phase began with a search for and insistence upon suitable social structuring. The patient would suggest nonhuman or inanimate pursuits, such as taking courses to learn about gems. I suggested she take up bridge again, learning that she knew how to play. This seemed to be a more social though still clearly structured activity. After much procrastination, inattention, and avoidance, her anxieties about trying a bridge club came clearly to the fore and were discussed. She then was able to join a club and pursue this activity with increasing skill as her major social involvement. She continued to feel undesirable as a partner, but the structure of the game engrossed her as she improved her game;

she bought a bridge table in the event that she would be hosting a game at her apartment, and she eventually did. She also developed a platonic friendship with a younger man from the club. I repeatedly credited her efforts to become involved and dealt with fears of being disliked while keeping up the pressure toward additional activities (such as church socials, dining with relatives, and taking courses). I explained how her protective defenses on an interpersonal level might alienate people around her. Only when well into this phase did I venture into the sensitive area of her demeanor and facial appearance. This included gently noting that she often looked not only surprised but quite literally supercilious. In addition to rather wide open eyes, she had very carefully plucked and raised her eyebrows, creating in the process two semilunar curves that seemed to pass a verdict of disapproval about everything within her field of vision. Later on her own she modified her hair color with a softer rinse and began to enjoy shopping for more colorful, sporty, and less formal clothes. Still later, she began wearing contact lenses.

LATE PHASE

More than two years after I had first seen her, during most of which period she had been maintained on 150 mg. of Thorazine® per day, the patient began a new phase in which she was addressing and revising certain fundamental relationships between herself and her social world. (I hesitate to suggest the term *"structural change"* in relation to this process since that is usually reserved for classical analysis of well-integrated patients.)

On one occasion she found herself in a store facing the reality that she could easily shoplift an item she had come to buy. She had never stolen before. This was not primarily a kleptomaniacal urge to reward herself with a symbolic object, but rather a need to question the rules of conscience. For the first time in her life she felt like buying something not out of blind obedience to rules learned in childhood but one of genuine respect for the social contract. She left the store with a feeling of great pride, not at having overcome temptation but at having revised her relationship with her conscience along more mature and autonomous lines. At about the same time she tempered her view of authorities so that she was able to decide that her bridge teacher could not "know all and see all," as she had always assumed teachers could do. These revisions were preceded by her trying to become involved in serious conversations. Usually she had remained an onlooker. She discovered with relief and surprise that everything did not revolve around her and that she also could be wrong sometimes! At the three-year point, she was rethinking her feelings toward groups in general, and in one of our sessions recalled a thought from childhood: "They don't want me because I'm a girl." By this time, acquaintances and coworkers had begun to remark how much she had changed and how much more "outgoing" she had become.

My role in the late phase was much more interpretive. We sought sources in her childhood experiences and personal fantasies with which to comprehend her typical defensive postures. These now became relatively freed up, with a new degree of "play" and potential for revision.

At one point, in view of her many gains, she asked whether she was ready to stop therapy. I replied that there was no compelling need to continue from the standpoint of personal survival, but that she had not yet reestablished an intimate companionship of any sustaining nature. She had, it is true, begun to enjoy some sexual affairs (she was not sexually anhedonic, despite the years of isolation and abstinence). I asked her if she felt satisfied with this level of human involvement and whether she had confidence (in view of her tendency to procrastinate and avoid) in her capacity to proceed on her own. She felt the answer to both questions was no, and decided to continue in treatment.

During the entire course of therapy, I placed very little direct emphasis on the major presenting symptom of her unrequited infatuation and her referentiality about it. This was because I felt she had been pinning her hopes upon a "safe" object, which fostered avoidance of the main areas of living. Challenging this system seemed contraindicated until she had developed other, healthier replacements. This hopeless infatuation and the paranoid defenses erected around it became transformed, as a result of her treatment, from an exquisitely painful area to a mild ache. All this occurred without much direct attention on our part to the old paranoid symptoms. This patient continued to require small amounts of chlorpromazine for her optimum ability to relate with others.

COMMENT

I chose this example to illustrate how, in the early phase of therapy, as Arieti (1974) points out, one must develop a relationship with the patient. The therapist's first duty, like the politician's, is to be elected. In the case of psychotherapy with a schizophrenic person, the race is not with another candidate, but with the patient's inwardly focused attention. The primary means of developing a relationship with a schizophrenic person is *to demonstrate practical competence in dealing with cognitive needs.* One's task is to show the patient that one understands and is familiar with his different ways of thought and can act accordingly with consideration and compassion. Add to this a low-anxiety manner on the part of the therapist, and the early phase is well underway.

11

Therapeutic Adaptations to the Affective Features of Schizophrenia

David V. Forrest, M.D.

While affects are present at all points in the course of schizophrenia, the therapist will usually find that cognitive features prevail in therapy early on and that the affects can be worked with only after the cognitive features have been able to relax their defensive grasp, ideally with the active help of the therapist. Although the dichotomy is somewhat artificial, I have discussed in Chapter 7 cognitive adaptations by the therapist in the early phase of treatment, and turn now to affective features as a matter for the middle phase.

As an aid to understanding the protean manifestations of affect in schizophrenia I favor a neurological analogy. If schizophrenia is considered as a *parapathia* (a disorder of substitute affective forms), rather than a *paraphrenia* (a disorder of substitute forms of thinking) or a *paraphasia* (a disorder of substitute forms of meaning), then the symptoms of schizophrenia can be seen as *unrealized affects,* or *proto-affects.* The profit in this, aside from its its being a simple way to arrange and remember these affective features, is that a built-in concept is provided of the direction in which to move therapeutically from each of substituted affect forms.

Preliminary Labors and the Goals of Therapeutic Work

Here I might note, as we now consider work with affects, that these are still preliminary labors en route to the psychodynamic interpretations that come in the later phase of treatment. Most residents and students, in my experience, have been tempted by the richly psychodynamic-sounding cognitive features encountered at the outset of treatment to begin dynamic interventions much too soon. The result is an edifice built on sand. Therapist and patient need to work on cognition together and they need to work on affect together so there is mutuality in the understanding and usage of these elements. Affects alone are not the goal; the significant pieces of psychodynamic reconstruction require assembly and shaping of both cognitive and affective ingredients if any worthwhile meaning is to emerge.

Treating Specific Affective (Parapathic) Features

A series of plain therapeutic directions are dictated by consideration of the substituted affect in schizophrenia:

1. *Interpret perceptions affectively.* We largely see what we expect to see, in accordance usually with the images and structures of which we have inner representations. The schizophrenic person does this, only more so (see Freud's model, 1895, of hallucinations and illusions resulting from the perception machine run in reverse), because of the preponderance of inner pressures and the priority of wishes over an external reality that can be validated. Schizophrenic patients may perceive worldly things in ways that are frankly animistic (reminiscent of Piaget's earliest childhood stage in which moving things in nature, such as clouds, sun, trees, and wind, move of their own volition and with their own purpose). Further, inanimate things may be strongly imbued with emotion, not just *passively,* which is usual (in the way that one has feelings for familiar old clothes or an jalopy one has driven for some time), but with active emotions in a kind of extended *pathetic fallacy* that is generally disdained in modern poetic metaphor. These ideas and affects are condensed or telescoped upon perceptions so that the latter are unregistered in a distorted form. These perceptions are said to be *cognitively tainted* in projective testing, but they are more properly considered to be *affectively tainted.* It is possible, and worthwhile, to treat perceptions as indexes of the affects they embody without dwelling particularly on the ideas they embody (often as intermediaries for more affect). Perceptive images lend themselves particularly as they are often in color (a good clue to affect) or involve movement that may be of a sort that indicates, feeling (e.g., anger by forceful or incessant motions, often noisy; hate by shattering, exploding, disseminating; fear by furtive, quick, short motions; or sadness by falling, drooping, etc.). Ecstatic perceptions are a category of special interest as they indicate the transformed fate of a pleasure capacity that cannot be shared in more human contexts. Such patients should not be

assumed to be anhedonic, and it is a good idea to remark upon how pleasurable are the images they see.

2. *Translate cognition into affect.* Much of the distortion of cognition in schizophrenia could be seen as the product of its being overloaded with affects that the schizophrenic person cannot tolerate feeling and, indeed, does not consciously feel. The system of blockade of affectivity in schizophrenic persons, whatever its sources, appears to shunt affects for storage and expression elsewhere, in the form of overprized and overloaded concepts. But the cognitive domain and the domain of language are insufficient to handle these affects and are embarrassed to the extent that they buckle and strain. The fantasies of obsessive persons are instructive analogues of the distortion by exaggeration that results. For example, a fairly straightforward anger at someone becomes transformed in the dreams or fantasies of obsessive persons into a gory idea or image of mayhem that may be more disturbing to the person than the recognition of mere anger. For schizophrenic persons the situation is worse because their boundary confusion is such that it is more difficult to tell if the fantasy has happened or would ever happen.

THE ANALOGY OF THE WRITER

Another, less extreme analogy to the schizophrenic transformation of affects into cognitive vehicles is writing. Many people who write a great deal, who are interested in making words sound and move and express feeling, are somewhat restrained, formal, or obsessive in speech habits. Those whose habits of speech are the most affect laden, moving, or inspirational—the ones who can stir a crowd to action—somehow have not had to or cared to develop the elaborate skills of writing, of making words carry the affect nicely and powerfully. For these people, voice tone and gestures have perhaps served their needs so well that they have not been motivated to acquire the differentiated skill of written language, which is surely a less direct and natural channel. In the case of the schizophrenic, the less direct, substitute channel of affectively flat speech with cognitive distortions may or may not involve differentiated skills; but the substitution occurs perforce and the affects are blocked or stymied to a much greater degree than in obsessive speech.

Generality and hyper-abstractness as expressed in religio-philosophic and sociopolitical ideas are common cognitive substitutions for affects and, when applied to ordinary interpersonal situations, are identifying features of schizophrenic language. It is usually not difficult to get a sense of diffuse hostility from references to social strife or of removed affection in many religious ideas.

Inventions are a category of cognitive embodiment of affects. The influencing machines of more paranoid schizophrenic origin are of interest not merely as concepts of the genital with its own will (an idea found by Tausk, 1933, in his original paper on the subject and perhaps presaged by Blake in his loathing of "artistic machines" [Eaves,J. 1977], Machines invented (or *described,* as they are seldom actually built, by schizophrenic patients are particularly likely, because of the propensity in schizophrenia to turn oneself inside out, to be models of the mental process and the defensive structure. To read the affective coloring with which they are laden, one looks for the intentionality they are designed to foster or prevent. Frequently anger and fear result from the threat of derangement or compulsion; correspondingly, the machine is often influenced as well as influencing. Other schizophrenic inventions or ideas may be approached similarly.

Schizophrenic language is the major domain of cognitive substitution for affect (see Chapters 7 and 17) and provides inventions in the form of neologisms (see Forrest, 1969), which are precise indicators of what is so special about the patient's experience that extant words won't serve. They seldom describe affect directly and are rather a lexicon for its substitutions. Schizophrenic persons share with others the giving of special emotional loadings to certain words of general language (Forrest, 1973) and the employment of the (more poetic) potentialities of language (sound, image, metaphor) to reinforce wish-fulfilling statements and to convince oneself that they are thereby fulfilled. The therapist may keep an ear cocked for phrases that seem well-worn by use and which seem to have been contrived or worked-over in their sound pattern (e.g., are alliterative or assonant) or the development of their images or metaphors.

3. *Interpret proto-affective sensations upward into affects.* One commonly notes in certain schizophrenic patients the substitution of sensations that are more *primitive* than affects in the ordinary sense of the word. Presumably these sensations were once experienced at some point early in infant development (i.e., before complex and positive affects have been induced by the first social interactions and before they acquire the socially relevant meanings that will later be attached to them, or which they later color and enrich). Some of these primitive sensations are:

(a) *All-consuming awe, serenity, removed ecstasy, union with nature, one's smallness seen against enormity.* These correspond first and foremost to the feelings of a baby beside the larger body of the mother. Secondarily the feelings reflect dependence on and love of parents and others, love of fellow humans, the development of social conscience, union with all humankind, mature religiosity.

(b) *The terrific thrill of falling unsupported, floating weightless, or whirling.*
These vestibular sensations, which have direct parallels in such activities as skydiving, scuba-diving, flying, spacewalking, trapeze
artistry, amusement park rides or dancing and skating, replicate
early sensations of floating in womb or bath, or of being carried,
tossed playfully, or dropped. Their role in character formation has
been explored by Balint (1959) particularly in his "philobatic" type.
But they have a great generality, as they are part of our basic protection against the ill effects of gravity, and they are frequently emphasized by schizophrenic patients as metaphors for the condition they
find themselves in as well as substitutes for affects. Flying may express exalted but conflicted joy; falling, sadness and hopelessness; or
dizziness, a lack of sure apprehension of any feelings or moral guide-
posts for action.

(c) *Exquisite aestheticism and a mystical appreciation of sensations* such as
smells, light and dark (especially great variegation), colors (especially as they seem to interact), warmth, textures, wetness, and the
incidental low noises that most people filter out. These seem often to
replace sexual love in the center of the schizophrenic stage, and
reach intensity with great estrangement and self-denial.

(d) *Eerie, creepy, chilling, flesh-crawling sensations, gooseflesh, formication, nau-
sea, and palpitations.* These suggest terror and revulsion, disgust and
loathing, dislike, and fears of sexual feelings of a tactile and oral nature.

(e) *Unutterably chaotic feelings of fragmentation or the multiplicity of sentient existence; or of nothingness, being nothing, non-being; or of having exploded or dis-
seminated oneself.* These usually signal the presence of anger that cannot be integrated, although any embarrassment of affects can be responsible. As the integration of affects and affiliation with others im-
proves, these lessen. Some societies (such as many Asian ones) may
preserve the feeling of being a fragment in normal adults by rearing
children not as integral individuals, but as parts of a more diffuse
identity (individuation within a group rather than individualism).
This is to be distinguished as a different mechanism in which talk of
being a single fragment expresses longing for union with the social
whole.

(f) *Synesthesias,* the experience of one sensory modality in terms of another (e.g., tasting colors). It is an extension of normal metaphorical
capacity enhanced by the more fluid cognitive associations of schizo-

phrenia. A particular perception is amplified by the awareness of its correlatives in other modalities, a resonance that suggests affective loading. The confluence of more than one perceptive modality may help specify the affect. A 35-year-old man whose speech was full of synesthesias and who regularly experienced and created in me proto-affective creepy sensations and piloerection spoke of there being "a blue point to your brain." When asked to explain this, he added, "It's like" (sucks breath in through his teeth) "a blue point, a cold projection, a cold down-up state. Others have had it on bummers; I've had it naturally." While this was all metaphor, the material of the metaphor is apprehended synesthetically.

(g) *Erotic sensations.* I find it of interest, and a reflection of our present society's pursuit of every form of sensation rather than of affective experience, that residents and medical students frequently must be reminded that erotic feelings are not per se emotions. Schizophrenic patients may have strong erotic feelings. They may not attach erotic feelings to positive emotional meanings, which used to be normal and is salutary; instead they may experience sex impersonally with inanimate objects or symbolic transitional objects, or they may experience erotic sensations as substitutes for affects. Again the sign of this is the distortion; the erotic sensations appear disproportionately intense for the situation or tortured and overloaded with anguished affects that the situation will often make clear to the therapist. The Japanese film *In the Realm of the Senses* was an exercise in obsession with erotic sensation by a couple driven by a murderous rage between them, to which they eventually succumb.

(h) *Suffocation versus aeration.* Suffocation, eroticized in the just-mentioned film, and the current interest in "aerobic" exercise (a buzzword that suggests that those who do not participate are anaerobic forms of life) are part of a dimension of respiratory kinesthetic sensations that often preoccupy schizophrenic patients. One messianic patient, interested in anatomy, felt that he would unify the world by integrating the two halves of the brain through his corpus callosum and that his very breathing would have curative effects on the world's ills. The salutary pleasant feeling of a deep breath is projected and shared as a form of love of humanity (the Greek *agapé* rather than *eros*). Another recovering and hopeful schizophrenic man, asked if he was now feeling more *emotions,* said, "Yes, I feel the blood flowing in my body rather than being cold; oxygen coming into my lungs and cells—it's invigorating, there's more purpose to my life. I can come in, breathe the air, and get ready for the day's work.''

(i) *Muscular tension and sensations of pressure within the body* (as from Valsalva maneuvers or intestinal gas). Such bodily tensions are often substituted for angry feelings and may be of sufficient distress to result in delusional complaints of physical disorders to nonpsychiatric physicians. The sensation of movement within the body (or of the body in catatonic immobility) is part of a substitution of *motion* for *emotion*. The behavior of obsessive patients in psychoanalysis, who for a long time give what I call ''boiler readings'' of bodily tensions until they are more at home with their angry affects, are a corresponding nonpsychotic phenomenon.

(j) *Pain* is a substitute for a wide gamut of unhappy affects in nonschizophrenic as well as schizophrenic persons. In fact, with a modicum of help the schizophrenic patient (as is so often the case) can, more frequently than most somatizers, distinguish the fact that what has been reported as a head pain is not head*ache* or a hurting of the head so much as emotional anguish.[1] In this and all the foregoing examples of sensations substituted for affects, interpretation of affects may produce more gratifying results with schizophrenic patients, I have found, than with neurotic patients. The latter have ordinarily been able to rigidify and overdetermine their substitutions in a complex of reinforcing motivations that have accumulated like riders on a congressional amendment. Here, for one example, the greater fluidity of the schizophrenic person can be turned to advantage.

(k) *Humor.* This may be classed with proto-affective sensations but was discussed in a separate section. (see Chapter 8)

4. *Call to attention abnormalities in the amplitude of voice and gestures.* One schizophrenic student, quite brilliant and well-read in philosophy, exhibited a progressive escalation of voice amplitude as he was able to find a subject, seize upon it, and begin expounding on it in a monologue. This appeared to derive from his mounting interest (which seemed to creep in belatedly), his need to command his own attention in pursuing a difficult line of thought, and his need to fend off possible interruptions. His facial display of affect was increasingly angry although he was unaware of this.

---

[1]Schizophrenic patients do not necessarily suffer from *alexithymia* (Sifneos, 1973), a lack of words for feelings common in those with psychosomatic disorrders. They lack instead feelings for their words.

Beneath the anger was fear of contention and also fear of being locked into this narrow corridor of thought down which he had committed himself and was accelerating.

Inappropriate facial affects such as grimacing smiles—in fact most facies—are not much in the awareness of schizophrenic persons. In fact most of us are aware of our moods, but often learn from others what our faces are showing; we should not expect more of our schizophrenic patients. Thus the discrepant facies should be reflected back to the patient, who will usually say, if he has been schizophrenic for some time, "oh, yes, that's my flat affect." Nevertheless they need to know when they are most flat (indicating a greater defensiveness and burying of affects) or inappropriate. In the latter instance the face is moving, literally, to a different music, and *is* appropriate to the affects upon an *inner* fantasy rather than to those of the interpersonal situation at hand.

5. *Mark and agree on affects.* The affects that do come through should be noted, named, and agreed upon. This is what Sullivan called consensual validation, and it is crucial to schizophrenic resocialization. Initially it may be useful to use such strong and value-laden words for affective concepts as the list of deadly sins, that is, scorn, wrath, sloth, lust, and so on. I have discovered that schizophrenic patients do not mind, and tend to seize upon, such words, perhaps because they are stronger substitutes for affects than most words and ideas.

6. *Translate affects into the more basic ones from which they originated.* From a practical therapeutic standpoint, certain affects are best considered derivative from other affects. It is of little use to tell a person that he or she is angry or to "let people know you are angry" or "be assertive" if one does not go beneath this and discover the fear or disappointment or feeling of impotence that hurt the patient and occasioned the anger. If possible, the patient should learn to avoid being angry by avoiding being hurt in the first place. Scorn is usually an angry defensive reaction covering envy of other persons' greater acceptance and sadness at not being included.

7. *"Calibrate" affects in regard to intensity and compounding or sequencing.* Opportunities to compare the readings of affects by patient and therapist should be pursued. The best and most available source of stimuli for use in comparisons is the therapy session, but other opportunities include movies both have seen and current events. Six basic affects for comparison are joy, fear, anger, shame, guilt, and sadness. Ratings of these affects in videotaped stimuli by comparison groups of professionals dem-

onstrate a natural reliability that crosses regions and cultures.[2] Unless the treating psychiatrist is severely deviant in the identification of affects, comparing them with the schizophrenic patient is valuably educative.

[2]For a preliminary report of my research in "Affect Calibration," see "Psychiatrist Develops System for Scoring Emotions," *Stethoscope* 36(9)4, October 1981 (Presbyterian Hospital, 622 W 168, N.Y.C. 10032). The report is also reprinted in *Selected American Expressions for the Foreign-Born Psychiatrist and Other Professionals*, revised 1982, available from Educational Research, 722 W 168, N.Y.C. 10032.

12

Varieties of Confrontation in Establishing Relatedness with Schizophrenic Patients

Michael H. Stone, M.D.

In the course of diagnostic and therapeutic work with schizoprenic patients, the clinician becomes aware of various methods—though they are not always as conscious and calculated as the term "method" would imply—employed by the patient to avoid genuine relatedness or to avoid imparting material of any real value or emotional conviction. Some of these methods are popularly considered defenses, by analogy with the catalog of defenses utilized by neurotic analysands (see Anna Freud, 1966). Included among these are denial, splitting, and several types of externalization, such as projection and projective identification (see Rosenfeld, 1965). Many of these "mechanisms" are encountered in work with borderline patients, also (Kernberg, 1975; Le Boit, 1979). Alongside these primitive defenses, other peculiarities of relatedness may occur, such as vagueness, evasiveness (as an example of withholding), and fragmentation. It has not always been clear to me how appropriate it is to designate vagueness or fragmentation as defenses, inasmuch as these tendencies seem more to be reflections of the basic integrative disturbance so noticeable in certain schizophrenics, rather than reflections of some conscious or unconscious strategy for dealing with conflict. To be sure, the vague or fragmented patient keeps the clinician in the dark about his conflicts, but *not* in a way that preserves some measure of adaptation. Unlike the reaction-formations or rationalizations of the healthier patient—defenses that keep life going, albeit in a less than optimal manner—vagueness and particularly *fragmentation* represent a *failure* to defend in any meaningful way.

Theoretical debate aside, however, schiophrenic patients will often present one with either the primitive defenses just mentioned, or, under conditions of even greater stress perhaps, with the bankrupt defenses of vagueness, unintelligible speech, or fragmentation, which, as I have argued, rob the very concept of "defense" of its meaning. The countermeasures that suffice in ordinary discourse or in work with classical analysands are of little use in the face of these mechanisms. Instead one finds oneself resorting, instinctively or as an outgrowth of one's training, to maneuvers that have a greater likelihood of getting through the barriers to relatedness erected by the patient. *"Confrontation"* is a term covering the set of verbal and gestural patterns, clinical strategems, and the like, that we employ in the hope of getting through or around the primitive avoidance mechanisms. Buie and Adler (1973) have outlined some of the confrontational means at our disposal and their potential misuses as well as uses.

It will give greater clarity to this topic of confrontational measures if we examine in some detail an actual interview with a recovering schizophrenic patient, one who nevertheless manifested considerable vagueness during the encounter, who was eventually able to respond to the different confrontations with an enhanced capacity for genuine relatedness.

The patient was a single woman of 33, who had worked fairly successfully for some years as an editorial assistant in a publishing house. She had suffered an overt break during late adolescence, and another the year before this interview. The latter had necessitated hospitalization. Productive symptoms had abated shortly thereafter; by the time of the interview she was functioning at the borderline level (as defined by Kernberg, 1977), and was beginning, albeit with trepidation, to contemplate returning to school for some courses she hoped would help further her career.

Pt:[1] (entering the room, preparing to shake hands with the interviewer) I'm glad to see there's no weapon in your hand!

T.: (after both are seated) Let me hear what's going on in you at the moment.

Pt: Well. . . . I guess I'm not too sure what I'm supposed to say. (This vague reply fulfils the obligation to say something in response to the question, but reveals nothing.)

T.: You *guess* you're "not too sure." You *may* be sure, but you're not quite *sure* you're sure!? (In this confrontation, Int. parodies her

[1]Pt.: = Patient   T. = Interviewer

seemingly deliberate indecisiveness; the hope is to compel Pt. to de-
clare her position with more precision.)

Pt.: (pause) I don't know what's important. I guess I could talk about
school. That's kind of important right now. (Her demeanor is very
tentative here; voice scarcely audible.)

T.: What's important to *me* , were you wondering? Or to you? (This response is at once a question and a mild confrontation, insofar as it is
directed at forcing her to become definite about something. Int.
knew, from case material presented by her therapist, that Pt. was
often caught up in conflicts about whether to remain loyal to her
mother's wishes or to pursue her own goals. The "you versus me"
question thus related, via the transference within the interview itself, to this older conflict.)

Pt.: I guess I wonder what's important to you.

T.: You do! But, then, you say it all so tentatively.

Pt.: I feel kinda nervous.

T.: Well, I'm reminded that before we shook hands you wondered did I
have a *weapon* of some sort! (Int. assumes she meant this metaphorically, since it had been some time since she had been in the grips of
the kind of irrationality where such a fear would be experienced at
the literal level.)

Pt.: (pause) Well, I don't know. . . . It's just that . . . other people
have said you can be very sharp.

T.: Uh huh. (wondering: does she mean cutting, insightful?)

Pt.: So far . . . you haven't been that sharp. (Spoken with a twinge of
disappointment—but at what? That Int. seemed not as cutting as
she would, for some paradoxical reason, have liked? Had she been
fond of a sarcastic parent, for example? Or was she dismayed at his
lack of cleverness . . .)

T.: You find me almost banal, in fact. (An indirect confrontation in the
form of a mild taunt. Int. intentionally uses an unusual word, for its
surprise value, in hopes it will challenge her to (1) agree or disagree
and in so doing (2) spell out more clearly just how she *does* experience
Int. Whichever way she responds, he will have learned of a transference distortion. He will get a measure of the discrepancy between
how he is and how she regards him. Later, he would hope to learn
whether the discrepancy reflected feelings toward some important
member of her family.)

Pt.: No.

T.: But it has been a bit of a disappointment, I gather. (Another challenging remark. It doesn't matter whether it was or was not. Either way, she almost surely must make a definite yes or no answer; she almost dare not resort to vagueness here.)

Pt.: No. I just don't feel that uncomfortable with you. (Still, this is spoken with a twinge of disappointment, as though it would have been so much homier, more familiar, if Int. were a carbon copy of whomever it was, in her past, who related to her with a sharp edge.)

T.: You did notice my hand was free of anything sharp and pointed.

Pt.: (beginning to look tearful and downcast) Sometimes people's words can be worse than a sharp weapon. (She is still vague here, but she seems readier to produce something definite. She doesn't specify which person, but she leaves Int. with the impression she can be coaxed toward such a revelation.)

T.: That brings to mind whom?

Pt.: (sighing) I guess my family. (The vagueness persists!)

T.: (pause) Who in particular?

Pt.: (Voice just above a whisper) My mother.

T.: Let me hear. (Grateful that she finally rewarded him with a *specific* reference!)

Pt.: She just has the ability to reduce me to nothing. (pause) I don't know why I'm thinking about her now.

T.: Were you wondering whether I'd be a duplicate of her in some way? (The question is aimed at establishing a possible transference connection between her anticipation of a fear-engendering interviewer and her experience with some important figure from the past—who really did make her anxious.)

Pt.: I guess so. (Her demeanor is now sad, almost despondent. But she is back to "guesses".)

T.: You keep saying "I guess." I'm beginning to assume your main intent is to *agree* with me—no matter what position I might take. Is it a fair statement to say that, in your book, as long as you keep agreeing with me, I'll, so to speak, put down my sword? (This confrontation is worded to appeal to her cognitive capacities and was done so in the belief that her having become more *reasonable* a moment earlier—she mentioned mother by name, finally—warranted such a confrontation. The specific confrontation here queried her about what Int. felt was a pronounced irony in her interaction: that she would rather agree even with something she didn't accept—out of fear that Int. (like her mother presumably was, in her eyes) would be a bully who allowed no one an opinion of his own.

Pt.: Well, I don't. . . .

T.: (going on with his train of thought, providing her with an analogy) If I were to say to you, "Well, it's certainly a lovely evening," and you were to come back with, "I guess so," that would be very different from standing your ground and telling me, "Look, you idiot, it's 10 in the morning!" But you wouldn't have been agreeing with me, either, which would be sheer madness. So you say "I guess so." An "in-between" comment. It allows both of us to exist. (Int. implies that her mother seemed to put her on the spot a great deal, demanding loyalty to untenable positions; she must expect Int. to treat her in the same way.)

Pt.: I guess I do that a lot.

T.: Like right now!

Pt.: (laughing) I just did it again.

T.: Um hmm.

Pt.: I was just going to say, "I guess I'm afraid to take a stand. . ." (Both participants chuckle over this. The previous confrontations have led to a turning point in the interview, and anxiety and vagueness have given way to a much more cooperative and comfortable attitude toward Int.)

Pt.: . . . but I thought better of it.

T.: (pause) Actually, what *is* so horrifying about taking a stand?

Pt.: It's like . . . like writing with indelible ink. (pause) Something to be avoided at all costs.

T.: Even if what you were about to write down was the Ten Commandments? (With this bantering confrontation, Int. shows the absurdity of her assertion that *nothing* dare be said in a definite way. Clearly, she would have to backtrack from such an extreme position—toward a more realistic one.)

Pt.: Kind of . . . ah . . . (pause) . . . I guess . . . ah . . . *yes* (now growing visibly anxious) . . . a person (note her retreat from 1st to 3rd person) has to be kind of . . . I guess . . . be careful.

T.: Perhaps! (alluding once again, via parody, to her maddeningly equivocal way of talking)

Pt.: (chuckling) Yeh.

T.: Or *else* what? What have you noticed to be the terrifying consequences of being definite?

Pt.: Well . . . I don't know if I've ever felt "definite." I always feel sort of smeared around the edges. (This is a highly idiosyncratic locution, one that seems to carry a considerable emotional charge. As such it triggers some vivid fantasies in the mind of Int., who wonders, what could she be alluding to with that phrase, "smeared around the edges?" It sounds like something connected with the bathroom —early memories involving excretion and messiness.)

T.: More or less. (again, an effort, through gentle parody, to urge her toward some degree of candor)

Pt.: Yes. But . . . when a person is *definite* it's as though . . . it comes back to the *ink* thing . . . (more evasion through solipsistic speech. Int. can't know what incident she may be referring to with the indelible ink image, yet she assumes he does know. This is a subtle example of primary-process thinking on her part.)

T.: OK, but all that doesn't tell me what you feel *happens* to whoever dares to be definite. I feel like asking, "So *then* what?"

Pt.: So now I just think of the likelihood of destruction being possible. (eyes now averted from Int., as she retreats into this elliptical and quite uncommmunicative speech)

T.: In what form?

Pt.: Well . . . (pause) . . . being *wrong*. Somehow, to be wrong is something I really can't tolerate. I . . . I was just going to say, "I guess" (pause) Sometimes I see things, and . . . the way I see them in my mind's eye is, like, *heavy* (she was actually looking at Int. with "heavy," nearly closed, eyelids at this moment) . . . and, uh, I always want to *stop* them . . . (she has by now become scarcely coherent.)

T.: You're aware, are you, of resorting to a rather private language just now? (A confrontation whose aim was to bring to a halt her attempts to hide behind vague or autistic language.)

Pt.: Well, I . . . I'm trying to say how I feel. (Pause) You didn't understand me? (She has little awareness how incomprehensible she was during the last few interchanges.)

T.: Did you want me too? (A mild confrontation aimed at getting her to take responsibility for the *opposite* to what her question implied; i.e., that she had more invested in *not* being understood.) The subject was, anyhow; what becomes of those who are *definite*? You convey the notion that they come to a bad end. But you don't tell be *what* bad end.

Pt.: (pause) It's kind of as though . . . I won't take a stand, so that . . . I could never be wrong. Or get hurt. Or hurt somebody else.

T.: What's the connection?

Pt.: Between taking a stand . . .

T.: Between being wrong and getting hurt.

Pt.: Somehow, it just comes to mind . . . of doing something and having it be kind of innocuous, and . . . (trails off)

T.: Such as?!

Pt.: (At last giving a specific example!) . . . like, once I wrote a letter to my therapist at the clinic when I was in college . . . which I thought I had a right to do. Only my mother found out about it. She got very upset with me.

T.: What sort of letter?

Pt.: It was while I was home for the summer. I was letting him know I was unhappy. I must have put the wrong address or no stamp or something, because it got returned, and my mother opened it.

T.: Would that have been typical of her?

Pt.: Yes. I think my family prefers me to be "smeared around the edges" anyway (again, this unusual phrase) because then anything they say can be appropriate, if I say nothing definite. And it ("it" = any vague remark she might make to them) fits into whatever they mean. I guess I get lost in the process. (A rather obscure way of referring to the ego-blurring quality of her overly deferential attitude, of agreeing always with any member of the family. The process is reminiscent of the "as-if" patients described by Helene Deutsch [1942].)

T.: You "guess" again, as though you'd prefer not to go on record even about that . . .

Pt.: Sometimes I just don't know what is true. (spoken in a monotone, without much conviction)

T.: I notice, by the way, you've used that phrase, "smeared around the edges," a second time. Does that have some special significance for you?

Pt.: I . . . uh . . . (pause)

T.: Perhaps some memory comes to mind. Having to do with smearing, etcetera.

Pt.: Well . . . there was this time when somebody in the family barged into the bathroom when I'd been trying to clean up after . . . to clean myself after going to the bathroom. Only I got startled, and lost track of what I was doing, and didn't do it properly . . . so there was stuff still dripping out of me, that got smeared onto me, onto my legs and all . . . (spoken with great embarrassment, just above a whisper) They taunted me a lot for that, afterwards. For years afterwards.

T.: So that expression becomes a sort of shorthand way of referring to your being in the "one-down" position at home, to being vulnerable. To be "smeared around the edges" is to be *no threat* to them, as you see it.

Pt.: (beginning to look very somber, almost tearful) That's me, all right. No threat to them . . .

T.: (after a long pause, in which both participants were sitting rather vacantly in their chairs, in a way that reminded Int. of two acquaintances on the porch of an old-age home) What's occurring to you right now?

Pt.: Well, mmm, just wondering about what I was wondering about . . . (the ultimate in noncommunicative communication)

T.: I was thinking, "Here we are, waiting for Grandma to die!" Does that bring anything to mind? (In this type of confrontation a personal fantasy, often a poignant one, is shared with a patient for tactical purposes: the clinician has the hunch his own mental image is a manifestation of having been empathically in tune with some warded-off feeling or affect-laden memory on the part of the patient. The hope is that the mentioning of one's personal reaction, something not ordinarily shared with a patient, will facilitate the surfacing—and the sharing—of the important but hitherto repressed material.)

Pt.: (She begins to sob, holding her head in her hands, and then cries quietly for several minutes before saying, with much emotion) Kinda too *late* to wait for her to die!

T.: "Kinda?" (Int. had not realized her grandmother had died, but now experienced the vague locution "kinda" as a way of perhaps denying that the death had really occurred. Hence the confrontative repetition of her indefinite wording.)

Pt.: It *is* too late!

T.: Well . . . could you have been thinking that if you just didn't say anything "definite"—anything, that is, that might offend anyone, that, somehow, *definite* things, like for instance *death* would never happen?

Pt.: (spoken very quietly; still crying) Yes . . . that's how it seems to be. I feel, sometimes, if I just shut my eyes, things'd all change.

T.: As though you might wake up in a different world.

Pt.: Mmm.

T.: What sort of world?

Pt.: A world where I wouldn't (crying once more) . . . I wouldn't be so afraid all the time.

T.: What are you mostly afraid of *these* days?

Pt.: Making a fool of myself at school. (pause) Or . . . I guess . . . losing Dr. J (Her therapist. In the patient's mind, there was still some question about whether or not the sessions could continue once she left the hospital—despite a firm promise from the therapist that there would be no interruption in their work.)

T.: Yes, that's what I was wondering about: would you and she talk in "guesses," so the issue of continuing therapy, or not, never got addressed in a definite way? Was that what you preferred—to what in your mind was the near certainty she could not continue. . .

Pt.: Yes . . . (pause) It surprised me your mentioning my grandmother. It really bothered me. I hadn't even been aware how much feeling I had for her. I really miss her . . . I mean . . . (again tearful) I miss her a lot!

T.: And to have lost Dr. J would be like losing your grandmother all over again.

Pt.: Yes (crying briefly) . . . I don't know how I'd be able to take it. She told me we'll be able to continue. But I can't bring myself to believe it.

T.: So you've been reacting as though you're about to lose her—even though that isn't very likely.

Pt.: I guess . . . (catching herself) . . . yes . . . at least that's what she tells me.

T.: Well, what would make the loss so unbearable . . . that you couldn't take it in stride? We're talking in the abstract here, because despite your pessimism it doesn't sound as if any interruption is going to take place. But "if" . . .

Pt.: (pause) I'd be very afraid.

T.: Of what?

Pt.: (pause) Falling apart. I feel like I'm a house of cards (Her fear, it would seem, is of *fragmentation*.)

T.: And she is one of the cards on the bottom?

Pt.: No, I . . . she's like a little glue.

T.: (pause) Have you considered that, in some way, you would *owe* it to her to collapse? That she might be rather taken aback at the idea you could survive without her? (This confrontation is delivered as a question, but one that compels her to ponder the *opposite* of what she as been conscious of. Her position, thus far, has been that she is weak and the "other"—whether mother, originally, or, transferentially, her therapist—is strong. She would tend to claim that she is terribly dependent on some "strong" figure, and therefore would "fall apart" after any separation. Int. wants her to contemplate what he has come to feel is an even more important—by virtue of being just as powerful, but hitherto *less conscious*—dynamic; namely, that she *isn't* so weak—and the other person isn't so strong. The problem may be: she *dare* not become autonomous and manage life on her own, lest mother/therapist fall apart in her absence. The mother might be considerably dependent on her daughter, but unable to admit this to herself—as few parents can, when they are dependent on their children—and unable to "let go." She continually undermines her daughter's confidence through excessive criticism, etc., so that now, even as an adult, the patient doesn't feel psychologically equipped to leave her mother, who, as a result never has to come to grips with her own dependency. Int. used a *surprise* maneuver—drawing attention to the opposite possibility—to help expand Pt.'s awareness about what may have been a long-neglected trend in her personal psychology: only by realizing that mother/therapist can survive without *her*, could she escape her heavy burden of guilt which, if Int. were correct in his assumption, impeded her progress toward autonomy.

Pt.: No, I never thought of it that way.

T.: You don't see her in the same light as your mother—who opens your mail and gets upset that somebody else mattered to you besides her?

Pt.: No, I . . . I've *wished* that I mattered to her. I don't feel I matter to Dr. J . She matters a great deal to *me* . . . I have wondered if she'd be upset if I were to kill myself . . . if she'd get depressed. I kinda hope she would, but it seems hard to believe I could affect her that much.

T.: Well, if you got very much worse and killed yourself, your relationship with her would be at an end. If you got very much better and could get along on your own, your relationship would be at an end. You can see that, for *your* sake, you feel you need to steer a course somewhere between suicide and self-reliance lest you lose her.

Pt.: Yes . . . I'm not in a hurry to get better, because I can't imagine doing without her. It would take the happiness out of getting well.

T.: But that Dr. J.'s losing *you* could affect her . . . that your relationship is a two-way street, not a one-way street . . . you seem never to have contemplated. I'm not trying to claim she would be as devastated by your success and independence as, according to what I sense about your home situation, your mother might be. To be truthful, I imagine your doctor would welcome your success, that her main reaction would be a positive one. But it doesn't seem as if you've even stopped to consider the other side the matter. Couldn't it be that what has held you back all these years from really gaining your independence is *not* your "stupidity," your laziness, or craziness—on which you place the blame at various times—but the tremendous fear I sense, of leaving your rather ill and lonely mother behind you, forlorn and disappointed? (These remarks combine confrontation with a transference interpretation. There is an appeal to her congnitive faculties here: the different aspects of the contradictory views Int. senses exist in Pt. are spelled out in detail, rather than merely hinted at, as in some of the more bantering or paradoxical interventions earlier in the interview. Int. hopes, in this manner, as the interview draws to a close, to leave something definite and something previously neglected, for Pt. to explore further with her therapist. For years Pt. has viewed herself—consciously—as weak, mother as strong. That her mother, and by transference, Dr. J., could have a hidden weak side that inhibits Pt.'s efforts to gain autonomy has up til now escaped Pt.'s attention.)

Pt.: (becoming tearful) Yes . . . (pause) I've always considered myself the weak one and mama the strong one. I thought I always failed at things because I didn't have what it takes (this despite her being almost consistently an "A" student, even during her recent coursework in the midst of her illness). You're saying I've failed—or gotten sick—to give myself a good excuse to stay home and keep mama company. (pause) There could be something to that. I'll have to think about that.

T.: Well, if we've gotten you to look at your situation in a new way, it's been a good morning's work. We'll stop at this point.

The example that follows stems from work with a woman in her twenties who had suffered a schizophrenic break several years before the time of the extract. Treatment (consisting of phenothiazines and a psychotherapy that varied between the expressive and supportive modes) had brought her to the point where she was coming to grips with ambivalent feelings toward the first therapist. This sector of her mental life was the only one remaining in which delusional thinking still held sway. Confrontation about the change into animal form she felt the therapist had undergone did not altogether dispel the primary-process ideation. For this reason, despite her rather good general level of function (she was working and maintaining an apartment at the time the session took place), her psychostructural level of function (cf. Kernberg, 1967) was "psychotic."

Pt.:[2] Oh, I had this exciting experience yesterday! I went to the fair, and there at the animal show I saw a pig, and it was Dr. Bond (her former therapist)! It was a case of . . . what were you calling it the other day when I spoke about . . . transubstantiation! That's what it was!

T.: I have a hunch that term is set aside for somewhat loftier conversions than the one you're talking about!

Pt.: What do you mean?

T.: I think "transubstantiation" is reserved for the Church . . . the wafers . . . that sort of thing.

Pt.: Oh.

---

[2] Pt. = Patient   T. = Therapist

T.: But did you feel Dr. Bond really underwent such a transformation, or . . .

Pt.: (interrupting) "Transformation"! Yes, that's what I meant in the first place . . .

T.: Anyway . . . you were sounding a moment ago as though you felt Dr. Bond was transformed *literally* into that piggy at the fair.

Pt.: Of course! That's no "feeling," Dr. Nelson, that's how it was! So I *saw* him at last. Isn't that marvelous?

T.: Uh . . . Tell me something: if he were *really* to evaporate in Oklahoma City (where she had been in treatment before) and recrystallize—as a pig , yet—in the city of New York . . . I mean, how do you even explain the physics and chemistry of it?

Pt.: Dr. Nelson, *you're* the scientist. *You* explain it! I know it was *him!* That's all!

T.: Have you consid . . . I mean, could it be, he had become a kind of "pig," in your mind's eye? After all, you had been criticizing him lately for certain things, where you felt he let you down, and so on. . . . Might you not be talking of a kind of *figurative* "piggishness" that got temporarily hardened in your mind while at the fair . . . as though . . .

Pt.: (interrupting again) Oh, Dr. Nelson—you're getting poetic! No, he's not "piggish", he's the most handsome man since Valentino! But at the *fair* . . . (pause) Yes! (raising her voice) He *was* a pig! (becoming somewhat tearful) He got my hopes up, and then . . . he left me high and dry. High and dry, goddammit.

T.: So in effect . . .

Pt.: No! I know what you're thinking, Dr. Nelson. I don't know how he got into that pig, or . . . or . . . however it was, but it was him!

The patient in this vignette readily grasped the symbolism of her allusion ("he was a pig: he left me high and dry"). But just as one imagines she is about to understand the connection between her having felt someone to be figuratively a pig and having then experienced him to change *literally* into a pig—she reverts to her initial stance.

There is also a highly playful and dramatic quality to her discourse, so that one can not always be certain whether she was really voicing a delusional idea or merely toying with the therapist. This patient was highly intelligent (verbal IQ 146), and was more able to appreciate the unrealistic nature of some of her distorted perceptions, or at least quicker than a less intelligent patient would be to grasp that her interviewer found a particular perception or conviction deluded. Since a patient's *response* to confrontation is a key element in the psychoanalytical diagnosis of structure (Kernberg, 1967, 1977), there is a good rationale for pursuing, via a confrontational technic, various statements made by a possibly schizophrenic patient that seem at first flush to reflect a weakened capacity to test reality. It was for this reason that the interviewer here was so persistent in probing her about her assertion that the pig at the fairgrounds was an actual, real transmogrification of her former therapist. The verbal duel ended in something of a draw: she grasped the figurativeness of her allusion (so far so good)—only to go on a moment later to claim ("No, I know what you're thinking . . .") that her doctor had turned into the pig after all.

. . . . .

The interview in the next example took place between the author and a hospitalized borderline schizophrenic woman of 26, about whose progress he had been asked to consult. Shortly before her admission, approximately three weeks before the interview took place, she had made an extremely serious suicide attempt from which she had been rescued only by chance, and with great effort. In the interview, I had been trying to understand the particularities of her life circumstances that may have acted as a precipitant to the attempt. A variety of confrontational measures were utilized.

T.: Was this, by the way, the first time you'd toyed seriously with the thought of killing yourself?

Pt.: Oh, no; I've thought about suicide ever since I was 14.

T.: Oh! What was particularly upsetting about that year?

Pt.: I don't know. Nothing I can think of. I really don't know.

T.: I find that hard to believe. (No subtlety here; Int. confronts her directly with his incredulity about the "absence" of any anxiety-provoking life events preceding an adolescent suicide attempt.)

Pt.: How come?

T.: Fourteen-year-olds don't become fixated on suicide over "nothing."

Pt.: Well, I can't think of anything. Really! . . .Apart from being ill . . . (The confrontation succeeded: she makes a passing reference, at least, to a probable precipitant.)

T.: Oh!? What did you have?

Pt.: Well, I have this retinitis condition, since even when I was younger. It seemed to be progressive; that year my vision got really bad, and I couldn't do sports any more. It got hard to read, also.

T.: That didn't figure into your feelings about suicide. (An ironic confrontation relying upon a deadpan elaboration by Int.—which he knows to be wildly untrue, and which Pat. almost dare not agree with, lest she appear absurd. Int. verbalizes the *opposite* to what is expected. With this maneuver, she is forced to reveal the truth.)

Pt.: Yes, it did. I'd have to say it did. (She responds, as expected, to the pseudo-naive interpretation—and admits what seemed obvious all along.)

T.: Um hmm.

Pt.: I felt life would be horrible if my vision got any worse, and I'd rather be dead.

T.: It goes without saying life as a blind person would be totally insupportable. (Again, the use of pseudo-naiveté and irony, along with an emphatic tone of voice. Int. speaks as if he identifies with Pat.'s viewpoint—while gently parodying this viewpoint at the same time.)

Pt.: Oh, absolutely! I'd certainly kill myself if that happened.

T.: You must wonder how come the Lighthouse has any live customers. (Here the confrontation relies on bantering humor.)

Pt.: It is puzzling. I know there are blind people who seem cheerful, though.

T.: According to your equation either *they* must be "crazy" or . . . (Here, Int. makes a confrontation that consists of a rephrasing and *dramatization* of Pat.'s grossly unrealistic, black-and-white views about the degree to which her handicap would drive any and every person—rather than just herself—to suicide.)

Pt.: Or *I'm* crazy! (nervous laugh) I know it's *my* craziness. But I still hold on to suicide as my "way out."

T.: Your trump card! (Int. restates her comment, using an unusual image—chosen for its ironic overtones—in an effort to highlight (1) her manipulativeness and (2) the pathetic nature of her manipulative act. Suicide "trumps" all cards, in the sense of compelling most people to accede to one's wishes. But it is ultimately a pathetic trump card, because, having played it, one doesn't survive to reap the "benefits" of one's coercive act.)

Pt.: Yeah!

T.: Well, but all this is "ancient history," so to speak. Were you getting any blinder the week or so before you took the Seconal?

Pt.: No.

T.: So what was happening?

Pt.: Well, my dog died.

T.: Uh huh.

Pt.: And I had a quarrel with my judo teacher.

T.: You see well enough to learn that?

Pt.: Yes. And I believe in building up my body. I also take yoga; I eat "organic" foods. I haven't smoked in three years . . .

T.: All this to make yourself a trimmer corpse?

Pt.: Huh!? (Shocked at this blunt confrontation; she saw no irony in making frantic efforts to perfect her body all the time she was plotting to kill herself.)

T.: You don't find it mildly contradictory that you perfect your body like an athlete's, and then kill it off with the Seconal? (This confrontation is phrased in a more readily understood way: appeal to emotion having failed, an appeal is now made to her cognitive powers. The language still has an edge to it ("kill it off"), the better to drive the interviewer's point home.)

Pt.: Well, I wasn't trying to kill my *body!* I *like* my body! I was trying to destroy my *mind!* To kill my *brain!*

T.: The two never got along anyway! (A playful challenge in which Int. purposely anthropomorphizes mind and body as a quarreling couple. Furthermore, the irony relies on the assumption that mind and body "seldom" get along and therefore her difficulty is—as she would claim—typical, nothing out of the ordinary. Implicit, however, is the comment that mind and body *are* supposed to function in an integrated fashion; her inability to make them "get along" is *not* at all normal or typical, and in fact constitutes a serious problem.)

Pt.: No! My brain doesn't even seem *connected* with me. It seems "out *there*" somehow (pointing to the air around her).

T.: Literally, out "there"? (Here the interviewer tries to test whether she is actually delusional about the location of her brain, or merely speaking metaphorically.)

Pt.: No, not "literally" out there; it's *in* me, all right. But it only gives me trouble . . . (She realizes she was speaking metaphorically—and this tends to establish her as having good reality testing, in keeping with *borderline,* rather than psychotic function, at this time.)

T.: What kind?

Pt.: Worries. Sadness. I'd just as soon *kill* it!

T.: As, indeed, you nearly succeeded in doing. With rather grave consequences for your body, too, I must say! (The confrontation here relies on the double entendre—"grave" consequences—to highlight a seriousness about her behavior that she ignored up till now.)

Pt.: Yes, I know. (Admitting, in a more reasonable way, that her mind and body are not so neatly separable as her behavior would suggest.) I almost died (said with some tearfulness).

T.: Are you sad you made it, or sad you almost didn't?

Pt.: I don't know. (more earnest and genuine, now, in her relatedness to the interviewer) I don't know if I can be happy. People frighten me. I don't get along with my folks. I can barely support myself, because there's only a few jobs I *can* do, what with my vision . . .

T.: And you're saving your trump card if things don't work out.

Pt.: Yeh. I couldn't give it up . . . the possibility of ending it all, I mean . . . unless I knew I could have some sort of decent life, a boyfriend, and stuff . . . but I *don't* know whether I can.

As often happens in working with borderline patients, whether schizotypal (as in this example) or otherwise, adroit use of confrontation—about the glaring discrepancies and areas of denial in their discourse—leads to a higher level of candor. The patient here began to "open up" about the painful issues that underlay her suicide attempt; at this point, a confrontative approach is no longer necessary. The consultant or therapist can relax into a more conventional kind of sympathetic, analytically exploratory style of interviewing.

13

Special Aids to Therapy: Contracts, Goal Setting, Diaries, Action, Metaphor

Harry D. Albert, M.D.

Relationship of the Contractual Mode to Coping Skills

We have seen that contractual negotiation between therapist and patient promotes self-observation skills, as well as contributing to the patient's realization that he can gain control of his everyday life, at least to some degree. These gains are over and above the immediate benefits derived from the practical aspects of therapy.

Meichenbaum (1966), a cognitive therapist, divides the process of personal change into three stages:

1. self-observation

2. recognition of incompatible perceptions and behaviors

3. planning regarding possible change

Negotiations around the therapeutic contract often will focus, of necessity, on the patient's more inappropriate defensive operations, to facilitate formation of the therapeutic relationship. Making the contract requires therapist and patient to define salient issues, to arrange them in a potentially solvable form, to take action, and to make further changes on the basis of results over time. This set of operations could just as well have been designated the *development of general coping skills.*

Schizophrenic persons may have difficulties with any or all of these steps. It is my experience, however, that patients will frequently attempt to adopt this format as a way of dealing more effectively with family members or with members of a hospital staff. This change, when it occurs, is prognostically a good sign. Often, we see this development even where the patient had not possessed self-control or self-observation skills to any marked degree when treatment began. The development of adaptive skills may not be welcomed by family members, who may, for various reasons, wish to maintain the old equilibrium in which the patient's wishes could be distorted and his problems largely ignored. (Sagers, 1976)

Example

A 21-year-old former student began to consider returning to school. Among his wishes was the idea of moving into an apartment in the disreputable East Village area of New York, not far from his old campus. It was impressive at joint meetings that his parents could almost literally not hear the patient's explanation. He emphasized that only in this area could he pay his own rent from a small trust fund and some part-time work. His parents' replies focussed only on their fears about "dangerous hippies and drugs." They required two later meetings to grasp the issue about financial independence. Even then, the mother angrily reproached the *therapist* for suggesting such a move, considering how her son was "so much safer" in their Fifth Avenue home.

When marital issues are of chief concern an approach like that of Sagers (1976) may be very useful. The first attempts at autonomy in patients may help expose (and begin to resolve) an impasse in treatment, to which this sort of pathological equilibrium with family, spouse, or therapist had originally contributed.

The process of negotiated stepwise change may be applied to the issue of certain primitive wishes which cannot reasonably be gratified in their original form. The process of negotiation may allow a gradual nudging of the patient up the gradient of social evolution to where partial expression (through less primitive mechanisms) of inner wishes may be possible.

Problems of Motivation

May Romm, in a personal communication, once defined a motivated patient simply as "a person who shows up at your office." Sometimes when we speak of poor motivation, the most important cause may lie in countertransference, or perhaps an inadequate definition of treatment goals. Or, one may be in the midst of some impasse in therapy not primarily of the patient's making. When one sees schizophrenic patients in consultation, it often emerges that they have been coaxed into treatment by parents, or other persons in authority, with the hope that they become "socialized"—rendered more acceptable to conventional society—rather than truly reintegrated along lines relevant to their psychological makeup. If this has been the case, the patient may come reluctantly and appear "unmotivated" to us.

Example

A 24-year-old college student was seen during a psychotic break in which he imagined himself pregnant as if from a "telepathic rape from God." With medication, his terrified agitation and much of the delusional material cleared. He then refused further medication or treatment of any kind, claiming that he was now able to return to his schooling (which was true). His real reason he revealed to me some time later, during a consultation. His therapist had urged further therapy as a means of dealing with this man's profound fear of others. To the patient this meant that he would be disarmed totally, inasmuch as he saw his life sustained only by a driving fear of others—from which he drew a kind of angry strength. As far as he was concerned, losing this fear would leave him "curled up in some state hospital like a dead cockroach." Once assured that therapy would help him be stronger and more purposive, and that he could keep his anger as long as he needed it, his "motivation" returned readily.

IMPROPER SETTING OF GOALS

Supposed failure of motivation may turn out to be a reflection of inappropriate goals. Therapists working with schizophrenic patients may overlook certain aspects of a case and be led into error for any of the following reasons:

1. the symptom may be ego-syntonic

2. the symptom may serve to ward off intolerable affect

3. the symptom may ward off intrusion of parental introjects

4. the symptom may represent the patient's (at present) best coping efforts

5. the symptom may be a necessary part of the patient's actual social equilibrium; any change may be vigorously opposed by significant people in the patient's life

6. the therapist's timing may be in error, in the sense that each loss of a symptom is mourned, and the rate of change tolerable for a given patient must not be exceeded

Principles Useful in Goal-Setting

The patient should be encouraged to set personal goals, either in positive terms (about future wishes), or in negative terms (about the avoidance of certain undesirable outcomes). Frequently the patient will elaborate goals in a highly abstract or autistic mode. Thus the therapist's earliest goal is mutual understanding of the shared task. Patients must be taught how to follow chains of causal thinking, so that even the most abstractly stated goal can be reformulated in such a way that patient and therapist will know what the objective is and when it has been achieved.

Example

A gifted 14-year-old schizophrenic girl told me her most basic wish was "self-understanding." When she had achieved this, it would no longer matter that she was prey to terrifying hallucinations, or that she mutilated her abdomen with a blade, and so on. Over the following two sessions I asked repeatedly what it was about herself that she was trying to understand. I offered a number of examples of what others meant by this (none of which apparently had any application to her). Finally, after much self-scrutiny and questioning me repeatedly—"What did I really mean?"—she shared with me her secret wish—that she "understand her bodily functioning." Behind this rather abstractly worded phrase was actually a desire to understand why she sweated at times, what the feelings in her abdomen really were, what her heart palpitations related to, and so on. She in the meantime had bizarre explanations for all these occurrences (and a bizarre explanation for just why she wished to explore bodily sensation further). On an everyday level of discourse, she was, of course, simply asking to understand why she felt as she did.

Because, as she told me, these feelings came and went unpredictably, we agreed that she would keep track of which feelings occurred at a given time and, as a later elaboration, what the external circumstance were. Initially she denied that outside events had any relationship to her bodily feelings, but was at this point willing to go along with our experiment. Still later, I offered the patient reading material on the experience of adolescence and on sexuality. Finally, her originally primitive list of sensations had metamorphosed into ''Susie's Feeling Book.'' This was a diary of emotions and their relation to the (often distorted) interplay between herself and others, and of her interpretations of the motivations behind other people's actions.

This program evolved over seven months of twice-weekly meetings, and was paced by the patient. Each increase in the observational detail of the diary led the patient to further curiosity about herself and others. The diary began as a largely autonomous activity and largely remained so.[1]

The principles illustrated in the preceding example include the following:

1. Goal-setting is primarily the patient's job.
2. Goal-directed activities must be pleasurable in themselves, must be largely ego-syntonic, must be relatively concrete and, ideally, should serve as a bridge to other, longer-range goals.

GOALS AND VALUES FOR PATIENT AND THERAPIST

If we assist the patient in setting goals, the nature of these goals (particularly those we establish first) will of necessity reflect to some degree our biases and values. Many therapists who pride themselves on ''value-free'' treatment of nonpsychotic persons will be troubled by this. It is also necessary to differentiate appropriate goal setting from what could constitute an undue interference in the life of the patient. On this topic, Fromm-Reichmann once wrote: ''There are legitimate values for every psychoanalyst. Unless he is clear on the importance and relevance of unconventional

---

[1] At times it had the quality of an ego-syntonic obsessional symptom, as the patient used diary keeping as a tool of distantiation and superiority. (See special techniques, below: Diaries)

standards, he is not likely to be alert to how his own values compare with the conventional evaluations which are promoted by the society that pays him for his services. The psychoanalyst's legitimate set of values should be the patient's growth and maturation of personality and helping the patient to gain the freedom and the courage to fulfill his needs and wishes as long as it can be done without hurting his neighbor" (1950, p.136).

As therapists of psychotic persons, it is incumbent upon us to develop an awareness of how "abnormal" are many of the features of so-called normal life. Various defenses are mobilized in the service of retaining composure, whether it be the callousness of walking around a fallen drunk on our way to the subway, denial of the all too obvious effects of a municipal garbage strike, or whatever. Our patients do not always share our repertoire of defenses, though they may possess others we quite lack. For therapists who are inexperienced with the realm of psychopathology on which we are focusing here, it may be useful to become familiarized with the lives of visionaries, revolutionaries, and philosophers. I am not suggesting, as Laing (1969) and others may, that the schizophrenic person necessarily has greater sensitivity or greater creativity than the rest of us, but rather that the therapist of a severely disordered person has a greater need to remember that the patient, "beneath" his disorder, may have a legitimate entitlement to much of his eccentricity.

Even Fromm-Reichman's view that it is not legitimate to have goals that "hurt one's neighbor" is under certain circumstances open to question.

Example

A 24-year-old physics graduate student was seen following a psychotic break that occurred while he was attempting to write 20 hours a day to complete a thesis. The patient felt doomed, because success in school would reward his parents, whom he hated; on the other hand, failure would doom him to life as a nonentity, especially since he was acutely aware of his social isolation and lack of "common sense." At the time I rendered a consultation, he was engaging a lawyer to obtain his hospital release and was refusing any treatment.

After he revealed the nature of his problem, along with some other, more bizarre thinking, I asked if he saw revenge upon his parents as a major motif behind his actions. I said that revenge was commonplace in the world, indeed the theme of many books and films, so I questioned why he, a man of obvious intelligence, was locked into such a self-damaging and primitive mode of revenge? I offered my services, with an initial goal of helping him to understand in greater depth the whole dynamism of revenge. Eventually this man went on to finish his degree. From my private point of view he remains to this day unduly preoccupied with envy, spite, and vengefulness, though less so than when I began working with him. He is, five years later, a functioning and creative scientist, with some social life through the Mensa organization.

GOALS SHOULD BE PLEASURABLE

A number of authors have written on the schizophrenic's deficit in experiencing pleasure (anhedonia; see Rado, 1962; Bellak, 1971; Searles, 1967). Be this as it may, almost all schizophrenic patients are able to offer us at least a brief list of personal pleasures. Such a list might have little more on it than a warm bath—offered, for example, as the "only enjoyment in life" by one 34-year-old schizophrenic man.

It will in any case be useful, when working with anhedonic patients of this type, to explore thoroughly what possibilities for pleasure may exist. Often the patient will at first deny there are any; we may need to encourage such a patient to indulge in fantasy (concretistic patients will find this step difficult), sharing with us what things or events *might conceivably* afford him some gratification. Our patients are all too familiar with grandiose and bizarre fantasies used as a retreat from action and contact. Many can be taught the technique of what one might call "creative day-dreaming" as an aid to future planning (of which we will have to say more below).

The Gradient Between Ego-Syntonic and Ego-Dystonic Action

Typically, the thoughts and actions of schizophrenic patients occur within the context of intense inner conflict. Because many of the dynamic and opposing issues are quite archaic, "preverbal" in their origin at times, and reside in disordered persons, their exploration and resolution will be a difficult and protracted business. Ultimately, as therapists, we must encourage those compromises (between inner wish and social restraint) which are to the greatest extent possible ego-syntonic, which will afford some pleasure and will reinforce the patient's capacity to maneuver comfortably in social settings.

In my experience, techniques that foster "regression" in the hope of retrieving a more solid integration seldom produce anything more than a prolonged period of increased disorganization (see Foster, 1975). The theoretical concepts for enhancing "regression in the service of the ego" are at least interesting, but in my experience patients are all too prone to regress without any urging on our part, and they experience all too much difficulty in returning later on to the status quo ante. Even in Sechèhaye's (1951) long treatment of Renée, with all the regression this patient exhibited, it is worth noting the importance attached by her therapist to simple pleasures: e.g., bathing, or viewing lovely scenes. Throughout, Sechèhaye encouraged the development of newer behaviors, despite her general emphasis on the symbolic aspects of the treatment.

Patients can divide problematical life events into those that disturb themselves and those that are disturbing to other people (some events are of course disturbing to others and oneself). If the patient is encouraged to work with this view, suddenly a fourth group will often appear: behaviors and thoughts that displease *others* (are "crazy"), but that the patient enjoys and wishes to hold onto. These typically involve dilapidation in personal habits, grandiose behavior, and belligerence. Discussion of such issues can be very useful as a prelude to the establishment of goals whose purpose is to achieve by other, more socially effective means what was hitherto accomplished in a "crazy" and socially alienating way. "Purpose," in this context, may be understood to be a combination of relatively sophisticated interpersonal wishes and some very primitive desires.

Example

A 23-year-old student presented with various psychotic manifestations, including a hand-washing compulsion. He cleaned his hands more than 60 times a day. Ostensibly he and his parents were desperate over this symptom. After a time he revealed to me that the only negative feature of the hand-washing, for himself, was that it prevented him from watching movies and sometimes made his hands raw. He was conscious of some pleasure, which he concealed, about the ability of his symptom to thwart all sorts of plans his parents might make for him or for themselves. His illness also afforded him some relief, by "justifying" avoidance of work. Similarly he was "spared" the problems he anticipated were he to date women. With respect to his symptom, he maintained the fiction that he could stop his hand-washing whenever he chose, as though this compulsion were really under his control.

Psychodynamically, it was noted that the earliest appearance of the hand-washing was connected with efforts to control masturbation, about which he felt especially guilty, the more so as he used to masturbate while spying upon his younger sister.

In dealing with his compulsion, our initial goal was to develop a

technique for getting him to a movie. In the past the patient went
to the theater and saw the film twice to view the complete movie
(what with all the interruptions to wash his hands). He now discovered that his washings could be "stored" by doing a few "extras"
each turn (see Franks, 1960). He also attempted, at my suggestion,
to get by merely with wipes of a handkerchief. This eventually
proved effective, especially if the movie was exciting.

The Ratcheting Effect of Small Gains in Treatment

The everyday tasks we engage in, our work, our social interactions—may
all be analyzed into complex sets of discrete acts, tasks within tasks, that can
be hierarchically arranged in terms of their relative difficulty. By "difficulty" I also have in mind their relative tendency to cause anxiety in sensitive persons like our schizophrenic patients. In the preceding example, we
dwelt on the overall task of helping a severely handicapped schizophrenic
man to sit through a movie. Each subtask involved in this goal had to be
identified and mastered. But each act of mastery advances the patient one
small step in a kind of ratchet-wheel of successful adaptation. Each advance, as on a real ratchet-wheel, protects against a reversal to lower points.
For the patient in the preceding vignette, there were a number of points to
be negotiated: he had somehow to get money; he needed to travel on public
transportation; he had to cope with the movie lines; he had to deal with the
possibility of becoming uncomfortably aroused, sexually, either by the film
or by other couples sitting nearby. Finally, he had to deal with the possible
disturbing effects on his parents that his gains toward autonomy and separation might stir up in them. Only when all these subjects were discussed,
the practical issues mastered, and the psychodynamic issues resolved, could
the patient advance enough notches on the ratchet-wheel to go, henceforth,
to the movies or to other forms of public entertainment without suffering an
outbreak of severe and inhibiting symptoms.

Actually, the alert therapist who examines his patient's activities closely
can see potential "ratcheting" aspects in virtually all behavior (Lidz, 1963,
pp. 110–113). This is a reflection of our awareness that schizophrenic coping behavior represents a dynamic equilibrium between withdrawal and attachment. In the above example there was a ratcheting effect up the scale of
social evolution, as we have outlined: (1) The patient must travel on public
transport. He will have to read maps, ask directions on occasion, and encounter other people in various ways. (2) He must obtain money and correctly apportion it for tickets, travel, and incidentals. Judicious work with

the patient's family can help establish a quid pro quo of reciprocal activities inside or outside the home to obtain this money. (3) He must deal with movie lines, which include people who may take his place, "street people" of various sorts, and social conversations around him. (4) He may be interested by social or even sexual aspects of the film or the audience around him. If he is aroused in some way by the film, this may provide an opportunity to discuss similar aspects of the patient's current life. (5) It is likely that the patient's relationships with others will be affected by his movie-going. In the case at hand, the patient's mother became depressed by his absences from home. Her difficulties in bearing loneliness led to subtle attempts to restrict her son's movements. These issues could easily be brought into the treatment. Hence, as it happened, the mother was involved in collateral treatment. Antidepressant medication was offered, along with further counseling around the issue of her own isolation and phobic avoidance.

Maintaining Alertness for Bridging Activities

Even profoundly regressive withdrawal into fantasy or compulsive masturbation can be utilized as starting places in therapeutic explorations of the functional meaning of that very behavior. Even grandiose fantasies tend to contain small elements that do permit a degree of gratification, with minimal effort. Such gratification will of course fall far short of what was desired in the total fantasy. Often, positive aspects of the transference will allow the therapist to address these primitive fantasies in such a way that small gains can be made in establishing a bridge to meaningful social activity. Patients in this situation will do well to be reminded of the adage that journeys of a thousand miles begin with a single step.

The chronically masturbating patient, for example, may be able to understand something about the reassurance this activity provides him, or about the hostile overture it may represent, etc. Exploration of the predominant fantasies connected with the masturbation will make clear whether its primary current meaning concerns tender feelings, or hostility, or the reduction of tensions from all sources, sexual and nonsexual.

Permission for Craziness (Crazy License)

There are times when a patient should be given explicit permission to retain a certain measure of symptomatic behavior. A great deal of time is usually necessary before the schizophrenic patient can exchange "symptomatic" for socially adaptive behavior. An explicit license will often defuse potential confrontation between patient and hospital staff or family. The explicit labeling of the symptom (one may even offer a written "license") serves as a concrete reminder that the current reality is changeable (albeit slowly): better alternatives may fall into place, but always with a timing and pacing suited to the patient.

Example 1: "Rampages"

An 18-year-old was prone to rages during which he smashed furniture and dishes. These rages were the product of complex family interactions. This insight was clear to the therapist, but intensely resisted by the family (in whose interest it was to keep an "identified patient" separate from the "normal" family).

The objects broken often satisfied one faction against another, with the patient as "agent." A "deal" was worked out in our treatment, specifying the hours and the nature of the objects and place for breakage. Thus, the patient saved pop bottles and maintained, for a time, "John's Bottle-Smashing Room." The rampages were now contained, in both time and place. No family members were gratified by the breaking of innocuous objects, and indeed, the patient experienced his increased control with considerable pleasure.

After some years of therapy the initial "rampage" tendency has been sublimated into target-shooting. This man now has a considerable reputation as a marksman and functions as a part-time instructor at a local gun range.

Example 2: "Sheep Dog"

During the recovery of a 16-year-old from her first acute psychotic break, much material of a delusional sort emerged concerning family incest, mixed with ideas of religious persecution. In reality the girl did have a physician-father who performed a gynecological examination on her. The family maintained an outward show of strictly orthodox Scotch-Presbyterianism. The young girl was strikingly attractive, and the family dynamics were inflexibly arranged to foster father-daughter sexual contact for ostensibly innocent reasons, while at the same time conventional demonstrations of affection were virtually nonexistent.

Thus, this girl had her break in the context of an overwhelming sexual threat from her father, which was nevertheless disavowed by the other members of the family. To compound matters, her privacy was nil, since her room actually formed a corridor for family traffic. Any objections she might raise to this situation led to accusations about her "evil thoughts" and also to threats of exclusion from the household. She was viewed as too ill to leave home except to live in a hospital, but this was against family policy. Early in treatment the patient had recurrent dreams of getting a large dog that would protect her from the demonic figures that peopled her head during her breakdown.

We discussed this dog first as a fantasy figure that could serve at once as a protector and as a provider of affection. With respect to actual pets, this family had always put a premium on order and cleanliness and had never permitted a dog or a cat in the house.

The patient and family were advised despite their fastidiousness to get an Old English sheepdog, which would be allowed to sleep in the patient's bedroom. This large, and frequently dirty, animal forced the family to close her door and give her, willy-nilly, a measure of privacy. Ostensibly this was to prevent the dog from shedding in other rooms. The dog's need for walks and grooming also allowed the patient convenient exits from family "hothouse" conversations. Her father found the dog's presence repugnant. The family clearly behaved as though the dog were a monitor for the therapist and, for dynamic reasons, "cleaned up their act" around the animal. The patient herself found the dog, and her association with others whom she met walking the dog, a great comfort.

Over the course of time, the ramifications of dog ownership were thoroughly explored with the patient, and this exploration contributed in various ways to redrawing generational boundaries along more appropriate lines, toward the fostering of social interactions, and to creating outlets for normal emotional experience. The unconscious aspects of possessing and controlling a large, hairy, male dog were also lifted into awareness, in a very useful way as well, once the dog had taken residence.

Modifying Socially Alienating Symptoms: Rendering Certain Ego-Syntonic Traits Ego-Dystonic

Some schizophrenic patients exhibit habits that exert a profoundly negative and socially alienating effect on other people—an effect scarcely registered by, let alone bothersome to, the patient. As therapists, we will recognize the need to convert such ego-syntonic traits into ego-dystonic ones, a task that requires of us considerable adroitness and forbearance. Occasionally, changes in the patient's environment will be enough to nudge him into an awareness of the alienating quality of his habits. Certain patterns of dress that were tolerated at home, for example, may offend roommates at college, who will eventually summon the courage to confront the patient.

How the patient responds to such confrontation is another matter: he may remain defiant or unconvinced of any need to change, or he may give in a bit. More often, we will have to rely on the therapeutic situation, whether the transference relationship in the case of individual therapy or the social pressures in group therapy, to push these syntonic symptoms toward the dystonic.

Example

A 35-year-old linguist remained dilapidated, and, to speak frankly, smelly, during our initial meetings. He presented this as the simple outcome of his sadness, not as behavior motivated by any feelings toward those colleagues or students whose eyes or noses might be offended. Actually he betrayed a certain pride in his being able to use his academic brilliance to force others to bear up with his "shit." I refused to go along with this arrangement. We discussed various means for dealing with his odor, including repeated cleaning of the chair, having a window open, or having the patient provide a plastic sheet to separate him from the upholstery. As one might suppose, he complained that the open window let traffic noise in, cleaning was too expensive, and a sheet, for which I had no storage space, was cumbersome. After this experimentation, he begrudgingly consented to a shower, once a week, "for me." This led quickly to a sheepish discussion of being shunned and of how much his decreptitude might be contributing to his loneliness. In time his hygiene improved without the grandiose and belligerent aspects of his behavior receiving much emphasis in our sessions.

COMMENT

Although the patient's poor hygiene seriously affected all his external relationships, our focussing only on how his habits affected *him* and *me* provided the greatest therapeutic leverage. Treating an issue, at least at the outset, strictly within the therapeutic relationship will often permit the patient to regard the changes he is being called upon to make—or to consider making—as stemming more from within himself. The patient can take greater pride in the eventual change; it feels more "autonomous" and saves face.

It is especially important for the therapist to avoid being pressured by ward staff (in the case of a hospitalized patient), or by the patient's relatives, into promoting change of some particularly unpleasant behavior before the issue has been addressed in the therapeutic encounter. This should protect against the regression of psychotherapy into a mere exercise in resocialization, based on other people's convenience, which carries too great a hazard of recapitulating early childhood pressures toward conformity.

Controlling the Pace of Therapy

Progress in the course of extended therapy tends to follow a saw-tooth curve characteristic of the response any homeostatic mechanism makes to disturbance. Schizophrenic patients may do well in one area of function and regress in another, simultaneously. One's judgment about the relative rates and direction of changes will influence every aspect of treatment. One may change the frequency or timing of meetings, dosage of medication, form of environmental manipulations, and the nature of some interventions within the therapy hour.

Generally, change must occur rapidly enough that patient and relatives do not become demoralized. Psychotic breaks typically occur at transition points (e.g., graduation, leaving home, childbirth). Thus, change must not occur so rapidly that a return of severe psychopathology occurs, by (an avoidable) duplication of the circumstances underlying the original break.

REGRESSION AND ADVANCE

The therapist must be alert to momentary regressions, which so often occur just after some significant step forward has been made in the therapy. The patient may react to his success—and to the new set of anxieties ushered in with it—by secretly stopping his medication. An adolescent might return to street drugs. In other patients, one might see the return of productive symptoms (delusions, hallucinations), or an increase in low-level disorder of thought (blocking, autistic statements).

Example

A 20-year-old schizophrenic woman who had been attending college used to exhibit very poor grooming: she would wear Army surplus clothing as well as Army boots. Over some weeks, she talked of returning to college (the scene of her breakdown). With this she began to appear in more conventional clothing and, finally, the Army boots were left behind in favor of conventional footwear. At this point her affect became constricted; she became less communicative and the therapist had less empathic contact wih her. Close questioning revealed that she was experiencing heightened feelings of alienation, along with some panic, from what she perceived as the therapist's excessive push toward conformity. One could see, microscopically as it were, the early shift of phases in the onset of a break (see Docherty et al., 1978).

The therapist reinstituted her medication, advised that the reasons for the change of clothing at this time be explored in therapy and suggested that the patient might consider either wearing Army boots or going to a few college classes, but not try just yet to do both simultaneously. She accepted this compromise, continued for a time to wear her boots, and grew more relaxed and less "symptomatic."

COMMENT

What does this example suggest for the clinician? First, the therapist should assemble a set of markers, or cues, which he will follow regularly to gauge change. These markers must be related to the important dimensions of change; i.e., social behavior, affect, and ego functions. Second, the therapist must be alert to signs of disintegration along any axis and must take steps to counteract the regressive tendency. Third, the clinician must be familiar with general patterns of schizophrenic illness and with corrective action appropriate to the phase of illness, or of recovery, in which the patient finds himself (see Arieti, 1971; Kayton, 1975).

MARKERS

Each therapist needs to select markers suitable for both the patient and himself. There is no point in a therapist becoming familiar with a complicated set of rating scales suitable for a research unit if they happen not to be well adapted to the variables encountered in the therapist's typical patient sample. One can select markers that can be observed, others that can be structured to appear in patient or family reports, and still others that may be followed up in a fairly formalized way at intervals of a few weeks.

Some widely used scales applicable to schizophrenic and other patients in office treatment include the Ego Function Scale of Bellak et al. (1973) and the Social Development Scale of Semrad (1969). The therapist is always at liberty, of course, to engineer a separate scale wedded to the particular set of symptoms and habits of any individual patient in his caseload. Thus, it may be useful to graph changes, in one patient, in such variables as number of hours slept, degree of delusory preoccupations, number of hours devoted to hobbies, etc.; while in another patient, one may want to chart number of aggressive outbursts toward family, degree of mannerisms in speech or dress, etc. Charting such items—which will not be found in the standardized instruments in current use—may help the therapist immeasurably in getting a feel for the evolution of his patient's progress, for rhythmical patterns, if any exist, and for *correlations* between certain life events and certain symptoms, which might be missed if careful graphing were not done.

As a general rule, one will want to keep tabs on affect, dress and grooming, sleep and dream disturbances, formal content of speech, and descriptions of social interactions. For the last, one's experience of the state of the transference provides the best clue to the patient's state. Incipient disorders of thought or affect will manifest themselves clearly within the transference experience.

Paradoxical Feelings of Loss in the Face of Clinical Gain

An event the therapist perceives as a gain is often felt as a loss by the patient. Why should this be so?

1. The gain may represent an increase in the social burden the patient will now have to bear. Sometimes, an advance may be experienced as a loss of (real or fancied) "specialness" in the relationship with the therapist.

Example

During a therapy hour with a young woman who had just begun work, I took a telephone call from a ward nurse about a psychotic patient who had cut her arms. The patient in my office experienced an urge to go back to the hospital so she could be my "sickest patient."

2. Gains (in personality development or in handling social situations) may entail, in the patient's eyes, the loss of a familiar setting in which long-held coping mechanisms have operated. The patient inevitably is exposed to new threats, often of a type that resulted in failures in the past.

3. Particularly for patients in their teens or twenties the return to a functioning life may confront them sharply with the feeling of years *wasted*. This is particularly true as they compare their school or occupational situation with that of people who were once their peers.

4. Schizophrenic patients are prone to experience certain otherwise postitive changes as a loss of some precious part of their accustomed

self—an occasion more for grief than gratitude. The following vignette
is illustrative:

A 20-year-old schizoprenic theology student felt his phenothiazines
to be extremely helpful in "clearing thoughts." He was, however,
very disturbed by the "loss of sensitivity" he noticed, in relation to
his 8-year-old nephew. The shift away from bizarre feelings of
union and fusion (coupled with mystical "total understanding")
was, as it turned out, quite a relief to the little boy. The actual relationship became closer as treatment progressed, but the patient
mourned his supposed "loss of understanding" for many months,
even while recognizing how much more comfortable with him his
nephew had become.

One encounters among schizophrenic patients many bizarre self-
conceptions. The internalized image of the self tends to be fragmented and
to consist, at times, of a hodgepodge of paradoxical and contradictory elements. As patients improve, some elements will become more clear as they
develop the courage to talk of aspects of their self that once had to be kept
hidden. In the course of struggling with their inner chaos, they may attempt
to simplify their difficulties by assigning aspects of their personality to some
vaguely external "nonself." The schizophrenic may take certain areas of
personality function and experience as somehow being intrusions, or alien
forces:

1. A 17-year-old girl, recovering from her first schizophrenic break, ac-
    cused me of being as "false" as she felt herself to be. This might occur
    merely in the course of my greeting her good morning. She experi-
    enced herself as profoundly "false" when even she greeted others, and
    pictured her frozen avoidance of casual human contact as altogether
    reasonable and realistic. Her understanding and use of everyday po-
    liteness had been walled off, or made into a "nonself" function. She
    regarded all forms of polite address as examples of extreme manipula-
    tiveness on the part of others.

2. A 32-year-old woman, a department store clerk, saw herself as a very
    angry and dangerous person, cornered by all manner of hostile forces.
    In the course of therapy she would become horrified at noticing herself
    liking me, or at catching herself looking forward to our meetings. She

said, "It's like a traitor opening the gates to the enemy. But there's one thing I want you to know: it isn't me!"

When schizophrenic patients are grappling with whether or not to integrate such hitherto repudiated and warded off ("dissociated") aspects of the self, it will often be useful to suggest that they are regaining lost aspects of themselves and becoming enriched in the process; they are not being "invaded," or "losing their will-power," etc., as they may view the process at first. There is a poignant passage in *I Never Promised You a Rose Garden* (Green, 1964), where the therapist admonishes her young patient, who was complaining that her mind was like the rubble of a collapsed building, that it is out of that very rubble that the new edifice of her restored self must be constructed.

• • • • •

Some schizophrenic patients cling to the idea that their personality can become simple and unchanging, regardless of time or circumstances. Nonreactivity to the environment becomes equated with "strength" of personality. Patients are slow to give up this comfortable notion of invulnerability, particularly when the psychological stresses to which they were once—and must once again be—vulnerable are severe and menacing. Schizophrenics from unusually chaotic homes or those who were victims of ridicule or physical abuse will be slow to expose themselves to such influences again.

Searles (1967) has suggested that fear of change among schizophrenic persons is often related to the fear of *death* (as *the* great "change"). In other instances the fear is related to general difficulties in maintaining a stable identity in the face of interpersonal and environmental changes.

Intervention with Appropriate Action and Metaphor

I choose to define as "effective" those interventions that can be seen as producing significant shifts in a patient's thoughts, feelings, or *behavior*. Some of our interventions appear to be profoundly moving to our schizophrenic patients yet lead to no discernible change in their relationships with others or in their feelings about themselves. These interventions, having produced more heat than light, cannot really be considered effective.

The majority of interventions illustrated in the various clinical examples of this chapter will be noted to have a strong appeal to the patient's *cognitive* faculty. There is in this connection substantial literature suggesting that the success of schizophrenic patients living in the community, their rehospitalization rates, and the level of their depression or nihilism correlates strongly with their cognitive difficulties (Helmsley, 1977; Serban, 1975).

Levels of Abstraction in Cognitive Interpretation

Intensive psychotherapy with schizophrenic patients, carried out within the context of a dyadic relationship, encourages by this very fact exploration of interpersonal behavior. Even at the outset, when the patient is apt to be least communicative, there is still plenty of "interaction" (even if this consists mainly of perplexed or hostile stares from the patient) right within the office on which the participants can work; not much information need necessarily be imparted from the patient's external world (and too great efforts on our part to effect such "impartation" may well violate the patient's already feeble trust).

It is well to function at a level of abstraction somewhat below the patient's current level of abstracting ability. When a schizophrenic patient finds me just a bit dumb, my analogies rudimentary, or the end of an example predictable, I believe that I am at exactly the correct level of abstraction for this person.

With respect to special cognitive difficulties in schizophrenia, there is a large literature (e.g., Bellak, 1960; Jerome Jaffe, 1964a; Forrest, 1976 and this book). Dealing with overabstraction, concreteness, blocking, autistic conceptualization, and so forth constitutes an art form in the daily treatment of schizophrenic patients. This art is more easily learned with the use of guidelines and with a format that points toward correct therapeutic intervention from the outset. The ideal format should be adapted to therapists of average ability and not depend upon extraordinary capacity for empathy or intuitiveness.

In the foregoing clinical vignette concerning the disheveled linguist, the initial encounter about his poor hygiene took the following form:

T:[2] Your dishevelment, you know, has an effect on me.

Pt: What is it?

T: Well, your body odor is more than noticeable to me; I can't help a certain concern about getting dirt—maybe even scabies—on my upholstered furniture.

[2]T = Therapist;   Pt = Patient

Pt: (goes off on a tangent about St. Francis of Assisi, holy poverty, and the Jain sect in India, who revere all forms of life, including insects and vermin, and who espouse poverty)

T: Personally, I don't happen to revere either poverty or bad smells. Would you consider bringing a plastic sheet to sit on, out of respect for my feelings?

Pt: (agrees to do so, but not without sneering at T's "bourgeois values")

T: I wonder if you haven't noticed similar concerns on the part of your students or colleagues?

Pt: (launches a long digression on the puerility of his colleagues; says unkind things about their intellect)

T: Well, perhaps they have equally acrimonious remarks to make about you—only not about your intellect (which they seem to acknowledge) but about your hygiene.

Pt: I can't be bothered.

T: Collect evidence for our next meeting illustrating the effect, for better or worse, their attitude has on you. It may be that you are above it all, or it may not be so. Evidence would be helpful.

Pt: Evidence? What do you mean? (digresses to epistemology)

T: Simple things: Who speaks to you, what is said, what interactions precede your cosmic-destruction feelings. That sort of thing.

Pt: Why should I waste my time with that sort of thing?

T: What, then, is all this crap you tell me about your *advanced curiosity* for the sake of *knowing*?

This example, slightly edited, illustrates the continued push on the part of the therapist toward

1. interpreting events in terms of the everyday, expectable world.
2. continued activity by the patient, who must bear responsibility for gathering information about specific issues.
3. a rather simple level of abstraction.

What is not illustrated are the continued countertransference problems: of wishing to hear more about the Jains or the aborigines of the Kalahari desert, and so on, rather than boringly making one's way through the process of social reeducation; also, of wishing to compete and to "prove oneself" when regularly told of one's slowness and ineptitude.

. . . . .

Only after the patient's information made clear the contempt he himself was exposed to, and the painfulness of this experience, was a bridging comment attempted:

> T: Perhaps some of the talk about the Jains and the bushmen is designed to elevate you above their stings?
>
> Pt: (long silence)
>
> T: Perhaps your disheveled hair, the dirt, and so on, is your way of rubbing their nose in it? Or—your being so *special* that they would have to tolerate in you what they would not tolerate from anyone else?
>
> Pt: (silence)
>
> T: We might wonder which is chicken and which is egg?
>
> Pt: Just like you! What a banal thing to say!

FORM OF THE THERAPIST'S ACTION

In the above example the therapist has already taken one action. He has insisted that the patient either bring in a sheet of plastic on which to sit, or that he wash his clothing before our meetings. In other examples, the therapist has insisted upon a "contract" relating to appropriate times for calling at night. Elsewhere, a time and place for breakage of objects was worked out.

These are active interventions the therapist has called for in the office meetings, and they constitute strategies for dealing with therapeutic impasses. The particular strategies were chosen because they fit naturally into a contractual format.

Typically, schizophrenic patients substitute thought or fantasy for activity. Therapists often make the mistake of tacitly fostering this emphasis on fantasy, insofar as they have adopted a therapeutic stance inappropriately derived from psychoanalytic techinques (see Buckley, 1979). We assume too readily that appropriate behavioral change will follow naturally if our interpretations have produced "insight." With the schizophrenic patient, we often cannot make this assumption.

The therapist must be assiduous in following an interpretive comment with methodical observations, later on, of any changes in behavior. Issues standing in the way of change, whether related to psychodynamic issues or to social skills deficits, must be dealt with in a stepwise fashion.

There have been reports of the use of therapeutic assistants (Federn, 1952; Arieti, 1955). These may even be patients of the therapist who have training as nurses or attendants. They serve as "real figures" in the patient's life and supply information, companionship, and training in social skills as well as encouragement before the start of new ventures. It is generally felt that family members cannot easily take on this function because they are so often involved, albeit unwittingly, in maintaining the patient's status quo as an ill person. In my experience, relatives who are *not* part of the nuclear family, or who did not have a direct influence in the rearing of the patient, can sometimes be of help in this role. Frequently it will be useful for patients to live temporarily with these relatives (who act as a kind of surrogate family), or to work for them for a time.

Unfortunately, many therapists are not comfortable with their skills in working with family members or in the creation of therapeutic "networks." Private practitioners, unless they specialize in working with psychotic patients, also tend to have little experience in a team approach involving therapists from the ancillary disciplines. Frequently, however, the therapist can "borrow" these skills from community resources. Halfway houses, occupational therapy centers, and some self-help groups may be available to the therapist, even in rural settings. These alternatives can provide some of the necessary bridging and educative skills necessary to help transform insight in the therapy hour into life changes. The therapist can often be his own agent in this process, provided he does not become ensnared by the idea that therapy involves only talk and can occur only within the confines of his office. The following example will illustrate:

> With further treatment the "dilapidated linguist" decided to purchase some new clothing. Discussions of menswear entered the therapy hour for some weeks, during which time the patient was as ill-clothed as ever. At one point he admitted that he had never bought clothing without his mother and was quite fearful of doing so now.
>
> We rehearsed the act of shopping and discussed what might be the appropriate behavior in relation to certain potential problems. He had to be taught when one does and does not use a check, whether or not to tip a clerk, how one determines clothing sizes, etc. We were able to dispel some anxiety through the use of role-playing (going through the motions of shopping without mother).

Over a further period of weeks the patient reported standing help-lessly in stores, paralyzed by various fears. We then painstakingly reviewed these fears, one by one. These included the fantasy that he would spend thousands of dollars and emerge from the store with an enormous amount of clothing, all of which would somehow be "wrong." Plans were made for the purchase of one tie, as a be-ginning. He was still rather fearful, but was able finally to pur-chase the tie. As a sign of his emancipation from his old fears, he now made plans to buy a suit at Brooks Brothers. This was particu-larly poignant, since his mother had taken him only to the cheaper stores of the Lower East Side.

He asked if I might meet him at the store to allay his anxiety, but without offering advice or assistance. We dwelt in session on one specific fear: that I would behave just as his mother used to. Fi-nally, a day was agreed on for us to go. The patient made his pur-chases quite comfortably and experienced the shopping tour as a significant victory that helped to desensitize him to his archaic fears.

COMMENTS

The successful outcome in this instance was predicated on a number of ther-apist actions: wariness lest traumatic early interpersonal experiences be-come inadvertently reduplicated in the treatment situation; thorough re-view of other possibilities that did not involve actual accompaniment of the patient; and so on. Our rehearsals alleviated much of his anxiety; so did the preliminary purchase of one small item. These stepwise changes permitted, eventually, a major gain; the stepwise approach was quite different from the "all-or-none" principle on which the patient habitually (and unsuc-cessfully—he ended up with "none") operated.

In summary, treatment proceeded along a path beginning with *interpreta-tion* ("It isn't an accident that you are dilapidated: you like to rub their noses in it"), followed by some clarification of the relevant themes and by cutting through to the underlying issues (as when the patient would admit—"I'm above them! They hate me! Why should I care if I smell or not?!") Some social causes and effects were then broached. (Therapist: "The more you feel locked out, the more you seek to annoy or embarrass them"; Patient: ". . .and the more I do it, the more they stay away from the crazy professor.") This leads to *prescriptions for action*, which are not at first actually carried out. The sequence follows the path of inquiry: sorting through issues of transference fears, assessments of reality, and miseducation. Finally, as much as possible is done at the level of talk (e.g., rehearsals and role playing) and, if necessary, the last residual interferences are resolved by direct assistance.

. . . . .

I do not wish to make this outline seem to have been derived from what would be the easy or the "natural" way events will happen within a correctly structured treatment setting. The "natural" way, in my experience, is for treatment to get bogged down over and over again by defensive maneuvers, including withdrawal, withholding, and the grossest sorts of repression and denial. There may be long silences, and little concrete information coming from the patient. When this is happening, therapists will experience considerable difficulty in understanding the essential facts of the patient's everyday life. It requires continued effort on the part of the therapist to pursue the active course decribed here. Passive listening, with appropriately spaced interpretations, is of course much easier—but, unfortunately, will be less effective than the approach described here.

A useful aid to treatment during the long middle phase is the patient diary.

Diaries

Somewhere in the early and highly resistive phase of treatment, I will find it necessary to relate that I do not understand very clearly what my patient has been telling me. This will evoke denial or withdrawal often enough, but I then simply emphasize how damaging lack of information is to our work. A therapist who is clear that he does not have an understanding of what actually happened (like Socrates, who "knew that he did not know"), or where hurt feelings have come from, will tend to keep the responsibility for explanation on the patient's side. This, after all, is where that responsibility belongs; we should not have to turn ourselves into omniscient beings who would, were we to become such, merely remove rather than enhance the patient's need to develop an observing ego.

When the lack of clarity becomes a continuing issue, as it commonly will, the keeping of a diary may be encouraged as a technical aid.

This diary may be written from one or more viewpoints: it may, for example, be presented as a catalog of actual life events or as a chronicle of inner thoughts that might otherwise be difficult to remember and to discuss.

CONVERSATIONAL DIARY

This diary records rather concrete descriptions of interpersonal events. I find it helpful with "empty" patients, particularly adolescents, who experience others as mysterious and threatening. These patients have little concept of how events interact. They frequently are quite resistant to developing this concept, since it would get in the way of the righteous indignation they enjoy feeling as they go about transferring responsibility for their social failures to others (whom they prefer to view as unpredictably hostile).

Some of the patient's denial may be sidestepped initially by creating a diary of this kind for *less* personal events (e.g., to explain events in a movie or book that they find incomprehensible). After a while the patient can transfer the analyzing of such events to some of the issues in his own life. Some safe distancing may be maintained by the patient through viewing his situation as a saga with elements common to a film or a book.

DIARY FOR RECORDING EVENTS AND FEELINGS

Many schizophrenic patients lose all contact with their feeling states during stressful situations. In this situation, a strictly psychodynamic approach can become inordinately difficult: the patient is very prone to resist interpretations linking events with feelings—by virtue of his "not having any feelings." Here, a diary of events constructed so that the patient makes an entry of what he *might have felt,* or what another person—an alter ego, as it were—might feel, can be very helpful.

Given the safe distancing this technique provides, patients are often able to describe their feelings in the most accurate and poignant ways. When the material is discussed later, the linking of the feeling state to preceding events, likewise the connection between subsequent behavior to the preceding feeling state, now becomes possible. Such a technique is particularly helpful for patients who deny feelings and reach an impasse around the issue of outbursts of various sorts that can be understood only in the context of antecedent feelings (see foregoing clinical example concerning "rampages").

DIARY OF "BACKSTAIRS THOUGHTS"

It is a common human experience to realize what one should have said or done only while descending the stairs following some confrontation. For schizophrenic patients who experience considerable helplessness and who find withdrawal a prime tool, this format—keeping a diary of backstairs thoughts—can be useful. In this instance, the patient is encouraged to maintain a journal of what he wished to have done or said in specific situations. The patient should be encouraged to record all his thoughts, however grandiose or unrealizable they may seem. This can be seen to have several advantages:

1. The patient's interest is focused on events that formerly elicited only a wish to withdraw.

2. Grandiose daydreams (e.g., ''I had a machine gun and I shot them all for talking to me that way'') are made available for exploration. The underlying feeling states can be exposed, often revealing yearnings for closeness or affection of which the patient was hitherto unaware.

3. Some constructive exploration of alternative coping strategies may emerge from the now expanded awareness of the patient's attitudes and feelings.

One may ask, in connection with these remarks about diarykeeping, ''Why do this at all?'' In the long run the material becomes available in the course of therapy anyway. Might it not be better to await the spontaneous unfolding of associational chains?

The answer is that the long run may be quite long. From my experience as therapist and consultant it has become clear that the wait may indeed be longer than the duration of available treatment. Also, the diary takes advantage of the same chains of association that would unfold spontaneously, except that the journal method often enjoys the advantage of training the therapeutic eye on situations that occur ordinarily outside the therapist's view. The diary functions both as an intensification and as an extension in time of the ordinary therapeutic process.

INTRAPSYCHIC FUNCTIONS OF DIARIES

The diary may be seen as embodying these functions at various times. It can be:

1. an auxiliary observing ego

2. an introjected therapist

3. an auxiliary superego, often of a permissive sort

4. an agent of modulating intensity of experience (or auxiliary stimulus barrier)

Schizophrenic patients who keep diaries often mention being able to observe or bring into consciousness material to which they had usually remained blind. A 17-year-old schizophrenic boy reported, ''It's like having you in my pocket helping me see what's really happening.'' Patients often are able to maintain themselves in situations that were previously intolerable, comforting themselves with the thought that they are merely a reporter, or that, whatever awful things may be happening ''out there,'' it is merely some new information for the diary. Many schizophrenic persons, unlike their neurotic counterparts, cannot adopt simultaneously the observer role and the participant role in tense life situations. If the schizophrenic is enmeshed in some stressful encounter, he is engulfed by powerful feelings and lacks the objectivity to see the other fellow's viewpoint, or to see better ways of adapting, etc. At other moments, the same patient will, in situations that would ordinarily be accompanied by strong emotion, remain detached and out of touch with his feelings. Devices like diary keeping may help the schizophrenic toward the goal of a more rewarding and full-bodied existence as participant-observer or observing participant.

Since the diary is often experienced as a portable and tangible bond to the therapist, it may help reduce the patient's feelings of aloneness and alienation. There may be a scoptophilic aspect to the reportage, and this may prove comforting and even enjoyable (especially to certain paranoid patients, who like to document everything and ''get the goods'' on their enemies). Patients will express some comfort at knowing that the diary is under *their* control—to be shared or kept hidden, as they wish.

Schizophrenic patients who bear heavy burdens of guilt may derive benefit from diary keeping, insofar as this activity may lead to a mellowing of their all too often excessively harsh superego. Through the diary, the patient may begin to identify increasingly wth the less primitive value system of the therapist and, out of this growing identification, derive a sense of permission, of entitlement, to engage in certain forms of behavior which, though socially appropriate, were once taboo for him.

Using the diary as an aid to observation and discrimination, the schizophrenic patient may become better able to see ways in which he is mistreated, and ways in which he invites mistreatment from others. Even patients with anhedonia or ''emptiness'' can benefit at times from diary keeping. The journal may help them retain a more vivid sense of having been alive, of having feelings, in the course of those very life events that have just become the subject matter of the last entry.

Example

A 17-year-old hospitalized schizophrenic girl was prone to outbursts of rage. In an effort to control these, her resident therapist eventually forbade her to shout at the ward nurses. Neither the various interpretations he had made earlier, nor the more exhortatory interventions he then instituted, had any effect. His dynamic understanding did, however, appear accurate: the outbursts constituted a displacement of rage at separation from mother to comparable ''separations'' within the hospital: her outbursts always occurred at the end of a nursing shift.

The patient was induced to begin a diary, chronicling her difficulties with the nurses. It quickly became clear that the patient maintained considerable aloofness from the nurses, even rebuffing their friendliness, until the moment just before they left their shift. At that point she would solicit a conversation in a most pathetic way and would then feel keenly rebuffed by their departure. She would then have a major tantrum. Next day, the cycle would be repeated.

After her therapist explored the stepwise events leading to each outburst, she promised that she would attempt to engage the nurses earlier in their ward shift.

14

Specific Technics with Dangerous or Armed Patients

Harry D. Albert, M.D.

It is well established that therapists do not predict the carrying out of violent threats at better than chance levels (A. Stone, 1978, 1979). Of course, threats of homicide, suicide, or other violence are not limited to a psychotic population. In fact, there is evidence that violence of all sorts may be less likely in a schizophrenic population than in other diagnostic groupings. Nonetheless, dealing with a threatening, let alone armed, psychotic person requires understanding of the particular dynamics of the situation but, more importantly, understanding of effective tactics for dealing with such persons. There are reported cases in which therapists or members of their families have been injured or killed in such circumstances.

Most therapists will deal with very few patients who arm themselves, unless they have an extensive hospital practice, or are located in a rural area where hunting is common. Threats of violence are more common, and domestic implements may be pressed into service as weapons. Evaluating a threat of violence differs from evaluating suicidal threats, and the tactics for defusing a potentially dangerous situation require handling issues of outsiders and of the therapist's apprehension, problems not posed by a potential suicide (Lion, 1973).

A PERSPECTIVE

During the ten-year period from 1970 to 1980 I treated eighteen persons who were referred for evaluation of their dangerous potential, all of whom were armed at some point. Four other cases were seen in consultation with psychiatric and medical colleagues who had been threatened. Of these twenty-two, fouteen required hospitalization, three with police intervention, one patient stabbed her former therapist during my vacation, and one continues to harass (nonviolently) another therapist and me after a lapse of four years and two hospitalizations. (Rofman, 1980).

Evaluation

First, we must distinguish the patient who ruminates about violence from the one who has actually taken steps toward carrying out an attack. This is similar in some ways to the assessment one does with a patient who has thoughts of suicide. With a patient who is armed, however, the situation may immediately become complicated by the therapist's fear, which may interfere with ordinary therapeutic judgment. With an armed patient it is necessary to structure the interview so that the patient disarms himself—a technique unfamiliar to most therapists.

At some point in their treatment many patients will speak of violent wishes toward others. The obsessional neurotic may present initially because of repetitive thoughts of violence (Salzman, 1980), which one may be reasonably sure will not take place.

When one is seeing a patient for an initial interview, there is of course no shared background of experience to draw upon. One does know, however, that the patient is at least ambivalent about his impulses. Otherwise he would not be there talking about them. One's best guide in this situation is an assessment of *past* episodes of violence, coupled with the patient's assessment of the likelihood of violence currently. The interviewer may ask the patient about the difficulties that have precipitated the current problem, and about how the patient has dealt with similar situations and inner feelings in the past. If the patient generally overcame these feelings without taking action, this suggests he will not behave violently in the here and now. The interviewer must get a sense of the frequency of past violent impulses and of their resolution. The direction of past resolution opens the inquiry to why the patient may not have been able to achieve a similar resolution now. The therapist may be of help in exploring avenues for similar solutions ("similar" in the sense of matching environmental manipulations to specific psychodynamic needs). It may be necessary to interview family members, police officers, and others in coming to a conclusion.

At the end of an interview in which the data suggest that the patient is not likely to pursue a violent course, the therapist will sometimes continue to experience considerable unease. The problem here is whether to consider these feelings as reflecting something subtle but valid, or as a problem of countertransference.

The therapist may review the data—specific actions the patient has taken in the way of observing the intended victim, obtaining maps or weapons, or the like. If the patient has taken steps of this kind, the therapist should consider sequestering the patient for observation. In some states there is a legal requirement to notify the intended victim about his danger. It should be emphasized again that the literature indicates poor predictive accuracy by even well-trained therapists. One should therefore consider a period of observation when significant doubt exists. It is a recurrent clinical phenomenon that therapists tend to deny danger to themselves (see clinical example 1, below) rather than experience appropriate fear.

Provided that hospitalization is handled openly and that one works with the patient from the onset, there will be a good possibility of establishing rapport and providing appropriate treatment (Whitman, 1976).

Countertransference Issues

A therapist who experiences strong dislike or fear of potentially violent patients ought not to treat them. These patients should be referred to others at least until the therapist has dealt with his personal issues in this area. Conversely, a therapist who does not experience *any* fear in working with violent patients is likely to blunder. In that situation the therapist's defenses may actually be serving to undermine his judgment. He may be denying the strength of the patient's impulses, denying the meaning of the patient's subtle communications, or indulging in grandiose fantasies about his omnipotence. Although studies on selection of therapists for particular kinds of patients are sparse, it seems that relatively active therpists who may be a trifle paranoid themselves (enough to appreciate a paranoid person's viewpoint, perhaps; see Gunderson, 1978) do better than others with the violent patient.

Therapists who deny their fears tend to overestimate the power of interpretive efforts, including those aimed at appraising the patient of "reality." Typically these interpretations take the form of discussions about the futility of violence or about the concerns one might have about future punishment. This is countertransference in its pure form. The proper focus is to clarify the patient's affects (fear and rage), relating them to whatever stimuli are provoking his violent impulses at this moment. Typically, one focuses on rage toward the therapist (see below). The problem for the therapist is how to make clarifications and connections that will defuse the anger, without the patient ever resorting to violence. Discussions about outside events are relevant only for purposes of overall assessment, or for helping the patient develop realistic and nonviolent solutions (Mackinnon and Michels, 1971, pp. 259–296).

Fear of a patient is an important early signal that rage has been impounded in the transference. Consultation with a colleague may be helpful in this situation. Appropriate measures may range from seeing the patient with an attendant, to forced hospitalization using the help of the police (see Salzman, 1960).

Example 1

A psychiatric resident, a woman in her twenties, sought consultation about a patient who had "blocked" through most of a meeting. Review of the ongoing treatment offered little clue, other than her uneasiness, to the problem. Arrangements were then made for the consultant to attend one session. During this meeting it was apparent that the patient spent much time gazing at the therapist's legs and breasts. During this time he would fall silent. It was noteworthy that the therapist made little attempt to have the patient reveal his thoughts during these silences. The therapist's office was on the deserted floor of an outpatient wing, and this man was seen at 7 P.M. Questioning by the consultant brought out the patient's tormenting sexual impulses, as well as his rage at women who teased men with their "sleaziness . . . they just tease men . . . they deserve to be punished." The consultant suggested that the therapy be moved to a daytime hour in an office in the busy Emergency Room. The patient revealed, after this was done, that he had begun carrying a knife weeks before, with a vague intention to punish one of these women who had tormented him.

The therapist had been using denial. She had screened out her impression of sexual menace. She had been able to report none of the patient's nonverbal behavior, and thus denied the reality of her vulnerability. The patient in turn worked as hard as he could to keep his impulses away from therapy, lest they be acted on with the therapist herself. The impasse was cleared when suitable security was available; the therapist could then actively pursue these disordered thoughts and the patient felt safe enough—from his own violence—to begin exploring his impulses.

COMMENT

The cardinal rule in dealing with the potentially violent patient is this: the clinician must take seriously all the information available about a patient's proneness to aggressive outbursts—statements, dreams, fantasies, nonverbal behavior, and observer-signs. Then, one must take active steps (that often go beyond verbal interventions) to defuse the situation. Often these will take the form of supplying external controls as a temporary aid to the patient, whose internal controls are still shaky. In the example above, a simple "change of venue" to a guarded office allowed the patient to talk about his impulses, to experience his desperate fear of and longing for women, and to become aware that the "omnipotent" woman therapist had human fears.

Paranoid patients in particular are often paradoxically gratified by the therapist's concern, or even by police intervention. Either will tend to redress the angry paranoid's wounded self-esteem by demonstrating that the therapist views the patient as a powerful person rather than as a helpless or passive creature. Operating from a position of strength, the paranoid individual can become conciliatory to a "weaker adversary" (see example 2, below).

Paranoid Reactions

In homicidal and other types of violent patients, the predominant personality features will be, in most instances, the paranoid.

Mechanisms of primitive denial (in delusional patients) and of reaction formation and projection (in all patients with a paranoid trend) are encountered with regularity in violence-prone patients of all types. The paranoid patient typically is struggling to control feelings of anger and hostility. He may experience his anger, if he can acknowledge the feeling at all, as totally appropriate, based on his many wounds from others. In other instances he may project his anger and resentment onto outsiders. In either case he attempts to rationalize his inordinate anger either by seeing it as justified retaliation or as a natural response to the jealousy of other people for his special talents.

The earliest warnings of an impending delusional state may be hypochondriacal concerns about the eyes or one or another of the bodily orifices. Concerns particularly about the buttocks or anus may (in males) signal the appearance of persecutory delusions, connected to primitive feelings about homosexual attack.

Violence within the context of pyschotherapy with paranoid patients may be precipitated primarily in these ways:

1. As the intimacy of the relationship grows, the paranoid patient may become threatened by fears of fusion or, if less regressed, by homosexual impulses. These are projected and may, in the more impulsive patient, lead to violence.

2. Threatened or actual loss of self-esteem. This may come in the form of loss (of job or money), competitive failure (e.g., loss of promotion) or rejection (e.g., divorce threat).

3. Experiences in which the patient is forced to adopt a passive or receptive role. This includes the therapeutic situation itself, studenthood, illness or injury (particularly to the back or genitals), or military service.

4. The experience of success. Here the mechanism is related to fear of retaliation from others. The paranoid patient assumes that others will be as consumed with envy and rage as he would be in their situation. This may have served as the psychological trigger for the persecutory psychosis that engulfed the jurist Schreber shortly after he was promoted to higher post (see Freud's "Schreber Case," 1911).

The problem for the therapist is that the psychotic patient tends to react out of all proportion to rather trivial incidents (whose meaning to the patient may easily be overlooked by the therapist). Violent impulses may be stimulated either by too much closeness within the therapeutic relationship, or by too abrupt withdrawal from closeness (Searles et al., 1973).

Example 2

A 28-year-old man was seen in a hospital emergency room, after trying to force his way onto the obstetrics floor to see his wife after her delivery. He quickly revealed an angry delusional system:

Pt: . . . and I know it's not my kid, so I have to kill her or I'm no kind of man.

T: Kill her? What do you mean?

Pt: I shoot the fuck.

T: Do you have a gun?

Pt: Here (indicates pocket).

T: That floor is full of women and babies. What if you hurt one of them—would you feel like a man then?

Pt: Women are shit. All of them. No damn good!

T: I see you are a strong man. Why not just beat the shit out of her? If you kill her she can't apologize or make up for what she did.

Pt: It's not enough.

T: Two men like us should be able to figure this out. The trouble is I'm afraid of guns ever since I was in the Army. Could you put the gun in the drawer while we talk so I can think straight?

Pt: No.

T: How about just the bullets? It's hard for me to think straight when I'm scared.

Pt: You're a good guy. I don't want you to be scared, doc. I'll put it in the drawer.

Notice that reminding the patient about reality provokes further rage ("women are shit!"). The therapist then explicitly makes their relationship equal ("Two men like us . . .") and finally suggests the patient is superior (". . . I'm afraid of guns"), at which point the patient can call him "doc" and relax his vigilance.

Transference Actualization Reactions

Therapists must be aware that there will be occasions when certain schizophrenic patients experience their therapist not merely as though he were *like* some figure from the past, but as though the therapist and that figure were literally one and the same, and interchangeable. Cues to this transformation are ordinarily present in the treatment setting. It may be, for example, that the patient cannot acknowledge a simple transference interpretation on the order of "You feel I treat you as your mother treated you," but reacts instead as though the therapist *were* the mother. Long silences in a tense atmosphere suggest this kind of impasse. The patient may also misidentify some other figure, including children or casual acquaintances. Psychotic misidentifications of this kind may provide the background for an outburst of violence, especially if the other figure is seen as a hostile or destructive force. This may be so, no matter how bizarre the misidentification may be.

Example 3

A 19-year-old woman was narrowly prevented from hurling her four-month-old baby from a ninth-story window in order to rid herself of the demons which, she felt, inhabited the infant. She believed the infant's crying and fussiness were attacks on her sanity and were designed to drive her to suicide. As later became clear, the baby was perceived to be a reincarnation of a hated younger sister for whom the patient had been responsible, and who was currently an object of jealously and hatred.

Fusion Wishes or Reactions

Patients who express active wishes to fuse or reunite with with others (usually parents) who have died may pose a serious threat. The patient may even wish that he and the therapist die together. Such a wish may be embedded within a delusional system—one that may be particularly difficult to resolve therapeutically. The delusion is uniquely comforting to the patient's sense of betrayal and emptiness, since it holds out the promise of blissful merger with a (fantasied) parent. Patients with this delusional wish sometimes seek membership in certain religious groups known to give credence or support to this kind of illusion. These patients may become a danger to themselves or others following some acute loss or the anniversay of such a loss.

This phenomenon is seen with some regularity in severely depressed people and occasionally in cases of drug reactions (PCP, LSD) as well as in schizophrenia (Fauman and Fauman, 1979).

When the therapist is threatened with an invitation to a suicide-murder pact, it will be important to let the patient know he does not wish to participate in such a venture and will not do so under any circumstance. When matters have reached this point, hospitalization is indicated: a patient comtemplating a murder-suicide pact, who then loses hope of the sought-after though fanciful reunion will become quite depressed and may go on to make a suicide attempt.

Example 4

A patient brought a straight razor to the office that she described as a memento of her father. When urged to discuss why she had brought the razor that particular morning, she went on to discuss her recent feelings of desertion during the therapist's vacation. She had thought of cutting herself, to show how hurt the absence had made her feel.

T: Had you thought of cutting me as well?

Pt: What would you do if I did?

T: Put the razor back in its case and hand it to me for the rest of this hour. Then you won't be so afraid. It'll be easier for you to talk. *I* won't have to be afraid, either.

Pt: Will you give it back? I *did* think of cutting you, too, of maybe cutting us *both,* so we could be together, hurt together . . .

T: If you cut me, we would never *be* together again, because I would not want to see you again. I will keep the razor for a time so you won't have to worry about hurting me and having me quit as a result. OK?

Pt: I wouldn't want you to quit.

T: I wouldn't want to quit, but I would quit if you hurt me. Why did you bring in the razor today, not last week or some other time? Why today?

The issue could not be resolved within the hour. The patient, who had surrendered the razor, was asked to return for another meeting later that day. The second meeting was set up in part to explore the idea that the relationship *could* be extended in ordinary ways, but not at all in extraordinary ways (by "fusing," etc.). The patient used the second hour to discuss feelings she had about her father and his desertion of the family. She also discussed her wish for hospitalization, which to her represented "entering the therapist's house."

Command Hallucinations

Psychotic patients of whatever diagnostic category may on occasion experience auditory hallucinations. At times these may become particularly vivid. The voices may, furthermore, present demands for actions of various kinds which the patient feels he must obey. The (presumably paranoid schizophrenic) man who smashed the Virgin's nose in Michelangelo's *Pietà* was acting in "compliance" with a command hallucination; likewise, the man who, a few years earlier, set fire to the El Aksa shrine in Jerusalem. The hallucinated voices, typically, will either threaten terrible punishment for disobedience or promise great rewards for compliance. Acts carried out in response to a command hallucination are often performed in a disassociated state. The patient may feel he has become a "puppet," as though he has relinquished all his autonomy. The degree of ego-alienness of the acts is generally not helpful in predicting whether the patient will or will not resort to violence.

Example 5

A 28-year-old schizophrenic music teacher appeared regularly with a large handbag that she kept on her lap. She revealed that she kept a knife in the bag to "defend" herself against my "sexual advances." She had recurrent hallucinations, in my voice, of proffered sexual acts. Similar delusory and hallucinated ideas had been woven about her previous therapist, who, she maintained, had "injected the most disgusting sex crimes into my brain."

A senior consultant advised not making an issue of the knife. He saw it as a security object that allowed the therapy to proceed. Over the following three months the patient returned to more normal function, although the delusion ebbed and flowed, and she still carried the knife.

My countertransference took the form of an ominpotent belief that I could predict her dangerousness, and that, if push came to shove, I could somehow evade her 300-pound bulk. It is significant that I remained aware of the hidden knife, and at times hated this patient intensely. I also neglected to verify that the patient took her prescribed phenothiazines.

Shortly before my vacation, the patient's delusion became "socialized" to the point that she discussed taking legal action against myself and former therapists for our "sexual misconduct." She did not focus at all on her long-standing feelings of helplessness and violation. She was even able to say that her plan sounded absurd, even crazy, as she thought of it. During my vacation, however, she sought out her therapist of four years before and stabbed him. Afterward I met her in the hospital to which she was then committed. She was now free of the delusion, somewhat remorseful, but still feeling victorious in having paid us (the former therapist and myself now fused into one) back for our "sexual torments."

Overview

As with suicidal ideation, any thoughts or impulses about taking violent action should be explored at once. It will be most useful, if not mandatory, to begin by making an effort to empathize with the patient's view of his situation. We put ourselves in the patient's shoes for the moment, and by this very process demonstrate to him our respect for his plight—and our capacity to comprehend what drove him in the first place to contemplate a violent solution.

In every clinical situation of this sort, we must find out what the immediate precipitants were. When violent impulses well up in the course of an ongoing therapy, we must determine if there are—as there will usually be—important transference aspects, and if so, what their specific nature is. Chances are, the patient is reexperiencing something in the transference that has revived archaic feelings of intense fear or anger. The therapist will be well advised to assume, until proven otherwise, and regardless of the anxiety this realization may provoke in him, that *he* is the target of the patient's wrath. This assumption will tend to prove valid even when the patient's wrath is directed ostensibly at someone else. To this end, the therapist should make an effort to discover some parallel that exists between the seemingly external events that are provoking the patient and dynamically related events in the recent therapy. This does *not* mean that the therapist, in the grip of his own anxiety, ought to offer some broad-based interpretation (along the lines of, ''perhaps you are really angry at me''), without having first obtained enough data to trace, step by step, the misunderstandings and transference distortions that have led to such anger. Many schizophrenic patients are sufficiently concrete to experience broad interpretations of this kind as either a *command* to be angry at the therapist, or as a *criticism* implying guilt of some wrongdoing. Some paranoid patients in particular, when already charged up with anger, will hear the broad interpretation as a challenge!

Example 6

A 48-year-old building contractor in his third month of treatment for a paranoid episode began to speak of arranging to electrocute his wife in a staged accident. He calmly discussed his plan to throw a lamp into her bath. He told me that she had recently begun to exert increasing control over his movements, and he again suspected that she was conducting an adulterous affair. The parallel in our relationship was that I had asked (''controlled'') this man to change a number of appointment hours in the preceding two weeks because of a birth in my family. He had been amenable to the changes, which in point of fact had been more convenient for him than his usual times. In discussion, he casually mentioned that his wife encouraged his evening meetings with me, and he felt that I was genuinely interested in him as evidenced by my care not to miss hours. He further revealed that he had heard by chance that my wife had just had a child. I asked him how this knowledge affected him. His first associations were about my sexual conduct while my wife was confined. He fantasied my having had an orgiastic bachelor interlude. He contrasted this with his own marital sexual dysfunctions. I drew a not quite direct connection between his thoughts about other men being sexually active, including myself, and his view that his wife could not be satisfied by him. He talked next about having fantasized, "since I asked," about what would happen if I met his wife, and even asked, with some diffidence, whether she and I had met. I drew his attention to his wife's praising me. He had considered this as evidence of her adulterous impulses. He volunteered that he had not really wanted to change his hours, but found it hard to say "no" to me. The patient spontaneously made the connection that this episode of anger at his wife was connected to his jealousy over my supposedly free-swinging life-style and also to having felt "put down" by the "forced" appointment changes. In our next appointment he was able to say to me: "You know, the way I was ready to kill Ann, that was really crazy!"

After uncovering the immediate precipitants, the therapist should now inquire into the details of the problems the patient hoped to resolve by resorting to violence. What does the patient expect he will experience differently if he is armed? How has he used violence in the past? How has violence been used against him? What alternatives has the patient considered, and why has he come to see violence as his only option? A nonpsychotic patient might be concerned with the possibility that his therapist may force hospitalization because of the violent threats. It is best, initially, in such situations to avoid making any hard and fast statements about hospitalization. The therapist may instead indicate that the patient must have some questions himself about what would be the best course of action, but he should also make it clear that truly uncontrollable impulses are, of course, best treated in a hospital. The therapist should also make it clear that the decision about this will be arrived at openly between the two participants.

Disarming the Patient

When dealing with an armed patient the most useful intervention for the therapist is the open use of his fear. With paranoids, for example, this helps establish the patient's active, superior position—thereby minimizing the feeling to which such patients are most vulnerable, namely, that of being helpless and subject to attack. The therapist also should search for any precipitants in the therapeutic relationship and should not hesitate to acknowledge making mistakes which the patient may have experienced as hurtful.

As in example 2 (concerning the *man with a gun*), patients should be encouraged to distance themselves from their weapons gradually or to disarm themselves piecemeal (e.g., as in first unloading the gun). One can usefully express concern for the break in the therapeutic relationship that would result, were the patient jailed for violence. But one ought *never* to ally oneself, after the manner of a parental figure, *with* the law and *against* the patient.

Patients subject to command hallucinations may be particularly dangerous to people around them. Even in the hospital such people must be carefully supervised and medicated. It is sometimes helpful for the therapist to indicate that the patient is to tell him (or a designated staff member) the content of such commands, so that hospital staff may apply their joint strength toward helping the patient resist the command. In my experience these patients are especially prone to resist taking their medication. For this reason, one should consider with such patients using liquid concentrates or injections of ataraxic medication.

15

Use of Humor in Therapeutic Work with Schizophrenic Patients

Michael H. Stone, M.D.

No one definition of humor would ever suffice to cover the multiplicity of its manifestations, its species, and its uses. Freud's lengthy essay on wit and its relation to the unconscious (1905) constitutes one of the most thorough and succesful attempts to explicate and analyze whatever it is we mean by "humor," although Freud was concerned with the use of wit by normal persons in everyday life, not by seriously disturbed patients or by their therapists. Although the reader of this chapter is not going to be rewarded by any brief formula containing the "essence" of humor, for that remains elusive, we can draw attention to some of its chief characteristics. Certainly one of the most common varieties of humor is the simultaneous allusion to both the obvious and the hidden connotations of certain words or phrases that happen to lend themselves to double entendres. Generally, *one* of the possible meanings will not only be unexpected, but will reflect sexual or aggressive feelings of a sort ordinarily kept under wraps—if not repressed altogether—by the auditor(s). If these socially embarrassing feelings are not too embarrassing, or too overwhelming, and if the joke is expressed in compassionate rather than in a purely hostile manner, the warded-off feelings may suddenly rise to the surface in the listener, who, now recognizing that the speaker truly accepts the embarrassing feelings, realizes at once he has *not lost face*. The atmosphere is friendly. All this permits (it would seem) the explosion of emotion, stemming from the sudden feeling of *relief* that all is still well, which we recognize as laughter.

With schizophrenic patients this mechanism is often rendered treacherous, especially in the presence of a strong paranoid component. Those schizophrenic patients who strike us as humorless, or before whom one's attempts at humor fall flat—if they do not outright offend—are not humorless because life has been so bleak. Patients of all diagnostic categories often have bleak pasts—and is there any large group of therapists not one of whose members has a past as sorrowful as our patients? Nor are schizophrenic patients humorless because of a want of intelligence.

I find two factors that may weigh more heavily in the balance, as we try to account for the phenomenon. To begin with, the thought patterns of many schizophrenic persons are remarkably constricted and concrete. Anxiety aggravates this tendency, which is, itself, presumably a by-product of the innate neurophysiological integrative disturbances which predispose one to whatever it is we call schizophrenia. This handicap in grasping meanings other than the strictly literal, surface ones makes the schizophrenic susceptible to missing the double entendre others see and laugh over. The other factor consists in the chronic lack of success in human relations that casts a pall over the lives of so many schizophrenic patients. It is only to the degree that we enjoy some modest success in friendship, in sex, in intimacy that we can see the humor in, and laugh at, our own awkwardness, our uncomfortable half-starts, our failures in these areas of life. Any joke about such matters will be experienced as a humiliation, a painful exposure, by a schizophrenic person who has not yet begun to have even modest success in love or friendship. This will be true whether the joke is directed at him or at someone else.

The following joke may serve as a springboard for discussing some of the points in the preceding paragraphs:

A traveling salesman invites a lady of the night to his Las Vegas motel room. Instead of conducting her to bed, however, he instructs her to fill the bathtub with water. He gets in the tub and a dialogue ensues:

He: Make waves!

She: Waves! How do I make waves?

He: Take your hand and run it through the water, like this . . . (which she does, making little ''waves'' in the bathwater)

He: Now make wind.

She: Wind? How do I make wind?

He: Bend over near the water and blow with as big breaths as you can!

She: Okay, okay. (blowing as hard as she can, according to his instructions)

He: Now make thunder!

She: (becoming rather impatient) *Thunder*!? How do I make thunder?

He: Pull the chain on the toilet and as soon as it fills up again, pull it again.

She: Okay, okay. (complying once more with his instruction)

He: Now make lightning!

She: *Lightning*!? How in the hell do I make *lightning*!?

He: Pull the light switch on and off with your other hand!

She: (exasperated by this time) Okay, okay! We make waves, we make wind, we make thunder, we make lightning . . . when do we make love!?

He: Make *love*!? Who can make love in this kind of weather?

In this example the "locus" of the humor lay not so much in special words with a double entendre as in the absurdity of the situation. The whole setting constitutes a double entendre: the scene is a motel room with participants—the salesman and the prostitute—whom the listener expects to be doing something sexual. But instead the salesman has the woman create an environment inimical to the carrying out of the very thing her presence would suggest. Another element of surprise stems from the absurdity of the salesman's behavior. Psychologically speaking the absurdity is only superficial. Below the surface, we suspect there is conflict, ambivalence. The salesman was divided, that is, between the wish to have sex and some inhibition that would oppose that wish. To appreciate the humor of his "story," the listener would have to grasp the essence of his apparent conflict, and would have to do so immediately. To enjoy the humor, to respond to it with relief rather than anxiety, a listener would probably have to have enough success in life—in the same sexual sphere where the salesman seems to be having such trouble—to hear the joke from a standpoint of distance and superiority. The listener would have to be able to say to himself, "I can appreciate the salesman's plight—he isn't very self-confident about sex; I've worried too at times, but, for the most part, I'm *more secure,* therefore I can laugh at the salesman's foibles." If the listener were as conflicted or as insecure as the salesman seems to be, my hunch is he would not experience the story as funny. It would strike too close to home. And this is precisely the point: many schizophrenic persons have had such chronic difficulties and lack of success in so many areas of life—social, sexual, occupational—that a large proportion of the jokes funny to the average person are not at all funny to them. The schizophrenic person is apt, in other words, to have too little distance from the "victim" of the joke to be able to enjoy it with safety. Instead, the joke will seem to refer to him and will be experienced as a verbal assault or a humiliation.

From the standpoint of a therapist, it would be risky to share with a schizophrenic patient jokes whose funniness depends on a mastery of life tasks not yet achieved by the patient. There are some jokes that *can* eventually be shared, whose meaning is highly relevant to the stage of psychic development at which the patient is currently situated, or has evolved *past*, on his way to a higher level.

There is, for example, a well-known joke about a man whose car gets a flat tire as he's motoring along a country road. He needs a jack before he can put on his spare. There seems to be no one in sight for miles around, but he espies a farmhouse off in the distance. Perhaps, he figures, the farmer can lend him a jack. But as he trudges toward the farmhouse, he begins to think, "I'll bet he'll say he doesn't have a jack even though he does." Next he thinks, "I'll bet he'll tell me he has one, but he'll charge me for it." Finally, as he's about to approach the house, he thinks, "I'll bet the son of a bitch isn't going to lend me the jack, money or no money." With that the door opens, the farmer asks what's the trouble—and the stranded driver punches him in the face, saying, "*Keep* your damn jack!"

This joke depends for its impact on its parody of the paranoid stance. The paranoid individual begins with a false assumption, or with an assumption that has only a grain—but no more so—of truth. Upon this fragile foundation, a logical train of thought ensues that would be "correct," were the assumption itself correct, but is wildly incorrect, given the faultiness of the original premise. The driver assumes the farmer will be stingy about the jack, and "therefore" is justified in his attack upon the unsuspecting farmer, who, in reality, would more likely have been accommodating. In dealing with paranoid patients, including schizophrenics with significant paranoid trends, I occasionally have recourse to this joke when I attempt to portray to them, in terms they can accept, the nature of their "logical" but ultimately irrational thought. Paranoid individuals are remarkably humorless, of course, so until a relationship of some solidity is built up between me and the patient, I keep this joke, and indeed all jokes, to myself. It is a sign of progress when I can finally use the joke by way of illustration, since this becomes possible only when the patient has begun to achieve some emotional distance from his paranoid tendencies.

Kubie (1971) actually cautioned against the use of humor altogether, in work with schizophrenic patients. Although it is better to err on the side of caution than to indulge in humor imprudently, Kubie's position appears to be extreme, and, more than that, if valid for certain therapists, not valid for others. This is an area where the therapist's personality and style come into play. In doing intensive psychotherapy with schizophrenic patients, much more so than with, say, neurotic analysands, we will feel the need to be candid and spontaneous, in much the same fashion that parents are compelled to be, with their children, "just themselves." With schizophrenic patients we must, of course, as with all our patients, be appropriately professional—but within this professional framework our "humanity," in all its aspects, will have to show through on many occasions. With respect to humor, we must be aware of our personalities, aware to what extent the use of humor would be a natural, as opposed to a contrived, attribute of our therapeutic style. This aspect of our personality must then be brought into line, usually through supervision, with the needs and the capacities of our patients. Since my own sense of humor borders on the irrepressible, I have had to work it into my therapeutic style. Rather than follow Kubie's dictum, which would have simplified matters greatly, I have had to develop a sense of timing: *when* is the use of humor legitimate? What kind of humor is appropriate? When must the temptation to laugh be suppressed? When may it be indulged safely or even therapeutically? These questions cannot be answered in a few pages, but some clinical vignettes may serve as a first step.

The following example was provided by Dr. Nehemiah Zedek (1978).

> A chronically ill, schizotypal borderline man was telling Dr. Zedek one day about an attractive woman he'd met, and whom he hoped to ask out. The patient said, "I was thinking of asking her to have coffee with me. But then I thought, if I ask her for *coffee*, the next thing is, I'll have to invite her to my apartment. And if she comes to my apartment—we could get into kissing and everything . . . and from there, we'd probably land in bed, to have sex. Only I'm *afraid* to have sex." "Well," Dr. Zedek said, in a purposely studied and ponderous manner, "you could have *tea!*"

Now this was a patient with whom Dr. Zedek had built up a good working alliance over a considerable period of time. In the therapist's judgment, the time was now right for an adroit use of humor, a bantering and rather dry sort of humor in this instance, as a confrontational device to help the patient get beyond his fears. For one thing, in a gentle, understated way, Zedek shows the patient the absurdity of his timorousness—without having in any way to humiliate the man. The concreteness of the patient is mirrored in the ''concreteness'' of Zedek's reply. The reply itself, however, by suggesting another alternative (tea instead of coffee) suggests to the patient, without saying it laboriously, that there are many options open to him. He could, after all, still ask the woman to have coffee, but tell her, ''I can't offer you much more this evening, unfortunately, because I have an important meeting I must get to early in the morning,'' thus buying time and helping to allay his anxiety. With the use of such spontaneous and compassionate humor, these volumes of information and insight are compressed into a sentence, and done so in a way that has a much greater degree of acceptability than if the analyst had spelled out the details at great length. Of course, if the patient had not grasped the humor, that would be another matter. Then one would have had no choice but to deliver the complicated message in painstaking detail.

At the correct time, gentle humor may be very useful in getting the patient to accept about himself some negative trait, some characterological quirk, that alienates people. If one confronted the patient about such matters bluntly, the patient might feel rejected.

I can mention as an example a schizoaffective patient who was, in general, extremely humorous herself. It was nearly impossible not to get caught up in this humor, which was really quite infectious. The patient said at one point that she was about to go to a certain halfway house. She had been reluctant to do so for a number of months. ''I don't know if I'll ever function again in my life,'' she said. ''I feel destined to be short-lived. I don't care what they've done—those horrible people at the halfway house. Nobody has done what I've done at a hospital. Nobody has been through and conquered so many problems. So they can bring everything to bear that they want to and I *still* won't get well,'' and I replied, ''You sure as hell aren't going to be Galatea to anybody's Pygmalion, right?'' And she said, ''I was supposed to be Dr. B.'s Galatea and it didn't work out too well,'' referring to her previous therapist, to whom she had grown quite attached over several years. When I then said, ''You make it plain you aren't going to be my Galatea, either,'' she retorted, puncturing my grandiosity in the process, ''*Your* Galatea! I never even *think* of *you*—you're Pygmalion suddenly?'' We were then able to use that interchange to explore how she repeatedly fended off any attempt to acknowledge my existence or my impact upon her, or how terribly overattached she had been to her former therapist.

When this same patient was originally referred to me, she announced that she had had a premonition she would have me as her therapist, by virtue of having seen a pebble on the rug in her parents' living room shortly before she was given my name. The magical thinking here consisted, of course, in the identification of "pebble" with "Stone." She said this in a cheery, optimistic tone, as though she had only pleasant expectations and no anxiety about the encounter with a new therapist. Since it was highly unlikely her attitude could be so positive at this stage of our work, I assumed she was covering up feelings of a quite different kind. To get around her denial, I asked her, using humor that relied on contrived naiveté, if she were not expecting—considering that a pebble is not exactly a boulder—a rather *insignificant* Stone?! This caught her by surprise, but had the happy result of enabling her—by legitimizing the possibility of my not being such a terrific therapist—to speak of her strong attachment to her still much-idealized former therapist and of her disappointment in ending up only with me.

The following example illustrates how I attempted, through the use of humor, to dramatize the crippling and seemingly inescapable sense of loneliness that one so often encounters among schizophrenic patients. By the way, the humor fell flat, since each of the patients was so concrete in his thought as to miss the punchline. The example thus also illustrates how difficult it is to use humor effectively with such a group.

About eight or nine schizophrenic patients, ranging in age from about 20 to 40, were gathered around the television set of their hospital unit. A few staff members, including me, were seated among them, since the weekly community meeting was to begin in a few minutes. One of the patients, having recently quarreled with another over the disruptiveness of the "noise" created by the set, had said: "I can't read while you're watching the damned thing; they ought to put in a jack for a set of earplugs!" His adversary cautioned: "Then, only *one* person could listen!"—to which the first retorted, "No, you could put in *two* jacks!" At this point, I interrupted with the remark, "Well, with enough jacks, we could all be alone, together." I had hoped, with this ironic, purposely absurd comment, to highlight, simultaneously, a number of impressions I had about this gathering of hermits. As part of the hospital staff, I wished to urge them on to some form of relatedness, however tentative. I wanted them to begin talking to each other. Activated by the most intense apprehension in the interpersonal encounter, they strove only to remain as isolated as possible—each man with his jack, freed from having to share even a TV show, let alone a personal thought. With my quip I hoped to pictorialize the futility of their quest—to remain alone in a group setting. I had thought the juxtaposition of "alone" and "together" would help some of them see the inherent contradictoriness of this electronic avoidance maneuver. I had also banked on the assumption that the bleakness conveyed by the image—of people around a TV set connected not to each other, but only, via wires, to the set—would strike them as so appalling and, given their proximity to one another, so unnecessary, that even the apparent dangers of human contact and relatedness would, in comparison, seem worth the risk.

Humor can sometimes be an effective weapon in combatting a patient's suicidal intentions. A therapist who was gifted in the use of irony related an anecdote to me concerning a young schizoaffective woman with whom he had been working for a year and a half in the hospital. She had made a number of serious suicide attempts both before and during her hospitalization. After many months of intensive psychotherapy, the patient had progressed from feeling "justified" in killing herself under certain stressful circumstances, to realizing that her threats of suicide could best be construed as a form of interpersonal "dirty pool" by which she tormented and manipulated the people who were important to her. She had not progressed so far, however, as to have parted company for good from this outrageous behavior. Her therapist had gone through various stages during his work with her—from the unquestioning sympathy for the "helpless victim," as he tended to regard her at the outset, to a more realistic attitude in which he could hold her responsible for the unspoken hostility and exploitativeness embedded within her suicidal proclivities. He also had grown courageous enough, no small feat, to confront her about this finally, whereas in the past he and the rest of the hospital staff would pussyfoot around her, whenever she announced one of her threats. After 18 or 19 months, then, the time had arrived where the therapist felt comfortable enough to use a confrontative approach—primarily because he sensed his patient had improved to the point where she could begin to see the absurdity of her suicidal threats. The next time she resorted to her old behavior—in connection with an upcoming vacation of her therapist, she taunted him with a threat that she would jump off a nearby bridge—the therapist quipped, "Well, before you make the leap, gimme about a half hour's notice beforehand, so I can have the firemen out there with a net." This sardonic comment, far from being heartless, as it seems to be on the surface, told her a number of things simultaneously: "Who are you kidding!?" and "If you're going to do something as childish and foolish as that, don't expect me to capitulate as everybody else, including myself, had done up 'til this moment. You want to destroy yourself? Then don't expect us to feel guilty; we expect mature behavior from you, just as we expect from any reasonable adult!" The comment worked because, among other things, the timing was just right. The relationship was solid enough that the patient could no longer deny the therapist's genuine concern. She thus realized, when he said what he said, that he *did* want her to live—but that he now expected her to grow up, in effect, and to abide by the same conventions of civility that the rest of the world gets along with. The days of her coerciveness were over. This patient, about whom my colleague has kept me informed over the past fourteen years, began to do very well following this confrontation. It constituted a turning point in her treatment.

A reasonable case could be made that a patient's sense of humor constitutes a prognostic sign of no mean significance, particularly in regard to social life. Some schizophrenic patients make excellent recoveries in the occupational sphere, without ever gaining ground in matters of socialization and intimacy. In such patients the paranoid component is usually rather pronounced, accompanied by standoffishness, concreteness, and humorlessness. It is as though the paranoid patient were rigidly defended against seeing life in any terms except his own. Presumably, this rigidity is a reflection of a markedly constricted behavioral repertoire. The patient who knows only a few ways of responding to various life events and crises is very much at the mercy of his own narrowness: to grasp social situations in all their complexity would force him to acknowledge myriad exceptions to the little book of rules that contains his prescriptions for behavior. The paranoid patient always strikes us as "legalistic" because he can govern himself only by the letter, never by the spirit, of the law. In this respect, he behaves like a traffic policeman who tickets a car even when he sees the owner running into a nearby shop to get change to put in the parking meter—because, in the 30-second interim, no coin had been placed in the slot.

How, one may ask, does the therapist gain entree into the private and heavily fortified citadel of the paranoid patient? In many instances, he cannot. A case in point is the patient from Clinical Vignette #23 in my book on borderline syndromes (Stone, 1980). Briefly, this vignette concerned an extremely suspicious college student who was so guarded during our consultative interview that he would seldom permit me to finish a sentence. He interrupted every attempt I made at a clarification of issues or interpretation of his behavior during our meeting with the words, "I disagree." He carried this to the point of caricature, so that when I said, "The most striking thing about this interview is that every time I begin to make a comment you yell, 'I disagree!,' " he immediately replied (as the reader has already suspected), "I disagree." Guardedness of this degree constituted an impenetrable barrier to dialogue.

If, however one succeeds over the course of time in helping a paranoid patient become more adroit in handling certain social situations and in understanding the usually harmless but, to him, hitherto menacing motives of others around him, he will gradually grow more relaxed. One sign of this evolution will be a burgeoning capacity for humor in areas that were formerly strictly off limits. Sometimes a therapist can test the waters with a bantering aside, which the patient may simply ignore, if still incapable of grasping its humor, or which may elicit a smile or chuckle. This can be illustrated by a clinical example:

A 27-year-old man had been referred for psychotherapy after having dropped out of law school because of inability to deal with the pressures either of the curriculum or of the expected social life among his colleagues. A schizotypal borderline patient, he had been a loner most of his life. There was a markedly suspicious and untrusting cast to his personality, stemming in part from well-documented experiences of physical abuse at the hands of his male family members. The distrust and righteous indignation he felt toward them spilled over into all relationships, including those with persons who meant him no harm and had high regard for his integrity and high moral values. He was notably lacking in humor. This lack was tested during the course of his psychotherapy by occasional asides in which the therapist would paraphrase one of the patient's remarks, using a word with a double entendre that highlighted in a humorous way the conflicting emotions with which the patient had just been grappling. For many months, these attempts came to nothing: the patient either missed the hidden meaning entirely or else was too set in his moroseness to permit himself a smile. After about sixteen months in this heavy and unrelentingly humorless atmosphere, he recounted a story one day, which happened to coincide with the Hallowe'en season, about some coworker whose sexual escapades evoked in him a mixture of contempt and envy: "He bragged to me," the patient related, "he'd gotten laid and ended up with a form of V.D. he'd never heard of—trichomonas." "Ah," the therapist interjected, "that was his way of trich-or-treating." On this occasion, the pun was greeted with an outburst of laughter—the first such response the patient had evinced in almost a year and a half. During this time, he had become rather more comfortable with himself and no longer had the crushingly low self-esteem that so overwhelmed him when he began treatment. And although he felt embarrassed about his own recent retreat from interpersonal, including sexual, life (which left him envious of those who continued to have active sexual lives), his feelings of moral superiority—to someone who gets a mild venereal infection—were a strong enough counterpoise to his embarrassment that he could, finally, laugh at the therapist's remark. The pun picked up, incidentally, on the specific conflicts about sex in this patient: sex was supposed to be a "treat," but somehow one ended up with the trick/trich. The patient's paranoid stance toward life by no means evaporated after this session, but the atmosphere in subsequent sessions did lighten appreciably and the work proceeded with a greater sense of relatedness and cooperation than before.

16

Management Issues in the Therapy of Schizophrenic Patients:

THE USE OF MEDICATION, HOME VISIT EQUIVALENTS, DEALING WITH SILENCE, TRIANGULATION, HANDLING THE TERMINATION PHASE

Harry D. Albert, M.D.

The Role of Medication

There is some controversy about the role of medication in the treatment of schizophrenia. Ten or fifteen years ago, prior to the influential studies of May (1968) and others, there were a substantial number of therapists who saw drug interventions as generally harmful. A considerable literature developed questioning the use of medication. Concerns were raised that the prescription of drugs would alter the delicate balance relating to transference and countertransference reactions, would increase patient dependency, and possibly even reduce motivation (Goldstein, 1970; Sarwer-Foner, 1970). Others, observing the emotional blunting patients may experience with medication, have been concerned with drugs as "symptom suppressors" that might prevent the sought-for "corrective emotional experiences" (Alpert, 1959) from therapy. Concerns have also been voiced that the medicated patient exhibited only "state dependent" learning and might thus fail to keep what had been gained from treatment, once medication was stopped (Searles, 1972).

In the nonmedical disciplines, such as clinical psychology, social work, and psychiatric nursing, one also encounters varying degrees of skepticism concerning the value of drug treatment. Nevertheless, by now it has been the experience of many that schizophrenic patients receiving the combination of psychotherapy plus medication are often better able to work in psychotherapy, and are more satisfied with the treatment, than those who receive psychotherapy alone.

Medication appears to exert beneficial effects independent of psychotherapy (May, 1968; Klein, 1973; Herz, 1979) and to be synergistic with it (Davis, 1975; Carpenter, 1977). Questions about selection of schizophrenic patients for this treatment still exist, as well as about titration of dosage and duration of treatment. There is evidence that some patients, in fact, do better if unmedicated. This may be true, for example, of paranoid men (Rapaport, 1978) and some "good premorbid patients" (Goldstein, 1970; Rosen, 1971; Rapaport, 1978).

None of our current treatment methods, it should be understood, has been unequivocally successful. In this context, medication is clearly best considered as one more resource among the several available methods for treating schizophrenic patients. Nonmedical therapists who may be philosophically opposed to psychotropic drugs should reconsider their views in the light of current evidence, rather than allowing practical difficulties or interprofessional concerns to interfere with the best interests of the patient.

In general, the course of treatment may be aided by relieving those psychotic symptoms that are amenable to drugs (e.g., panicky feelings and productive signs like hallucinations). The decreased thought disorder and return of specific ego functions can then make communication more easy and direct (Bellak, 1972). Social rehabilitation and various forms of group therapy can be used most effectively only *after* delusions and hallucinations have been diminished or dispelled. Proper attention to dosage (see below) can leave the patient quite sensitive to ongoing events so that he can make the best use of psychological treatment. At the same time, there is good evidence that appropriate dosage will also lessen the schizophrenic's vulnerability to stress-induced decompensation (Hogarty et al., 1974; Carpenter, 1977).

SELECTION OF PATIENT, DRUG AGENT, AND TARGET SYMPTOMS

"Selection of patient" and "compliance with treatment" are phrases that imply an active therapist and passively receptive patient. Unfortunately, in some overburdened hospital facilities this may be an accurate description. Ideally, of course, medication must not be administered in such a way as to interfere with the growth of trust and mutual respect in the therapeutic relationship. It should be remembered that the patient's self-esteem, as well as issues of transference and countertransference, are bound up in the choice and timing of drug and dosage. The therapist must remain aware that medication may signify meanings to his patients much different from those he intended to convey (see Chapter 7). Some of these meanings are along the following lines:

Illness: Some schizophrenic patients will interpret the use of medication as an indication that they are "sick" or "crazy"—to an extent quite beyond their actual level of incapacity. They may, as a result, become increasingly demoralized, or may refuse medication as a way of denying their difficulties.

Magical Powers: Patients may experience the medication as a gift of love or strength from the therapist or, depending on the current transference situation, as an indication of poisonous hatred.

Control: Patients may experience the use of medication as an attack upon their humanity or individuality. They may fear losing aspects of their personalities under influence of the drug. Physical side-effects, especially impotence, add greatly to these concerns.

Intrusion: The taking of pills or, more especially, receiving injections (e.g., of depot-phenothiazines) may engender concerns about bodily boundaries. Certain male schizophrenics may experience a surge of homosexual concerns in relation to either form of medication.

Dependency: Many patients, apprehensive about opposing or questioning the use of medication, will experience taking drugs as an act of submission to a parental figure. Such patients may eventually be disposed to dissimulate about how faithfully they take their prescribed drugs and may even resort to "street drugs" to make a sort of declaration of independence.

Countertransference: Certain therapists may *under*medicate out of personal fears along lines similar to those we have just described, or out of an overidentification with the patient's fears. Others may *over*medicate to control chaos within the patient of a sort that threatens their own stability (see below). Some may fail to medicate appropriately as an expression of some inner need to be the savior; still others omit medication because of a professional identification with a therapeutic school of thought that is inflexibly opposed to the use of drugs (such as that of R. D. Laing).

Some therapists also pay insufficient attention to the *side effects* of psychotropic drugs, both the physical and the emotional, out of unconscious sadistic impulses toward "difficult" patients (see below).

The Contractual Format and the Use of Medication

The treatment framework I have been advocating places therapist and patient in the role of collaborators on mutually agreed-upon sets of problems.

This viewpoint can be successfully applied to the use of medication so that the identification of distressing symptoms, titration of dosage, and management of side effects can also be a collaborative effort. These shared responsibilities can be ego enhancing to the patient, furthering in this way the therapeutic relationship. The experience of having his concerns taken seriously, and of being included as an active participant in the design of the treatment he is "buying," usually enhances a patient's sense of autonomy as well. Within this format, schizophrenic patients in my care have rarely experienced the use of neuroleptics as "meaning" that they are "hopelessly sick," nor have they interpreted temporary dosage increases as meaning they are becoming still more hopelessly sick.

INTRODUCING THE SCHIZOPHRENIC PATIENT TO PSYCHOTROPIC MEDICATIONS

Patients can be asked to trace the symptoms of their illness that have been particularly troublesome. Among these are likely to be some of the difficulties for which neuroleptic drugs are often helpful. Patients are frequently troubled by disorders in their thinking, by hallucinations and delusions, and by episodes of depersonalization and derealization.

Disorders of thought (such as blocking, tangentiality, neologisms, autistic allusions, etc.) are particularly troublesome to those schizophrenic patients who are, in their treatment, making serious efforts to be understood by others and to understand others in turn. In contrast, paranoid ideation is often quite satisfactory to the patient, and usually is not seen as something in need of change. There is some evidence as well that paranoia per se does not respond well to medication and that paranoid individuals may be better off unmedicated (Rappaport, M. et al., 1978).[1]

At times a patient who is apprehensive about starting on medication will find it helpful to read articles, often from lay publications, about the use of psychotropic drugs. The personal experience of other patients who have taken these medications is discussed in some of these articles. Paradoxically, it may also be useful for some patients to consult literature or organizations opposing the use of medications. Respect for the therapist generated by his making available all the relevant information—pro and con—may, in my experience, be gained even by the more disordered patients.

Having compiled their own list of disturbing symptoms and pairing this with the expectable benefits and deficits of drug treatment, the patient may then regard the use of medication as now comfortably consistent with his need for autonomy and self-respect. This is in contrast to the commonly encountered attitude that taking medication is something done for a quasi-parental therapist.

Within this format the patient is not obliged to continue his medication. Each is told, however, that as a collaborator in this work, I, as therapist, should be told when he does not take medication, lest I become hopelessly

---

[1]Some schizophrenic patients with paranoid delusions at the height of an acute psychotic episode, but whose premorbid personality is not (or only slightly) paranoid, do respond favorably to neuroleptics; those with markedly paranoid personalities, whether acutely delusional or not, tend to be, with respect to medication, in the poor-response group.

confused about what is going on clinically. Estimates of "noncompliance" with drug regimens range from 30% to 50% of patients (Davis, 1971). Within my practice the proportion of patients not taking medication while reporting that they are, is less than 10% (by urine test), and most of these are adolescents (a notoriously noncompliant group; see Blackwell, 1976).

Apart from these advantages, the therapist can help the patient focus on issues amenable to drug treatment in a way that facilitates proper dosage. With outpatients small changes in dosage can be made to ensure adequate drug action with minimal side effects. For relatively compensated patients the most troublesome side effect is a sense of disconnection or deadness in their feelings and in their responses to the events and people around them. This deadness is often, though not always, dose related: small decreases in dosage will often ameliorate this condition. For other patients this detachment may be therapeutically essential. Such patients may be encouraged to tolerate the lack of feeling as a temporary expedient before they will be ready to reenter, with the full complement of emotions, certain problematic areas of their lives. Here detachment may be treated as a kind of shield permitting reexposure and thus a measure of desensitization to noxious events that otherwise might exert a grossly disruptive influence on the patient's function.

Therapists may also be surprised by certain psychotic symptoms that some schizophrenic patients may wish (in our view, paradoxically) to retain. The following example will illustrate:

Example

> A 24-year-old schizophrenic woman decided not to take medication because she feared it would prevent her from obeying the commands of her persecutory voices. She reasoned that she would be terribly sinful if not "kept in line" by her hallucination and that punishment for these sins would surely follow. Gradually we worked our way toward the idea that the voices had no special link to a punishing agency, and that one goal of her therapy was to make her conscience independent of external influences. Apart from her psychosis, her fundamentalist religious upbringing lent itself to the use of biblical readings and attendance at evangelical meetings as a substitute for the voices.

A patient's avowed or concealed wish to retain a symptom may alert the therapist who becomes aware of this mechanism to the need for attention to important conflicts that might otherwise be overlooked.

Since, in my practice, the patient regulates his dosage with my advice and consent, changes in his dosage will tend to highlight specific issues. Patients commonly will raise (or at times lower) their medication when they sense a rise in psychotic symptoms. The events serving to trigger these changes can be seen in a clear temporal relationship. It may be fruitful to alter the situation either by reworking of insight or by direct environmental change. This may be more helpful than simply allowing the patient to continue in the stressful situation while we attempt to override the stress with increased levels of medication.

There will be occasions when the clinician may permit a schizophrenic patient, stabilized on a certain regimen of medication, to live through a crisis on a patient-initiated *lowered* level of medication. If done with the right timing, this may enhance a patient's self-esteem in situations previously stigmatized by coping failure and decompensation.

Example

A 19-year-old schizophrenic man was taking instruction in carpentry as preparation for working. His original psychotic break was occasioned by leaving home for college. He had been in treatment and on medication for seven months before recompensating to the point where this prevocational training could be seriously considered. He was generally pleased with the lessening of his disordered thinking, the return of his ability to concentrate, and the absence of bizarre dreaming—all of which he attributed to the medication. During his apprenticeship, however, he revealed that he had always spent several hours a day absorbed in half-awake daydreaming. This had been very satisfying, and in these fantasies he had redressed his failures of the day and had triumphed over all obstacles in a grandiose way. In the present he found these fantasies unrewarding: he was not able to enter them as readily or as engrossingly as before. Furthermore, his apprenticeship was considerably more demanding of his time (and of an orientation reality) than school had been. He experimented with his medication and discovered that whether or not he could effect a comfortable retreat into his fantasy-world was dose related. Under the pressure of his prevocational training, he was eager to reenter this dreamlike state (at the peril, of course, of not completing his training). This regressive wish became the major topic in his sessions over a period of some months. Ultimately, he developed enough objectivity and enough strength to face new situations to take note of momentary increases in his wish to withdraw as a warning sign that some new issue or conflict was surfacing in his treatment and needed our closer scrutiny and attention so that he not become overwhelmed.

As termination nears (see below) the patient's awareness of the relationship between symptoms, events, and medication ought to be quite clear. It is often helpful for patients to develop an awareness of the stepwise stages of relapse. This awareness may arise either from their own personal experience or from reading relevant articles such as those of Herz (1980) or Docherty et al. (1978).

SIDE EFFECTS

Patients who are alert to potential side effects of their medications are much more likely, in my experience, to take proper precautionary measures. They will not unduly expose themselves to sunlight (if they happen to be taking chlorpromazine or other phenothiazines) and are quite conscientious about reporting any abnormality of movement or coordination. Also, patients who have become cooperative partners in the therapeutic enterprise will not be embarrassed to report impotence or failure of ejaculation (which may be associated, for example, with thioridizine or other phenothiazines).

It should be remembered that the occurrence of side effects is specific to the medication and may constitute a good reason to change agents or even class of agent (e.g., from a phenothiazine to a butyrophenone). Despite earlier hopes, there are few clear-cut reasons to choose one agent over another, apart from the risk of certain side effects, and from the general rule of thumb that panicky patients may do better on a more sedating drug (like chlorpromazine) and withdrawn patients may do better on more "activating" drugs (like fluphenazine or another compound from the piperazine group of phenothiazines).

Apart from the physical side effects (photosensitivity, dyskinetic reactions, and so on), it is commonplace for patients to complain of a sense of emotional blunting.

Transference-Countertransference Issues

From the patient's standpoint taking medication often represents a special connection to the doctor. Schizophrenic patients frequently experience the medication as an intrusion on their already fragile body boundaries. Concerns of this sort may underlie certain pseudorational and protracted discussions of drug side effects. With some patients, taking a drug may be experienced as ingesting the therapist, or as the "therapist's milk." Thus a patient's decision to stop medication may be predicated on having simply entered a phase of negative transference, regardless of the events in the patient's external life.

Patients commonly stop taking medication just before or just after a success or a return to a more complicated social milieu. In the latter instance the medication may be discontinued by the patient because he feels overwhelmed and perceives the medication as one of the factors contributing to his new troubles.

Conversely, a patient who feels a powerful need to please the therapist may unduly increase his dosage to deal with an anxiety-provoking life situation in which he believes his efforts toward mastery will gratify his therapist. He may do this even at the risk of upsetting a newly found equilibrium for a relatively trivial cause.

The therapist must also be alert to manifestations of countertransference that may announce themselves by way of peculiarities in his drug dosage and in his choice of drugs.

Sarwer-Foner (1970) describes the psychodynamics of prescribing medications in various clinical settings. Particularly for therapists relatively unaccustomed to schizophrenic patients, the power of hatred, love, erotic feelings, and rescue fantasies elicited by these patients may lead to overmedication as a means for the therapist to regain his own emotional equilibrium. This is especially true with patients who are perceived as dangerous, either because they truly are dangerous in some way or because their situation reawakens important unresolved conflicts within the therapist.

This kind of problem is prone to occur during a time of unusual stress in the life of the therapist (marriage, divorce, illness, and so on). Greenson (1974) discusses these kinds of countertransference phenomena in considerable detail.

Similar conflicts in a therapist may lead to a failure to medicate, particularly with therapists who have a bias against medication generally, or who have powerful needs to feel in personal control of their patients' situation or to feel personally and omnipotently "curative."

MAINTENANCE AND REINSTITUTION OF MEDICATION

Maintenance of drug treatment, as with dosage, must be individualized. To my knowledge there have been few controlled studies of maintenance treatment in schizophrenic persons who have had one or more brief, florid psychotic episodes with relatively quick recovery. Some studies done near the beginning of the neuroleptic era suggest that these people are likely to do well without continuous medication (Langfeldt, 1969; Stephens, 1963).

In any event one usually has considerable time to evaluate the patient's course relative to the interaction of external stress and the need for medication.

Example

> A 24-year-old man was treated for three years following his second psychotic break. The first break had been triggered by leaving home at 18 to attend college. The second began at 21 when the patient attempted to move out of the parental home to live with a girl friend. During the course of treatment the patient was medicated for eight months. Following the cessation of medication, he was able to complete college and enter a local optometry school. Family treatment was used to loosen the parent-child bonds. Finally, the patient married, prior to the end of treatment. As of this writing (six years after treatment stopped) the patient had reinstituted treatment and medication for premonitory symptoms shortly before the birth of his first child some three years ago. His treatment consisted of five meetings during which the main themes were fear of an emotional separation from his wife and competitive concerns about her relationship with the infant-to-be. His medication consisted of the eqivalent of 200 mg. of chlorpromazine daily for two months. He is currently well.

In making decisions about medication, consideration must be given to the rate and nature of relapse in those patients who have had several episodes of decompensation during the course of therapy. Some are prone to sudden and precipitous breaks with reality; with others, the therapist will witness the slow dissolution of ego functions side by side with the increasing domination of psychotic thought and behavior. In the latter instance, it will usually be possible to increase the level of medication before total decompensation occurs. With the sudden-break patient, episodes of acute psychosis cannot always be circumvented.

Another factor when considering discontinuing a drug is the patient's current level of function. Paradoxically, one may be more unwilling to chance a break in a patient who has returned to a high level of function (for whom the break is less likely) than in a patient who, though improving, may be socially and occupationally withdrawn. For the recovered patient, a new break may be socially and occupationally disastrous. For the patient who has not reentered ordinary life the damage done socially by a second break will ordinarily not be as great.

Equivalents of a Home Visit

During the long mid-course of treatment there are likely to be situations in which patients ask for direct intervention by the therapist or else for some very personal response. One patient may wish to have an artistic production looked at and admired; another may wish to have the therapist visit an apartment or house the patient hopes to rent, etc. These requests must be carefully considered, each on its own merits, in line with our previous discussion about goal setting and rates of change. Due consideration must of course be given to the realities of the therapist's situation. His scheduling, experience and comfort with such activities, and his training all play a role here.

Tape recordings of important interactions, school experiences and the like, may bring an immediacy and wealth of detail that can be very welcome in one's work with isolated people. Similarly, photographs can add emotional aliveness, provide clarifying detail, and be useful in correcting perceptual distortions.

Example

A 44-year-old chronically paranoid physician was in despair over his growing isolation from his work. His therapist requested a consultation. Work had come to represent this man's total connection to life. His situation had deteriorated to the point where suicide or some danger to his colleagues were real possibilities. As his work lost meaning, this man ruminated on "plots" his colleagues were hatching allegedly to prevent his "greatness" from becoming more widely appreciated.

At our initial meeting this doctor wondered if someone with an office as "gaudy" as mine could be of any help to someone like him. He emphasized that he lived a life of Spartan efficiency, immersing himself totally in the study of neurology.

The precipitating event for his increased paranoia appeared to be his "exclusion" from a newly formed journal seminar. Discussion foundered on the puzzling fact that, as best I could piece together, the patient had seemingly excluded *himself* from the seminar. In the next meeting even more concern was voiced about the "display" my actually rather plain office made. The patient then said, as if to explain why he could not participate in the seminar, that his own office-apartment was "too efficient." He felt a person like me could not understand this concept and moved to end the consultation. Our dialogue continued in this fashion:

T: You may be right. You might enlighten me if you took some pictures of your home and office. I can certainly understand how inclusion in the seminar was important to you, since Dr. M and Dr. B are important to your career.

Pt: It might do *you* some good to be more efficient!

As one might expect, his home (as I learned after he brought in some photos) contained a bed, one chair, one table and many, many books. He had no window shades, no rugs, no decorations, and, quite remarkably, nowhere for anyone to sit but himself! This led to some further discussion:

T: These pictures sure do look efficient for solitary study. Nothing to clean, nothing to move around.

Pt: Exactly. That's my life—to know everything in neurology, that's it.

T: But for the seminar—where would the others sit?!

Pt: Is that why you have all these chairs—for seminars?

T: Sometimes. More often for families and such. Also, I sit a lot, and moving around keeps me from a backache.

Pt: You should have an orthopedic chair.

Over the course of three additional meetings we discussed his discomfort at the prospect of people invading his privacy, and how this discomfort was affected by his need at the same time to share his ideas widely in order to become famous. We focussed on the practicalities of getting his apartment in appropriate shape for meetings and seminars. We also dwelt on his "spartan" office and the effect this might be having on his practice. We then explored a number of "next step" issues: his having to deal with "contemptible" furniture clerks, his rage at spending money on "crap," and, of course, the difficulties his having to rub shoulders with his colleagues would provoke, once he went ahead and invited them to meetings at his place.

The photographs proved tremendously helpful because this patient had been so extremely guarded about exposing his impoverished surroundings to either therapist or consultant. All the material related to this complicated avoidance mechanism was thus unavailable for use in therapy and had remained an unanalyzable barrier to social relations.

Example

A 20-year-old schizophrenic man had many abdominal surgical procedures done in childhood. His scarred abdomen was used as the reason for avoiding dating, sports, the beach, and so on. In fact, the abdominal scarring became the explanation for virtually every anxiety and failing.

The patient was unwilling to expose his abdomen to me because, he was convinced, the sight would be too horrible. A long period of negotiations followed, in the course of which the patient was asked to provide at least a sketch of his abdominal topography, so that I could appreciate his problem more fully. One sketch led to another, as each proved inadequate in portraying the horrible. The sketches progressed to Polaroid photos, which he also felt failed to convey a true picture of how repellent a sight his belly would prove to be. The patient was asked to study these snapshots and to attempt different positions, or perhaps a different lighting, in order, finally, to make clear to me how loathesome he appeared. Much as he labored at it, the photos simply were not disgusting enough to mirror the "true" state of affairs.

The patient was caught now in the ironic situation of struggling to present his "horribleness" to a highly receptive therapist, willing to bow to the "truth" once he saw it, and whose only interpretive efforts, for a long time, were directed (paradoxically) at helping the patient figure out how come the "horrible" didn't seem to come through. This led eventually to the following interchange, for which he now seemed much more ready, and which proved quite beneficial. It will be noted how much I relied on pseudo-naiveté, irony, and a line of reasoning that took the patient by surprise, since it did him one better at his own "game."

Pt: I'm going to show you the goddam scars right now!

T: Wait a minute! Let's think this through. What if you do, and I *am* disgusted—that would be awful for us both! Or, if I'm *not* bothered, you'll just tell me *again* that I'm lying to you—just like before.

Pt: But I can't make any sense out of this—maybe *you* can, if you see them?

T: You hit it on the head! The problem is for *you* to make sense of it. *My* sense of it isn't at all important. Please stick to the camera, though, at least a while longer.

Pt: If you won't let me show you the scars, I'll show them to someone else: I've got to have help!

T: Well, maybe I'm wrong in not looking—but I don't think the time is right yet. I think you can do more yourself—but if you *insist* in showing your scars around, well, O.K. But what will you do, if no one is horrified—only you?

Silent Patients

The question, in working intensively with schizophrenic patients, of how best to manage prolonged periods of silence is frequently raised in consultative work.

Refusal to speak is of course a form of communication, much as any behavior is. Long silence runs counter, nevertheless, to our training (especially if this has been psychoanalytic training) about the nature of therapy. Typically it is the therapist who experiences mounting anxiety, and perhaps anger, during dry spells of this sort.

Theories about silence as a means of "nonidentification" have been propounded by Jackson and his group (1960). They demonstrate that some schizophrenic persons will go to extreme lengths to avoid *defining* themselves, resorting instead to mutism, denial of name, sex, and so on.

Searles (1965) discusses some of the rage-bound issues one tends to find buried underneath the silence and mentions, as well, typical schizophrenics' fears about specific "destructive powers" of speech. Arieti (1955) understood the schizophrenic's silence as, often enough, a fearful withdrawal from contact. He advocates an expectantly waiting attitude while making remarks on neutral and nonthreatening topics.

In actual practice, each of these dynamics—fear, rage, fears of destruction, fears of intrusion, and wishes to control—may be present, separately, sequentially, or together. For this reason, the wish that some "technic" be demonstrated for dealing with silence is no more likely to be discovered, than would be a universal remedy for "headache."

It is possible, however, to speak of an orientation that will help therapists understand some of the communicational and therapeutic values silent periods may have.

First, the therapist must consider his wish that the patient talk to him. Anger at the silent patient—a common enough countertransference reaction—may stem from the feeling that the patient is being sadistically *controlling*. Therapists who react to the silence with intense anxiety may well be responding to free associational material within themselves, which may have a chaotic or disruptive quality. In any event, the most important first questions the therapist must put to himself are: What is this patient communicating in this indirect way, and, what emotions and memories is the silence evoking within myself?

Once the therapist has achieved some degree of inner comfort with the silent patient he can ask the second question: What does this patient wish to achieve by remaining silent? This is the interpersonal form of the related *intrapsychically* focused question: What is going on within this patient which causes him to be silent? The issues are not synonymous. Patients may at any given time be enmeshed largely within their internal dynamic problems or within more strictly interpersonal issues; the nonspeaking must be examined from both perspectives. During this process, the patient should not be chastised for being silent. The therapist should make known his awareness that the patient is at the moment trapped within himself, that he probably wishes, at some level, to talk with the therapist, else why would he have come to the meeting?

If a review of the past material and of the therapist's internal observer-signs suggest that fear is the primary issue, one may usefully begin to investigate the problem from this perspective.

The patient may be offered some questions for him to consider. For example: "Without telling me anything right now which you are afraid to mention, perhaps you can tell me what you fear my reaction would be? That is, I understand that there is something you fear to tell me. It is more important that we understand what you fear I will feel, or do, than for you to tell me this secret." Patients can often respond to this, voicing their concern that the therapist might feel "disgust," "anger," or whatever. This can now be dealt with, as one would in exploring how the patient makes such predictions to begin with. Transference material that may be relevant can also be explored more profitably once the patient has provided the outlines of what his anxiety may be centered on.

If the threat posed by the "secret" seems overwhelming, one can give explicit permission to the patient that he retain the secret until some later time. One can also suggest alternative means of communication. The patient can write a note, for example. This should be read in the patient's presence, to avoid his having to reveal the secret out loud to his therapist before he feels ready to do so. Certain nonverbal features of the patient's communication may offer clues to the ongoing issue. This communication includes facial expression, of course, but may also involve bodily posturing, gestures, and the like (see Birdwhistle, 1970). It may be helpful in this context for the therapist to imitate the gestures or postures of his silent patient, in order to get a better sense of what they would mean for himself. The patient may be present during this attempt. In my experience, patients are often gratified by the effort the therapist is making to understand them and occasionally are moved to speak, to help him out.

Example

A 37-year-old woman with borderline schizophrenia would regularly perch on the arm of a waiting room chair. Although she spoke, she could not explain this oddity, which was repeated regularly. When I imitated this posture it felt as though I were poised for flight. Only with care could I avoid making a run for the office door. When I made an interpretation to this effect, the patient was able to confirm her fears that I might not be inside—which in turn prompted a wish to rush into the office to see if I were still there. She also observed that I must really care about what she thought and felt to have noticed this behavior, and then taken the effort to understand it.

Increased distance can also be obtained by moving the chairs further apart, or by having patient and therapist simply face away from each other. If the issue is fear of attack from the therapist, the door can be opened, or some other protection found for the patient. In such a case the therapist should indicate that the protective step was taken to foster some movement around the therapeutic impasse—not because he took the patient's fears of attack as in any way realistic.

Auxiliary Therapeutic Contacts

In the era of phenothiazines, true catatonic, global silences are very rare. With this exception, other ''silent'' patients may very well talk with their social workers, with other patients (in the case of a hospitalized schizophrenic), in group meetings, and so on. Often the therapist can develop some awareness of whatever issues are rendering the patient silent with *him,* provided he has retained good channels of communication with those who are involved with the patient in other settings.

Among hospitalized schizophrenic patients, prolonged silence will occasionally be a reflection of anxiety—whether realistic or quite exaggerated—about certain unharmonious relationships within the therapeutic ''family'' (nurses, occupational therapists, psychiatrists, etc.) that has come to surround them. Some patients will manipulate various staff members into an unwitting reenactment of their central conflicts, but the converse will also occur: staff members will at times (and at first quite unconsciously) involve certain patients in the playing out of some ''drama'' related to unresolved conflicts within their own lives (Stanton and Schwarz, 1954). This process, sometimes referred to as "triangulation," may be seen as one of the disadvantages inherent in the otherwise advantageous situation in which many staff members devote themselves to the treatment of one schizophrenic patient. Silence may, in the beginning at least, be the only coping device the schizophrenic knows to preserve the intactness of his new "family" against some perceived threat. Indeed, the patient may see a need to remain silent—and to remain ill—as the same sacrificial offering he once felt constrained to make to keep peace in his original family (cf. Searles, 1965).

Where staff rivalries or other difficulties do appear to be the major factor underlying a period of protracted silence in a hospitalized schizophrenic patient, it will often be helpful for patient and staff to discuss the situation jointly. As an "outsider" with respect to disharmony among staff members, the patient may have some acute and perceptive observations to make, which may prove valuable in the unraveling of the staff's entanglement. For a patient to have something to contribute in this very adult level will of course make for a most rewarding experience—and may help significantly to undo old feelings of childishness and worthlessness. Furthermore, it can be very moving—and very beneficial—to hear earnest discussion among the staff about their feelings of competitiveness, anger, uncertainty, etc.—to witness the *resolution* of their intercurrent conflicts at close range. Many schizophrenic patients will have come from families where candid discussions of this sort simply never took place, much less progress toward some workable resolution. Patients who have remained strangers to the normal process of airing and settling problems in an amicable way will be found in particularly dense concentration in families emphasizing the polite facade and surface sociability over genuine relatedness.

SELF-REVELATION AND THE SILENT PATIENT

When confronted by silence, therapists are somtimes prone to break the silence with personal anecdotes. They may reveal certain problems in their own lives comparable to what the patient seems to be struggling with, or they may try to compare their feelings with those the patient seems to be in the grips of. The rationale for this has been "humanizing the therapy," or else "reducing the intensity of the transference."

In practice, a period of silence is rarely the right time for such a shot in the dark. The patient is already burdened enough, one can assume, without having to hear the therapist's troubles. Similarily, the "real" facts of the therapist's life probably have little relevance to the intense and turbulent emotions that are affecting the (currently) primitive person in his office. All this does not preclude some neutral comments by the therapist about shared interests. This talk may have a distancing and temporizing quality, with respect to the anxiety-engendering material that underlies the silence. Premature and inappropriate revelations about the therapist's personal life can only serve to reinforce the patient's belief that silence is a terribly powerful tool, the more so because the therapist seems unable to tolerate quiet.

Termination

Termination of an intensive psychotherapy ordinarily implies the end of regularly scheduled meetings. The treatment relationship tends, nevertheless, to be maintained—and this is true irrespective of the patient's diagnosis—for years or even decades, via impromptu meetings, telephone calls, or letters relating to important life events or holidays.

In one's work with schizophrenic patients, termination is generally even less "final" than what we have just outlined above. Some therapists, in fact, make no effort to discharge their convalescent schizophrenic patients from continuing care (Hansell and Willis, 1977), tapering the contacts, instead, until they are scheduled only on an "as needed" basis. Others do mark an ending to formal treatment, though with a clear understanding about arrangements for future contacts should the occasion arise.

Much of the literature on continuation and maintenance of therapy is not actually applicable to well-integrated patients who have completed intensive psychotherapy or classical psychoanalysis. The better integrated, intensive therapy patients will presumably have achieved a solid grasp of the circumstances, intrapsychic and external, that precipitated their original symptoms. Such patients can reasonably be expected to handle future stressful social and occupational situations with competence and effectiveness. By the termination phase, these patients should also have developed better reflective skills for evaluating novel situations, as well as a a repertoire of more adaptive behavioral strategies.

In the ideal situation, where the patient has a good integrative capacity, whatever functions the therapist may have performed transitorily for his patient should become internalized after the intensive therapy, and thoroughly assimilated, emerging as (strengthened) ego functions in the patient. Certain "reality-functions" of the therapist should, when treatment has neared an end, be lodged, if not in the patient himself, in various other experts and organizations that help form the patient's external world.

The question of how completely resolved the transference should be at the end of treatment is a matter of some debate. Certainly, the patient should come more and more to see and to behave toward the therapist in a realistic manner. But it is not clear how nearly completely even a neurotic analysand can totally resolve transference feelings by the end of therapy, even though the analytic pioneers once spoke of "complete resolution" as a goal of the analytic endeavor. A counterpoint to that no longer so widely accepted rule, is the remark of Arieti, "The patient cannot cease to have positive feelings for the former therapist, just as a child does not cease to love his parents when he grows and does not need them any longer" (1974). Intensive psychotherapy concerns, of course, an interaction between two people. When the active phase of treatment has drawn near a close, the schizophrenic (and no longer psychotic) patient will have carved out a special niche in the feelings of his therapist.

This will have derived partly from sources that are not based in reality—counterparts of the tender but, strictly speaking, irrational, or not wholly rational, feelings the patient will have developed for the therapist. In the course of intensive psychotherapy, the therapist will have learned much and experienced much about the inner recesses of his own being. Strong feelings of attachment will, in any case, persist after a successful treatment outcome; care must be exercised lest this residue of warm feeling constitute a "rationale" to continue treatment at an intensive level when it is no longer necessary. The cautionary note is especially applicable to the situation of intensive therapy with schizophrenic patients, since the latter will almost always show *some* disabilities in various life functions: this renders it difficult to draw a dividing line between the stage where frequent sessions are still likely to be productive and the stage where *enough* independence has been gained that frequent sessions are no longer really necessary.

· · · · ·

Schizophrenic patients recuperating through any of the various treatment modalities are at greatest risk of recurrent illness during the first two years after breakdown (Herz, et al., 1980). During this high-risk period, a patient needs to maintain an extra measure of vigilance for any sign of impending decompensation. It may be hoped that each patient will have learned through the intensive therapy to recognize both the specific situations to which he is vulnerable, and the premonitory signs of adaptive failure. The latter may include inordinate anger or suspicion, bewilderment, a sadness that goes beyond the magnitude of the stress, or perhaps a particular type of sleep disturbance, difficulty in concentration, or sense of alienation (or "distantiation").

MANAGEMENT OF TERMINATION: METICULOUS PLANNING, TERMINATION IN MINIATURE

Sullivan (1956) wrote that the psychotherapy of schizophrenic persons required a preparation for termination from the very beginning. Each brief separation during the course of treatment serves as an ending in miniature. Schizophrenic patients tend to have pronounced reactions to the end of a session, to a weekend, or to the therapist's vacation. Many therapists remain blind to the impact these brief and seemingly unimportant separations may exert. This countertransference problem may lead a therapist to neglect mention of a forthcoming separation until there is very little time to adjust to it. On the part of some therapists this may be an expression of hidden sadistic impulses directed toward the patient. More often, the omission may represent a turning away from the pain of the temporarily broken bond—which is after all a mutual bond, formed out of a cherishing of the other that exists on both sides, not just on the patient's.

This break may provoke angry ''acting out'' in both parties. The therapist may find himself longing to be rid of the patient and, while he remains in this frame of mind, may allow his attention to wander—even to the point of forgetting to inform the patient of an impending vacation. The patient, meantime, may regress, exhibiting symptoms or behavior patterns that seemed to have been long outgrown. Some patients will suddenly stop taking a medication in this situation, contributing to the emergence of a crisis ''requiring'' (at least in the patient's fantasy) the presence of the therapist, just as he was about to go.

These events foreshadow the kinds of issues that may arise around the time of a more definitive, if not final, parting.

THE NEED FOR A DEFINED ENDING

Depending on one's clinical judgment, the final parting may be more or less explicitly final. It is clinically commonplace to meet less frequently toward the end of the treatment. One often speaks here of ''tapering off.'' Saying a final goodbye when the time comes (or at least a ''so long'') will be appropriate. Each previous separation had a planned reunion. Resolution of the painful feelings connected with parting is facilitated by the definiteness of a last goodbye. If there is a formal, official ''ending,'' even though meetings may well go on later as needed, the work of resolving the important transference and countertransference issues can move more easily toward completion.

Having an officially defined end also allows the former patient to experience himself as an autonomous being, freed, perhaps for the first time, from any outside interference of a parental sort. This awareness has several potentially beneficial effects.

Schizophrenic patients who have hitherto refrained from fully committing their energies toward realistic goals in order to defeat parents or their surrogates may now be able to work to their fullest capacity. Whatever success they now have is theirs alone. During the course of therapy this issue

relating to *autonomy* will come up again and again, but it is often not resolved until the termination phase has been entered and worked through.

In a similar fashion, other schizophrenic patients do not experience their
life as the "real thing" until at or near the end of treatment.

Example

A 28-year-old schizophrenic man had difficulty managing his fi-
nances throughout a three-year treatment. He lived on the proceeds of a half-million dollar trust, but found himself without funds
by the third week of every month. This symptom of "carelessness"
was resistant to investigation and interpretation. Toward the end
of the fourth year, it remained the only significant disturbance in
his everyday functioning. Apart from this problem, termination
was now indicated. Two weeks before our last meeting, the patient
called from an emergency room. He had gone to the nearest hospital while having an attack of hyperventilation (his first)—which he
imagined to be a heart attack. He had begun hyperventilating
while sitting in the park thinking about what he would do in his life
without me. For the first time the thought occurred to this man
that "treatment was over." His thought was: "I'll never be 21
again—this is *real* time now!" At our next meeting he linked his
carelessness with money to the underlying feeling that it didn't
count. Dollars were like play money in a rehearsal. He had an impulse, when this idea occurred, to take the money in his pocket and
scatter it to the wind—which would have fortified his illusion that
he still had "time out." He also experienced a wish to become
crazy again, in order to preserve his "time out" (and thus neither
leave me nor grow old and die). All these issues had been explored
in some detail over the four years, but had not hit home until near
the moment of ending.

COMMENT

For this man, neither our previous separations nor the planning leading up
to them had seemed quite "real" enough. In contrast, for most patients,
the details of their lives and a framework of various supports (including
those that will help them tolerate separation better) are fully in place by the
time of termination. As an example, when patients talk with me about the
strong feelings of loneliness and despair they anticipate in connection with
the Christmas holidays, I try to get them to focus on the possibilities they

have for positive experiences that will not be marred by being an "outsider." I might encourage them to be a "good parent" to themselves (by buying something they always wanted, taking a trip, etc.). We explore all the possibilities, real and fantasied, of what they may be doing from December 24th through New Year's Day. Ultimately, patients develop realistic plans and learn how to minimize the loneliness they would otherwise have felt. The same kind of planning around activities and contacts with people is to be encouraged for any other separation. The people, organizations, hobby groups, etc., to which the patient can turn in these times eventually become the stable and expanded set of resources upon which the patient, like the rest of us, can rely in good times and in bad. Almost any plan we make with a patient, however narrowly conceived it may have been initially, can be broadened to include human contacts and self-sustaining elements.

Example

A 17-year-old schizophrenic woman, profoundly withdrawn, when confronted with the task of having to get through the holidays alone, was only able at first to think of attending movies. Even so, she anticipated feeling worse, because most others in the theater would be with friends. This would emphasize her isolation. An alternate possibility she finally settled on was that of attending a film-lecture series at a local college. In this classroom-like atmosphere, she could manage to identify with the other students. During a question-and-answer period she could write down the things she would have said, had she had the courage. In this way, she felt she could be at one remove less from the others. In the course of the film series she was asked to join a music group by a woman who noticed the flute case my patient was carrying. This fortuitous invitation (which the patient was not yet ready to accept) formed a real opening in treatment to discuss her isolation, which had previously been defended as though it were her "choice" (to avoid contamination from the "lower elements").

FURTHER CONTACT BEYOND TERMINATION

Patients frequently will want contact of some continuing sort with the therapist. This may be only episodic, but nonetheless very important to the patient. In my practice these contacts have tended to occur in quite appropriate ways, at times of unusual stress or after a success (which can itself be an unusual stress). The return of symptoms under stress is, in my experience, more prone to occur during the first two years after termination. It cannot be taken for granted that the patient should resume therapy with the same therapist. Contact itself may be supportive, but problems unresolved after a completed course of intensive therapy may represent an area of counter-transference difficulty within the therapist. In this situation a consultation with a colleague is essential.

Example

A 28-year-old man completed a course of four years of twice weekly meetings and membership in a therapeutic group. After having suffered three psychotic episodes and a year of demoralized loss of function, he had, at the end of this therapy, ostensively re-covered. During the four years following treatment, he married and obtained a CPA degree. Under the stress of working and studying for his CPA boards, however, he began to drink. He re-turned to consult me about this. Review of his course through my notes indicated that he actually had never totally stopped drinking while he had been in therapy. His drinking had not been disabling at that time because he was then functioning at a (lower) level, which permitted some loss of work time. The issues of magicality, denial, and self-destructive impulses that were connected to his drinking had been jointly avoided. Searching self-examination re-vealed an overinvestment on my part in his unusual success in hav-ing recovered from a profoundly ill, ''state hospital'' psychosis to become a married professional. This overinvestment was accentu-ated by a connection between this patient and a renowned supervi-sor who had been important to me in my early training. With a col-league I reviewed my reactions of anger and disappointment as well as my continued wish to deny the seriousness of his drinking problem. The conclusion we reached was to have the patient re-turn for additional treatment while I continued in supervision, the better to deal with those various countertransference issues within myself.

17

Schizophrenic Language:

VANTAGES FROM NEUROLOGY

David V. Forrest, M.D.

Neurological disorders as paradigms to compare with schizophrenic psychopathology are attracting renewed interest in psychiatric medicine. Benson (1975) has noted the useful differential diagnostic point, derived from the evaluation of cortical function in the aphasias, that the presence of anomia (a disorder of word finding on formal testing) weighs against the diagnosis of schizophrenia, and for the diagnosis of aphasia. Gerson, Benson, and Frazier compared 15-minute verbal samples from eight posterior aphasics and ten acute schizophrenics. They found that neologisms were absent and other paraphasic substitutions were rare in schizophrenia, whereas the aphasics all produced neologisms (though they were not common) and commonly made paraphasic substitutions. The authors concluded that:

> expressed most simply, the verbal output of the posterior aphasic is a disorder of language, whereas that of the schizophrenic derives from a disorder of thought. . . . Unlike the disordered verbal output of schizophrenia, which appears to derive from subcortical dysfunction, aphasia results from damage to the cortex [of the dominant hemisphere] (1977, pp. 968–969).

I question whether a neurological approach is able so facilely to distinguish and locate language and thought. The authors distinguish a language disorder, "an abnormality of verbal output in which the patient has difficulty manipulating the semantic and syntactic structures necessary to express his ideas," from a thought disorder, "the expression of abnormal ideas thought disorders represent abnormalities of ideation that are reflected in verbal output" (ibid., p. 969).

These distinctions from a neurological standpoint are a useful contribution to a rough stage of differential diagnosis, but they appear to oversimplify and ultimately to obscure description at the level of the mental process. Complexities remain that can be considered as a series of still unsettled questions:

1. Is thought disordered in schizophrenia?
2. Is language disordered in schizophrenia?
3. What is the relation of language to thought in schizophrenia?
4. What is the relation of language to emotion in schizophrenia?
5. From a neurological vantage point, how might the impairment of schizophrenia be described?
6. Could aphasia be a coexisting element in some schizophrenia?

1. *Is thought disordered in schizophrenia?* If one were to accept for the moment that schizophrenia is not a disorder of language, one would be tempted to say that, in the strict sense of a lack of logical procedure, there is no thinking disorder either. From the standpoint of Aristotelian logic, the "identification by predicates" described by Von Domarus in schizophrenic "paralogic" is not a lack of logical manipulation, but rather a problem of grasping the objects of thought to be manipulated. One or a few attributes are accepted for identification, instead of all or most attributes of an object. This is a lower level of statistical approximation leading to identification errors, but not a lack of logic. A fitting analogy with which to grasp the relation of thoughts to language and to other cognitive objects (e.g., percepts, images, symbols, concepts) in schizophrenia is the vagueness, shallowness, and inconstancy of relations with human "objects" (in the psychoanalytic sense). Misidentification leads to problems in categorization, which in turn lead to logical problems. The logical problems are not primary. Careful studies of the logical sorting process (as Livingston and Blum, 1968, have made) show not disorder or illogic but a missing of the mark, the lower level of statistical approximation again.

In paranoia especially there is a preservation of logical processing or even a hypertrophy of logical ability, and the disorder is less a thinking disorder than a *premise disorder,* a disorder of premise choice. The statistically unlikely premise or idea is overvalued in much the same way that objects (persons) may be overvalued (and often later devalued) in psychotic personalities, borderline syndromes, and pathological narcissism.

In other schizophrenias a more general *valuation disorder* may be apparent. The patient has trouble weighting the manipulable elements or "freight" of thought, trouble loading words, images, concepts, and percepts with emotion. The integration of these elements is difficult because of blocked, incoherent, or conflicted emotions attached to them, and because of attitudes toward them. Both schizophrenic and severely depressive persons can devalue the world as a whole, as can depersonalized patients. But a general devaluation of things, so that the whole world seems profoundly to lack color or vividness, suggests depression, whether or not the adjective "schizophrenic" can also be applied. Schizophrenic valuation problems, on the other hand, are characterized by inconsistent and intermittent senses of absurdity, incongruity, scorn, or esthetic fascination with and awe of the inanimate world.

2. *Is language disordered in schizophrenia?* In the crude clinical neurological sense schizophrenic language can usually be found intact, especially if one defines the schizophrenic syndrome widely and will accept compensatory cleverness, intermittent lucidity of meaning, and fluency (rapidity both of retrieval of elements and generation of linguistic productions) as evidence of intactness. Lecours and Vanier-Clément summarized a series of distinctions between the overlapping categories of jargonaphasia and "schizophasia," by which they mean the deviant language said to be schizophrenic in "a small proportion of subjects considered to be schizophrenics":

> A distinction is made between deviations testifying to diminished ability, which betray the speaker's intention, and deviations testifying to singular but rigorous use of ability, which are adapted to the speaker's intentions. The former are contended to be common in the jargonaphasias and occasional in standard discourse and schizophasia, the latter to be characteristic of schizophasia and of various forms of "literary" language, but incompatible with aphasia. In lapidary terms, this implies that ordinary speakers think and talk standard, that (most) jargonaphasic speakers think standard but talk deviant, that schizophasic speakers think quaint and talk accordingly. It is further suggested that the differential diagnosis of jargonaphasia and schizophasia, when made on the sole basis of tape recorded samples of discursive language, resorts mainly to quantitative appraisal of different types of deviant segments on one

hand, and, on the other, to the listener's interpretations of the speaker's mode of ideation. Within the realm of pathological language production, nearly exclusive and important production of phonemic transformations is said to be characteristic of conduction aphasia; combined production of numerous phonemic and verbal transformations, and of neologisms, is said to be characteristic of Wernicke's aphasia proper; nearly exclusive and important production of verbal transformations is said to be possible in so-called transcortical sensory aphasia; and predominant production of morphemic transformations and of glossomaniac utterance is said to be characteristic of schizophasia (1976, p. 516).

"Glossomania" is a term Lecours and Vanier-Clément borrow from Cénac (1925) to describe "a linguistic behavior characterized by production of sentences the verbal components of which are chosen (mainly) on the basis of phonological kinship to one another (alliteration, assonance, homophony, and so forth)" (ibid., p. 524). Glossomania could be included within my own concept of *poiesis* (Forrest, 1965). Poiesis is a "making" of linguistic systems or the seeking of order within the language itself, with the purpose of lending authority to wish-fulfilling statements, or creating a rival universe; a world of words taken as things to be played with at will, away from the insistent reality of real things. Not only sound but such dimensions of language as the material of metaphors and what I. A. Richards (1935) once referred to as the image-bodies of words (sensual, perceptual connotations) were included in poiesis; Lecours and Vanier-Clément divided glossomania into formal versus semantic types. (Glossomania may be an especially appropriate word for the frequently assonant stream of manic speech, with its punning, listing, and babbling play. Some of the best examples of "schizophrenic" language, loosely defined, are found in mania, and are not easily distinguished, in and of themselves, from hebephrenic silliness or even frontal lobe *Witzelsucht*).

Sometimes one has a clear feeling the language is schizophrenic but not impaired. Is this the same as the thought being impaired? An intelligent schizophrenic adolescent girl I once saw interpreted the proverb "Two heads are better than one" as "With two heads you can think twice." She spoke grammatical English, but the meanings one may derive suggest schizophrenia. So does the very multiplicity of possible meanings. For her "underlying" schizophrenic thinking we might trot out the old saw of concreteness, so often misleading in defining schizophrenicity (which is as often hyper-abstract; it is more often not recognizing the level of social relevance the situation calls for; see Forrest, 1976). The developmental psychoanalytic model might be applied, to show poor boundaries between self and others. Cognitive approaches such as Piagetian object constancy and schizophrenic temporal disorganization (Melges and Freeman, 1977) and discontinuity might be invoked, to say the two heads are both the patient's at different times. Perhaps the language was "made" passively, a strong but unintended association overcoming the meaning. Perhaps language itself generated the patient's language, by donating the available and facile phrase, "to think twice," e.g., "before leaping". If this had been the case, the patient would have been saying something not wholly of her ownership. But all these approaches strike me as a disservice to the facilitation and alacrity of schizophrenic thought which, if the delivery were funny (in this typical case it was not), might be considered rather dazzling wit. To paraphrase Freud's comment on dreams as a royal road, and on whatever level it makes sense to speak of a logistics of thought, schizophrenic thought is a royal six-lane freeway to the unconscious. Almost the polar opposite of every type of aphasia is suggested by such a comeback, by "With two heads you can think twice." The patient answers the posed problem of responding to the doctor's seemingly silly proverb game and in the same blinking of an eye compresses into a single utterance many dimensions of the deeper structure of her pathology for the doctor to marvel at and decipher later.

Similarly the elegant and perfectly syntactic sentence "A growing pattern had climbed on me" that I have cited elsewhere (Forrest, 1976), so descriptive of the passive thought experiences that are characteristic of schizophrenia, contains a weirdly infelicitous phrase, "climbed on me", which makes the sentence schizophrenic in its language as well as its meaning. The "pattern" the patient refers to becomes animated, almost an incubus before our eyes, and we can quite easily become awed at how economically he conveyed his schizophrenicity of thought.

The "schizophrenic savant" neologist (Forrest, 1969), who coined such terms as "stereosociopathology," defined as "the solid form of study of friendship and diseases"; "pyrocardiology," "the study of a heart on fire, also study of a heartburn"; and "orthophototitubation," a "straight failure (staggering) that is done by light," was also apparently retrieving his linguistic elements without aphasic interference and coining new words by the same rules followed in general language. Yet his language is schizophrenic, as was the language in the previous examples, and because the linguistic means of expression have been so intimately appropriated into the meaning process, I am reluctant to write it off simply as "normal" language carrying abnormal thought. Asked to sort his words, the neologistic patient used his word elements (suffixes, prefixes, etc.) to classify them.

Because Gerson and his colleagues used acute schizophrenic patients in their study, they are likely to have also selected for certain features that would affect the language. Acute schizophrenic patients tend to be more affectively disordered, to have a better prognosis, and genetically may be more heterogeneous and less related to the chronic cases, as Kety's (1968) work has suggested. They also tend to be more anxious, and given to the kind of speech errors that anxious or tired or other distracted people have, i.e., mispronunciations and substitutions of words without attempts to correct them. However, Gerson found little such substitution in their schizophrenic subjects, which might raise the question of how acutely disturbed they were. Indeed, although all were "loose" at the time of testing and had at least three of Schneider's first rank symptoms, the authors note, "Most were medicated at the time of evaluation." Acute patients may also not reflect what Rado (1956) referred to in his term, "the schizotypal adaptation," a career that promotes more fully developed maladaptive defensive structures, which in chronic schizophrenia more than in acute schizophrenia may be associated with things done with language to order experience and lend comfort. In acute schizophrenia, peculiar and idiosyncratic language, including habitual circumlocutions, stereotypy, condensations, and the coinage of neologisms, may not be developed yet and perhaps may never develop.

A lot of the difficulty, and by this I mean the oddity and incomprehensibility, of language in chronic schizophrenia could derive from the patient being so "out of it" in the interpersonal sense, out of the consensual lexicon, out of tune with the current shibboleths of diction and tone. If your "head is in another place," it is hard to learn the language extant in *this* place. The idiosyncrasy, deviance, or errors (by criteria of social acceptability) of schizophrenic persons may resemble those of nonnative speakers of English, especially those who have been taught by other nonnatives or self-taught from books. Deprived by their interpersonal distance of the normal reinforcing effects of consensual validation by the communal lexicon, some schizophrenics seem to get out of practice, especially in such areas as word definition, affective tone, and colloquial usage.

3. *What is the relationship of language to thought in schizophrenia?* In another way the schizophrenic person is *more* dependent on the communal language, on mere words and not the underlying appropriate sense. A number of features of schizophrenia are contributory, namely, (a) a decrease in conative ability because of an inability to mount emotionally unconflicted, forceful propositions about wants, about the self in needful relation to the world; (b) a passive openness to the perceptual determination of thought; and (c) a retreat from the complexities of personal closeness with others, with an overreliance upon the literal word. A phenomenon that frequently emerges

in schizophrenia is the generation of thought by language. I find this concept is more congenial to those who have studied literature seriously or attempted creative writing. When I first encountered schizophrenic patients,
I found parallels between their language and literary language; my overview of the studies of schizophrenic language then extant (Forrest, 1965)
has recently been borrowed back and applied by a literary critic to understand the elaborate fantasy creations of the linguist J.R.R. Tolkien (1977)
in an instructive analogy for the understanding of schizophrenia:

> No doubt when the adolescent Tolkien first began to create private
> languages, he had things to say that he could not permit himself to
> say: his mother had just died; he was interested in a girl; and a
> priest was his guardian. Like any adolescent, he probably exhib-
> ited neurotic behavior; but, like any artist, he turned that behavior
> into art. Continually applying more stringent rules to his artificial
> languages, he transformed them into a creative activity. But as his
> private world became more lucid, it became more independent,
> more demanding, and more real; Tolkien was beset by two elves
> who kept talking about Middle-earth, and he was forced to listen:
>
> The schizophrenic's thought, like the poets, may be determined
> more by the exigencies of his language than thought usually is. The
> autonomy of automaticity of schizophrenic thought has been suc-
> cinctly put by (one researcher) who remarks that "it thinks" in the
> patients. "It" may in part be predetermined relationships which
> inhere in language. —David Forrest, *Poiesis and the Language of
> Schizophrenia.*
>
> The thought behind *The Lord of the Rings* is obviously that of the
> poet, not the schizophrenic, but it did proceed in Tolkien's head
> "automatically"; I chose the passage because it singles out the pro-
> cess by which thinking can proceed independent of its thinker, by
> "the exigencies of his language." This is, I think, the central fact
> of Tolkien's genius. Because he was not only highly sensitive to lin-
> guistic structure, but was consciously applying these rules to his
> private languages, the "predetermined relationships which inhere
> in language" operated on those special languages with redoubled
> force, so that they grew and independently generated a world,
> without Tolkien's volition. All he had to do was to find it.

There is indeed always a contributory element drawn from the demands
of the patient's particular language "usage pool" to the effort of commu-

nication. One's "own" language is as individual as one's fingerprint; I have employed the word "onymy" to describe the portion of the common lexicon (as well as idiosyncratic terms) that one makes one's own by investing it with personal feelings and private meanings (Forrest, 1973). In the case of schizophrenic language, the degree of idiosyncrasy of the onymy is greater and words are used less as coins of common value, but the reliance of thought on the particulars of the language the patient happens to speak is greater. Even in cases in which there is a communication disability of more clearly neurological rather than "functional" origin, the nature of the patient's language contributes. Recently in the *Archives of Neurology* (1977) a case was reported of a crossed aphasia in a Chinese- and English-speaking dextral who lost his earlier-acquired Chinese, in contrast to the usual greater sparing of the earlier-learned tongue. The authors suggested that the pictographic nature of the Chinese characters explained the apparent anomaly. Similarly Japanese language forms, one pictographic (*kanji*) and the other a phonetic script (*kana*), are differentially spared according to the posterior or anterior site of the lesion (Geschwind, 1972). Cross-national studies of schizophrenic language might show differences of difficulty for schizophrenic persons in the use of languages that differ in the channels and substance of their signification.

4. *What is the relation of language to emotion in schizophrenia?* When emotions do not find their direct expression in evident affects, gestures, facial expressions, and variations in voice tone, and instead take thoughts as their vehicle, as frequently occurs in obsessive rigidities of character as well as in schizophrenia when the state of removal from affects blocks emotional expression, then language and thought must strain to carry more than their usual burden. As a result, an escalation occurs in the translation from emotion to cognition, and the language may become more extreme, exaggerated, bizarre, or tortured. This is seen in the choice of metaphors, which became relatively grand or drastic in comparison with the emotions from which they originated; and in the choice of words (diction), which becomes stronger in degree than the situation calls for. In the obsessive person the language is watered down as a reaction formation, but the obsessions themselves and such dreams as may occur are exaggerated in their images. In the schizophrenic person, the language is exaggerated, "conceited" in the literary sense that was applied to the extravagant metaphors of some Elizabethan and metaphysical poets, for example. In schizophrenia, as William Blake said, "A tear is an intellectual thing/And a sigh is the sword of an angel king."

5. *From a neurological vantage point, how might the impairment of schizophrenia be*

described? If schizophrenic affect conveyance overrelies on cognitive channels, the perspective of aphasia with which we began may have much to offer here. For if the schizophrenic person is not merely apathetic and anhedonic in the sense of being *empty* of affects, but rather blocked in many aspects of affective expression by a combination of neurochemical and functional, conflictual factors, then it may be appropriate to think of schizophrenic emotional expression as an *apathia* (a loss of feeling, on analogy with aphasia, a loss of speech); or if this sounds too much like "apathy," as a *parapathia*, the diverted and substituted expression of affects, both in inappropriate facial displays and in the cognitive and linguistic spheres. Schizophrenic language is a parapathic phenomenon because the language has more to bear than language should: a compounded simultaneity of unassimilated and conflicted emotions and preaffective sensations that the affective faculties of the neuraxis—for whatever reason—cannot process and deliver.

6. *Could aphasis be a coexisting element in some schizophrenia?* As a syndrome, it most likely can. Aphasic syndromes affecting the final common pathway of language processing with little motor involvement may be difficult to distinguish from schizophrenia, especially when both are present and the schizophrenia affects cooperation with the examination. Paraphasias and neologisms appear in posterior cortical aphasia and in schizophrenia as well. The classical descriptions of schizophrenic language by Kraepelin (1919) and Sechèhaye (1951)—who described such neologisms as "icthion," "gao," "itivare," "gibastown," and "ovede"—offer examples that sound like aphasia, even jargon; and Weinstein's descriptions (1964) of word substitutions in lesions of the nondominant hemisphere, diencephalon, and midbrain resemble schizophrenic language in their condensation, symbolization, and personalization. In aphasia the emotionality attempts to overcome the blockage of thought or language, the difficulty in *operating* language, while in schizophrenia the language and thought attempt to overcome the blockage of emotion, and the emotional input appears to contribute to the schizophrenicity of the thought or language.

7. *Conclusion.* Schizophrenia is here redefined as a disorder derivatively of both thought and language, but primarily of neither: schizophrenia is a disorder of the *emotional apprehension* of the elements of thought and language. There is a missing of the mark in the appropriate affective loading or valuation of those elements that are both the freight and vehicle of thought. This *valuation disorder* is akin to the poor (human) object relations. There is also an overreliance upon and consequent distortion of elements of thought and language to express blocked affects that have been diverted into cognitive

channels. In this regard schizophrenia is a *parapathia,* and many of its symptoms are substitutions for and transformations of affects. Schizophrenic processes might also be considered transducers of affects into unlikely and interesting affective equivalents, much as cartoonist Rube Goldberg's apparatuses were unlikely transducers of kinetic and motivational energy.

References

Abraham, K. (1924) A short study of the development of the libido, viewed in the light of mental disorders. In *Selected Papers*. New York: Brunner/Mazel, pp. 418-501.

Abraham, K. (1927) *Selected Papers*. (Tr. by D. Bryan, A. Strachey.) New York: Basic Books.

Alpert, A. (1959) Reversibility of pathological fixations associated with maternal deprivation in infancy. *Psychoanal. Study of the Child* 14:169-185.

Anthony, E. J. (1971) A clinical and experimental study of high-risk children and their schizophrenic parents. In Kaplan, A. R. (Ed.), *Genetic Factors in Schizophrenia*. Springfield, Ill.: C. C. Thomas, pp. 380-406.

April, R.S. and Tse, P. C. (1977) Crossed aphasia in a Chinese bilingual dextral. *Arch. Neurol.* 34:12:766-770.

Arieti, S. (1955) *Interpretation of Schizophrenia*. 1st edit. New York: R. Brunner.

Arieti, S. (1970) The concept of schizophrenia. In Cancro, R. (Ed.) *The Schizophrenic Reactions*. New York: Brunner/Mazel, pp. 25-40.

Arieti, S. (1971) Current ideas on the problem of psychosis. In Doucet, P. and Laruin, C. (Eds.), *Problems of Psychosis*. Excerpta Medica, pp. 6-21.

Arieti, S. (1974) An overview of schizophrenia from a predominantly psychological approach. *Amer. J. Psychiat.* 131:241-249.

Arieti, S. (1977) Parents of the schizophrenic patient: a reconsideration. *J. Amer. Acad. Psychoanal.* 5:347-358.

Arlow, J. A. and Brenner, C. (1969) The psychopathology of the psychoses: a proposed revision. *Int. J. Psychoanal.* 50:5–14.

Balint, M. (1959) *Thrills and Regressions.* London: Hogarth.

Balint, M. (1967) Sandor Ferenczi's technical experiments. In Wolman, B. (Ed.), *Psychoanalytic Techniques.* New York: Basic Books, pp. 147–167.

Bateson, G., Jackson, O. D., Haley, J., and Weakland, J. (1956) Toward a theory of schizophrenia. *Behav. Sci.* 1:251–264.

Beavers, W. R. (1972) Schizophrenia and despair. *Comprehen. Psychiat.* 13:561–572.

Belfer, M. L. and d'Autremont, C. C. (1971) Catatonia-like symptomatology. *Arch. Gen. Psychiat.* 24:119–120.

Bellak, L. (1960) The treatment of schizophrenia and psychoanalytic theory. *J. Nerv. and Ment. Dis.* 131:39–46.

Bellak, L. (1971) Research on ego function patterns, a progress report. In *The Schizophrenic Syndrome,* L. Bellak and L. Loeb (Eds.), New York: Grune and Stratton.

Bellak, L. (1976) A possible subgroup of the schizophrenic syndrome and implications for treatment. *Amer. J. Psychother.* 30:194–205.

Bellak, L., Hurvich, M., and Gediman, H. K. (1973) *Ego Functions in Schizophrenics, Neurotics and Normals.* New York: John Wiley.

Bender, L. (1959) The concept of pseudopsychopathic schizophrenia in adolescents. *Amer. J. Orthopsychiat.* 29:491–512.

Benson, D. F. (1975) Disorders of verbal expression. In Benson, D. F. and Blumer, D. (Eds.), *Psychiatric Aspects of Neurologic Disease.* New York: Grune and Stratton, pp. 121–135.

Berger, M. M. (ed.) (1970) *Videotape Techniques in Psychiatric Training and Treatment.* New York: Brunner/Mazel.

Bergson, Henri (1900) Why do we laugh? In McClintock, M. (Ed.), *The Nobel Prize Treasury.* Garden City, N.Y.: Doubleday, 1948, pp. 248–259.

Bion, W. R. (1954) Notes on the theory of schizophrenia. *Int. J. Psychoanal.* 35:113–118.

Bion, W. R. (1957) Differentiation of the psychotic from the non-psychotic personalities. In *Second Thoughts.* London: Heinemann.

Birdwhistle, R. L. (1970) *Kinesics and Context: Essays on Body Motion Communication.* University of Pennsylvania Press.

Bjerre, Poul (1912) Zur Radikalbehandlung der chronischen Paranoia. *Jahrb. für psychoanal. und psychopatholog. Forschungen* 3:759–847.

Blake, W. (1804–1820) Jerusalem. (Chap. 2, Sec. 52.) *Complete Poetry of John Donne and William Blake.* New York: Modern Library, 1941, p. 957.

Bleuler, E. (1950) *Dementia Praecox or The Group of Schizophrenias.* (Tr. by J. Zinkin.) New York: International Universities Press.

Breuer, J. and Freud, S. (1937) *Studies in Hysteria* (Tr. A. A. by Brill.) Boston: Beacon Press.

Brill, A. A. (1930) Schizophrenia and psychotherapy. *Amer. J. Psychiat.* 9:519–541.

Broen, W. E. (1968) *Schizophrenia: Research and Theory*. New York: Academic Press.

Brown, G. W., Birley, J. L. T., and Wing, J. W. (1972) The influence of family life on the course of schizophrenic disorders: a replication. *Brit. J. Psychol.* 121: 241–258.

Brown, James A. C. (1961) *Freud and the Post-Freudians*. Middlesex: Penguin Books.

Brunswick, R. M. (1929) Psychoanalysis of a case of paranoia. *J. Nerv. and Ment. Dis.* 70:1–22 and 155–178.

Bryce-Boyer, L. (1961) Provisional evaluation of psychoanalysis with few parameters employed in the treatment of schizophrenia. *Int. J. Psychoanal.* 42: 389–403.

Bryce-Boyer, L. (1966) Office treatment of schizophrenic patients by psychoanalysis. *Psychoan. Forum* 1:337–356.

Bryce-Boyer, L. (1971) Psychoanalytic technique in the treatment of certain characterological and schizophrenic disorders. *Int. J. Psychoanal.* 52:67–85.

Bryce-Boyer, L. (1978) Countertransference experiences with severely regressed patients. *Contemp. Psychoanal.* 14:48–72.

Bryce-Boyer, L. and Giovacchini, P. L. (1980) *Psychoanalytic Treatment of Schizophrenic, Borderline and Characterological Disorders*. 2nd edit. New York: Jason Aronson, Inc., pp. 131–170.

Buber, M. (1953) *I and Thou*. Edinburgh: Clark.

Buckley, P., Karasu, T. B., Charles, E., and Stein, S. P. (1979) Common mistakes in psychotherapy. *Amer. J. Psychiat.* 136:1578–1580.

Buie, D. H. Jr., and Adler, G. (1973) The uses of confrontation in the psychotherapy of borderline patients. In Adler, G. and Myerson, P. G. (Eds.), *Confrontation in Psychotherapy*. New York: Science House, pp. 125–146.

Bychowski, Gustav (1928) Ueber psychotherapie der schizophrenie. *Nervenarzt* 1:478–487.

Bychowski, G. (1953) The problem of latent psychosis. *J. Amer. Psychoanal. Assoc.* 4:484–503.

Cameron, N. (1944) Experimental analysis of schizophrenic thinking. In Kasanin, J. S. (Ed.), *Language and Thought in Schizophrenia*. Berkeley: University of California Press, pp. 50–64.

Cancro, R. (1970) A review of current research directions. In *The Schizophrenic Reactions*. New York: Brunner/Mazel, pp. 180–196.

Carpenter, W. T. Jr., Gunderson, J. G., and Strauss, J. S. (1977) Considerations of the borderline syndrome: a longitudinal and comparative study of borderline and schizophrenic patients. In Hartocollis, P. (Ed.), *Borderline Personality Disorders*. New York: International Universities Press, pp. 231–253.

Cazzullo, C. L. (1976) The drug approach to therapy: treatment of acute schizophrenia. In Kemali, D., Bartholini, G., and Richter, D. (Eds.), *Schizophrenia Today*. Oxford: Pergamon Press, pp. 161–172.

Cénac, M. (1925) Les glossolalies. Thèse, Faculté de Médecine, Université de Paris.

Clayton, P., Rodin, L., and Winokur, G. (1968) Family-history studies: III.

Schizoaffective disorder, clinical and genetic factors including a one to two year follow up. *Comprehen. Psychiat.* 9:31–49.

Cohen, S. M., Allen, M. G., Pollin, W., and Hrubec, Z. (1972) Relationship of schizo-affective psychosis to manic-depressive psychosis and schizophrenia. *Arch. Gen. Psychiat.* 26:539–545.

Coriat, I. H. (1917) Treatment of dementia praecox by psychoanalysis. *J. Abnl. Psychol.* 12:326–330.

Dahl, H. (1978) A new psychoanalytic model of motivation. *Psychoanal. and Contemp. Thought* 1:373–408.

Davis, J. M. (1975) Overview. Maintenance therapy in psychiatry: I. Schizophrenia. *Amer. J. Psychiat.* 132:1237–1245.

Davis, M.D. (1971) Variation in patient compliance with doctor's orders: Medical practice and doctor-patient interaction. *Psychiatric Medicine.* 2:31–54.

De Alarcon, R. (1975) Detection and management of affective disturbances in schizophrenia. In Lader, M. H. (Ed.), *Studies of Schizophrenia.* (British Journal of Psychiatry Special Publication No. 10) Ashford, Kent: Headly Bros., pp. 137–141.

Diagnostic and Statistical Manual of Mental Disorders: 3rd Edition (1980) American Psychiatric Association.

Docherty, J. P., VanKammen, D. P., Siris, S. G. et al. (1978) Stages in the onset of schizophrenic psychosis. *Amer. J. Psychiat.* 135:420–427.

Eagle, M. and Wolitzky, D. L. (1981) Therapeutic influences in dynamic psychotherapy. In Slipp, S. (Ed.), *Curative Factors in Dynamic Psychotherapy,* New York: McGraw-Hill, pp. 349–378.

Eaves, M. (1977) Blake and the artistic machine: an essay in decorum and technology. *Publications of Mod. Lang. Assoc.* 92:903–927.

Eissler, K. R. (1951) Remarks on the psychoanalysis of schizophrenia. *Int. J. Psychoanal.* 32:139–156.

Electronic Textbook of Psychiatry (1973) *IV: Schizophrenic Language.* (D. Forrest, Ed.). New York State Psychiatric Institute: Education Research Laboratory.

Elliott, Page, and Quastel, (1962) *Neurochemistry.* 2nd edit. Springfield, Ill.: C. C. Thomas.

Erlenmeyer-Kimling, L. (1975) A prospective study of children at risk for schizophrenia. In Wirt, R. D., Winokur, G., and Roff, M. (Eds.), *Life History Research on Psychopathology* (Vol. 4). Minneapolis: University of Minnesota Press.

Fairbairn, W. R. D. (1946) Object-relations and dynamic structure. *Int. J. Psychoanal.* 27:30–37.

Fauman, M. A. and Fauman, H. J. (1979) Violence associated with phencyclidine abuse. *Amer. J. Psychiat.* 136:1584–1586.

Federn, P. (1928) Narcissism in the structure of the ego. *Int. J. Psychoanal.* 9:401–419.

Federn, P. (1943) Psychoanalysis of psychoses. I: Errors and how to treat them; II: Transference. *Psychiat. Q.* 17:3–19.

Feighner, J. P., Robins, E., Guze, S. B., Woodruff, R. A. Jr., Winokur, G., and

Muñoz, R. (1972) Diagnostic criteria for use in psychiatric research. *Arch. Gen. Psychiat.* 26:57-63.

Ferenczi, S. (1926). *Theory and Technic of Psychoanalysis.* (Vol. 2) New York: Basic Books. Chap 16: The further development of an active therapy in psychoanalysis (1920); Chap. 17: contraindications to the 'active' psycho-analytical technic (1925), pp. 199-230.

Fleck, S. (1976) A general systems view of families of schizophrenics. In Jorstad, J., and Ugelstad, E. (Eds.), *Schizophrenia 75.* Oslo: Universitetsvorlaget, pp. 211-228.

Flor-Henry, P. (1976) Lateralized temporal-limbic dysfunction and psychopathology. *Ann. N.Y. Acad. Sci.* 280:777-795.

Forrest, D. V. (1965) Poiesis and the language of schizophrenia *Psychiatry* 28:1-18.

Forrest, D. V. (1969) New words and neologisms, with thesaurus of coinages by a schizophrenic savant. *Psychiatry* 32:44-73.

Forrest, D. V. (1969a) The patient's sense of the poem: affinities and ambiguities. In Leedy, J. J. (Ed.), *Poetry Therapy.* Philadelphia: Lippincott, pp. 231-259.

Forrest, D. V. (1973) On one's own onymy. *Psychiatry* 36:266-290.

Forrest, D. V. (1976) Nonsense and sense in schizophrenic language. *Schiz. Bull.* 2 (2):286-301.

Foster, B. (1975) The recapitulation of development during regression: a case report. In Gunderson, J. G., and Mosher, L. R. (Eds.), *Psychotherapy of Schizophrenia.* New York: Jason Aronson, Inc.

Franks, C. M. (1960) Conditioning and abnormal behavior. In Eysenck, H. J. (Ed.), *Handbook of Abnormal Psychology.*

Freud, A. (1966) *The Ego and the Mechanisms of Defense.* Rev. Edit. New York: International Universities Press.

Freud, S. (1895) Project for a scientific psychology. *S.E.* 1:283-397.

Freud, S. (1905) Wit and its relationship to the unconscious. *S.E.* 8:3-238.

Freud, S. (1908) Discussion of Stekel's paper of Jan. 8th. In Nunberg, H., and Federn, E. (Eds.), *Minutes of the Vienna Psychoanalytic Society.* New York: International Universities Press., 1962, pp. 279-280.

Freud, S. (1911) Psychoanalytic notes on an autobiographical account of a case of paranoia. *S.E.* 12:1-82.

Freud, S. (1914) On narcissism. *S.E.* 14:69-102.

Freud, S. (1917) Mourning and melancholy. *S.E.* 14:239-258.

Freud, S. (1918). Turning in the ways of psychoanalytic therapy. In Riviere, J. (Ed.), *Collected Papers of Freud.* New York: Basic Books. Vol. 2, p. 401.

Freud, S. (1918a) From the history of an infantile neurosis. *S.E.* 17:3-122.

Freud, S. (1923) The Ego and the id. *S.E.* 19:3-66.

Freud, S. (1926) Inhibitions, symptoms and anxiety. S.E. 20:87-172.

Fromm-Reichmann, F. (1939) Transference problems in schizophrenics. *Psychoan. Q.* 8:412-426.

Fromm-Reichman, F. (1950) *Principles of Intensive Psychotherapy.* Chicago: University of Chicago Press.

Frost, J. (1969) Paraphrenia and paranoid schizophrenia. *Psychiatrica Clinica* 2:129–138.

Gardiner, M. (1971) *The Wolf Man.* New York: Basic Books.

Garmezy, N. (1974) Children at risk: the search for the antecedants of schizophrenia. I: Conceptual models and research methods. *Schiz. Bull.* 8:14–90.

Gedo, J. E. (1964) Concepts for a classification of the psychotherapies. *Int. J. Psychoanal.* 45:530–539.

Gedo, J. E. (1979) Theories of object relations: A metapsychological assessment. *J.A.P.A.* 27:361–373.

Gedo, J. E. (1980) Reflections on some current controversies in psychoanalysis. *J.A.P.A.* 28:363–383.

Gerson, S. N., Benson, D. F., and Frazier, S. H. (1977) Diagnosis: schizophrenia versus posterior aphasia. *Amer. J. Psychiat.* 134:966–969.

Geschwind, N. (1972) Language and the brain. *Scientific American,* April, pp. 76–83.

Gill, M. (1981) The analysis of the transference. In Slipp, S. (Ed.), *Curative Factors in Dynamic Psychotherapy,* New York: McGraw-Hill, pp. 104–126.

Giovacchini, P. L. (1969) The influence of interpretation upon schizophrenic patients. *J. Psychoanal.* 50:179–186.

Giovacchini, P. L. (1980) Psychoanalytic treatment of character disorders. In Bryce-Boyer, L., and Giovacchini, P. L. (Eds.), *Psychoanalytic Treatment of Schizophrenic, Borderline and Characterological Disorders.* 2nd edit. New York: Jason Aronson, chap. 6, 7, 8.

Goffman, E. (1961) *Asylums: Essays on the Social Situation of Mental Patients and Other Inmates.* Garden City, N.Y.: Doubleday Co.

Goldberg, A. (1980–81) Self psychology and the distinctiveness of psychotherapy. *Inter. J. Psychoan. Psychother.* 8:57–70.

Goldstein, M. J. (1970) Premorbid adjustment, paranoid status and patterns of response to phenothiazines in acute schizophrenia. *Schiz. Bull.* 3:24–37.

Green, A. (1975) The analyst, symbolization and absence in the analytic setting (on changes in analytic practice and analytic experience). *Int. J. Psychoanal.* 56:1–22.

Green, H. (1964) *I Never Promised You a Rose Garden.* New York: Signet Books.

Greenson, R. (1974) The decline and fall of the fifty minute hour. *J. Amer. Psychoanal. Assoc.* 22:785–791.

Grinberg, L. (1962) On a specific aspect of countertransference due to the patient's projective identification. *Inter. J. Psychoanal.* 43:436–440.

Grinspoon, L., Ewalt, J. R., and Shader, R. (1967) Long-term treatment of chronic schizophrenia. *Int. J. Psychiat.* 4:116–141.

Groddeck, G. (1926) *Das Buch vom Es: Psychoanalytische Briefe an eine Freundin.* Leipzig: Int. Psychoan. Verlag.

Gunderson, J. G. (1977) Drugs and psychosocial treatment of schizophrenia revisited. *J. Contin. Educ. Psychiat.* December, pp. 25–40.

Gunderson, J. G. (1978) Patient-therapist matching: A research evaluation. *Amer. J. Psychiat.* 135:1193–1197.

Gunderson, J. G. (1980) A reevaluation of milieu therapy for nonchronic schizophrenic patients. *Schiz. Bull.* 6:64–69.

Guntrip, H. (1962) The manic-depressive problem in the light of the schizoid process. *Int. J. Psychoanal.* 43:98–112.

Guntrip, H. (1967) The concept of psychodynamic science. *Int. J. Psychoanal.* 48:32–43.

Gur, R. E. (1978) Left hemisphere dysfunction and left hemisphere overactivation in schizophrenia. *J. Abnl. Psychol.* 87:226–238.

Hansell, B., and Willis, G. L. (1977) Outpatient treatment of schizophrenia. *Amer. J. Psychiat.* 134:1082–1086.

Helmchen, H. (1975) Schizophrenia: diagnostic concepts in the I.C.D.-8. In Lader, M. H. (Ed.), *Studies of Schizophrenia.* (British Journal of Psychiatry Special Publication No. 10) Ashford, Kent: Headley Bros., pp. 10–18.

Hemsley, D. R. (1977) What have cognitive deficits to do with schizophrenic symptoms? *Brit. J. Psychiat.* 130:167–173.

Herz, M. I. and Melville, C. (1980) Relapse in schizophrenia. *Amer. J. Psychiat.* 137:801–805.

Hinsie, L. (1929) The treatment of schizophrenia. *Psychiat. Q.* 3:5–39

Hoch, P. H., and Polatin, P. (1949) Pseudoneurotic forms of schizophrenia. *Psychiat. Q.* 23:248–276.

Hogarty, G. E., Goldberg, S., and Schooler, N. (1974) Drug and sociotherapy in the aftercare of schizophrenic patients, II: Two-year relapse rates. *Arch. Gen. Psychiat.* 31:603–608.

Hollander, M., and Hirsch, S. J. (1964) Hysterical psychosis. *Amer. J. Psychiat.* 120:1066–1074.

Horwitz, W. A., Polatin, P., Kolb, L. C., and Hoch, P. H. (1958) A study of cases of schizophrenia treated by "direct analysis." *Amer. J. Psychiat.* 114:780–783.

Huey, L. Y., Zetin, M., Janowsky, D. S., and Judd, L. L. (1978) Adult minimal brain dysfunction and schizophrenia: a case report. *Amer. J. Psychiat.* 135:1563–1565.

Jackson, D. D. (1960) *The Etiology of Schizophrenia.* New York: Basic Books.

Jackson, D. D. (1967) The transactional viewpoint. *Int. J. Psychiat.* 4:453–457.

Jacobson, E. (1953) Metapsychology and cyclothymic depression. In Greenacre, P. (Ed.), *Affective Disorders.* New York: International Universities Press, pp. 49–83.

Jacobson, E. (1967) *Psychotic Conflict and Reality.* New York: International Universities Press.

Jaffee, J. (1964) Verbal behavior analysis in psychiatric interviews with the aid of digital computers. In Association for Research in Nervous and Mental Diseases, *Disorders of Communication.* Baltimore: Williams Wilkins, pp. 389–399.

Jaynes, J. (1976) *The Origin of Consciousness in the Breakdown of the Bicameral Mind.* Boston: Houghton and Miflin.

Jones, E. (1957). *The Life and Work of Sigmund Freud.* 3 volumes. New York: Basic Books.

Kasanin, J. (1933) Acute schizoaffective psychoses. *Amer. J. Psychiat.* 97:97–120.

Kayton, L. (1975) Toward an integrated treatment of schizophrenia. *Schiz. Bull.* 12:60–70.

Kempf, E. J. (1919) The psychoanalytic treatment of dementia praecox: report of a case. *Psychoanal. Rev.* 6:15–58.

Kernberg, O. F. (1967) Borderline personality organization. *J. Amer. Psychoanal. Assoc.* 15:641–685.

Kernberg, O. F. (1975) *Borderline Conditions and Pathological Narcissism.* New York: Jason Aronson.

Kernberg, O. F. (1977) Clinical observations regarding schizophrenic patients. In Chiland, C. (Ed.), *Long-Term Treatments of Psychotic States.* New York: Human Sciences Press, pp. 332–360.

Kernberg, O. F. (1977a) The structural diagnosis of borderline personality organization. In Hartocollis, P. (Ed.), *Borderline Personality Disorders.* New York: International Universities Press, pp. 87–121.

Kety, S. S. (1977) Genetic aspects of schizophrenia: observations on the biological and adoptive relatives of adoptees who became schizophrenic. In Gershon, E. S., Belmaker, R. H., Kety, S. S. and Rosenbaum, M. (Eds.), *The Impact of Biology on Modern Psychiatry.* New York: Plenum Press, pp. 195–206.

Kety, S. S., Rosenthal, D., Wender, P. H. et al. (1968) The types and prevalence of mental illness in the biological and adoptive families of adopted schizophrenics. In Rosenthal, D., and Kety, S. (Eds.), *The Transmission of Schizophrenia.* New York: Pergamon Press.

Kinzel, A. (1971) Violent behavior in prisons. In Fawcett, J. (Ed.), *Dynamics of Violence.* American Medical Association.

Klein, D. F., Rosen, B., and Oaks, G. (1973) Premorbid asocial adjustment and response to phenothiazine treatment among schizophrenic inpatients. *Arch. Gen. Psychiat.* 29:480–484.

Klein, M. (1940) Mourning and its relation to manic-depressive states. *Int. J. Psychoanal.* 21:125–153.

Knight, R. (1954) Management and psychotherapy of the borderline schizophrenic patient. In Knight, R., and Friedman, C. (Eds.), *Psychoanalytic Psychiatry and Psychology.* New York: International Universities Press, pp. 110–122.

Kohut, H. (1971) *The Analysis of the Self.* New York: International Universities Press.

Kohut, H. (1977) *Restoration of the Self.* New York: International Universities Press.

Kohut, H., and Wolf, E. S. (1978) The disorders of the self and their treatment: an outline. *Int. J. Psychoanal.* 59:413–425.

Kolb, L. C. (1956) Psychotherapeutic evolution and its implications. *Psychiat. Q.* 30:579–597.

Kraepelin, E. (1919) *Dementia Praecox and Paraphrenia.* (Tr. by R. M. Barclay.) Edinburgh: E. S. Livingstone.

Laing, R. D. (1969) *The Divided Self.* New York: Pantheon.

Langfeldt, G. (1969) Schizophrenia: diagnosis and prognosis. *Behav. Sci.* 14:173–182.

Langsley, D. G., Pittman, F., and Swank, G. (1969) Family crisis in schizophrenics and other mental patients. *J. Nerv. and Ment. Dis.* 149:270–276.

LeBoit, J. (1979) The technical problem with the borderline patient. In LeBoit, J., and Capponi, A. (Eds.), *Advances in Psychotherapy of the Borderline Patient.* New York: Jason Aronson, pp. 3–62.

Lecours, A. R. and Vanier-Clément, M. (1976) Schizophasia and jargonaphasia: a comparative description with comments on Chaika's and Fromkin's respective looks at "schizophrenic" language. *Brain and Language.* 3:516–565.

Lidz, R. W., and Lidz, T. (1952) Therapeutic considerations arising from the intense symbiotic needs of schizophrenic patients. In Brody, E., and Redlich, F. (Eds.), *Psychotherapy with Schizophrenics.* New York: International Universities Press, pp.

Lidz, T. (1963) *The Origin and Treatment of Schizophrenic Disorders.* New York: Basic Books.

Linn, M. W., Klett, C. J., and Coffey, E. M. (1980) Foster home characteristics and psychiatric patient outcome. *Arch. Gen. Psychiat.* 37:129–132.

Lion, J. R., and Pasternak, S. A. (1973) Countertransference reactions to violent patients. *Amer. J. Psychiat.* 130:207–210.

Little, M. (1957) "R"—the analyst's total response to his patient's needs. *Int. J. Psychoanal.* 38:240–254.

Little, M. (1966) Transference in borderline states. *Int. J. Psychoanal.* 47:476–485.

Livingston, P. B., and Blum, R. A. (1968) Attention and speech in acute schizophrenia: an experimental study. *Arch. Gen. Psychiat.* 18:373–381.

London, N. J. (1973) An essay on psychoanalytic theory: Two theories of schizophrenia. I: Review and critical assessment of the development of the two theories. II: Discussion and restatement of the specific theory of schizophrenia. *Int. J. Psychoanal.* 54:169–178, 179–193.

London, N. J. (1980–81) Toward a further definition of psychoanalytic psychotherapy. *Int. J. Psychoanal. Psychother.* 8:71–84.

MacKinnon, R. A., and Michels, R. (1971) *The Psychiatric Interview in Clinical Practice.* Philadelphia: W. B. Saunders.

Maeder, A. (1910) Psychologische Untersuchungen an Dementia praecox-kranken. *Jahrb. für Psychoanal. und Psychopatholog. Forschungen.* 2:234–245.

Maher, B. (1966) *Principles of Psychopathology: An Experimental Approach.* New York: McGraw-Hill.

Maher, B. (1968) The shattered language of schizophrenia. *Psychology Today,* November, pp. 30.

Mahler, M. S. (1971) A study of the separation-individuation process, and its possible application to borderline phenomena in the psychoanalytic situation. *Psychoanal. Study of the Child.* 26:403–424.

Masterson, J. F. (1975) The borderline syndrome: the role of the mother in the genesis and psychic structure of the borderline personality. *Int. J. Psychoanal.* 56:163-177.

Matte-Blanco, I. (1976). Basic logico-mathematical structures in schizophrenia. In Kemali, D., Bartholini, G., and Richter, D. (Eds.), *Schizophrenia Today.* Oxford: Pergamon Press, pp. 211-233.

May, P. R. A. (1968) *Treatment of Schizophrenia.* New York: Science House.

McCabe, M. S., Fowler, R. W., Cadoret, R. J., and Winokur, G. (1971) Familial differences in schizophrenia with good and poor prognosis. *Psychosom. Med.,* 33:326-332.

McGlashan, T. H., and Carpenter, W. T. Jr. (1976). Post psychotic depression in schizophrenia. *Arch. Gen. Psychiat.* 33:231-233.

Megaro, P. A. (1981) The paranoid and the schizophrenic: the case for distinct cognitive style. *Schiz. Bull.* 7:632-661.

Meichenbaum, D. H. (1966) The effect of social reinforcement on the level of abstraction in schizophrenics. *J. Abnl. Psychol.* 71:354-363.

Meissner, W. W. (1981) The schizophrenic and the paranoid process. *Schiz. Bull.* 7:611-631.

Melges, F. T., and Freeman, A. M. (1977) Temporal disorganization and inner-outer confusion in acute mental illness. *Amer. J. Psychiat.* 134:874-877.

Menninger, K. A., and Holzman, D. S. (1973) *Theory of Psychoanalytic Technic.* New York: Basic Books, pp. 15-38.

Morrison, J. R. (1979) Diagnosis of adult psychiatric patients with childhood hyperactivity. *Amer. J. Psychiat.* 136:955-958.

Morse, S. J. (1972) Structure and reconstruction: a critical comparison of Michael Balint and D. W. Winnicott. *Int. J. Psychoanal.* 53:487-500.

Mosher, L. R., and Keith, S. J. (1980) Psychosocial treatment. *Schiz. Bull.* 6:10-41.

Mudd, J. W. (1978) Conceptual aids in the teaching of psychiatric fundamentals. *Psychiat. Ann.* 8:90-95.

Munkvad, I., Fog. R., and Kristjansen, P. (1976) The drug approach to therapy. Long term treatment of schizophrenia. In Kemali, D., Bartholini, G., and Richter, D. (Eds.): *Schizophrenia Today,* Oxford: Pergamon Press, pp. 173-182.

Nacht, S. (1962) The curative factors in psychoanalysis. *Int. J. Psychoanal.* 43:194-234.

Nacht, S. (1963) The non-verbal relationship in psycho-analytic treatment. *Int. J. Psychoanal.* 44:328-333.

Nacht, S., and Viderman, S. (1960) The pre-object universe in the transference situation. *Int. J. Psychoanal.* 41:385-388.

Nicol, C. (1977) The reinvented word. *Harper's* 255:1530; 95-103.

Nunberg, H. (1961) *Practise and Theory of Psychoanalysis* Vol. 1. New York: International Universities Press.

Nunberg, H., and Federn, E. (1962) Minutes of the Vienna Psychoanalytic Society. *Vol. I: 1906-1908.* New York: International Universities Press.

Ogden, T. H. (1979) On projective identification. *Int. J. Psychoanal.* 60:357-374.

Ollerenshaw, D. P. (1973) The classification of the functional psychoses. *Brit. J. Psychiat.* 122:517–530.

Pao, P.-N. (1979) *Schizophrenic Disorders.* New York: International Universities Press.

Paul, G. L. (1980) Comprehensive psychosocial treatment: beyond traditional psychotherapy. In Strauss, J. S., Bowers, M. et al. (Eds), *The Psychotherapy of Schizophrenia.* New York: Plenum Books, pp. 167–179.

Piaget, J. (1930) *The Child's Conception of Physical Causality.* London: Routledge.

Pope, H. G., Lipinski, J. (1978) Diagnoses in schizophrenia and manic depressive illness: a reassessment of the specificity of "schizophrenic" symptoms in the light of current research. *Arch. Gen. Psychiat.* 35:811–828.

Pribram, K. H. (1971) *Languages of the Brain.* Englewood Cliffs, N. J.: Prentice Hall.

Procci, W. R. (1976) Schizo-affective psychoses: fact or fiction. A survey of the literature. *Arch. Gen. Psychiat.* 33:1167–1178.

Rado, S. (1956) *The Psychoanalysis of Behavior.* Vol. 1. New York: Grune and Stratton.

Rado, S. (1962) Schizotypal organization. In *Psychoanalysis of Behavior.* Vol. 2. New York: Grune and Stratton.

Rank, O. (1924) *Das Trauma der Geburt und seine Bedeutung für die Psychoanalyse.* Leipzig: Int. Psychoanal. Verlag.

Reich, A. (1960) Further remarks on countertransference. *Int. J. Psychoanal.* 41:389–395.

Reich, W.(1925). *Der triebhafte Charakter.* Leipzig: Int. Psychoanal. Verlag.

Reich, W. (1967) *Reich Speaks of Freud.* (K. Eissler, Ed.) New York: Farrar, Straus & Giroux.

Reiss, D., and Wyatt, R. J. (1978) Family and biologic variables in the same etiologic studies of schizophrenia: a proposal. In Cancro, R. (Ed.), *Annual Review of the Schizophrenic Syndrome,* Vol. 5. New York: Brunner/Mazel, pp. 441–466.

Rey, J. H. (1979) Schizoid phenomena in the borderline. In LeBoit, J. and Capponi, A. (Eds.), *Advances in Psychotherapy of the Borderline Patient.* New York: Jason Aronson, pp. 449–484.

Richards, I. A. (1935) *Science and Poetry.* 2nd Edit. London: K. Paul, Trench, Trubner.

Rinsley, D. B. (1977) An object-relations view of borderline personality. In Hartocollis, P. (Ed.), *Borderline Personality Disorders.* New York: International Universities Press, pp. 47–70.

Ritzler, B. A. (1981) Paranoia: prognosis and treatment. *Schiz. Bull.* 7:710–728.

Rofman, E. S., Askinazy, C., and Kant, E. (1980) Prediction of dangerous behavior in emergency civil commitment. *Amer. J. Psychiat.* 137:1061–1065.

Rosen, J. (1947) The treatment of schizophrenic psychosis by direct analytic therapy. *Psychiat. Q.* 21:3–37.

Rosenfeld, H. A. (1965) *Psychotic States: A Psychoanalytic Approach.* New York: International Universities Press.

Rosenfeld, H. (1969) On the treatment of psychotic states by psychoanalysis: an historical approach. *Int. J. Psychoanal.* 50:615–631.

Ruitenbeck, H. M. (1973) *Freud as We Knew Him.* Detroit: Wayne University Press.

Sagers, C. J. (1976) *Marriage Contracts and Couple Therapy.* New York: Brunner/Mazel.

Salzman, L. (1960) Paranoid state, theory and therapy. *Arch Gen. Psychiat.* 2:101.

Sarnoff, C. (1976) *Latency.* New York: Jason Aronson.

Sarwer-Foner, G. J. (1970) Psychodynamics of psychotropic medication: an overview. In DiMascio, A., and Shader, R. (Eds.), *Clinical Handbook of Psychopharmacology.* New York: Jason Aronson.

Savage, C. (1961) Counter-transference in the therapy of schizophrenics. *Psychiatry* 24:53–60.

Schneider, K. (1959) *Clinical Psychopathology* (Tr. by M. W. Hamilton.) New York: Grune and Stratton.

Schulz, C. G. (1976) An individualized psychotherapeutic approach with the schizophrenic patient. In Jorstad, J., and Ugelstad, E. (Eds.), *Schizophrenia 75.* Oslo: Universitetsvorlaget, pp. 135–144.

Schulz, C. (1980) History of the psychotherapy of schizophrenia at the Chestnut Lodge. Presented at Meeting of the American Psychoanalytic Association, December 1980, New York City.

Schweitzer, L. (1979) Differences of cerebral laterization among schizophrenic and depressed patients. *Biol. Psychiat.* 14:721–733.

Searles, H. F. (1958) The schizophrenic's vulnerability to the therapist's unconscious processes. *J. Nerv. and Ment. Dis.* 127:247–262.

Searles, H. F. (1960) *The Nonhuman Environment.* New York: International Universities Press.

Searles, H. F. (1961) Phases of patient-therapist interaction in the psychotherapy of chronic schizophrenia. *Brit. J. Med. Psychol.* 34:169–193.

Searles, H. F. (1965) *Collected Papers on Schizophrenia and Related Subjects.* New York: International Universities Press.

Searles, H. F. (1967) The schizophrenic individual's experience of his world. *Psychiatry* 30:119–131.

Searles, H. F. (1972) Intensive psychotherapy of schizophrenia: a case report. *Int. J. of Psychoanal. Psychother.* 1:30–51.

Searles, H. F. (1979) *Countertransference and Related Subjects.* New York: International Universities Press.

Searles, H. F., Biscu, J. M., Goutu, G., Gillies, E. et al. (1973) Violence in schizophrenia. *Psychoan. Forum* 5.

Sechèhaye, M. (1951) *Symbolic Realization.* New York: International Universities Press.

Sechèhaye, M. (1951a) *Reality Lost and Regained: Autobiography of a Schizophrenic Girl.* (Tr. by Grace Rubin-Rabson.) New York: Grune and Stratton.

Sechèhaye, M. (1956) The transference in symbolic realization. *Int. J. Psychoanal.* 37:270–277.

Sechèhaye, M. (1956a) *A New Psychotherapy in Schizophrenia.* New York: Grune and Stratton.

Segal, H. (1975) Psychoanalytical approach to the treatment of schizophrenia. In Lader, M. H. (Ed.), *Studies of Schizophrenia.* (British Journal of Psychiatry Special Publication No. 10) Ashford, Kent: Headley Bros., pp. 94–97.

Semrad, E. V. (1969) *Teaching Psychotherapy of Psychotic Patients.* New York: Grune and Stratton.

Serban, G. (1975) Functioning ability in schizophrenic and normal subjects. *Comprehen. Psychiat.* 16:447–456.

Shakow, D. (1967) Understanding normal psychological function: contributions from schizophrenia. *Arch. Gen. Psychiat.* 17:306–319.

Shapiro, S. A. (1981) *Contemporary Theories of Schizophrenia.* New York: McGraw-Hill, pp. 141–151.

Shields, J. (1976) Genetics in schizophrenia. In Kemali, D., Bartholini, G., and Richter, D. (Eds.), *Schizophrenia Today.* Oxford: Pergamon Press, pp. 57–70.

Sifneos, P. (1973) The prevalance of "alexithymic" characteristics in psychosomatic patients. *Psychother. Psychosom.* 22:255–262.

Silverman, J. (1964) Scanning-control mechanism and cognitive filtering in paranoid and non-paranoid schizophrenia. *J. Consult. Psychol.* 280:383–385.

Simmel, E. (1929). Psychoanalytic treatment in a sanatorium. *Int. J. Psychoanal.* 10:70–89.

Singer, M. (1979) Some metapsychological and clinical distinctions between borderline and neurotic with special consideration to the self experience. *Int. J. Psychoanal.* 60:489–499.

Spitzer, R. L., Andreason, N., and Endicott, J. (1978) Schizophrenia and other psychotic disorders in DSM III. *Schiz. Bull.* 4:489–509.

Spitzer, R. L., Endicott, J., and Gibbon, M. (1979) Crossing the border into borderline personality and borderline schizophrenia: the development of criteria. *Arch. Gen. Psychiat.* 36:17–24.

Spohn, H. E., Thetford, P., and Cancro, R. (1970) Attention, psychophysiology and scanning in the schizophrenic syndrome. In Cancro, R. (Ed.), *The Schizophrenic Reactions.* New York: Brunner/Mazel, pp. 259–269.

Stanton, A. H. and Schwartz, M. S. (1954) *The Mental Hospital.* New York: Basic Books.

Stierlin, H. (1976) Perspectives on the individual and family therapy of schizophrenic patients: an introduction. In Jorstad, J., and Ugelstad, E. (Eds.), *Schizophrenia 75.* Oslo: Universitetsvorlaget, pp. 295–304.

Stone, M. H. (1971) Therapists' personalities and unexpected success with schizophrenic patients. *Amer. J. Psychother.* 25:543–552.

Stone, M. H. (1973) Commentary on current studies on schizophrenia. *Int. J. Psychiat.* 11:58–61.

Stone, M. H. (1977) Dreams, free association and the non-dominant hemisphere: an integration of psychoanalytical neurophysiological and historical data. *J. Amer. Acad. Psychoanal.,* 5:255–284.

Stone, M. H. (1980) *The Borderline Syndromes.* New York: McGraw-Hill.

Stone, M. H. (1981) Vulnerability to schizophrenic and affective disorders: implications for psychoanalytic therapy in borderline patients. In Klebanow, S. (Ed.), *Changing Concepts in Psychoanalysis.* New York: Brunner/Mazel, pp. 61–88.

Stone, M. H. (1981a) Psychotherapy with borderline schizophrenic patients, II: Description of patients and recommendation for psychotherapy. Presented at meeting of the American Academy of Psychoanalysis, May 10, 1981, Houston, Texas.

Stone, M. H. (1981b) Analytically oriented psychotherapy with borderline patients: a report on the best and the worst outcomes. Presented at the Chicago Psychoanalytic Institute Symposium on Borderline Syndrome, December 5, 1981.

Strupp, H. (1978) Suffering and psychotherapy. *Contemp. Psychoanal.* 14:73–97.

Sullivan, H. S. (1940) *Conceptions of Modern Psychiatry.* Washington, D.C.: William Alanson White Psychiatric Foundation.

Sullivan, H. S. (1953) *The Interpersonal Theory of Psychiatry.* New York: W. W. Norton.

Sullivan, H. S. (1956) *The Collected Works.* New York: W. W. Norton.

Sullivan, H. S. (1956a) *Clinical Studies in Psychiatry.* New York: W. W. Norton.

Sullivan, H. S. (1962) *Schizophrenia as a Human Process.* New York: W. W. Norton.

Sutherland, J. D. (1980) The British object relations theorists: Balint, Winnicott, Fairbairn, Guntrip. *J. Amer. Psychoanal. Assoc.* 28:829–860.

Szalita, A. (1958) Regression and perception in psychotic states. *Psychiatry* 21:53–63.

Tausk, V. (1918). On the origin of the "influencing machine" in schizophrenia. In Fliess, R. (Ed), *The Psychoanalytic Reader.* New York: International Universities Press, 1948.

Taylor, M. A., Redfield, J., and Abrams, R. (1981) Neuropsychological dysfunction in schizophrenia and affective disease. *Biol. Psychiat.* 16:467–478.

Vaughn, C. E., and Leff, J. P. (1976) The influence of family and social factors on the course of psychiatric illness: a comparison of schizophrenic and depressed neurotic patients. *Brit. J. Psychiat.* 129:125–137.

Volkan, V. D. (1981) Identification and related psychic events: their appearance in therapy and their curative value. In Slipp, S. (Ed.), *Curative Factors in Dynamic Psychotherapy.* New York: McGraw-Hill, pp. 153–176.

Von Bertalanffy, L. (1968) *General System Theory.* New York: George Braziller.

Von Neumann, J. (1958) *The Computer and the Brain.* New Haven: Yale University Press.

Watson, C. G. (1965) WAIS profile patterns of hospitalized, brain-damaged, and schizophrenic patients. *J. Clin. Psychol.* 21: 294–295.

Weingarten, L., and Korn, S. (1967) Psychological test findings on pseudoneurotic schizophrenics. *Arch. Gen. Psychiat.* 17:448–454.

Weinstein, E. A. (1964) Affections of speech with lesions of the non-dominant hemisphere. In *Disorders of Communication,* Vol. 43, Chap. 15. New York: Association for Research in Nervous and Mental Disease.

Welner, A., Croughan, J. L. and Robins, E. (1974) The subgroup of schizoaffective and related psychoses. Critique, record, follow-up, and family studies, I: a persistent enigma. *Arch. Gen. Psychiat.* 31:628-631.

Wexler, B. E. (1980) Cerebral laterality and psychiatry: a review of the literature. *Amer. J. Psychiat.*, 137:279-291.

Wexler, M. (1971) Schizophrenia: conflict and deficiency. *Psychoanal. Q.* 40:83-99.

Whitman, R. M., Armao, B. B., and Dent, O. B. (1976) Assault on the therapist. *Amer. J. Psychiat.* 133:426-429.

Wild, C. M., Shapiro, L. N., and Goldenberg, L. (1978) Transactional communication disturbances in families of male schizophrenics. In Cancro, R. (Ed.), *Annual Review of the Schizophrenic Syndrome, 1976-1977.* New York: Brunner/Mazel, pp. 501-527.

Wing, J. (1978) Social influences on the course of schizophrenia. In Wynne, L. C., Cromwell, R. L. and Matthysse, S. (Eds.), *The Nature of Schizophrenia.* New York: J. Wiley and Sons, pp. 599-616.

Winnicott, D. W. (1949) Hate in the countertransference. *Int. J. Psychoanal.* 30:69-75.

Winnicott, D. W. (1960) Countertransference. *Brit. J. Med. Psychol.* 33:17-21.

Winnicott, D. W. (1965) *The Maturational Processes and the Facilitating Environment.* New York: International Universities Press.

Wynne, L. C. (1974) Family and group treatment of schizophrenia; an interim view. In Cancro, R., Fox, N., and Shapiro, L. (Eds.), *Strategic Intervention in Schizophrenia.* New York: Behavioral Publications, pp. 79-98.

Wynne, L. C. (1980) Paradoxical interventions. In Strauss, J. S., Bowers, M. et al. (Eds.), *The Psychotherapy of Schizophrenia.* New York: Plenum, pp. 191-202.

Yozawitz, A., Bruder, G., Sutton, S., Sharpe, L., Gurland, B., Fleiss, J. and Costa, L. (1979) Dichotic perception: Evidence for right hemisphere dysfunction in affective psychosis. *Brit. J. Psychiat.* 135:224-237.

Zedek, N. (1978) Panel Discussion, American Academy Psychoanalysis, December 10, 1978, meeting.

Zilboorg, G. (1941) *A History of Medical Psychology.* New York: W. W. Norton Co.

Index

353

o

About the Authors

MICHAEL H. STONE, M.D., is Associate Clinical Professor of Psychiatry at the University of Connecticut and the author of *The Borderline Syndromes*.

HARRY D. ALBERT, M.D., is Associate Professor of Clinical Psychiatry, College of Physicians and Surgeons, Columbia University.

DAVID V. FORREST, M.D., is Assistant Professor of Clinical Psychiatry and Liaison Psychiatrist in Neurology, College of Physicians and Surgeons, Columbia University.

SILVANO ARIETI, M.D., (Deceased) was a world-renowned psychiatrist and the author of *The Interpretation of Schizophrenia* which won the National Book Award in 1974.